CONTENTS

COVER PHOTO:
Grain Elevator, Aberdeen, Saskatchewan ©Shutterstock / Scott Prokop

I

THE TEAM

DIRECTORS
Russell Mussio
Wesley Mussio

VICE PRESIDENT
Chris Taylor

EDITOR IN CHIEF
Russell Mussio

GIS & CARTOGRAPHY

MANAGER
Andrew Allen

GIS SPECIALISTS
Farah Aghdam
Sal Kahila
David Mancini

CARTOGRAPHERS
Courtney Fry
Oliver Herz
Dale Tober

MARKETING & CREATIVE SERVICES

MANAGER
Lee Ann Pughe

GRAPHIC & LAYOUT DESIGN
Elisa Codazzi
Nicky England
Farnaz Faghihi

SOCIAL MEDIA
Carly Watson

CONTENT WRITERS
Sean Anderson
Leslie Bryant
Colin Hughes
Mike Manyk
Russell Mussio
Stepan Soroka

SALES
Basilio Bagnato
Chris Taylor

ADMINISTRATION
Shaun Filipenko
Jo-ana Maki

TECH SUPPORT
Matthew Steblyna

ACKNOWLEDGEMENTS

This book could not have been compiled without the dedicated and talented people at Backroad Mapbooks. Thanks to Sean Anderson, Leslie Bryant, Lorne Collicutt, Colin Hughes, Mike Manyk and Stepan Soroka who continued with the work of Trent Ernst and Linda Aksomitis of digging up new recreational opportunities and describing them in a creative, yet appealing way. Combined with the talented efforts of Farah Aghdam, Andrew Allen, Basilio Bagnato, Elisa Codazzi, Nicky England, Farnaz Faghihi, Shaun Filipenko, Oliver Herz, Sal Kahila, Jo-ana Maki, David Mancini, Lee Ann Pughe, Matthew Steblyna, Chris Taylor, Dale Tober and Carly Watson we are able to produce the most comprehensive guidebook for Saskatchewan.

As always, we could not have done this book without the help that was provided to us by various folks who live, work, and play in this area. This addition we would like to thank Dominique Clincky with her help in confirming what parks and recreation sites are active within the Saskatchewan Parks system. We are also indebted to Kelly Harle from Tourism Saskatchewan for proving access to the photo library and photo credits and Don Ewart for sending his GPS tracks and updates. In addition, many great resources were utilized in our research including Tourism Saskatchewan, Saskhiker.com and the Saskatchewan Border. Merging their information with our maps and other sources has certainly enhanced and expanded our recreational coverage in the province.

We would also like to express our gratitude to Geogratis, and Statistics Canada for their help as data source providers. Our maps also contain public sector Datasets and contain information licensed under the Open Government Licence – Canada. When combined with the countless updates, GPS tracks and map links loyal customers sent us over the years, we were able to provide the most up to date information for virtually every corner of the province.

Finally, we would like to thank Allison, Devon, Jasper, Nancy, Madison, and Penny Mussio for their continued support of the Backroad Mapbook Series. As our family grows, it is becoming more and more challenging to break away from it all to explore our beautiful country.

Sincerely,

Russell and Wesley Mussio

Library and Archives Canada Cataloguing in Publication
Mussio, Russell, 1969– , author
Saskatchewan Backroad Mapbook / Russell Mussio.

Includes index.

ISBN 978-1-926806-41-9

1. Recreation areas—Saskatchewan—Maps. 2. Outdoor recreation—Saskatchewan—Guidebooks. 3. Saskatchewan—Maps. 4. Saskatchewan—Guidebooks. I. Title.

G1160.S68E63M79 2013   796.5097124   C2013-903706-3

DISCLAIMER

HELP US HELP YOU

A comprehensive resource such as Backroad Mapbooks for Saskatchewan could not be put together without a great deal of help and support. Despite our best efforts to ensure that everything is accurate, errors do occur. If you see any errors or omissions, please continue to let us know.

* ALL UPDATES WILL BE POSTED ON OUR WEBSITE

CONTACT US

☎ 604-521-6277
toll free 1-877-520-5670

✉ updates@backroadmapbooks.com

🖷 604-521-6260

📍 Unit 106- 1500 Hartley Ave
Coquitlam, BC, V3K 7A1

f facebook.com/backroadmapbooks

instagram.com/backroadmapbooks

🌐 backroadmapbooks.com

INTRODUCTION

Buffalo Pound Lake, Saskatchewan
© Shutterstock / Pictureguy

WELCOME

Welcome to the second edition of the Saskatchewan Backroad Mapbook!

▶ **THE AREA:** Saskatchewan is much more than just prairies, although they are one of its greatest assets, allowing for endless scenic vistas and a bigger, bluer sky than visitors could possibly imagine. The Trans-Canada Highway runs west to east across the prairies and, if you leave this ribbon of asphalt, within minutes you can find yourself on the banks of the South Saskatchewan River, Lake Diefenbaker or the chain of lakes in the Qu'Appelle Valley. Travelling north and south along the Alberta-Saskatchewan border presents opportunities to visit the highest point of land between the Rockies and Labrador in the pine forest covered Cypress Hills, as well as the shifting desert landscape of the Great Sand Hills.

Regina, the province's capital, sits on the Trans-Canada Highway and is famous for its small-town charm and big-city attractions. The Highway makes up part of the province's 256,000 km (158,720 mi) of roads, or 22% of all the roads in Canada! As you travel this road network you will pass through a charming town or hamlet roughly every 15 km (9 mi). Heading north, the number of roads starts to dwindle as the prairie landscape gives way to the rugged Canadian Shield. North of Prince Albert there are only a handful of major highways and, finally, at the tiny hamlet of Stony Rapids, the roads end (ice roads do continue north in the winter).

▶ **THE ACTIVITIES:** Whether it is fishing, hunting, ATVing or snowmobiling, there are plenty of opportunities to explore the wilderness. In the north, extended river systems make the province a world-class paddling destination. Saskatchewan is also a major destination for bird watchers, with numerous unique opportunities to focus your binoculars on rare or endangered species.

Hikers and campers can check out some of Saskatchewan's incredible parks, including Cypress Interprovincial Park in the west, Moose Mountain Provincial Park in the east, Grasslands National Park in the south and La Ronge Provincial Park in the north. All in all, Saskatchewan has over 225 national, provincial, regional parks and provincial recreation sites.

Although Saskatchewan is a four-season outdoor recreation destination, visitors should be prepared for extreme cold in the winter and heat in the summer. Throughout the year, temperature can readily drop to below -40°C (-40°C) or climb above 40°C (104°C).

▶ **THE BOOK:** As always, we have spent hundreds of hours updating the maps to provide you with the most comprehensive coverage possible. New to this edition, we have added 20 smaller scale maps for the north of the province, as well as new Oil & Gas facilities as well as expanding on road and trail networks throughout the province. Each Adventure section has been updated and expanded with countless new POIs and activities.

We are extremely proud to present the most detailed and easy-to-use outdoor recreation guide for the province of Saskatchewan you can find anywhere. We hope you enjoy using this book as much as we did creating it!

BACKROAD HISTORY

The Backroad Mapbook idea came into existence when Wesley and Russell Mussio were out exploring. They had several books and a few maps to try to find their way through the maze of logging roads around southern BC. The brothers were getting very frustrated trying to find their way and eventually gave up. Not to be outdone, the two ambitious brothers started brainstorming. Eventually the Backroad Mapbook idea was born.

They published their first book in January 1994 and it quickly sold out. Rather than simply reprinting it, they listened to the feedback of customers and made several alterations that helped improve the book. This formula of continuing to make the product better continues today and has helped establish the Backroad Mapbook series as the top selling outdoor recreation guidebook series in the country. From the tiny beginnings in that Vancouver apartment with maps strewn all over the walls, to one of the most sought-after outdoor products in the country, the Backroad Mapbook series has truly come a long way.

NAVIGATING

Each of our Backroad Mapbooks is filled with amazing experiences that show you how to enjoy the outdoors and create unforgettable memories. Visit backroadmapbooks.com for our other great products, tips & tutorials, features and updates to further enhance your outdoor experiences.

INTRODUCTION

Along with an informative overview of the region, you will find a comprehensive legend to guide you through our maps.

ADVENTURES

Exclusive to Backroad Mapbooks, this section is filled with adventure write-ups, put together by our team of outdoor researchers and with the help of local residents & communities. From backroad attractions to fishing hotspots and winter adventures, you have access to the most comprehensive backcountry planning tool available on the market.

MAP & ADVENTURES INDEXES

A full map and adventures index of the guide's contents is included with page numbers and map coordinates for easy reference.

TOPO MAPS

Containing the core foundation of our Mapbooks, this section begins with a regional map key and leads into our nationally-acclaimed topographic maps, with hundreds of thousands of kilometers of backroads, backcountry trails and points of interest.

TRIP PLANNING

Everything you need to know before heading into the outdoors, including important contact information for general services, parks, wildlife, club & association contacts, distance chart, alongside a list of advertisers featured in the mapbook.

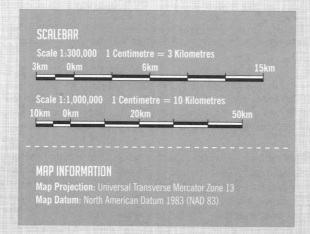

SCALEBAR

Scale 1:300,000   1 Centimetre = 3 Kilometres

3km   0km   6km   15km

Scale 1:1,000,000   1 Centimetre = 10 Kilometres

10km   0km   20km   50km

MAP INFORMATION

Map Projection: Universal Transverse Mercator Zone 13
Map Datum: North American Datum 1983 (NAD 83)

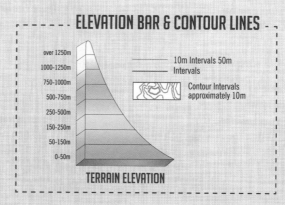

ELEVATION BAR & CONTOUR LINES

over 1250m
1000-1250m
750-1000m
500-750m
250-500m
150-250m
50-150m
0-50m

10m Intervals 50m Intervals

Contour Intervals approximately 10m

TERRAIN ELEVATION

MAP LEGEND

AREA INDICATORS

National / Provincial Parks

Ecological Reserve / Fish & Wildlife Dev Fund / Game Preserve / National Wildlife Area / Regional Park / Special Management Area

WMZ (Wildlife Management Zone)

Canadian Forces Base / Mining / Restricted Area / Water Supply

City

Water

Swamps

County / Municipal / District

First Nations

LINE CLASSIFICATIONS

Freeways

Highways

Secondary Highways

Arterial Paved Roads

Local Paved Roads

Railways

Forest Service & Main Industry Roads

Active Industry Roads (2wd)

Other Industry Roads (2wd / 4wd)

Unclassified & 4wd Roads

Deactivated Roads

Ferry Routes

Trans Canada Trail

Long Distance Trails

Snowmobile Trails

Motorized Trails ATV/OHV & Snowmobile

Developed Trails

Routes (Undeveloped Trails)

Portage Routes

Lake / River Paddling Routes

River Paddling Routes

Transmission Lines

Pipelines

Cut / Seismic Lines

MAP SYMBOLS

ON THE TRAIL

- ATV / OHV / Motorbiking
- Cabin / Chalet / Hut / Shelter
- Campsite (backcountry / water access only)
- Campsite / Limited Facilities
- Cross Country Skiing / Backcountry Ski Touring
- Cycling / Mountain Biking
- Hiking
- Horseback Riding
- Picnic Site
- Ranger Station / Patrol Cabin
- Rock Climbing
- RV Campsite / Trailer Park
- Shooting Range
- Ski Area
- Snowmobiling
- Snowshoeing
- Trailhead
- Viewpoint / Forestry Lookout (abandoned)
- Wildlife Viewing

ON THE WATER

- Anchorage
- Beach
- Beacon
- Boat Launch
- Canoe Access Put-in / Take-out
- Ferry
- Fish Hatchery
- Float Plane Landing
- Marsh
- Paddling (canoe-kayak)
- Portage
- Portage Distance
- Waterfall
- Windsurfing

OTHER

- Airport
- Airstrip
- Arrow / Location Pointer
- Caving / Spelunking
- City, Town, Village Indicator
- Compressor
- Customs
- Gate
- Gas Plant
- Golf Course
- Hang-gliding
- Highway: Trans Canada
- Highway Interchange
- Information Centre
- Microwave Tower
- Mine Site
- National Historic Site Park
- Outfitter
- Parking

OTHER

- Point of Interest
- Refinery / Well Disposal Site
- Resort
- Wilderness Area / Wildlife Area / Wildlife Reserve

Visit backroadmapbook.com to see tutorials on how to use different elements of our legend

BACKROAD NAVIGATOR
EXPLORE THE CANADIAN OUTDOORS

 COLLECT MEDIA AND STATS

 OFFLINE MAPS

 **1,000s OF POINTS OF INTEREST**

 **TRIP PLANNING & SUMMARY**

ADVENTURE LAYERS

10+ adventures available in each province. See detailed trails, points of interest, trailheads and much more. Be your own guide!

 BACKROADS

 FISHING

HUNTING

 PADDLING

 PARKS

RECSITES

 **TRAILS**

 ATV [OHV]

SNOWMOBILE

 WILDLIFE

 WINTER

 FREE TO EXPLORE

 MANAGE YOUR TRIPS

 IMPORT GPX FILES

 SOCIAL MEDIA

brmbnavigator.com

TOPOGRAPHIC MAPS

MAP KEY

NOAB
NORTHERN ALBERTA MAPBOOK

MBMB
MANITOBA MAPBOOK

CEAB
CENTRAL ALBERTA MAPBOOK

SOAB
SOUTHERN ALBERTA MAPBOOK

ALBERTA

MANITOBA

Fort Smith

Fort Chipewyan

Fort McMurray

Cold Lake

St Paul

Vegreville

Vermilion

Wainwright

Hanna

Medicine Hat

Ingalls Lake

Selwyn Lake

Kasba Lake

Fond-du-Lac

Lake Athabasca

119

Athabasca Sand Dunes Prov Park

Black Lake

120

Black Lake

121

Wollaston Lake

Brochet

116

Clearwater River Prov Park

Wasekamio Lake

La Loche

Turnor Lake

Cree Lake

117

Reindeer Lake

118

Pine Lake

Lynn Lake

Leaf Rapids

South Indian Lake

Thompson

Churchill Lake

106

107 St George Hill

108 Buffalo Narrows

109 Knee Lake

110

111 McIntosh Lake

Sandfly Lake

112 McLennan Lake

113

Steephill Lake

114

115

Pukatawagan

Nelson House

96

Primrose Lake

97

98 Ile-a-la-Crosse

99 Lac la Plonge

100

101 La Ronge

Pinehouse Lake

Lac La Ronge Provincial

102 Stanley

Trout Lake

103

Wood Lake

104 Pelican Narrows

Sandy Bay

Kinibigan Lake

105

Snow Lake

86

Pierceland

87 Meadow Lake Prov Park

Goodsoil

88 Waterhen Lake

Doré Lake

89

90 Weyakwin Lake

91 Weyakwin

Wapawekka Lake

92

Deschambault Lake

93

94

Jan Lake

Creighton

Flin Flon

95

Cranberry Portage

The Pas

Norway House

76 Little Fishing Lake

77 St Walburg

78 Chitek Lake

Meadow Lake

79 Big River

80 Waskesiu Lake

Prince Albert Nat Park

81 Candle Lake

Montreal Lake

82 Narrow Hills Prov Park

83 Squaw Rapids

Cut Beaver Lake

84 Cumberland House

85

Cedar Lake (Reservoir)

Grand Rapids

66 Lloydminster

67 Edam

68

Glaslyn

69 Shell Lake

70 Shellbrook

71 Prince Albert

72 Choiceland

73 Nipawin

Red Earth

74 Wildcat Hill Prov Park

Mountain Cabin

75

Leaf Lake

Lake Winnipeg

North Battleford

Melfort

Tisdale

Hudson Bay

Macklin

56

Unity

57

Wilkie

58

59

Rosthern

60

Wakaw

61

62

Greenwater Lake Prov Park

63

64

Porcupine Plain

65

Langham

Saskatoon

Swan River

Winnipegosis

45 Major

46 Kerrobert

47

Biggar

48 Delisle

49

50 Colonsay

Humboldt

51

Quill Lakes

52

Wynyard

53 Kelvington

54 Preeceville

Duck Mountain Prov Park

55

Winnipeg

Alsask

34

Kindersley

35

Rosetown

36

37

38

Douglas Prov Park

39 Davidson

40

Strasbourg

Last Mountain Lake

41 Punnichy

Foam Lake

42

Canora

43 Yorkton

Kamsack

44

Dauphin

Minnedosa

Neepawa

Portage la Prairie

WINNIPEG

South Saskatchewan

Leader

23

Abbey

24

Saskatchewan Landing Prov Park

25 Swift Current

26 Herbert

27

Central Butte

28 Moose Jaw

REGINA

29

Fort Qu'Appelle

30

31 Indian Head

Melville

32

Esterhazy

Langenburg

33

Moosomin

Virden

Brandon

Crane Tompkins

12

Maple Creek

13

14

15 Vanguard

16 Gravelbourg

Mossbank

17

18 Milestone

19

20 Stoughton

Moose Mountain Provincial Park

21

22

Souris

Cypress Hills Interprovincial Park

Eastend

1 Consul

2

3

Mankota

Val Marie

4

Grasslands National Park

5 Wood Mountain

6

7 Bengough

Weyburn

8

9 Estevan

10 Oxbow

Carnduff

11

Boissevain

Killarney

Scale 1:300,000

2.5km 0 5km

© Backroad Mapbooks

Eastend

2

Scale 1:300,000

© Backroad Mapbooks

See Map 2

See Map 4

WMZ 2W

WMZ 2E

WMZ 3

Val Marie

Frenchville

Driscol Lake

Beaver Valley

Hillandale

Climax

Canuck

Bracken

Masefield

Orkney

Port of Climax

Monchy

Port of Morgan

Grasslands National Park (West Block)

Grasslands NP Visitors Centre

Ecotour Scenic Drive

70 Mile Butte Trail

Prairie National Wildlife Area Unit 15

Prairie National Wildlife Area Unit 14

Rosefield Grid Rd

CANADA
USA

SASKATCHEWAN
MONTANA

USA

3 Val Marie

2.5km   0   5km

Scale 1:300,000

© Backroad Mapbooks

Mankota

4

Scale 1:300,000

2.5km 0 5km

© Backroad Mapbooks

Scale 1:300,000

© Backroad Mapbooks

Scale 1:300,000   2.5km 0   5km

Big Muddy

Scale 1:300,000

© Backroad Mapbooks

Estevan

Scale 1:300,000

© Backroad Mapbooks

Forget

Kisbey
Rae
BALMORAL
Armilla

RED

COAT

Arcola

Fremantle

Carlyle
Carlyle
Airfield

Steppes

WMZ
33

gas
plant
Johnstone
Shelter
Kisby
Oil Field

Arcola
Airfield

Queensdale
Oil Field

Viewfield
Oil Field

Tecumseh

Brock

Clarilaw
Oil Field

Woodsworth
Oil Field

Moose Mtn
Creek
Route

Wordsworth

Moose Mountain

Moose Mtn
Snowmobile
Trails

Morrisview
Oil Field

Blue
Line
Shelter

Fish & Wildlife
Development
Fund

Estevan
Snowmobile
Club Snow
Trails

Browning
Oil Field

Estevan
Snowmobile
Club Snow
Trails

Wildwood
Oil Field

WMZ
32

Minard
Oil Field

Willmar

Dalesborough
Oil Field

Bryant
Oil Field

Willmar
Shelter

Moose Creek

Browning

Browning

Woodley

Douglaston

Benson

Minard

WMZ
16

Oxbow
Shelter

Wilmar
Oil Field

Luxton
Lampman
Lampman
Airfield

Steelman
Oil Field

Moose
Mtn
Creek
Route

Breeze

SE Sask
Stubble
Jumpers
Snow
Trails

Domex

Steelman

Alameda

West Kingsford
Oil Field

Deborah

Moose
Creek
Regional
Park

Kingsford

Alameda
Dam

Oxbow

Oxbow
Airfield

Bow
Valley
Regional
Park

Bienfait
Oil Field

Frobisher

Alameda
Oil Field

Souris
River
Route

Hirsch

Enniskillen

Foeda

Openshaw

Bienfait

Glen Ewen
Oil Field

Coalfields

WMZ
31

Estevan

Bienfait Percee
Coalfields Historical
Museum

Fish & Wildlife
Development
Fund

Souris
River
Route

Shand

Coalfields

Souris
Rec Site

Roche Percee
Sandstone Caves
& Hoodoos

Roche Percee
Rec Site

Pinto

Elcott

Roche
Percee

Pinto
Oil Field

Heritage
Cemetery

Short
Creek
Cairn

La Roche Percee
Provincial
Historic Site

Northgate
Oil Field

North
Portal

CANADA
USA

SASKATCHEWAN
NORTH DAKOTA

Port of
Northgate

INTERNATIONAL

Portal

USA

© Backroad Mapbooks

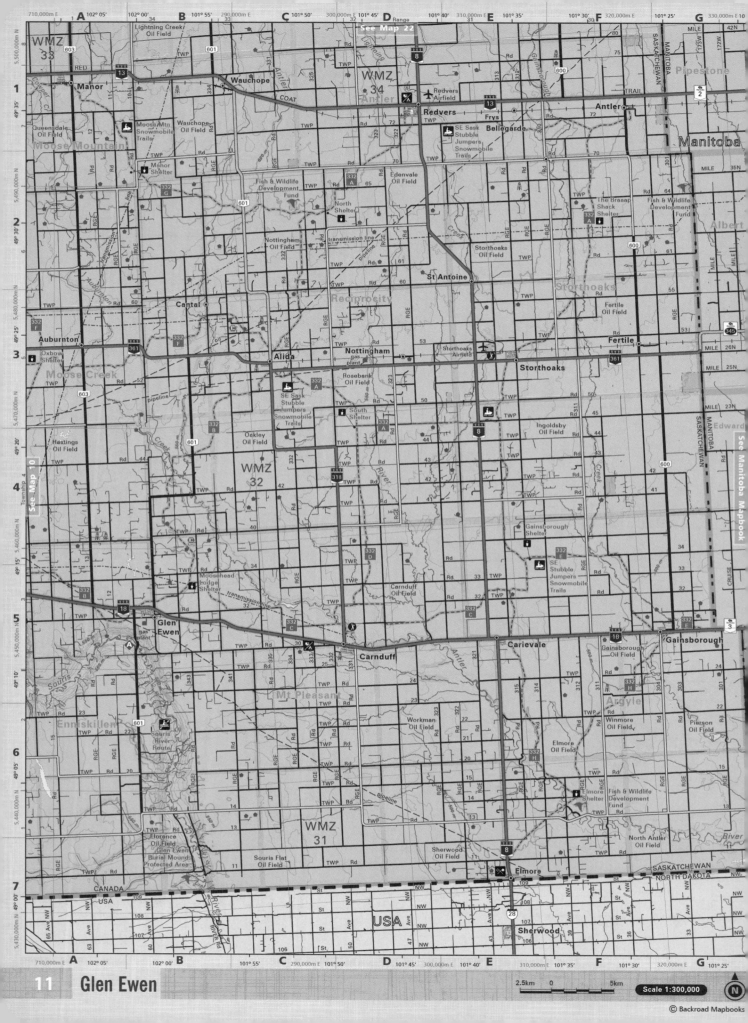

Scale 1:300,000

2.5km 0 5km

© Backroad Mapbooks

Scale 1:300,000   2.5km   0   5km

Swift Current 14

Scale 1:300,000   2.5km 0   5km

© Backroad Mapbooks

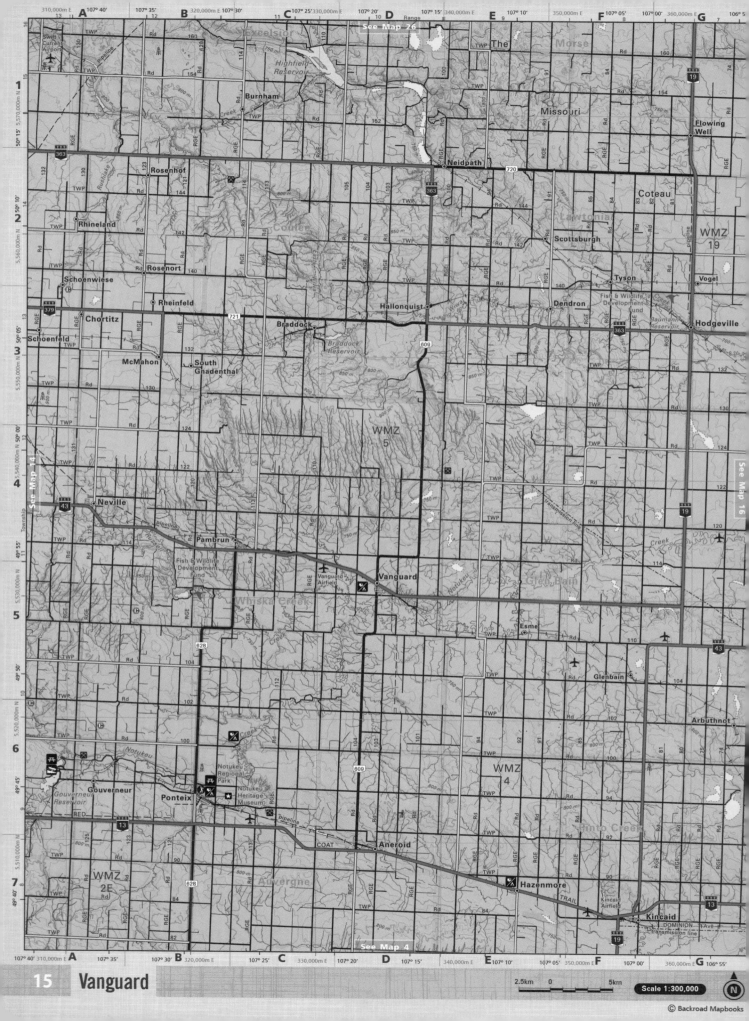

15 Vanguard

2.5km   0   5km

Scale 1:300,000

© Backroad Mapbooks

Scale 1:300,000   2.5km   0   5km

Scale 1:300,000

2.5km 0 5km

© Backroad Mapboo

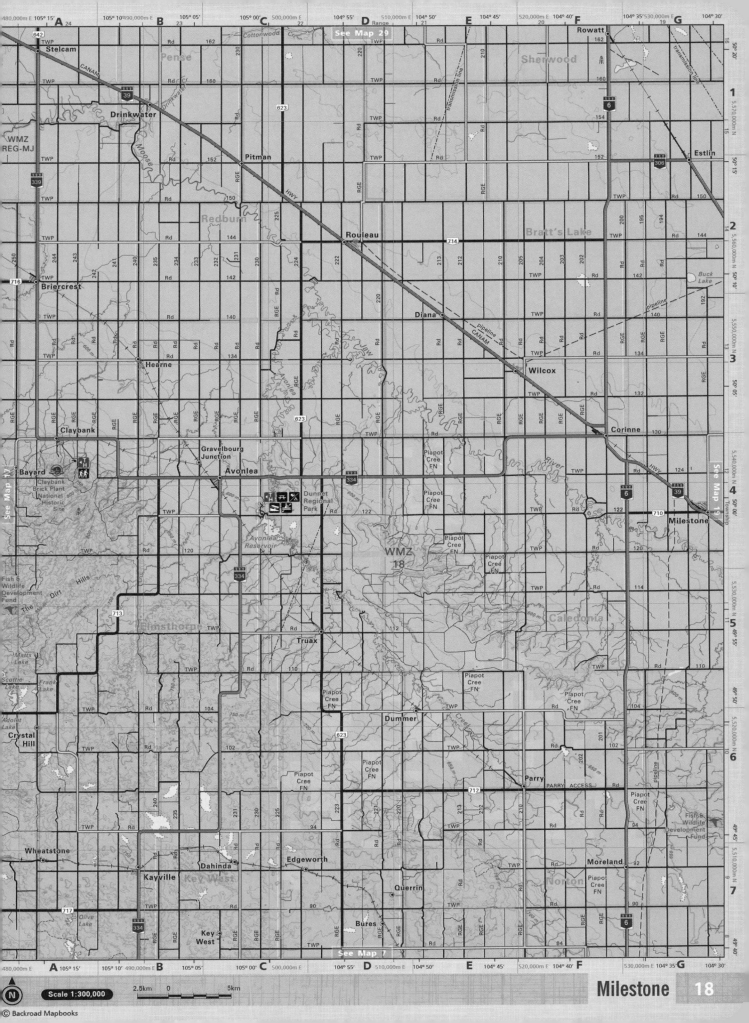

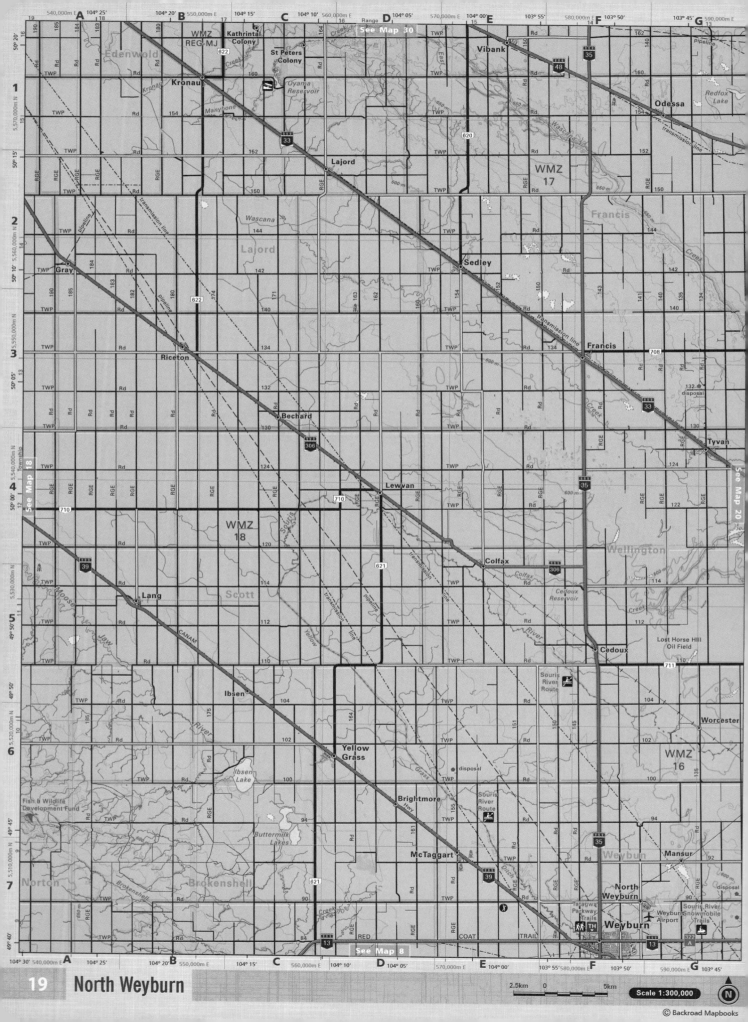

Scale 1:300,000

© Backroad Mapbooks

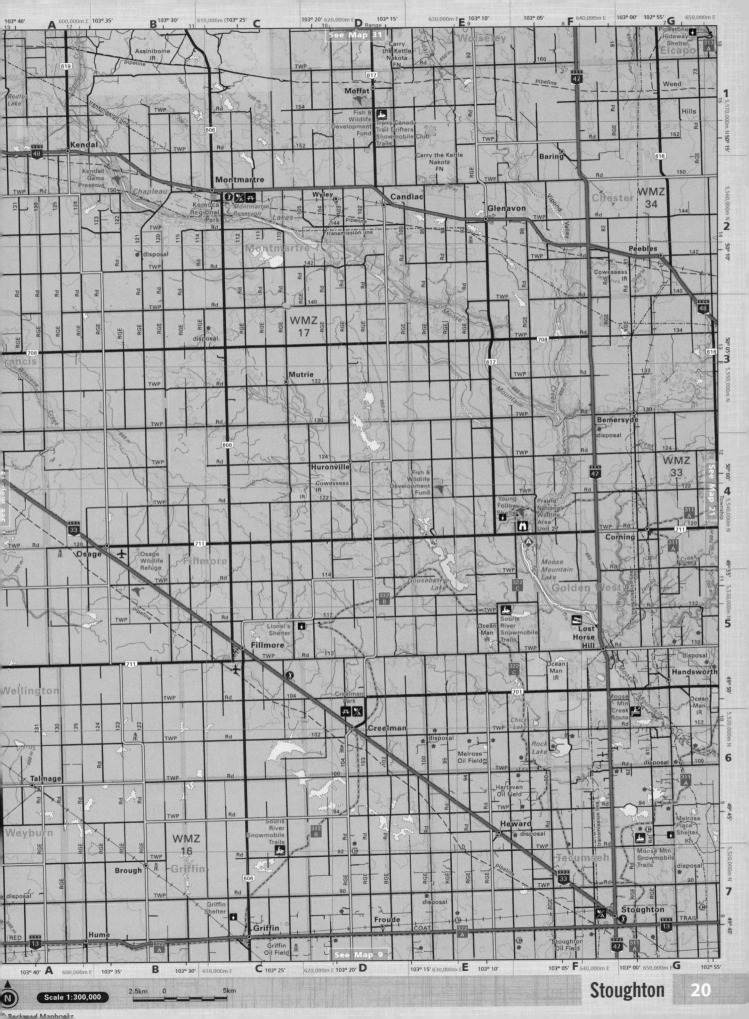

Moose Mountain Provincial Park

Scale 1:300,000

2.5km   0   5km

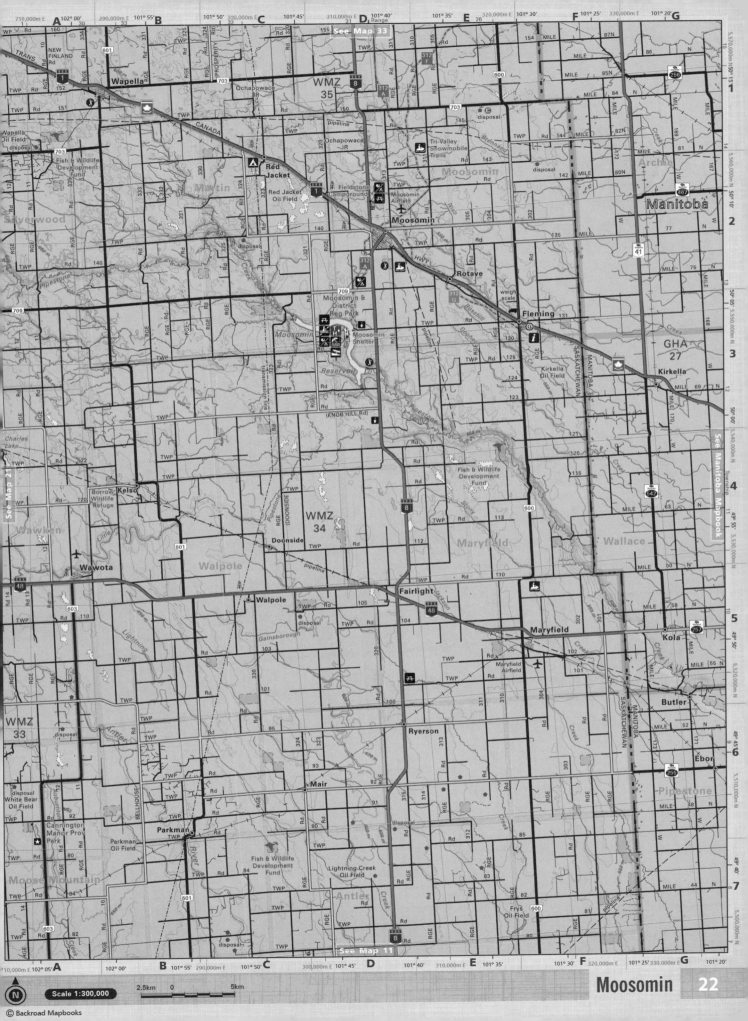

Scale 1:300,000

© Backroad Mapbooks

Great Sandhills Museum

Sceptre

Lemsford

Trans Canada Adventure Trail

Portreeve

Cramersburg

Lancer

WMZ 12

South Saskatchewan Route

Carry the Kettle Nakoda First Nation

WMZY 14E

Fairdale Coulee

Prairie National Wildlife Area Unit 21

Great Sandhills Viewing Area

Great Sandhills Ecological Reserve

Clinworth

Great Sandhills

Great

Abbey

Shackleton

Miry Creek

Prairie National Wildlife Area Unit 20

Great Sandhills Ecological Reserve

Pipeline

WMZ 10

transmission line

Sand

Ingebrigt Oil Field

Trans Canada Adventure Trail

Roadene

Fox Valley

Freefight Lake

Pittville

Hills

Hazlet Park

Hazlet

Standing Rock

MILLIE TRAIL

disposal

Martin Lake

WMZ 9

Piapot

Nadeauville

Gull Lake

Verlo

Delta Oil Field

STEELE

Bigstick Lake

See Map 13

See Map 25

Scale 1:300,000   2.5km   0   5km

Great Sand Hills   24

Backroad Mapbooks

Saskatchewan Landing Provincial Park

2.5km 0 5km

Scale 1:300,000

© Backroad Mapbooks

Scale 1:300,000

2.5km   0   5km

Scale 1:300,000

© Backroad Mapbooks

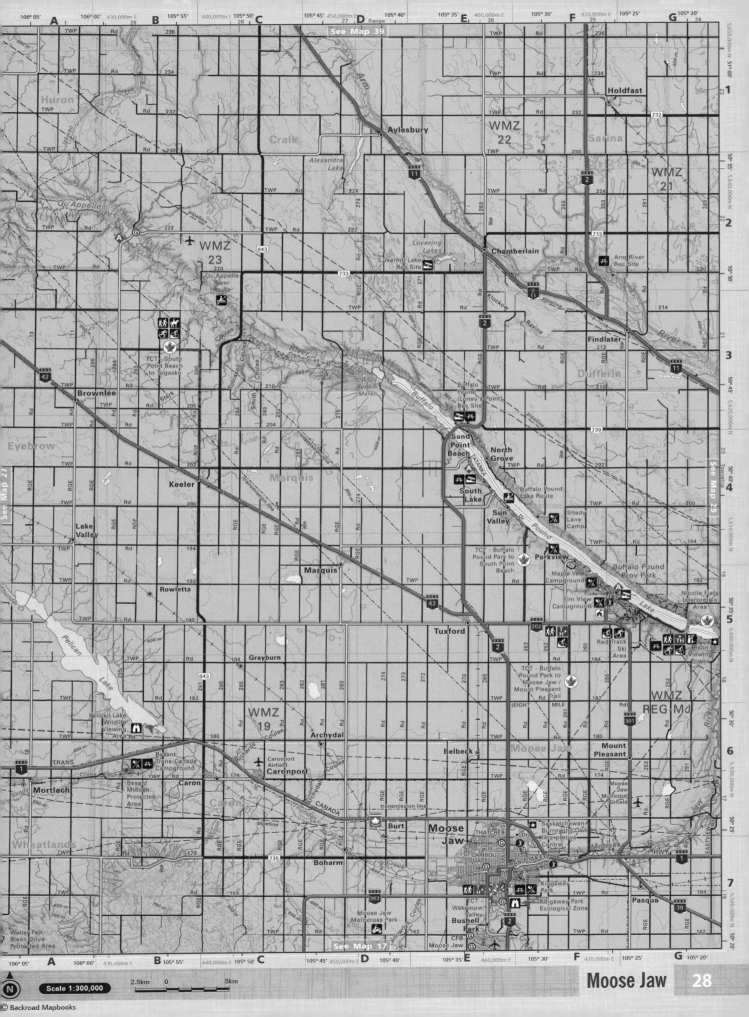

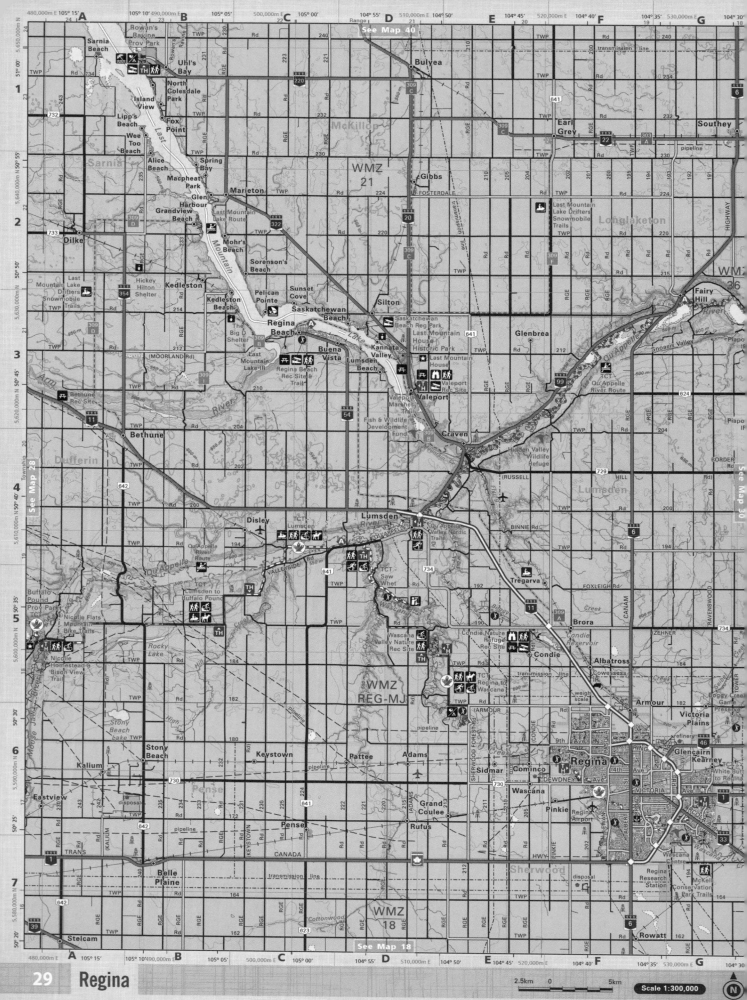

Scale 1:300,000

2.5km 0 5km

© Backroad Mapbooks

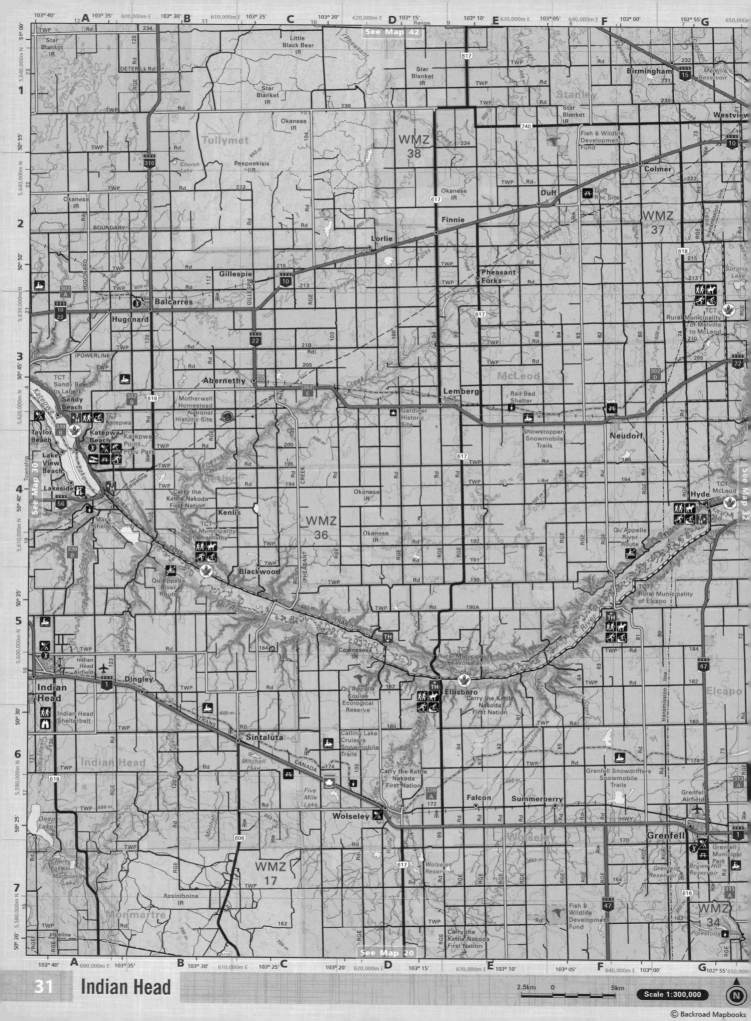

Scale 1:300,000

© Backroad Mapbooks

Scale 1:300,000

2.5km   0   5km

Melville   **32**

See Map 31

See Map 33

WMZ 37

WMZ 36

WMZ 35

WMZ 34

Qu'Appelle River Route

Scale 1:300,000

© Backroad Mapbooks

Alsask 34

Scale 1:300,000

© Backroad Mapbooks

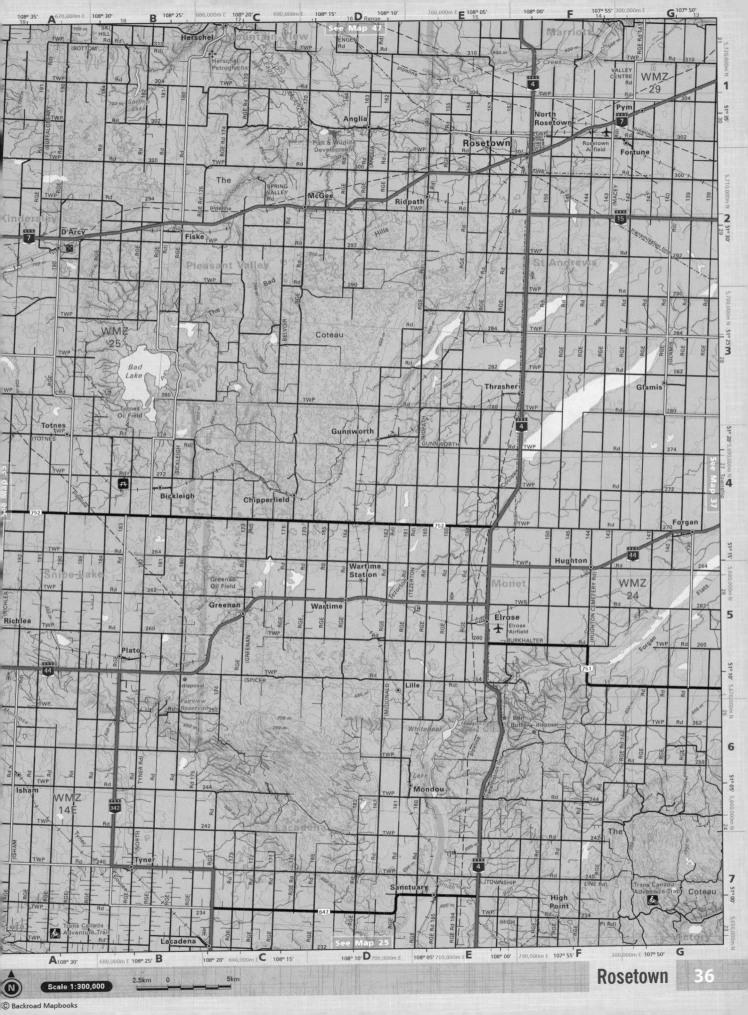

© Backroad Mapbooks

Outlook

Scale 1:300,000

© Backroad Mapbooks

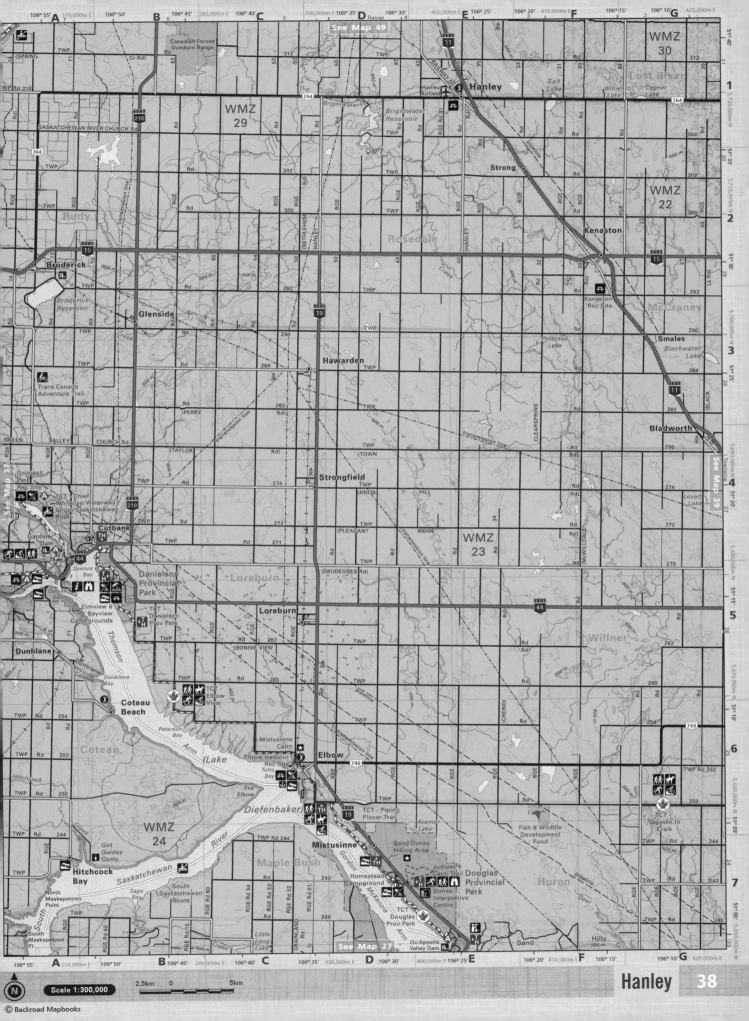

See Map 49

WMZ 30

WMZ 29

WMZ 22

Hanley

Strong

Kenaston

Rosedale

McCraney

Smales

Broderick

Glenside

Hawarden

Bladworth

Trans Canada
Adventure Trail

Strongfield

WMZ 23

Coldwell
Park
Rec Site

TCT Chief
Whitecap Waterway
South Saskatchewan
Route

Cutbank

Danielson
Provincial
Park

Loreburn

Willner

Elmview &
Bayview
Campgrounds

Danielson
Prov Park

Loreburn

Dunblane

Coteau
Beach

TCT - Elbow
View

Mistusinne
Cairn

Elbow

Elbow Harbour
Rec Site
Tufts Bay

Diefenbaker

TCT - Piping
Plover Trail

Fish & Wildlife
Development
Fund

TCT -
Tugaske to
Craik

WMZ 24

Girl Guides
Camp

Mistusinne

Sand Dunes
Hiking Area

Hitchcock
Bay

Maple Bush

Homestead
Campground

Juniper &
Cacti Trail

Douglas
Provincial
Park

Huron

North
Maskepetoon
Point

South Saskatchewan
Route

Sage Bay

Dunes
Interpretive
Centre

TCT
Douglas
Prov Park

Sand
Hills

South
Maskepetoon
Pt

Little Long
Lake

See Map 27

Qu'Appelle
Valley Dam

Scale 1:300,000

2.5km   0   5km

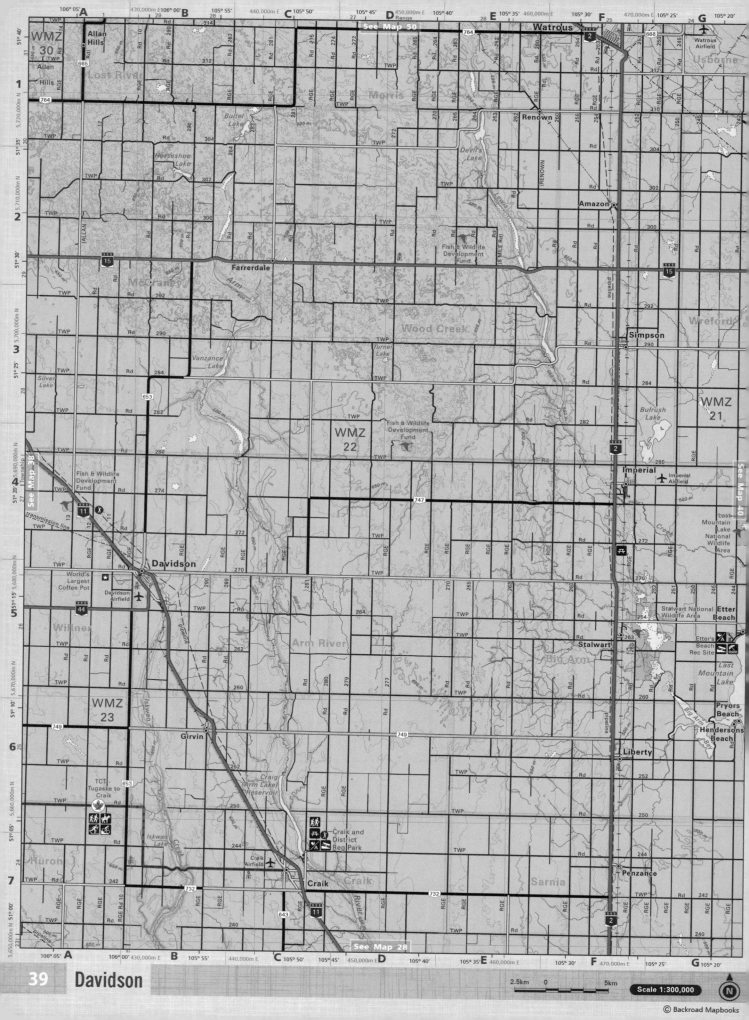

Scale 1:300,000

© Backroad Mapbooks

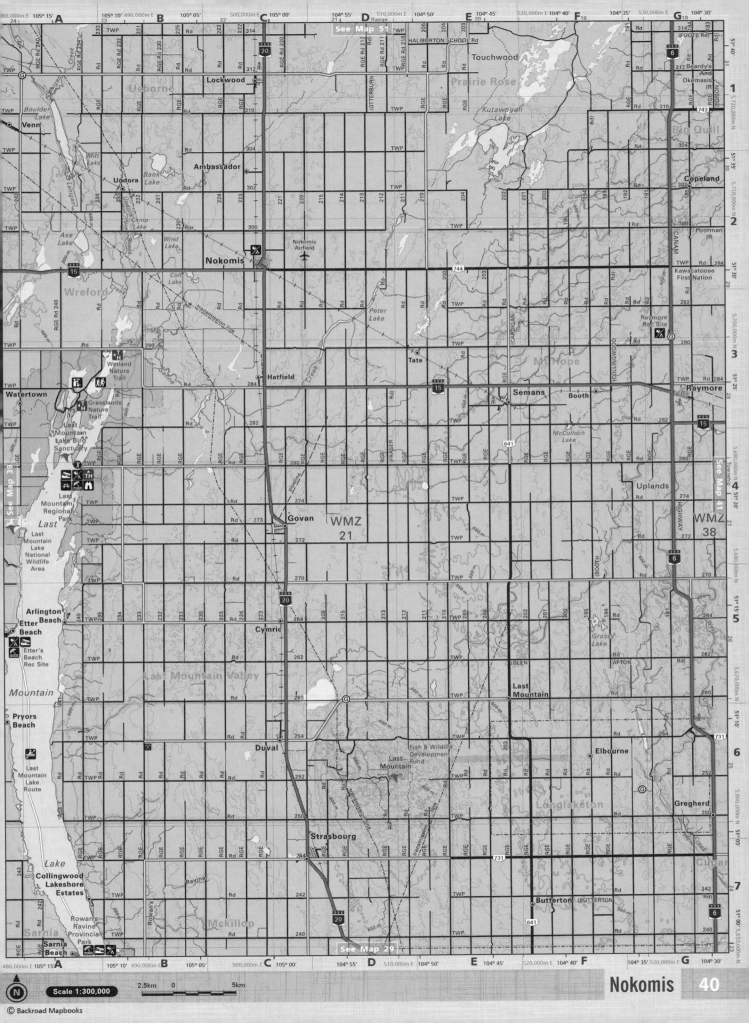

Scale 1:300,000

2.5km 0 5km

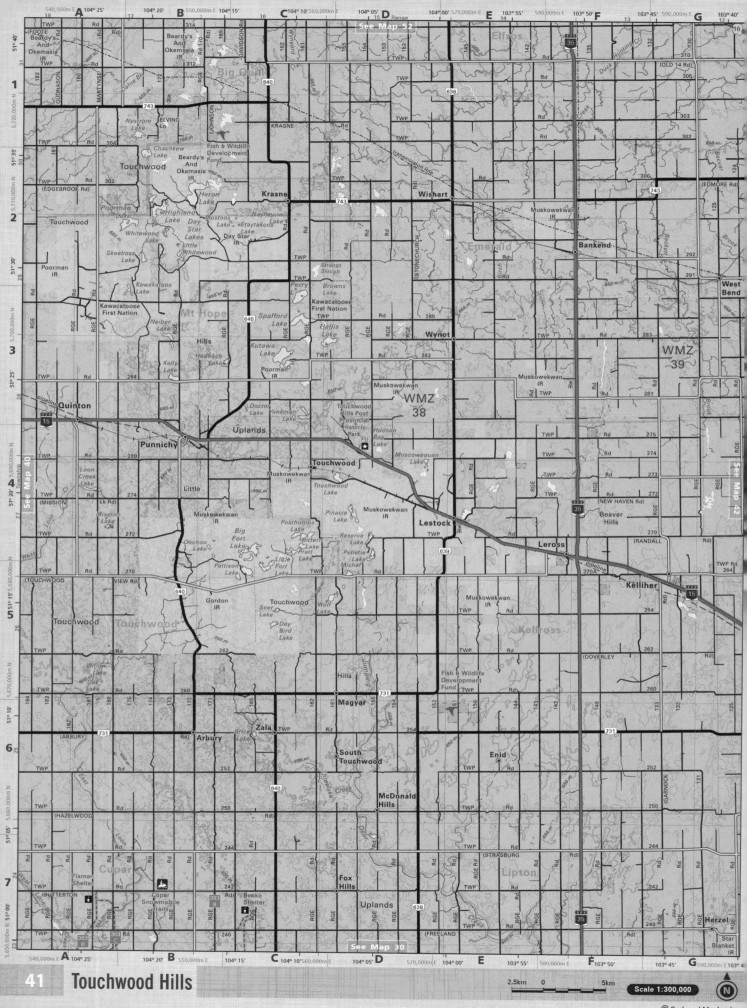

Scale 1:300,000

© Backroad Mapbooks

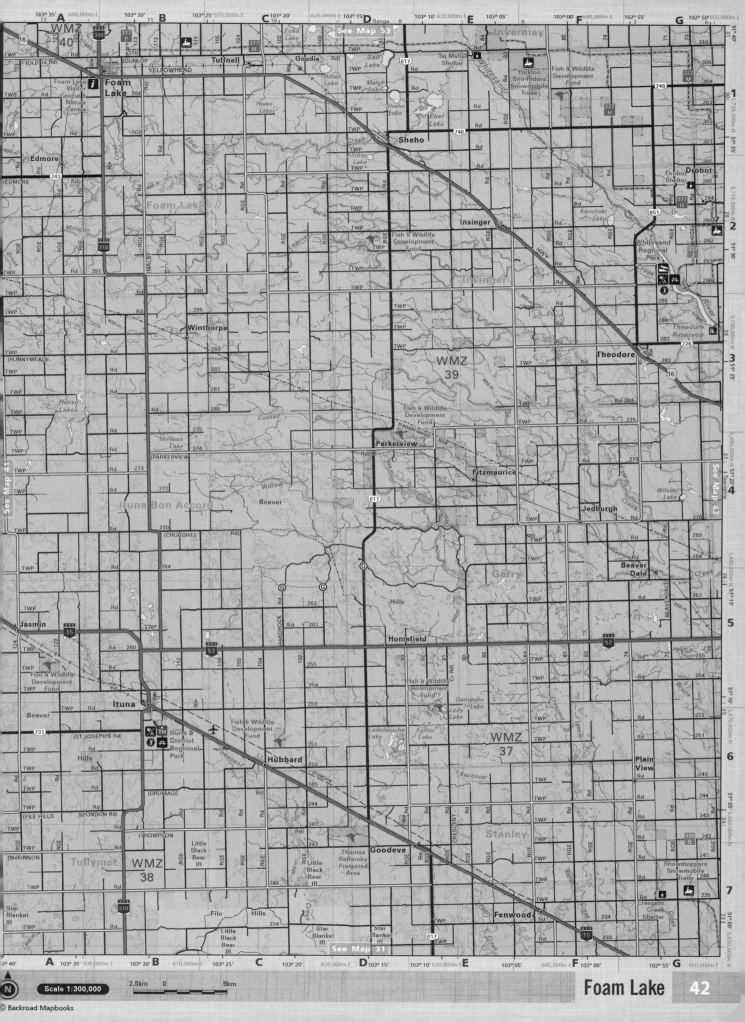

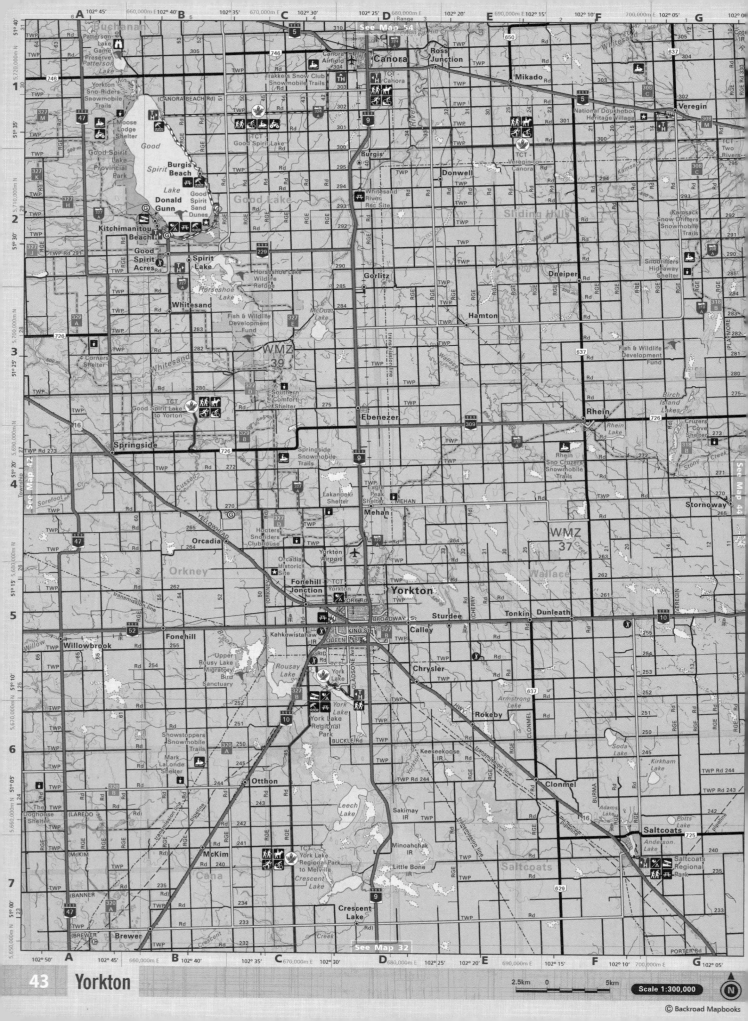

See Map 42
See Map 44
See Map 32

43 Yorkton

2.5km 0 5km

Scale 1:300,000

© Backroad Mapbooks

Major

Scale 1:300,000

© Backroad Mapbooks

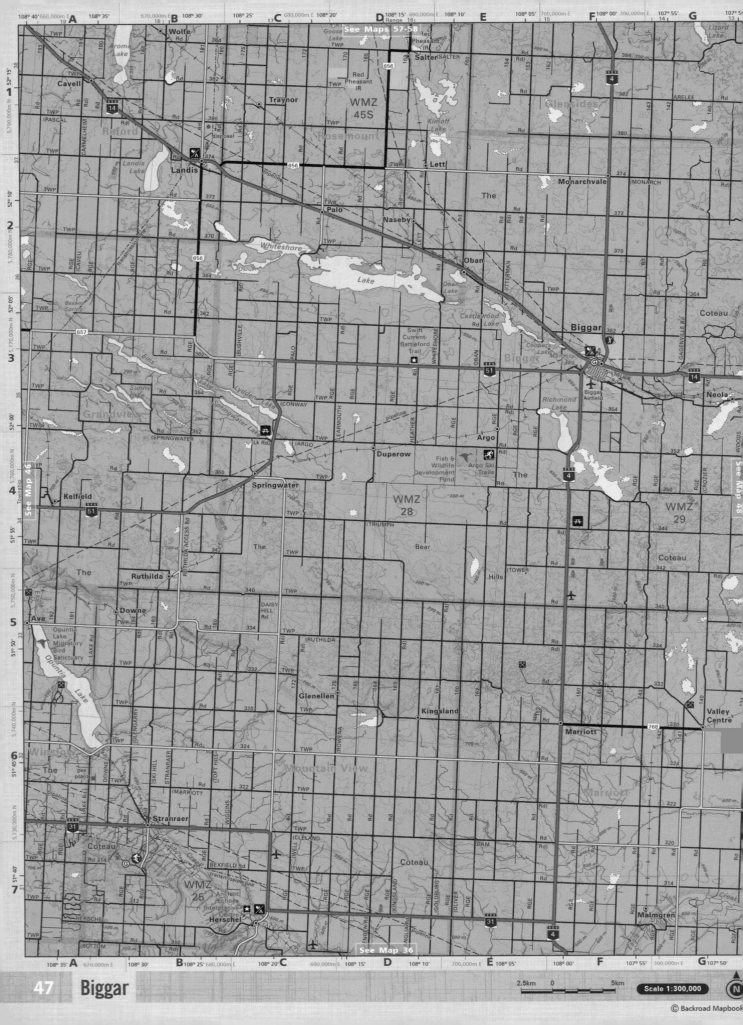

Scale 1:300,000

© Backroad Mapbook

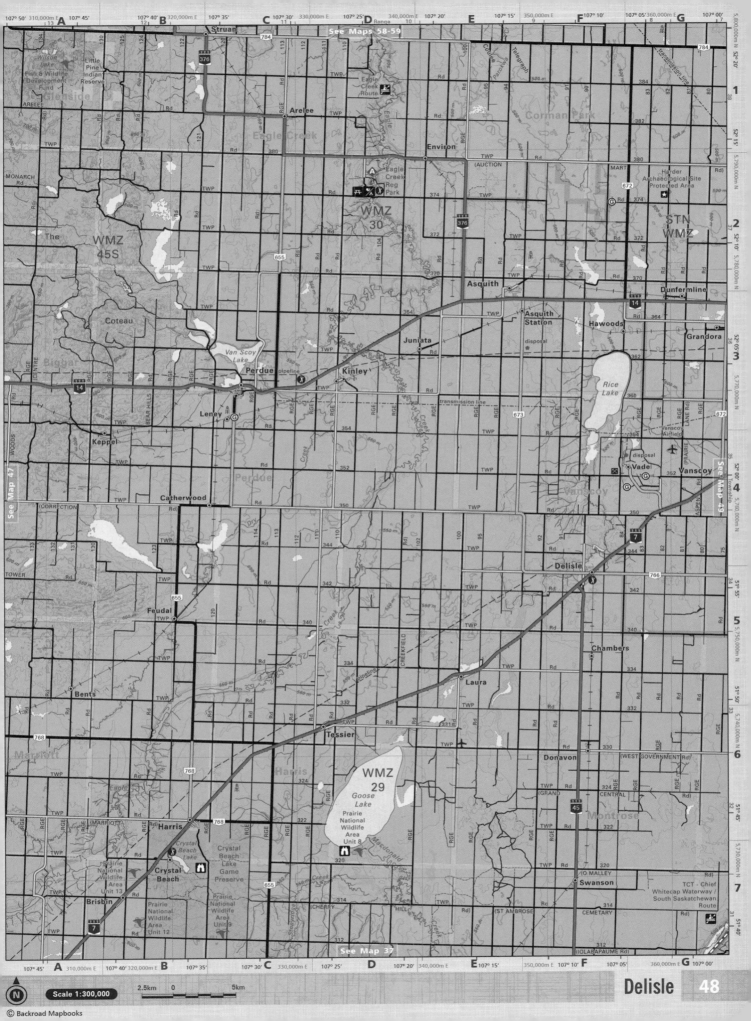

See Map 47

See Map 49

WMZ
45S

The

WMZ
30

STN
WMZ

WMZ
29
Goose
Lake

Prairie
National
Wildlife
Area
Unit 8

Scale 1:300,000

2.5km   0   5km

© Backroad Mapbooks

Delisle   48

Scale 1:300,000

© Backroad Mapbooks

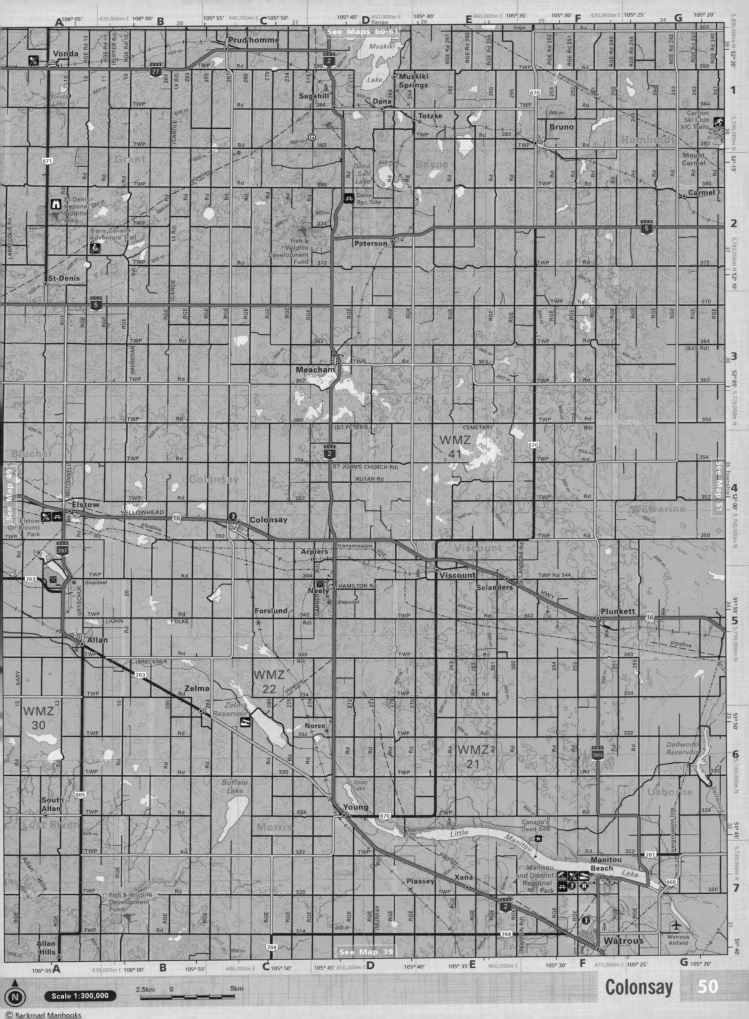

Scale 1:300,000   2.5km   0   5km

© Backroad Mapbooks

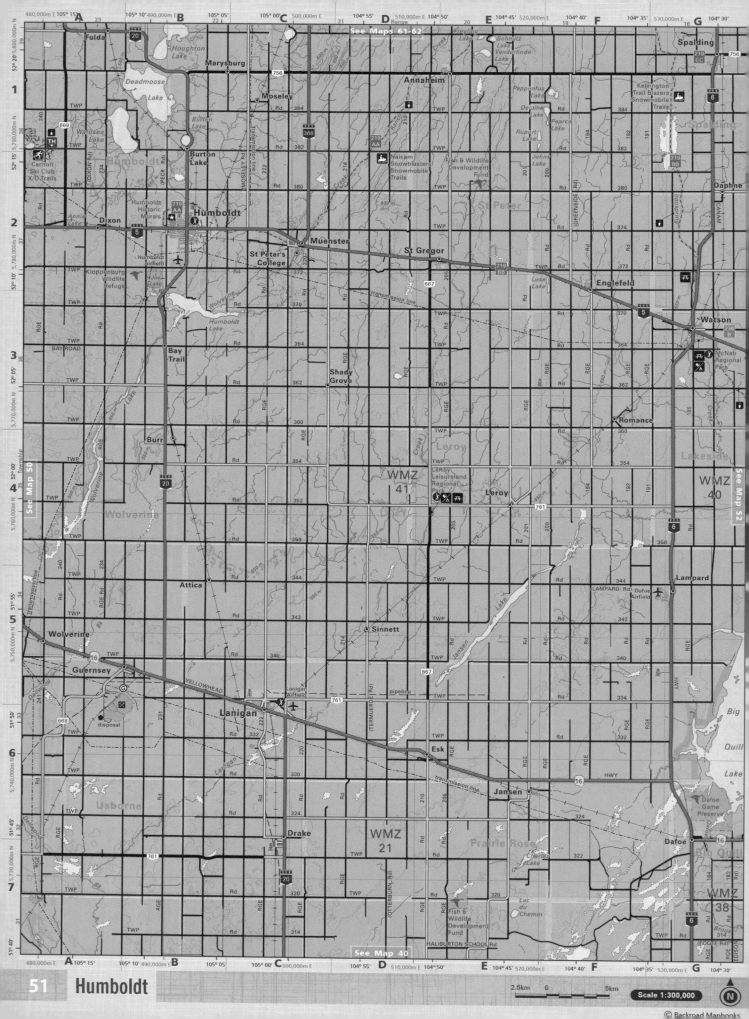

Scale 1:300,000

© Backroad Mapbooks

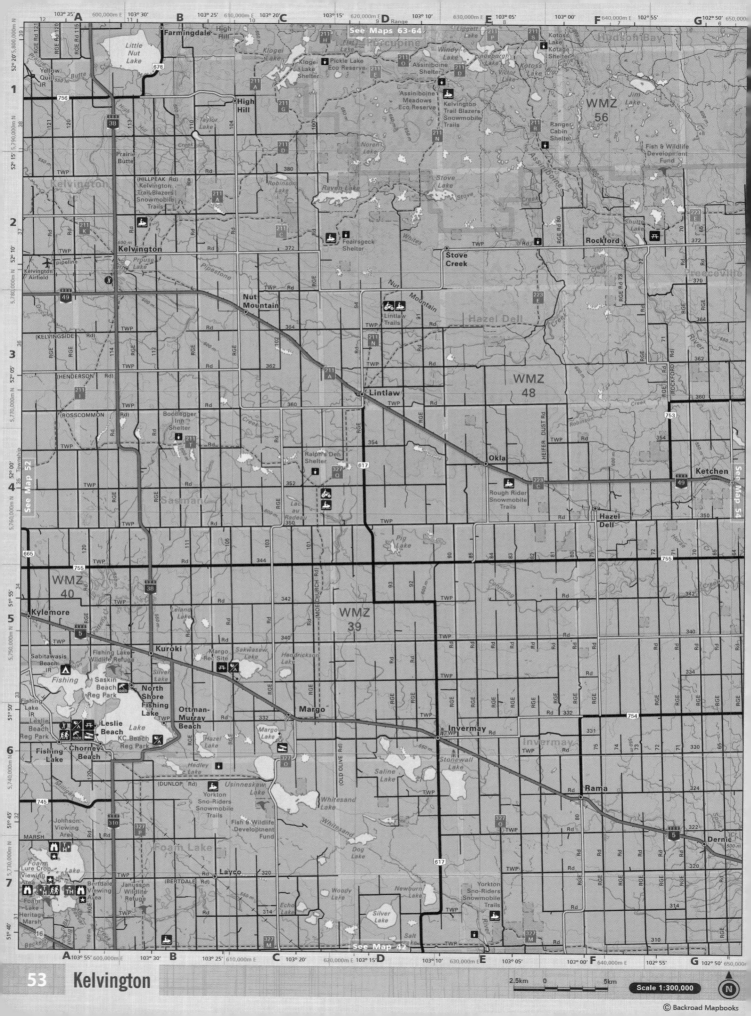

Scale 1:300,000

© Backroad Mapbooks

Duck Mountain Provincial Park

Scale 1:300,000

© Backroad Mapbooks

Scale 1:300,000

© Backroad Mapbooks

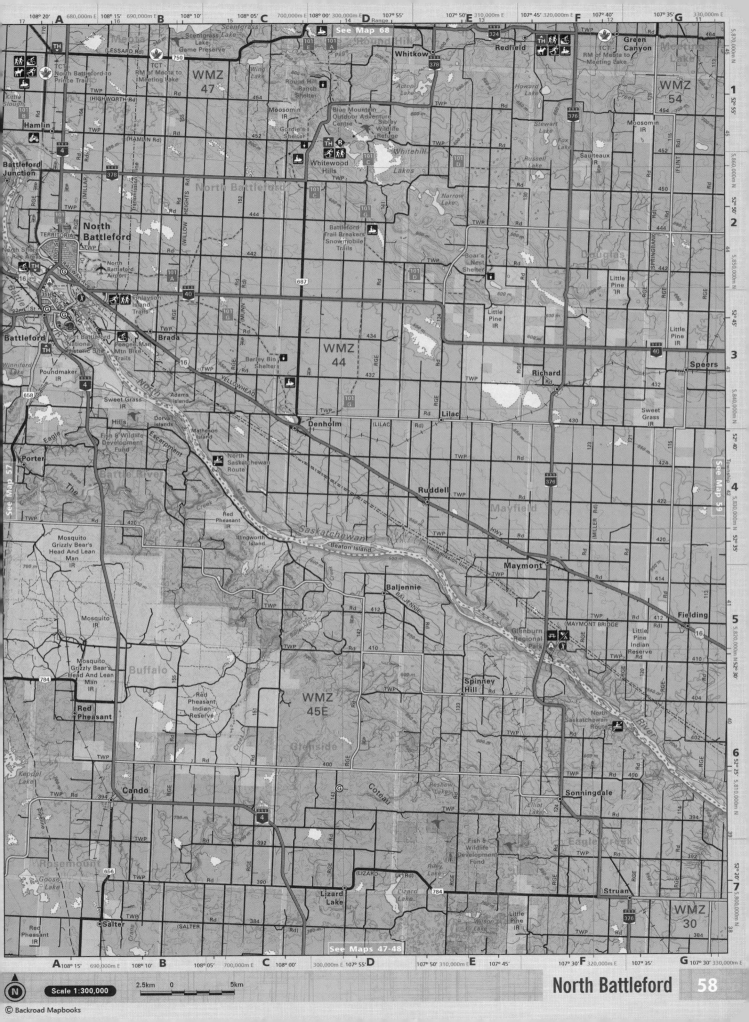

Scale 1:300,000

© Backroad Mapbooks

2.5km   0   5km

Backroad Mapbooks

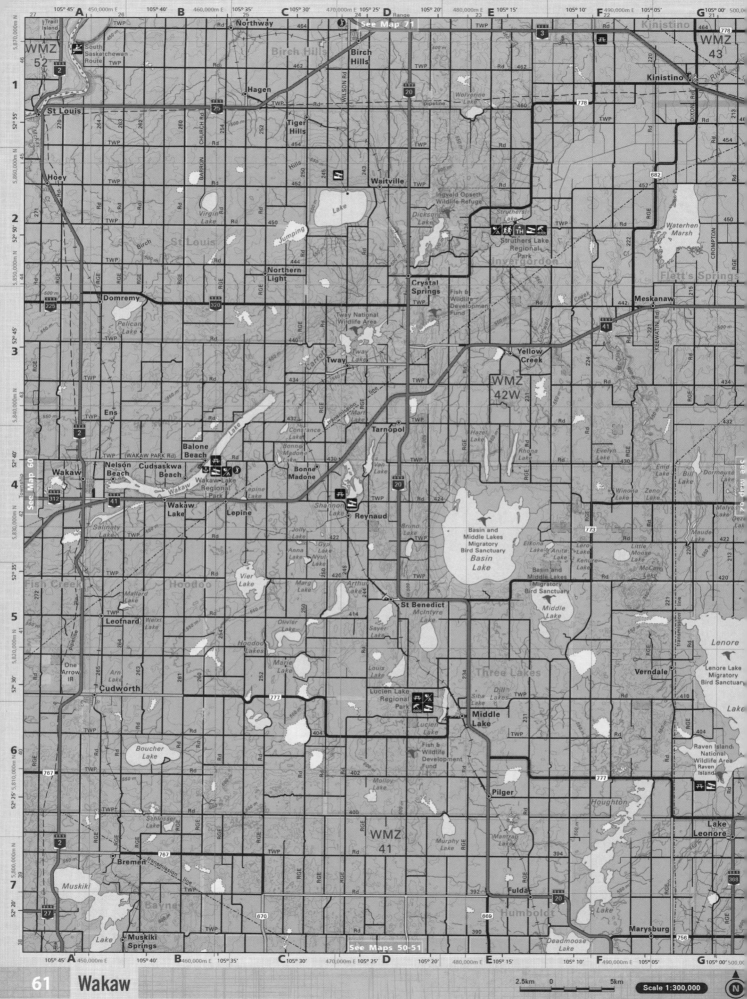

Scale 1:300,000

© Backroad Mapbooks

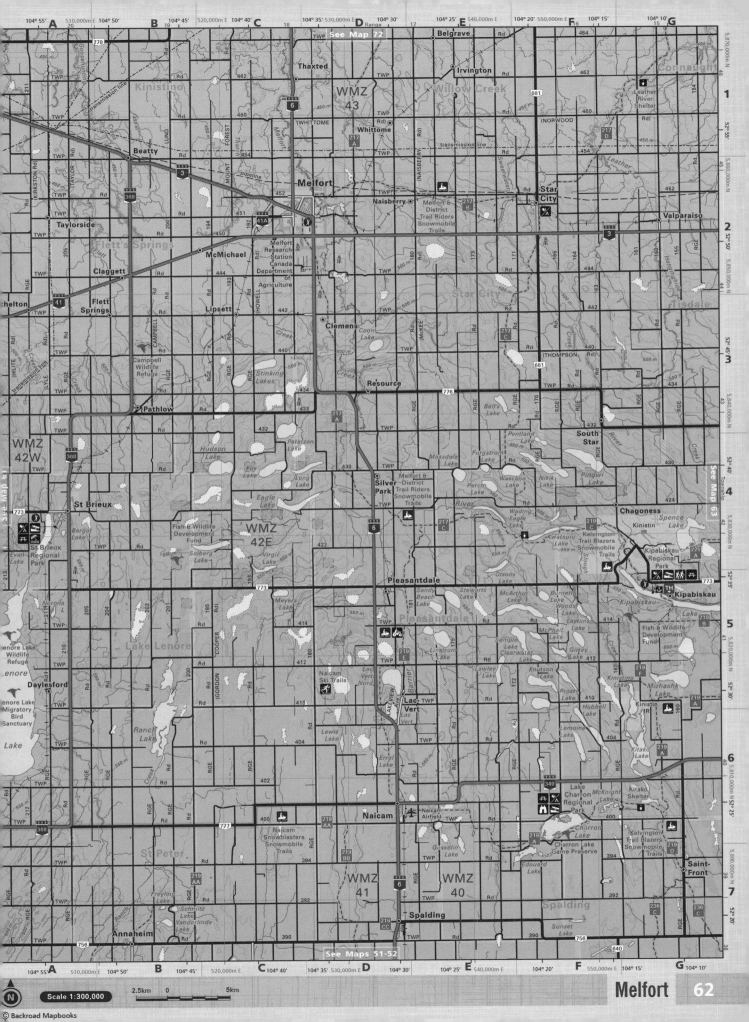

See Map 72
See Maps 51-52

Melfort 62

Scale 1:300,000

Scale 1:300,000

2.5km 0 5km

© Backroad Mapbooks

WMZ 59

WMZ 49

WMZ 48

WMZ 56

Arborfield

Pasquia

Hills

Prairie River

Bjorkdale

Muskeegan

Neely Lake Bird Sanctuary

Neely Lake

Porcupine

McElhanney

Lens

Porcupine Plain

Carragana

Somme

Weekes

Dillabough

Doncrest

Hudson Bay

Bertwell

Clemenceau

Veillardville

Mutchler

Akosane

Greenbush River Eco Reserve

Greenbush River Rec Site

Greenbush Shelter

Challange Camp Shelter

Fish & Wildlife Development Fund

Hudson Bay Trail Riders Snowmobile Trails

Hudson Bay Trail Riders Snowmobile Trails

Shawage Game Preserve

Fir River Eco Reserve

Wolfhide Lake

Tank Lake

Greenwater Lake Prov Park

Mistatim Snopackers Snowmobile Trails

Carragana Swamp Eco Reserve

HudsonBay Trail Riders Snowmobile Trails

Piwei River Rec Site

Piwei Lake Eco Reserve

Big Valley Lake Eco Reserve

Kelvington Trail Blazers Snowmobile Trails

Pickle Lake Eco Reserve

Pickle Lake

Timberwolf Shelter

Weldon Lake

Liggett Lake

Lindeburgh Lake

Kotoss Lake

Kotage Shelter

Kotoss Lake

Windy Lake

Assiniboine Meadows Eco Reserve

Assiniboine Shelter

Victor Lake

Hazel Dell

WMZ 56

Big Valley Lake

Alterson Lake

Eagle Lake

Ravine Creek

Arps Lake

Roy Lake

Atnfield Lake

Gara Lake

Tall Pines

Kelvington Trail Blazers Snowmobile Trails

Ushta Shelter

Preeceville

HudsonBay Trail Riders Snowmobile Trails

Reserve Shelter

Reserve

Reserve Reservoir

McBride

Eldredge Lake

McBride Lake

Mekin Lake

Sweeney Lake

Chinook Lake

Kidney Lake

Menesachin Lake

Arthur Lake

Toboggan Lake

McKinnon Lake

Rogal Lake

Wells Lake

Flat Lake

MacMurchy

Iogei Lake

Shelter

See Maps 53-54

See Maps 74

See Map 65

N

Scale 1:300,000

2.5km   0   5km

Porcupine Plain **64**

© Backroad Mapbooks

See Map 64

See Maps 54-55

WMZ 59
WMZ 58
WMZ 49
WMZ 58
GHA 12
WMZ 57
WMZ 56
GHA 13 Manitoba

Ruby Beach
Ruby Lake
Hudson Bay Regional Park Ruby Lake
Hudson Bay Trail Riders Snowmobile Trails
Red Deer River Eco Reserve
Smoky Ridge
Rendek Elm Forest Nature Sanctuary
North Armit River Eco Reserve
Lower Armit River Eco Reserve

Hudson Bay
Erwood
Smoking Tent
Roscoe
Armit
Westgate
National Mills
Armit River Rec Site

Hudson Bay Regional Park
Hudson Bay Airfield
Red Deer River Route
Pineview X/C Trails

Loiselle
Etomami
Fish & Wildlife Development Fund

Smoking Tent Creek Eco Reserve
Ice Road Inn Shelter

Upper Armit River Eco Reserve
Little Armit River Eco Reserve

Armit River Canyon

Dagg Creek Rec Site

Hudson Bay Trail Riders Snowmobile Trails

Hudson Bay

Hills

Brockelbank Hill Protected Area
Brockelbank Hill

Porcupine Provincial Forest

Porcupine

Swan Valley Shelter
Saginas Lake Rec Site
Saginas Lake

Alleri Lake
Killian Lake
Halliday Lake
Isbister Lake
Midnight Lake
Island Lake

Spirit Mtn
Spirit Lake
Spirit Lake Campground
Muakeg Lake
Little Armit Lake

McBride Lake Rec Site
Swallow Lake
McBRIDE
McBride Lake
White Lake

Bill's Lake

Nelson
Trickett Lake Shelter
Trickett Lake

Isbister Lake Campground
McSherry Lake
Townsend Lake Campground
Woody River Recreation Site
Townsend Lake

Elbow Lake
Elbow Lake Day Use
Woody Lake Day Use
Zapfe Lake
Picker Lake

Pepaw Lake Rec Site
Wapsim Lake
Pepaw Lake

Porcupine Hills Trails

Otter Lake
Prairie & Pine Snowmobile Trails
Smallfish Lake Campground
Smallfish Lake
Thunder Snowmobile Trail

Little Swan River
Parr Hill Springs
Parr Hill Lake
Parr Hill Lake Rec Site
Hudson Bay Trail Riders Snowmobile Trails
Boiler Junction Shelter
Decorby Lake

Little Swan River Viewpoint
Stewart
Marder Lake

Woody Lake
OOPS Boundary Shelter
Whitef Lake Prov P
Whitef Lake

Hamilton Lake
Clayton

Twin
Kenney Lake

TENNANT
Moose
Tennant Lake
Georger Lake
Livingston

65 Hudson Bay

2.5km 0 5km
Scale 1:300,000
© Backroad Mapbook

Lloydminster   66

Scale 1:300,000

2.5km   0   5km

© Backroad Mapbooks

Scale 1:300,000

2.5km 0 5km

© Backroad Mapbooks

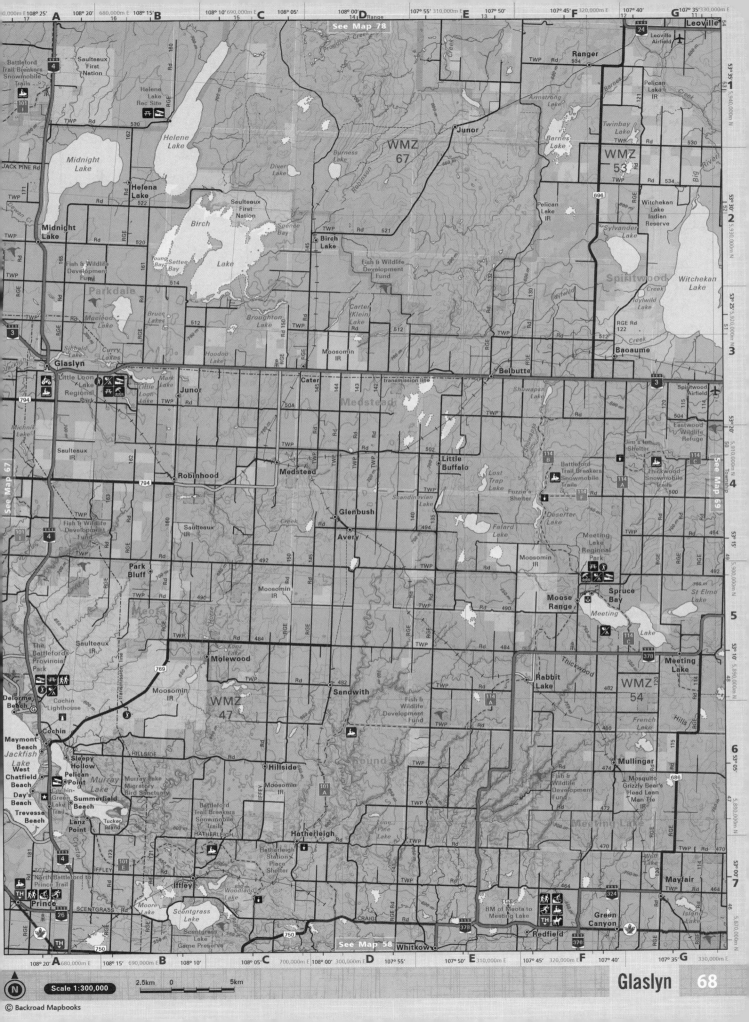

Scale 1:300,000

2.5km 0 5km

© Backroad Mapbooks

Glaslyn 68

Scale 1:300,000

2.5km   0   5km

© Backroad Mapbooks

Scale 1:300,000

2.5km   0   5km

Scale 1:300,000

© Backroad Mapbooks

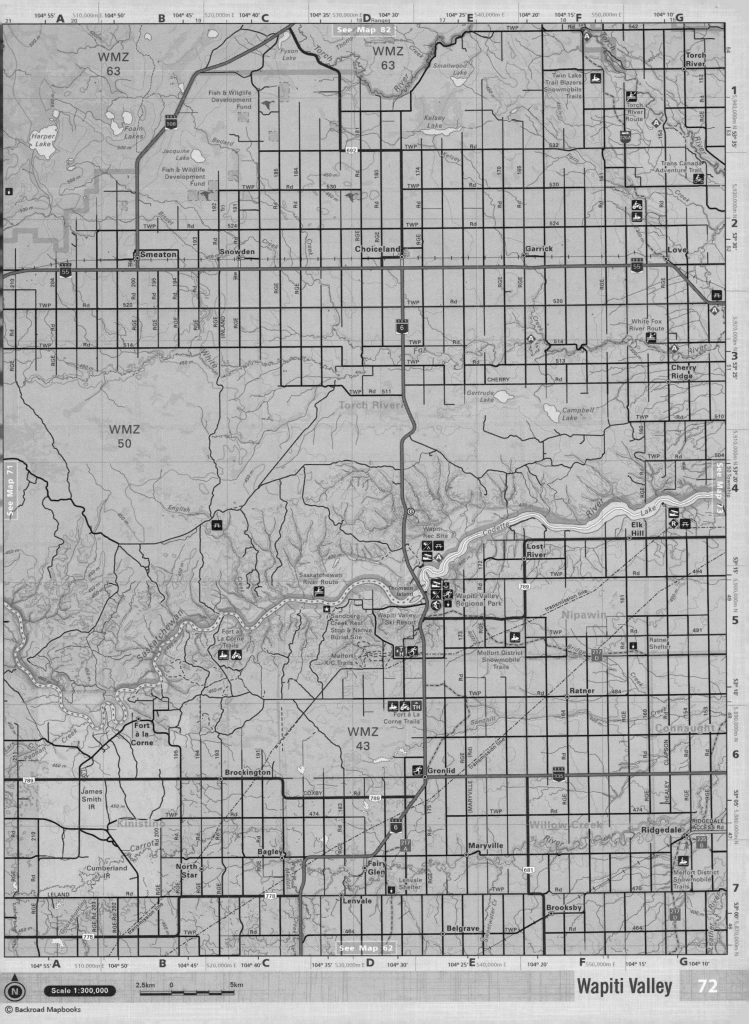

Scale 1:300,000

2.5km 0 5km

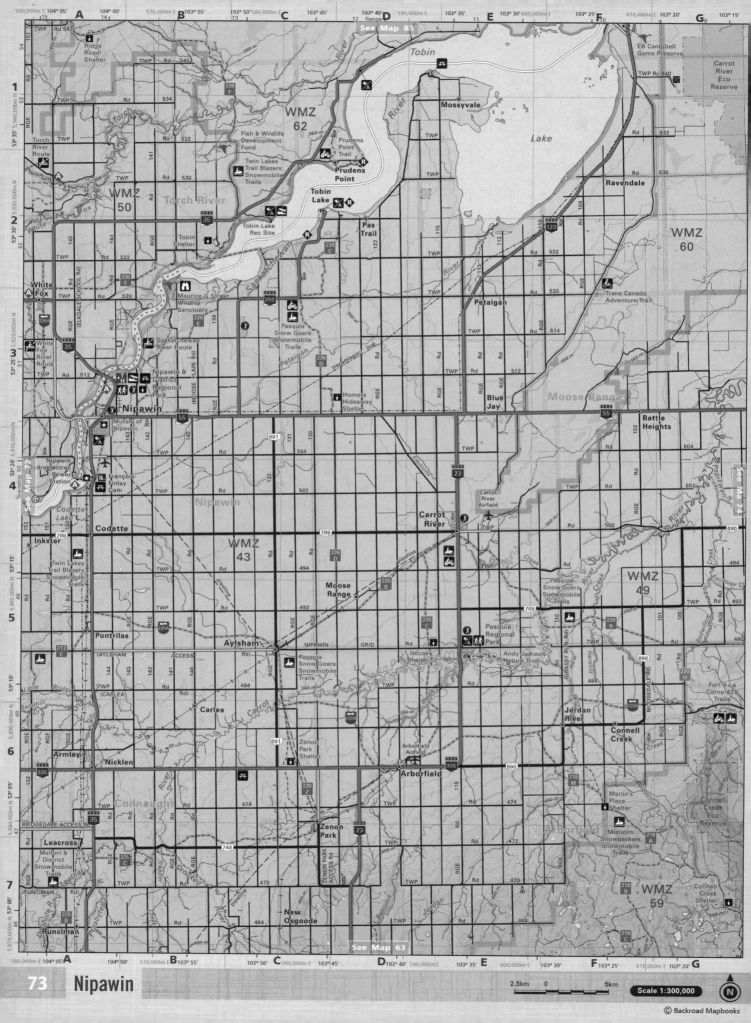

560,000m E 104° 05' A 104° 00' B 570,000m E 103° 55' C 103° 50' 580,000m E D 103° 45' E 103° 40' F 590,000m E G 103° 35' E 103° 30' 600,000m E F 103° 25' G 610,000m E 103° 20' G 103° 15'

Carrot River Eco Reserve

Ridge Road Shelter

Torch River Route

WMZ 62

WMZ 50

Torch River

Tobin Lake

Mossyvale

Tobin Lake

Lake

Ravendale

WMZ 60

Fish & Wildlife Development Fund

Twin Lakes Trail Blazers Snowmobile Trails

Prudens Point Trail

Prudens Point

Pas Trail

White Fox

Tobin Shelter

Tobin Lake Rec Site

Petaigan

Trans Canada Adventure Trail

Maurice G Street Wildlife Sanctuary

White Fox River Route

Saskatchewan River Route

Pasquia Snow Goers Snowmobile Trails

Moose Range

Nipawin & District Regional Park

Blue Jay

Battle Heights

Nipawin

Homers Hideaway Shelter

Murals of Nipawin

Nipawin Hydroelectric Power Station

François Finlay Dam

Codette Lake

Nipawin

Carrot River

Carrot River Airfield

Codette

WMZ 43

Moose Range

WMZ 49

Inkster

Twin Lakes Trail Blazers Snowmobile Trails

Pasquia Snow Goers Snowmobile Trails

Pontrilas

Aylsham

NIPAWIN GRID

Pasquia Regional Park

Andy Jamault Nature Trail

Jordan River

Fort 'A La Corne ATV Trails

Carlea

Pasquia Snow Goers Snowmobile Trails

House Shelter

Connell Creek

Armley

Nicklen

Zenon Park Shelter

Arborfield Airfield

Arborfield

Marlin's Place Shelter

Connell Creek Eco Reserve

Connaught

Zenon Park

Mistatim Snowbackers Snowmobile Trails

Leacross

Melfort & District Snowmobile Trails

BRIDGEDALE ACCESS Rd

WMZ 59

Connell Creek Shelter

Runciman

New Osgoode

560,000m E 104° 05' A 104° 00' B 570,000m E 103° 55' C 580,000m E 103° 50' D 103° 45' 590,000m E E 103° 35' F 103° 30' G 600,000m E 103° 30' 103° 25' 610,000m E 103° 20'

73 Nipawin

2.5km 0 5km

Scale 1:300,000

© Backroad Mapbooks

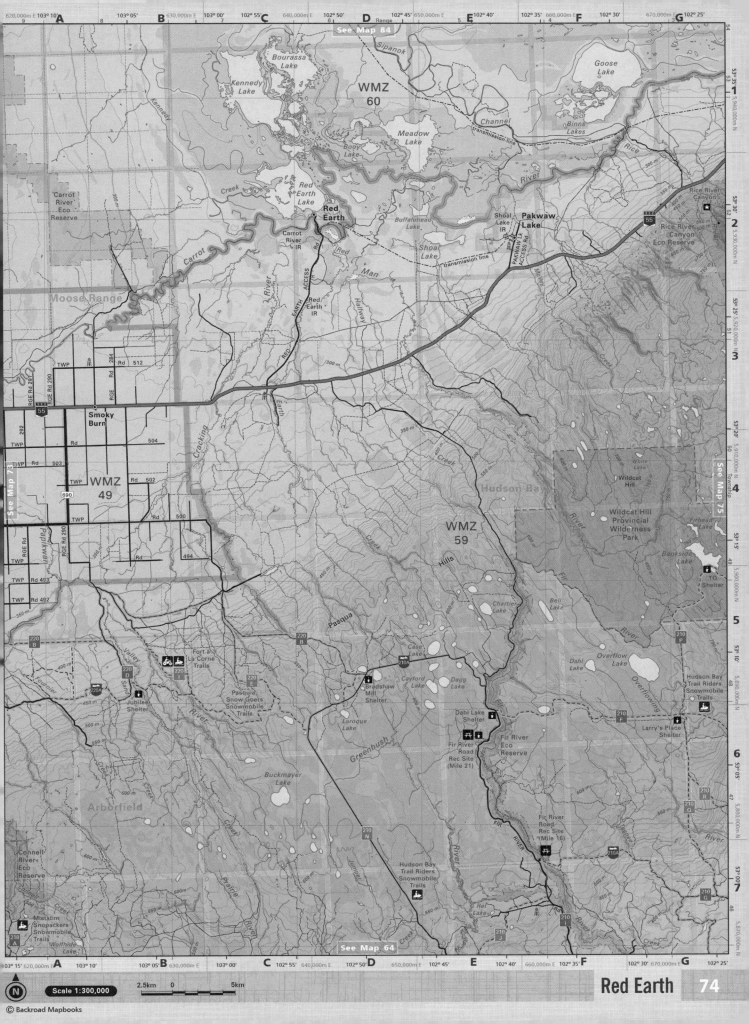

© Backroad Mapbooks

Scale 1:300,000

2.5km   0   5km

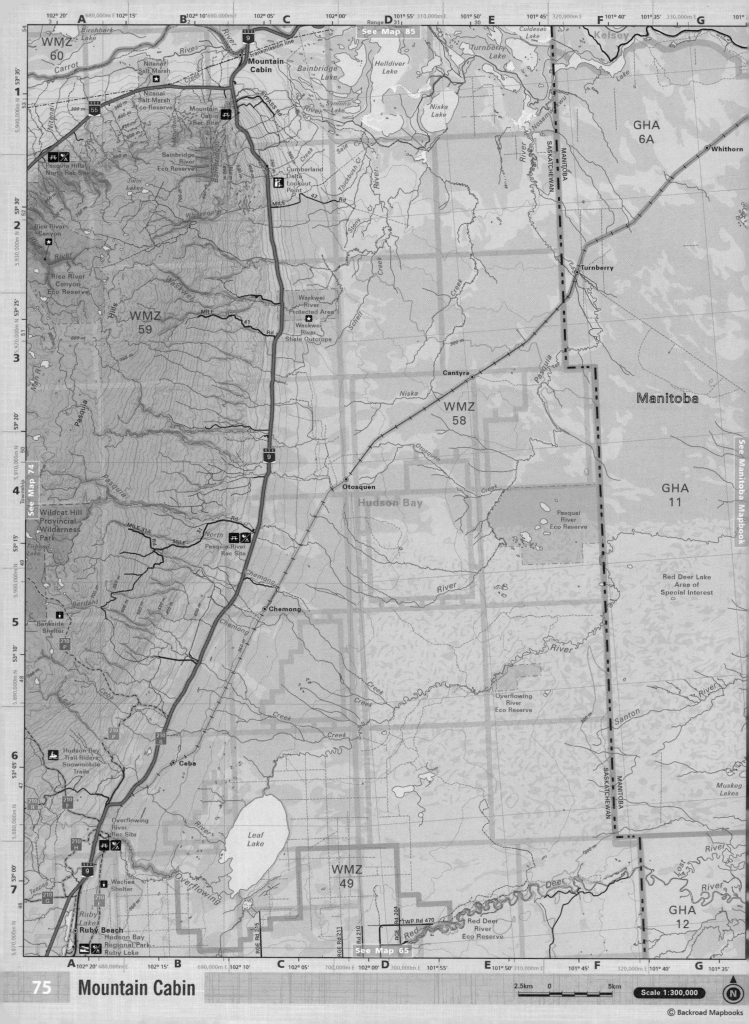

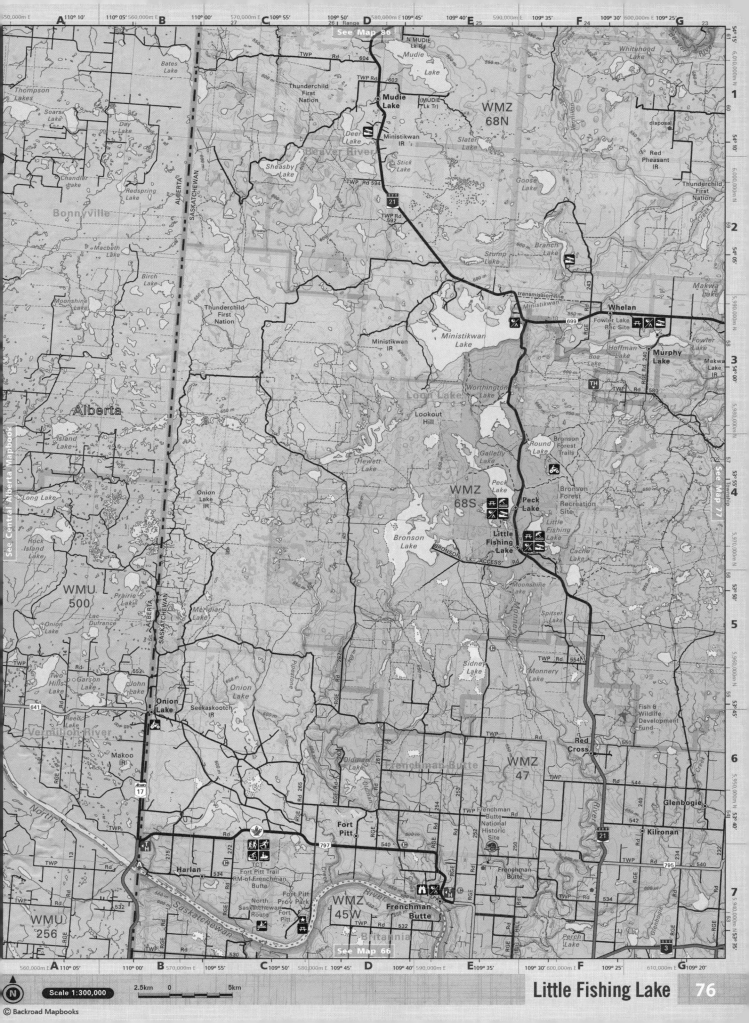

St Walburg

2.5km 0 5km Scale 1:300,000

© Backroad Mapbooks

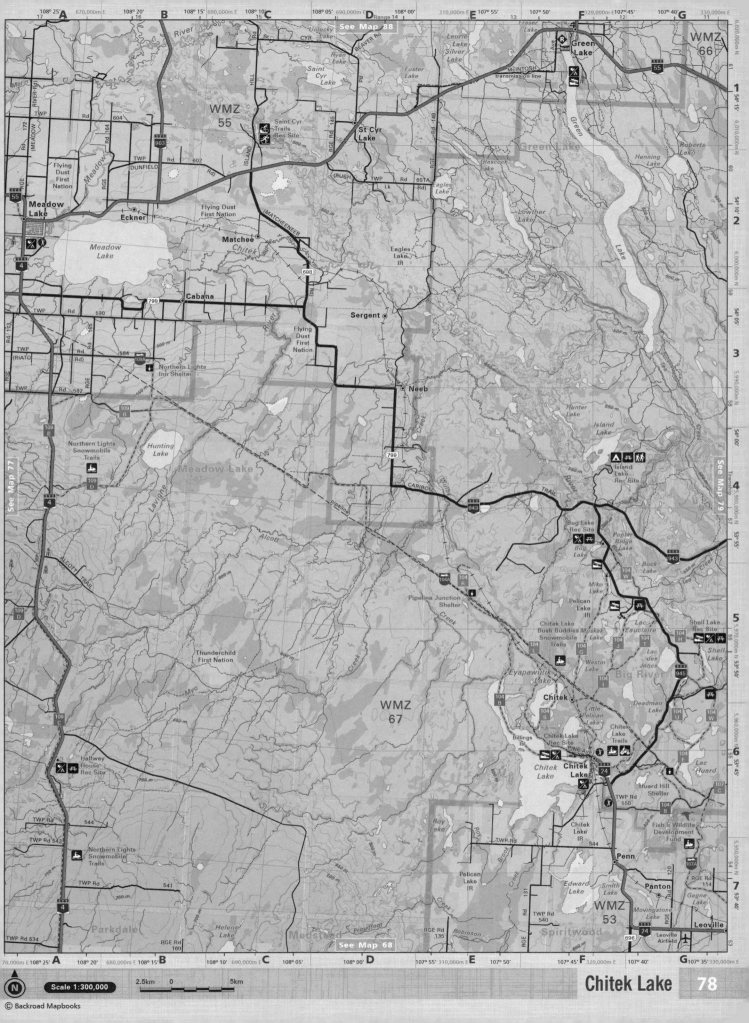

WMZ 66

WMZ 55

WMZ 67

WMZ 53

Green Lake

GreenLake

Meadow Lake

Chitek Lake

Big River

Spiritwood

Leoville

Penn

Panton

Neeb

Sergent

Cabana

Matchee

Eckner

Meadow Lake

St Cyr Lake

Scale 1:300,000

2.5km   0   5km

© Backroad Mapbooks

Chitek Lake

78

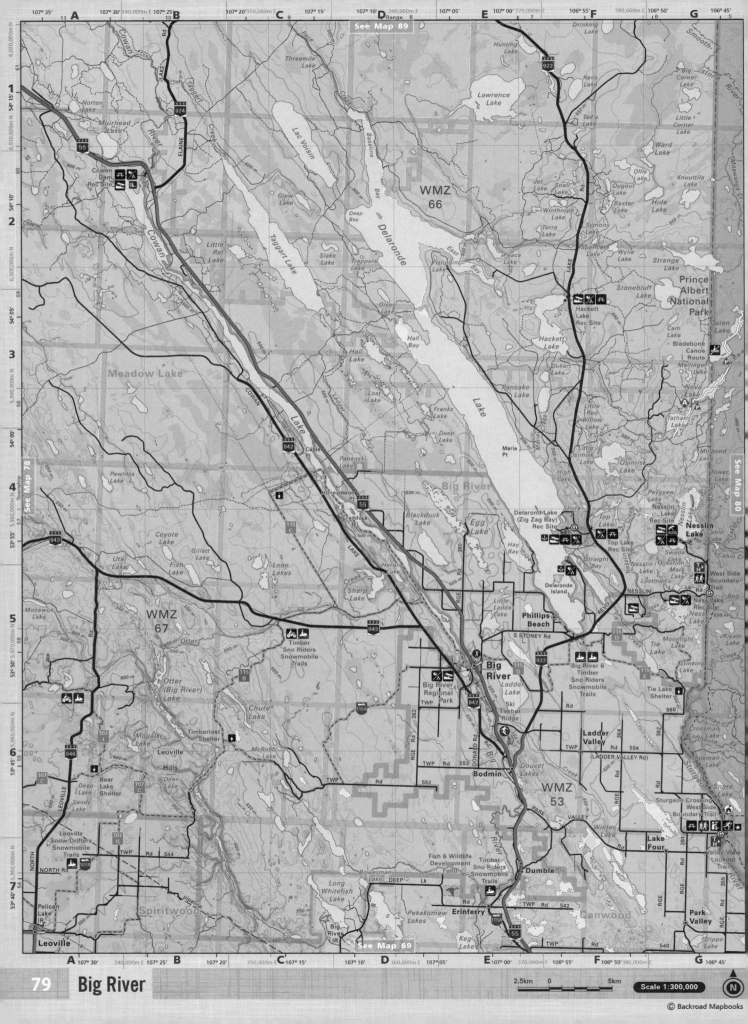

Scale 1:300,000

© Backroad Mapbooks

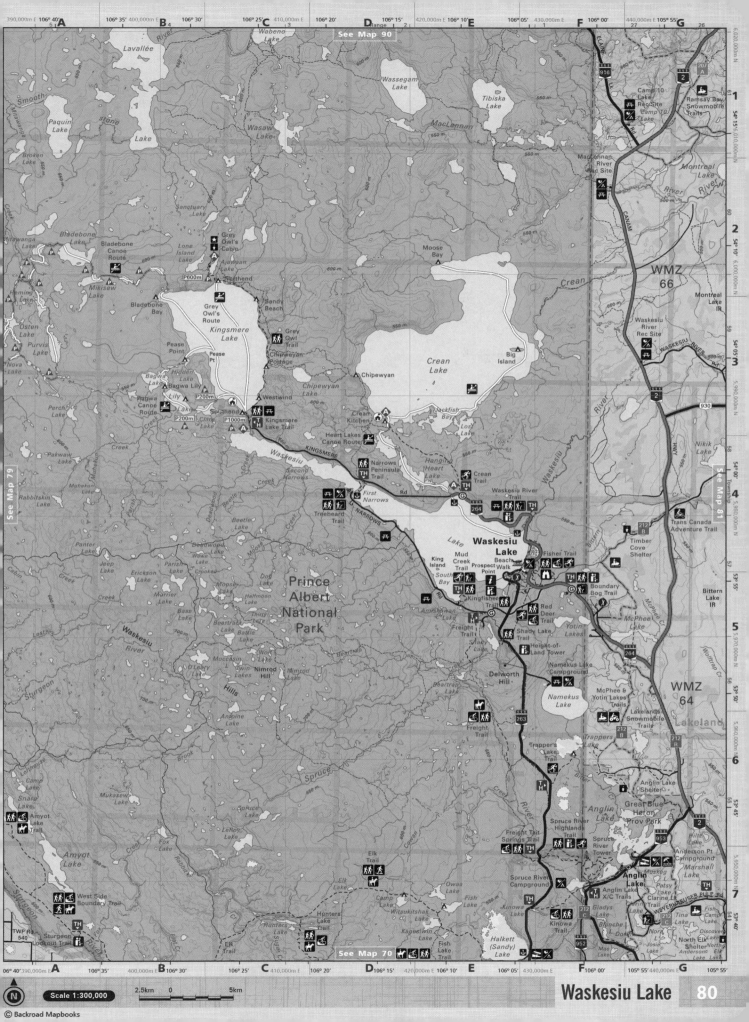

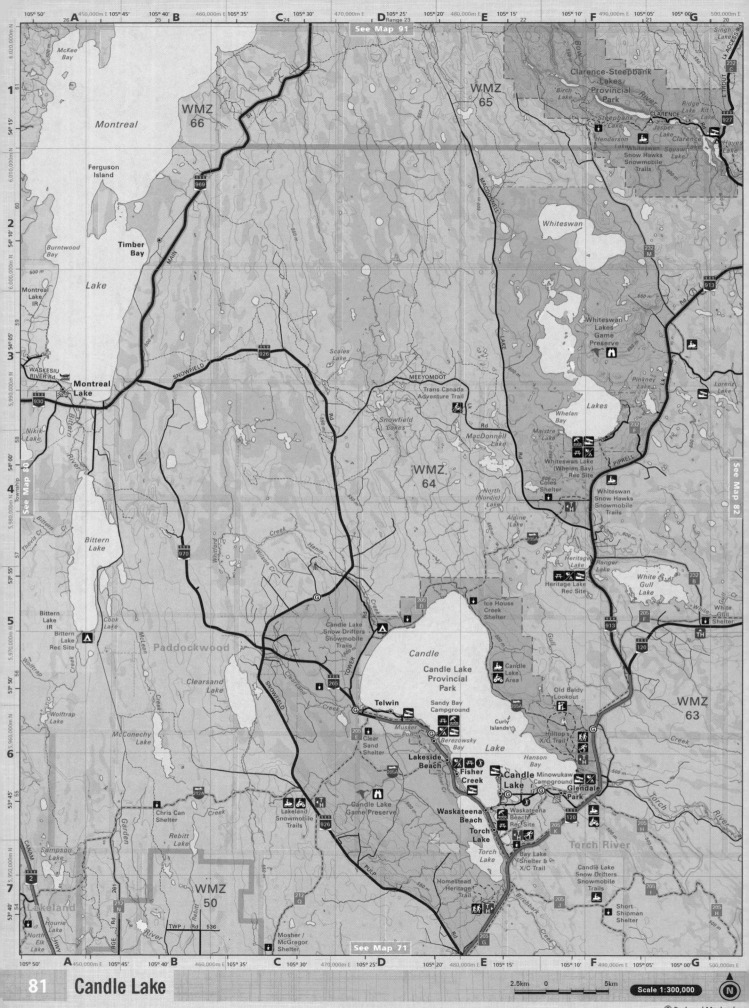

WMZ 66

WMZ 65

WMZ 64

WMZ 63

WMZ 50

Montreal Lake

Ferguson Island

Burntwood Bay

Timber Bay

Montreal Lake IR

Waskesiu River Rd.

Montreal Lake

Nikik Lake

Bittern River

Bittern Lake

Bittern Lake IR

Bittern Lake Rec Site

Cook Lake

Paddockwood

McLean Creek

Wolftrap Lake

McConechy Lake

Clearsand Lake

Clearsand Creek

Chris Can Shelter

Rebitt Lake

Sampson Lake

Lakeland

Hourie Lake

North Elk Lake

Scales Lake

Snowfield Lakes

Trans Canada Adventure Trail

Meeyomoot

MacDonnell Lake

North (Nordic) Lake

Alpine Lake

Ice House Creek Shelter

Candle Lake Snow Drifters Snowmobile Trails

Candle

Candle Lake Provincial Park

Candle Lake Area

Old Baldy Lookout

Hilltop X/C Trail

Telwin

Clear Sand Shelter

Musker Pond

Sandy Bay Campground

Berezowsky Bay

Lakeside Beach

Fisher Creek

Candle Lake

Minowukaw Campground

Glendale Park

Curly Islands

Lake

Hanson Bay

Lakeland Snowmobile Trails

Candle Lake Game Preserve

Waskateena Beach

Torch Lake

Waskateena Beach Rec Site

Bay Lake Shelter & X/C Trail

Torch Lake

Homestead Heritage Trail

Birchbark Rd

Mosher / McGregor Shelter

Candle Lake Snow Drifters Snowmobile Trails

Short Shipman Shelter

Torch River

Clarence-Steepbank Lakes Provincial Park

Birch Lake

Steepbank Lake

Clarence

Ridge Lake

Kit Lake

Henderson Lake

Jasper Lake

Clarence

Whiteswan Snow Hawks Snowmobile Trails

Squawky Lake

Hayes Lake

Whiteswan

Whiteswan Lakes Game Preserve

Whelan Bay

Maistre Lake

Coles Shelter

Whiteswan Lake (Whelan Bay) Rec Site

Whiteswan Snow Hawks Snowmobile Trails

Heritage Lake

Ranger Lake

Heritage Lake Rec Site

White Gull Lake

White Gull Shelter

Pinkney Lake

Lorenz Lake

Singh Lake

Trout

McKee Bay

2.5km 0 5km

Scale 1:300,000

© Backroad Mapbooks

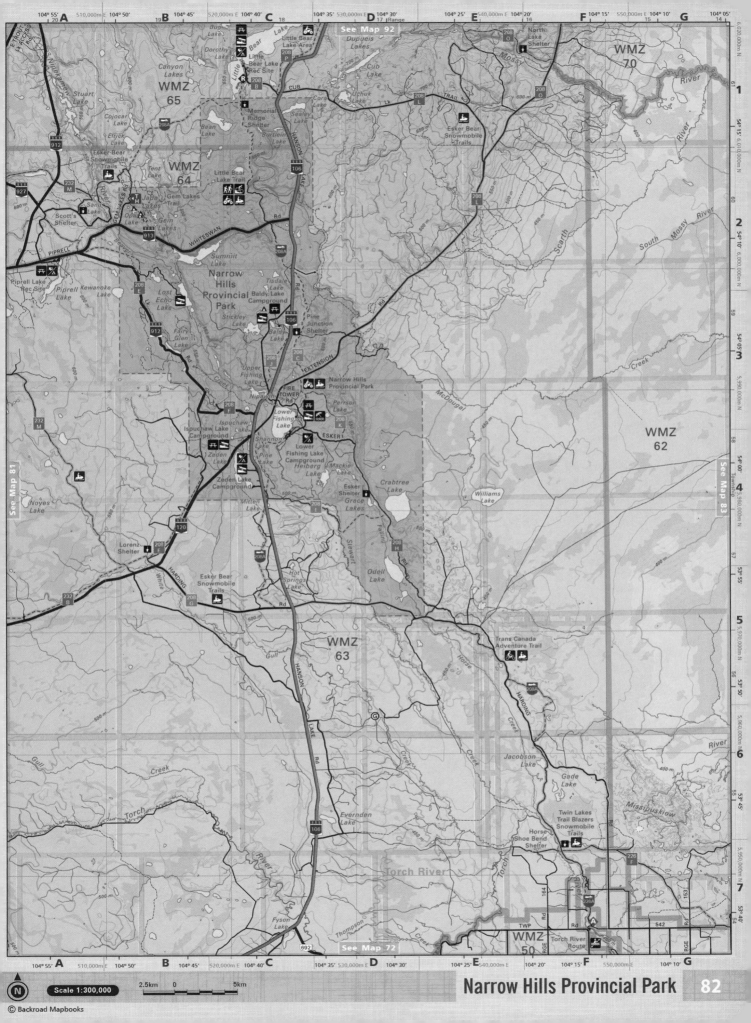

Scale 1:300,000

2.5km 0 5km

© Backroad Mapbooks

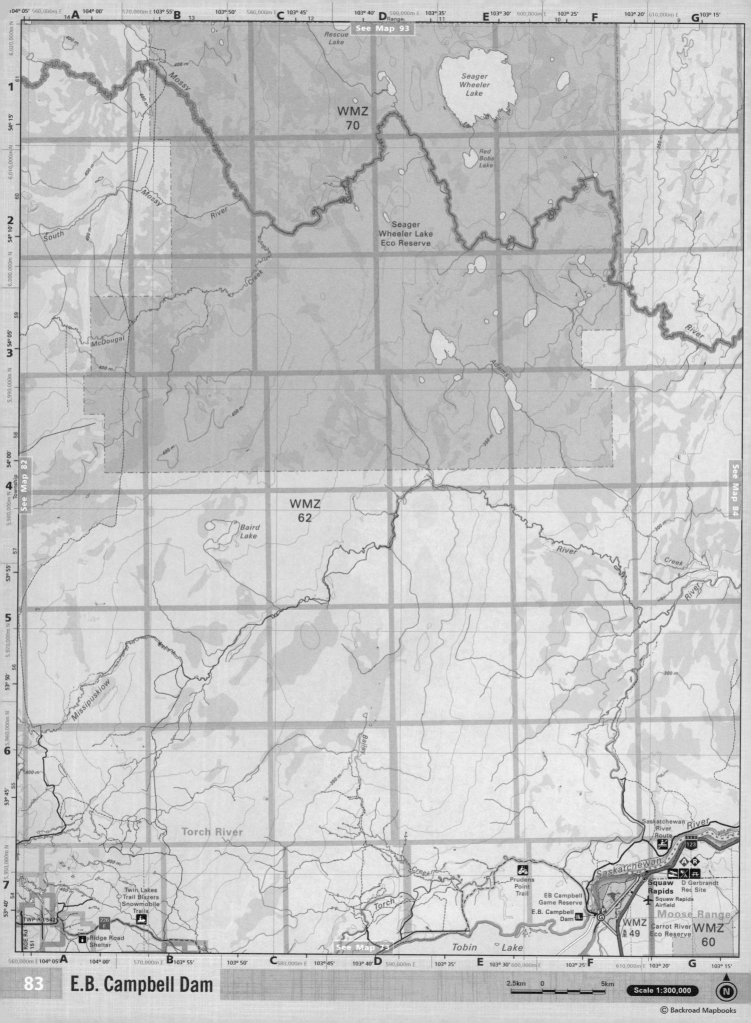

WMZ
70

Seager
Wheeler
Lake

Rescue
Lake

Red
Bobs
Lake

Seager
Wheeler Lake
Eco Reserve

Mossy

Mossy

River

South

Creek

McDougal

400 m

350 m

River

Moose Range

Adams

WMZ
62

Baird
Lake

River

Creek

350 m

300 m

Missipuskiow

Bailey

300 m

Torch River

Torch

Creek

Prudens
Point
Trail

Saskatchewan
River
Route

Saskatchewan

River

123

Twin Lakes
Trail Blazers
Snowmobile
Trails

226
F

Ridge Road
Shelter

RGE Rd
151

TWP Rd 542

EB Campbell
Game Reserve
E.B. Campbell
Dam

Squaw
Rapids

Squaw Rapids
Airfield

D Gerbrandt
Rec Site

WMZ
49

Carrot River
Eco Reserve

WMZ
60

Tobin   Lake

E.B. Campbell Dam

2.5km   0   5km

Scale 1:300,000

N

Marquis Lake

Burns Lake

Silcox Lake

Suggi Lake

WMZ 70

Tyacke Lake

McKenzie Lake

Mossy

Brougham

Ferguson Lake

McOrmond Lake

Erickson Lake

Loyns Lake

Pine Bluff IR

Grassberry

Muskeg River IR

River

Mossy

Channel

Pine Island

See Map 83

Ball Lake

Weasel Lake

Steamboat

Ratroot

Cadotte

Angling

Muskeg Lakes

Angling

Saskatchewan River Route

Dinner Point

Cumberland Lake

River

See Map 85

Hill Island Lake

Ben Lake

South

Channel

Angling

Dumbell Lake

WMZ 61

Bigstone Cutoff

Elm Portage

123

Bigstone Cutoff Rec Site

McAuley Lake

Cook Lake

River

Burntwoods

New

Zig

Zag

Creek

Old

Channel

Mink

Grassy Lake

Waterhen Lake

Egg Lake

Torch

River

Creek

Budd Island

Dragline Channel Rec Site

Dragline Channel

Moose Jaw Lake

Bloodsucker Lake

Highbank Lake

Cow Lake

Junction Lake

Saskatchewan River Route

Cut

Beaver

River

Deep Lake

Creek

Bloodsucker

Creek

Anderson Island Protected Area Anderson Island

Cut Beaver Lake

Paul Lake

Clark Bay

Wapisew

Lake

Saskatchewan

Sipanok

123

Brown Bay

Brown Lake

Moose Range

transmission line

WMZ 60

Dead

Moose

Creek

Birch

Creek

Petabec Cr

Creek

Kennedy

Bourassa Lake

Kennedy Lake

Hudson Bay

Goose Lake

Scale 1:300,000

© Backroad Mapbooks

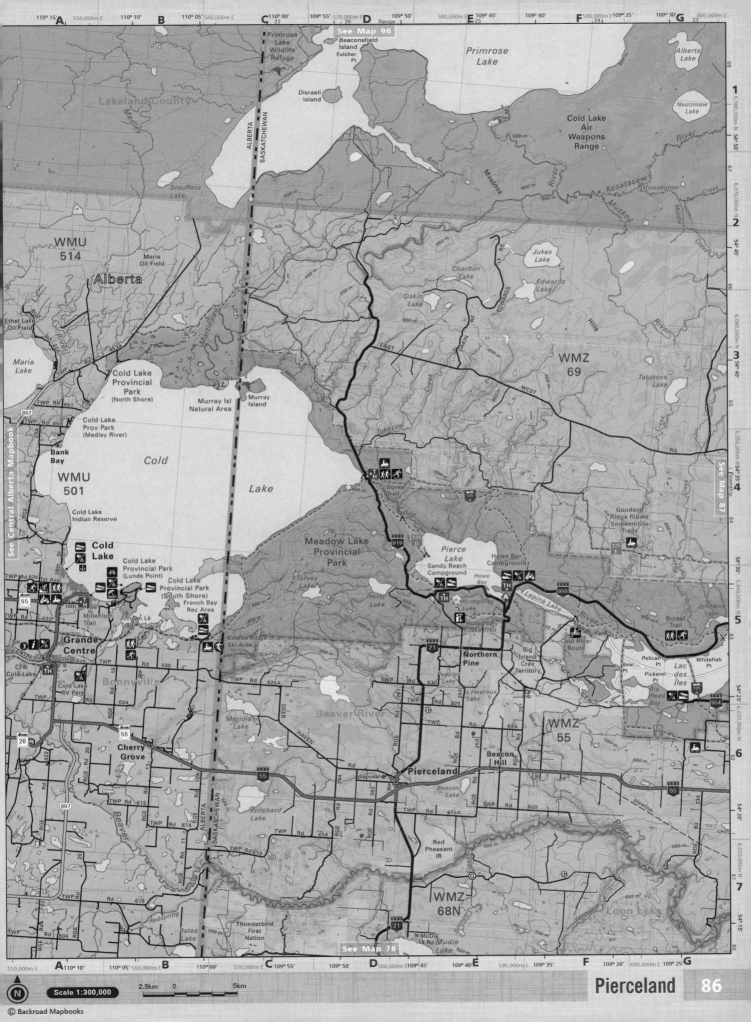

Cold Lake
Air
Weapons
Range

McCusker Lake
Eco Reserve

Kesatasew Lake
Little Caribou Lake
Sooneyaw (Silver) Lake
Rock Lake
Wuchusk Lake
Matisekawe Lake
Pimple Lake
Wye Lake
Tee Lake

Mostoos

River

Ustookumin

Askew Lake

Knox Lake

Ethelwyn Lake

Lost Lake

Hills

Minnowin Lakes

Middle Creek
Halfmoon Lake
South Twin Lake
North Twin Lake
Muskeg Lake
House Lake
Bib Lake
Hedle Lake
Sekip Lake
Pipe Lake
Coupland Lake
Trask Lake
Wotherspoon Lake
Armour Lake
Arnold Lake
Creek

Muskeg

Porcupine Lake
Tamarac Lake
Ten Lake
Sukaw Lake
Muskeg Island Lake
Kukuka Lake
Little Muskeg Lake
Mallard Lake

Flotten Lake
Clay Island
White Birch Nature Trail

EAST

Gold Lake
Creek

See Map 86

Township 1

WEST Rd

MUSKEG
Kewatinook
Tarawich

MISTOHAY

WMZ 69

Rush Lake
Sergent Lake
Jeanette Lake Trail
904
Jeanette Lake
Fifth Lake
941
Hildred Lake
Waterhen Lake

Murray Doell Campground
950
De Balinhard Lake
De Balinhard Lake Trail
Mistohay Lake Campground
Mistohay Lake
Meadow Lake Provincial Park

Third Mustus Lake
Fourth Mustus Lake
Hansen Bay
Greig Lake Campground
Greig Beach
Meadow Lake

Lac des Îles
Misikitew (Big) Island
Hinger
Lac des Îles
26
954
Goodsoil Airfield
625
Goodsoil
225
Bousquet Lake
EMBERVILLE
Rd
Waterhen River Route
Boreal Trail
Mistohay Lake Trail
224
Peitahigan Lake
Goodsoil Ridge Riders Snowmobile Trails
100A
Waterhen
Matheson Lake
Vivian Lake Trail
Vivian Lake
Second Mustus Lake
Hub Lake
Newbanch Boreal Trail
South Greig Picnic
First Mustus Lake
Stanley Lake
Kimball Lake Trails
Kimball Lake
1st Mustus Lake Trail
Rusty Lake
Rusty Lake Day Use
Little Raspberry Lake
Greig Lake
Hildred Beach
Waterhen River Picnic
Hay Meadow Tr
Waterhen Lake Campground
Waterhen River Picnic
A

6

Peerless
55
Beaver River
TWP
222
220
WATERHEN
215
RIVER
212
211
213
TWP
Rd
623A
21
779
193
192
185
184
624
181
Waterhen River Route
A
Dorintosh
4

Fish & Wildlife Development Fund

Flat Valley
TWP
Golden Ridge
55
614
RGE
FOUR CORNERS
612
615A

pipeline
26
612
Beaver
Pine Woods Rec Site
Loon Lake

Woolsrd Lake
Beaver River Rec Site
Blind R

WMZ 55

River

2.5km 0 5km

Scale 1:300,000

WMZ
73

Cold Lake
Air
Weapons
Range

McCusker Lake
Eco Reserve

Wepuskow
Sahgaiechan
IR

Keeley
Lake

Marshy
Bay

Wiggins
Bay

Durocher
Lake

Grand
Rapids

Atchison
Lake

Utikumak
Lake

KEELEY Lk
ACCESS

Fern
Lake

Dubé
Lake

Barnett
Ridge

Big Plate
Lake

Rude
Lake

Ingleby
Lake

Funk
Lake

Gallant
Lake

WMZ
69

Waterhen River
Route

Waterhen
River
Rec Site

Hillyer
Lake

Meadow
Lake
Provincial
Park

Shallow
Lake

Stewart
Lakes

Gergley
Lakes

Aubichon
Lake

White Birch
Nature Trail

Little
Lake

Nesootao
(Twin
Lakes)

WMZ
66

Waterhen
IR

ACCESS

Waterhen
Lake

Waterhen

Meadow Lake

Jarvis
Lake

Gaudry
Lake

Boire
Lake

Minnow
Lake

Lake

Beatty Lake
Rec Site

Beaver
River Route

Waterhen
River
Route

Redmond
Lake

Niven
Lake

Waterhen
IR

Beaver/Cowan
Rivers
Rec Site

Matkin
Lake

Kisayinew Lake

Iskwayach
Lake

Keskuchow
Lake

Jackman
Lake

Seguin
Lake

Ferguson
Lake

Horseshoe
Lake

Charles
Lake

Ross
Lake

Cassidy
Lake

Watt
Lake

Walter
Lake

Pagan Lake
Rec Site

Pagan
Lake

Herlen

Kerr
Lake

Money
Lake

WMZ
55

Swiderski
Lake

Green
Lake

Waterhen
IR

Island
Hill

Unlucky
Lake

Braba
Lake

Laurie
Lake

Beaver River
Sand Cliffs

Blind R

Waterhen Lake   88

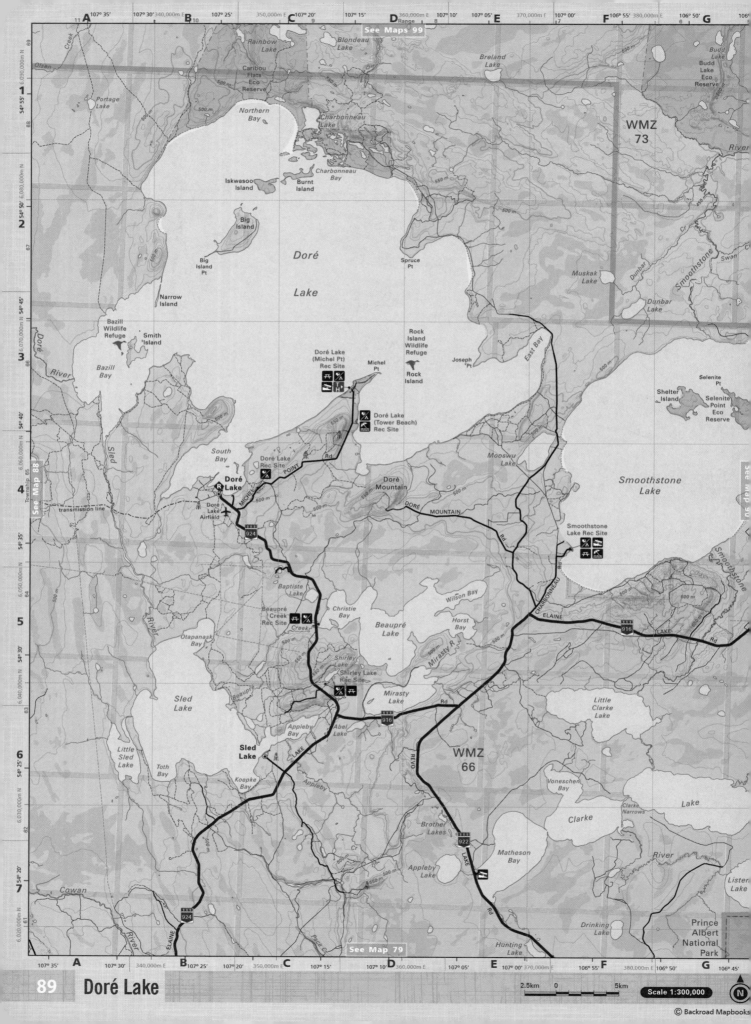

Scale 1:300,000

© Backroad Mapbooks

WMZ
73

WMZ
66

See Map 89

See Map 91

Smooth-
stone

Selenite
Bay

Selenite Point
Eco Reserve

Budd
Lake
Eco
Reserve

Little
Emmeline
Lake

Emmeline
Lake

Twoforks

Meyakumew
Lake

Caldwell
Lake

Cardinal
Lake

Swan Lakes

Mahigan
Lake

Little
Mahigan
Lake

Mahigan

Pear
Lake

Hines
Lake

Hurtean
Lake

Philion Lake

Davies
Lake

Little
Phillon
Lake

Thunder

Randall
Lake

Hills

Rock
Lake

Weyakwin

Muskakowun
Lake

Wasyluk
Bay

Lake
Weyakwin Lake
(Ramsey Bay)
Rec Site

Peterson
Bay

Buhl

Buhl
Lake

Pease
Lake

Elaine
Lake

Elaine Lake
Rec Site

MacLennan
Lake

Musquash
Lake Shelter

Musquash
Lake

Home Hay
Lake

Karaloff
Lake

Dore
Lake

Sedge
Lake

Ramsey Bay
Snowmobile
Trails

Cheeyas
Lake

WEYAKIN

Wanner
Lake

Edgelow
Lake

Clarke
Lake

Lone
Lake

Glass
Lake

Tourist
Lake

Labiuk
Lake

McClure
Lake

Leadley
Lake

George
Lake

George
Lake
Shelter

Listen
Lake

Lavallée
Lake

Wabeno
Lake

Prince Albert
National
Park

Wassegam
Lake

Ashley
Lake

Scale 1:300,000   2.5km 0   5km

© Backroad Mapbooks

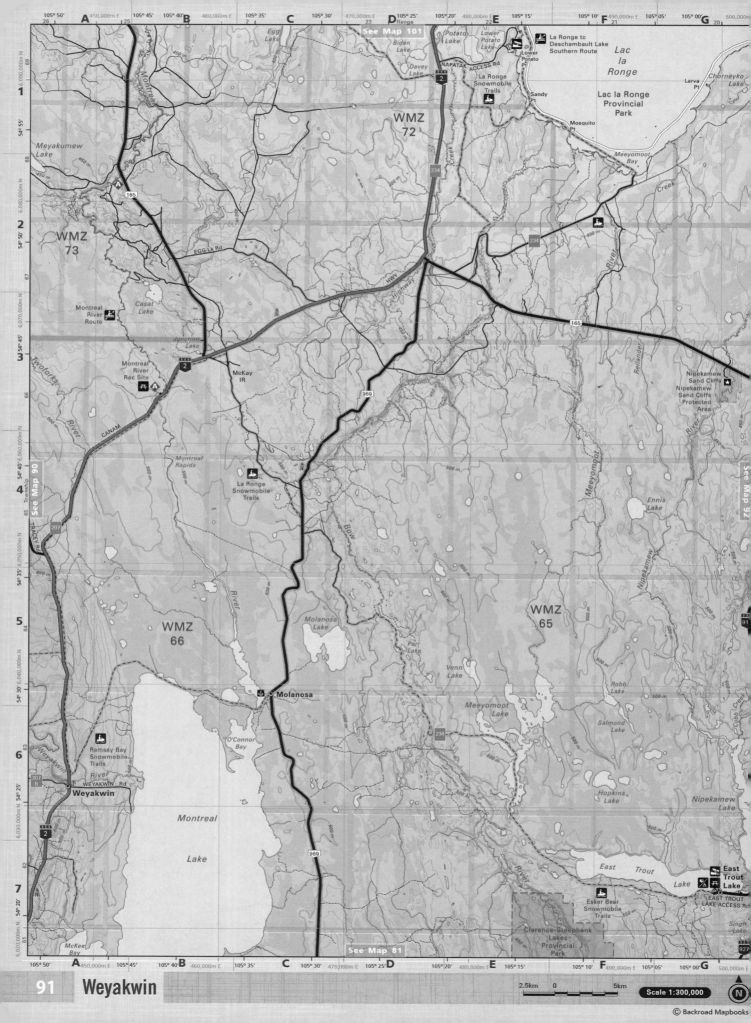

Montreal

Meyakumew
Lake

450 m

450 m

WMZ
73

See Map 101

Egg
Lake

Biden
Lake

Davey
Lake

NAPATAK ACCESS Rd

2

Potato
Lake

Lower
Potato
Lake

La Ronge to
Deschambault Lake
Southern Route

Lower
Pt

Sandy
Pt

La Ronge
Snowmobile
Trails

Lac la
Ronge

Larva
Pt

Chorneyko
Lake

Lac la Ronge
Provincial
Park

Mosquito
Pt

Meeyomoot
Bay

WMZ
72

234

234

165

EGG Lk Rd

Casat
Lake

400 m

Montreal
River
Route

Junction
Lake

Montreal
River
Rec Site

2

McKay
IR

500 m

969

165

Nipekamew
Sand Cliffs
Nipekamew
Sand Cliffs
Protected
Area

Twotorks

River

CANAM

500 m

Montreal
Rapids

La Ronge
Snowmobile
Trails

500 m

Bow

500 m

Reindeer

River

Ennis
Lake

500 m

See Map 90

207

800 m

WMZ
66

River

500 m

Molanosa
Lake

Parr
Lake

Venn
Lake

WMZ
65

500 m

Robb
Lake

600 m

See Map 92

91

207
B

Weyakwin
River

Ramsey Bay
Snowmobile
Trails

O'Connor
Bay

WEYAKWIN Rd

Weyakwin

2

234

Molanosa

Meeyomoot
Lake

Salmond
Lake

500 m

Montreal

Lake

969

500 m

Hopkins
Lake

600 m

Nipekamew
Lake

River

East Trout
Lake

East
Trout
Lake

EAST TROUT
LAKE ACCESS Rd

McKee
Bay

Esker Bear
Snowmobile
Trails

550 m

Clarence-Steepbank
Lakes
Provincial
Park

Singh
Lake

027

See Map 81

2.5km 0 5km

Scale 1:300,000

© Backroad Mapbooks

N

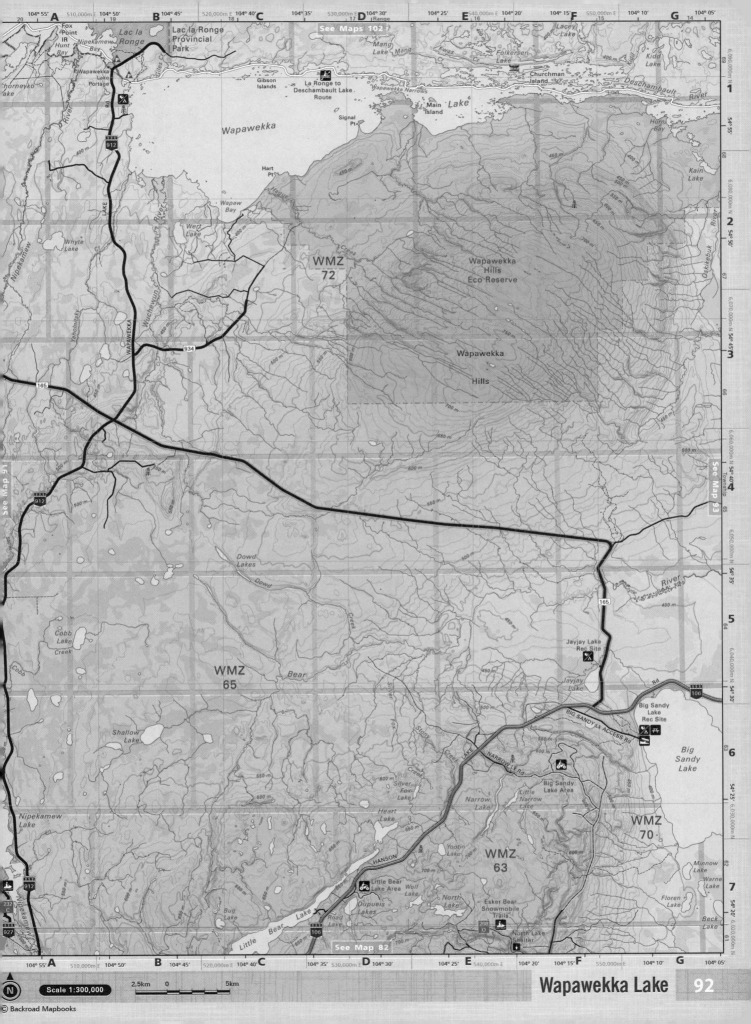

WMZ
72

Wapawekka
Hills
Eco Reserve

Wapawekka

Hills

WMZ
65

WMZ
63

WMZ
70

Jayjay Lake
Rec Site

Big Sandy
Lake
Rec Site

Big
Sandy
Lake

Big Sandy
Lake Area

Lac la Ronge
Provincial
Park

Lac la Ronge

La Ronge to
Deschambault Lake
Route

Wapawekka

Whyte
Lake

West
Lake

Wapaw
Bay

Nipekamew
Lake

Cobb
Lake

Shallow
Lake

Dowd
Lakes

Silver-
Fox
Lake

Heart
Lake

Little Bear
Lake Area

Dupueis
Lakes

Wolf
Lake

North
Lake

Yootin
Lake

Narrow
Lake

Little
Narrow
Lake

Esker Bear
Snowmobile
Trails

North Lake
Shelter

Minnow
Lake

Warne
Lake

Floren
Lake

Beck
Lake

See Map 91

See Map 93

Scale 1:300,000

2.5km   0   5km

N

© Backroad Mapbooks

Wapawekka Lake

92

WMZ 71

WMZ 72

Deschambault Lake

Kimosom Pwatinahk IR

Robertson Island

La Ronge to Deschambault Lake Route

Oskikebuk Lake

Wapawekka Hills Eco Reserve

Wapawekka Lake

Jira Lake

Povol Lake

Wuchusko Lake

Muskose Lake

Merritt Lake

Vance Lake

Deschambault Channel

Twin Bays

Viney Lake

Vagg Lake

Crooked Bay

Southeast Arm

Tower Island

Hidden Bay

Portage Bay

Carey Island

Ellis Island

La Ronge to Deschambault Lake Northern Route/ Deschambault Lake to Maligne Lake Route

South Arm

Unser Lake

Deschambault Lake (South East Arm) Rec Site

Limestone Lake Rec Site

Fisher Bay

Clarke Pt

Pisiwiminiwatim IR

La Ronge to Deschambault Lake Routes

Bear Pt

Muskwaminiwatim IR

Deschambault Lake

Ballantyne Bay

Williams Island

Renown Lake

Grassberry

Puskwakau River Rec Site

Limestone Lake

Twigge Lake

WMZ 70

Big Sandy Lake

Ballantyne Creek

Hanson

Herman Lake

Puskwakau River

Goulden Lake

Beck Lake

Seager Wheeler Lake Eco Reserve

Rescue Lake

Platt Lake

Seager Wheeler Lake

Red Fife Lake

See Map 92
See Map 94
See Map 83

93 Deschambault Lake

2.5km 0   5km

Scale 1:300,000

© Backroad Mapbooks

A   103° 05'   B   630,000m E   102° 55'   C   102° 50'   640,000m E   102° 45'   D   Range 5   102° 40'   650,000m E   E   102° 35'   660,000m E   102° 30'   F   102° 25'   670,000m E   G   102° 20'

Northeast
Arm

Pelican
Lake

Wilkin
Bay

Reid
Lake

Cooper
Lake

Corneille

McDonald
Lake

McMaster
Lake

Wildnest
Lake

69

Busteed
Island

Pelletier
Lake

Carter
Bay

Ripley-Kibzey
Lake

Judiquer
Lake

Nichol
Lake

68

Deschambault
Lake

Jan

Lake

Doupe
Bay

Jan Lake
Rec Site

Birch
Portage
IR

Iskoonikun
Lake

Pelican
Narrows to
Mile 190 Bridge

Granite
Lake

Apetow
Lake

1

La Ronge to
Deschambault Lake
Northern Route;
Deschambault Lake
to Maligne Lake
Route

La Ronge to
Jan Lake
Route

Jan Lake
Eco
Reserve

JAN LK ACCESS Rd

135

Rightangle
Lake

Onikup
Lake

Garnet
Lake

La Ronge &
Maligne Lake
Route

Waskwaynikapik
IR

GRANITE LK ACCESS Rd

106

Rd

Maskunow
Lake

Johnson
Lake

54° 55'

McIntyre
Island

Harper
Island

Phaneuf
Lake

McBride
Lake

Kistapiskaw
Lake

Ziporkin
Lake

Granite Lake
Rec Site

275km

Baht
Lake

Ahrens
Lake

54° 50'

Brock
Bay

Bryans
Lake

Delorme
Lake

Nakiskatowaneek
IR

Leaf Rapids
Rec Site
190mi Mid
Lake

Maligne
Lake

Martin
Lake

67

Church
Lake

Crawford
Lake

Winteringham
Lake

Gillingham
Lake

Jan
Lake
Airfield

Wyllie
Lake

Matheson
Lake

Wildfong
Lake

Welsh
Lake

Neagle
Lake

WMZ
71

LAKE

Sewap
Lake

Morton
Lake

Morton River

Sturgeon-Weir

Abbott
Lake

Jardine
Lake

54° 45'

6,070,000m N

Tulabi
Lake

Jackpine
Lake

Wakisew
Lake

Shkwarok
Lake

Errington
Lake

Neagle
Creek

3

Unser
Lake

Sarginson
Lake

HANSON

Bertrum
Bay

Hanson
Lake

Attree
Lake

Halfway
Lake

Steeprock
Lake

54° 40'

6,060,000m N

106

Hand
Lake

Bad
Carrot
Lake

Winn
Island

Blackduck
Lake

Mitoskwun
Lake

Sturgeon-Weir

Maligne Lake to
Amisk Lake

Wolf
Lake

Oddan
Lake

Limestone
Lake
Rec Site

Pasowun
Lake

Side
Lake

Hanson
Lake
Rec Site

Winn
Bay

Sturgeon
Weir
Eco Reserve

Burton
Lake

Amisk
Lake

54° 35'

6,050,000m N

Limestone
Lake

Guyader
Lake

Shuttleworth
Lake

Spruce
Rapids

Amisk
Lake IR

Muskeg
Bay

Hayes
Island

64

See Map 95

4

See Map 93

Chisolm
Lake

Philmitchell
Lake

Ministik
Lake

McDermott
Lake

Leskiw
Lake

Oskatukaw
Lake

Balsam
Lake

McKenzie
Bay

Lake

5

Riecke
Lake

Hollingdale
Lake

Oatway
Lake

Miskat
Lake

Hobbs
Lake

Craig
Lake

Stringer
Lake

Kerr
Lake

Usinne
Lake

54° 30'

6,040,000m N

63

Bigstone
Lake

Acheninni
Lake

Grassberry

WMZ
70

Balsam Brook

54° 25'

6,030,000m N

6

Harrington
Lake

Apex
Lake

Brougham

Sinclair Creek

River

Foy Creek

62

Saunders
Lake

Suggi

Windy
Lake

Nejedley
Lake

54° 20'

6,020,000m N

7

Marquis
Lake

Creek

Charles
Bay

Hill
Bay

Lake

Grassberry River

61

A   103° 05'   B   630,000m E   103° 00'   102° 55'   C   640,000m E   102° 50'   D   102° 45'   650,000m E   E   102° 40'   102° 35'   660,000m E   F   102° 30'   G   102° 25'   670,000m E   102° 20'

N

Scale 1:300,000

2.5km   0   5km

Jan Lake   94

© Backroad Mapbooks

Scale 1:300,000

© Backroad Mapbooks

WMZ
73

Wood Buffalo

Royemma
Lake

Dillon

River

Calder

650 m

650 m

700 m

Nisbet
Lake

Winefred
Fire
Lookout

Clarita

Creek

Creek

800 m

700 m

650 m

Gray

Creek

650 m

850 m

Watapi

Neath

Creek

Taskum

Creek

700 m

700 m

Hathaway
Lake

700 m

Lake

850 m

See Northern Alberta Mapbook

700 m

Foster

Creek

700 m

700 m

Tamarack
Lake

Alberta

700 m

Victor

ALBERTA

SASKATCHEWAN

700 m

Holmes

Creek

850 m

850 m

Mostoos

850 m

Hills

See Map 97

Lakeland County

Cold Lake
Air
Weapons
Range

Scheltens
Lake

700 m

700 m

Farrall

850 m

River

Cr

Cold Lake
Air
Weapons
Range

Brett

Bouvier

Shaver

Medley

Creek

700 m

650 m

850 m

700 m

700 m

700 m

Creek

Primrose Lake
Wildlife
Refuge

Bailey
Island

Baker
Island

Wilson
Pt

Francis
Bay

Backes
Island
Wildlife
Refuge

Backes
Island

Shinnan
Island

Primrose

Lake

Alberts
Lake

River

Beaconsfield
Island

Fulcher
Pt

See Map 86

Scale 1:300,000

2.5km   0   5km

N

© Backroad Mapbooks

Primrose Lake   96

WMZ
73

McCusker
Lake
Ecological
Reserve

Cold Lake
Air
Weapons
Range

Scale 1:300,000

© Backroad Mapbooks

Île-à la-Crosse

98

Scale 1:300,000

© Backroad Mapbooks

Dockerill Lake

Binnie Lake

Dutertre Lake

Degryse Lake

Seymour Lakes

Pedersen Lake

Alstead Lake

Belton Lake

Wysoski Lake

Musqua Lake

Glen Lake

Senyk Lakes

Harry Lake

500 m

Zbytnuik Lake

River

Chilton Lake

Brewer Lake

Agumik Lake

Agumik Cr

400 m

Learn Lake

Grant

Creek

Lavale Bay

918

Pinehouse Lake

Cinder Lake

450 m

500 m

Pine

WMZ 73

Massinahigan

914

WMZ 72

Mitchell Lake

460 m

See Map 98

River

La Plonge IR

Bella Lake

Wylie

165

Massinahigan

Jones

River

Maurice Lake

R

Creek

Van Nes Lake

Tippo Lake

Tippo

500 m

Sanderson X/C Trails

Lac La Plonge Rec Site

Weber Isl

Lac la Plonge

Weber Bay

Voakes Lake

Lorimer Lake

R

Beaval

Riv la Plonge

165

La Plonge IR

Beaver

LeBlanc Bay

Buchanan Peninsula

Lac la Plonge

500 m

McLurg

Creek

Budd Lake Eco Reserve

Carragher Lake

550 m

Olsen

Creek

500 m

500 m

Rainbow Lake

Caribou Flats Eco Reserve

Blondeau Lake

Budd Lake

2.5km   0   5km

Scale 1:300,000

© Backroad Mapbooks

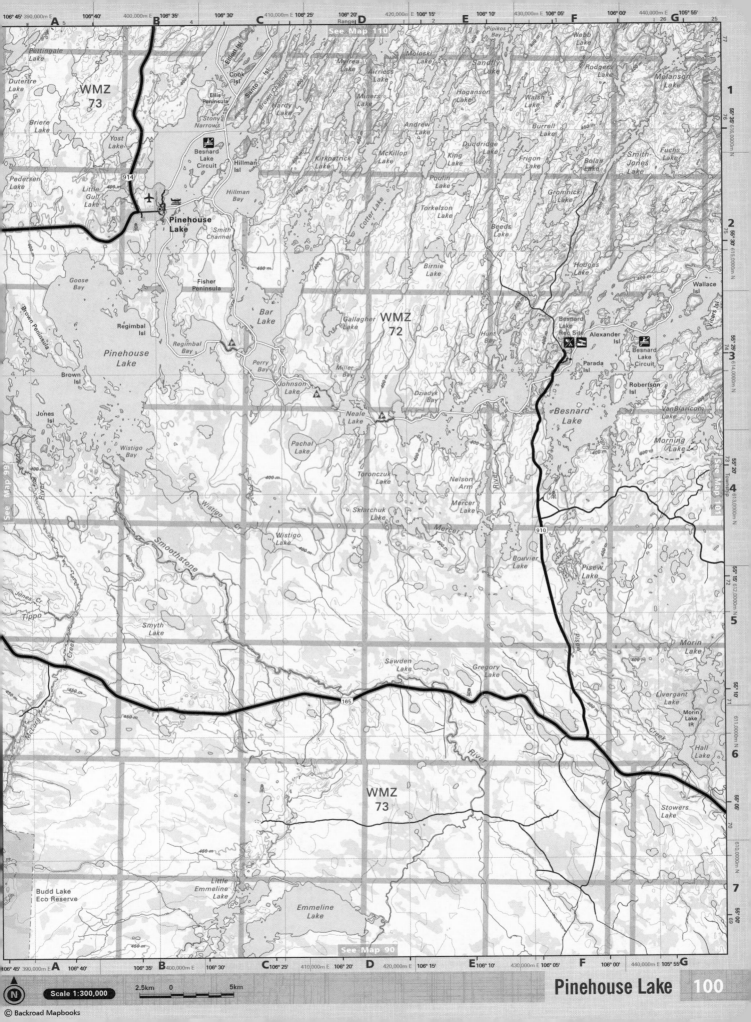

WMZ
73

WMZ
72

WMZ
73

Pettingale
Lake

Dutertre
Lake

Briere
Lake

Pedersen
Lake

Yost
Lake

Little
Gull
Lake

914

Goose
Bay

Brown Peninsula

Brown
Isl

Jones
Isl

Regimbal Isl

Pinehouse
Lake

Wistigo
Bay

Smoothstone

Jones Cr.
Tippa

McLeod

Smyth
Lake

Budd Lake
Eco Reserve

Little
Emmeline
Lake

Emmeline
Lake

Cook
Isl

Ellis
Peninsula

Santo Isl

Brown Channel

Hardy
Lake

Elliot Isl

Besnard Lake
Circuit

Hillman
Isl

Pinehouse
Lake

Fisher
Peninsula

Hillman
Bay

Smith
Channel

Regimbal
Bay

Bar
Lake

Perry
Bay

Johnson
Lake

Neale
Lake

Pachal
Lake

Wistigo
Lake

Wistigo Cr.

Sawden
Lake

Kirkpatrick
Lake

Myrea
Lake

Airless
Lake

Miners
Lake

Andrew
Lake

McKillop
Lake

Gallagher
Lake

Miller
Bay

Toronczuk
Lake

Sklarchuk
Lake

Cotter Lake

Birnie
Lake

Dziadyk
Bay

Moloski
Lake

Hoganson
Lake

King
Lake

Poulin
Lake

Torkelson
Lake

Nelson Arm

Mercer
Lake

Gregory
Lake

Sandfly
Lake

Duddridge
Lake

Walsh
Lake

Burrell
Lake

Frigon
Lake

Beeds
Lake

Hunt
Bay

Mercer River

Mercer

165

Pipikos
Bay

Webb
Lake

Rodgers
Lake

Melanson
Lake

Smith-
Jones
Lake

Fuchs
Lake

Gromnicki
Lake

Bolan
Lake

Hodges
Lake

Besnard Lake
Rec Site

Alexander
Isl

Parada
Isl

Besnard
Lake
Circuit

Robertson
Isl

Besnard
Lake

VanBlaricom
Lake

Morning
Lake

910

Bouvier
Lake

Pisew
Lake

Pisew

Morin
Lake

Livergant
Lake

Morin
Lake IR

Hall
Lake

Stowers
Lake

Wallace
Isl

Vian Isl

400 m

450 m

Scale 1:300,000

2.5km   0   5km

© Backroad Mapbooks

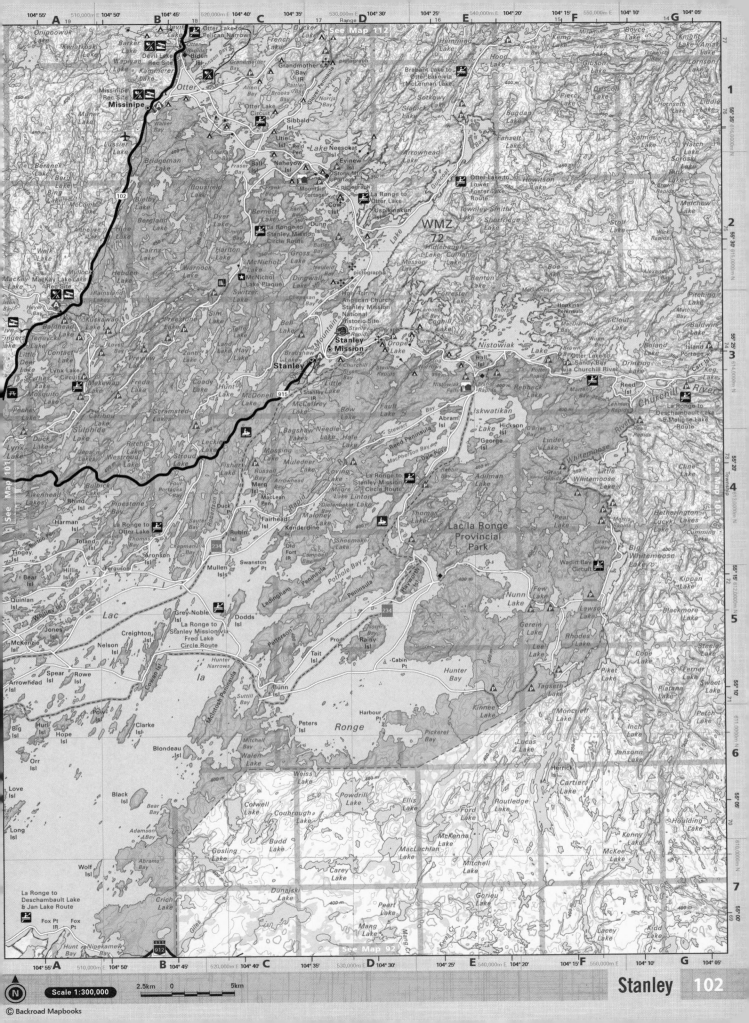

Scale 1:300,000

2.5km 0 5km

Scale 1:300,000

© Backroad Mapbooks

Scale 1:300,000

© Backroad Mapbooks

WMU
529

WMU
517

WMZ
73

Alberta

North
Watchusk
Lake

South
Watchusk
Lake

Kimowin
(Hook)
Lake

Kimowin

Fornby
Lake

Brown

Finlay
Lake

McAdam
Lake

Brown
Lake

Winefred

River

Acaster
Lake

Barney
Lake

Graham
Lake

Lakevold
Lake

Dillon
Lake

McAlister
Lake

Cowper
Lake

Alberta

Saskatchewan

109° 35' 590,000m E   109° 30'   109° 25' 600,000m E   109° 20'   109° 15' 610,000m E   109° 10'   D   109° 05' 620,000m E   109° 00'   108° 55' 630,000m E   108° 50'   108° 45' 640,000m E   108° 40'

A   B   C   Range   D   E   F   G

Nimowin
River

Brown

Grizzly

Bear

Creek

WMZ
73

Hills

Martin

Williard

Dillon
Lake

Chain
Lake

Lessard

Lockwood
Lake

Loche

River

Michel
Village

Buffalo
River
Dene
Nation

Dillon
Bay

Creek

St George's
Hill

River

Dillon

Nipin

Vermette
Lake

Vermette

River

Hay
Pt

Peter

Pond

Willow
Pt

Dillon

Turnor
Lake
IR

Buffalo
River
Dene
Nation

925

Little
Point
Lake

Eadie
Lake

Cumins
Lake

Bear

Creek

155

Huddleston
Lake

Clearwater River
Dene Band
IR

Taylor
Lake

Taylor Lake
Rec Site

Lac La Loche
to Ile-A-La Crosse

Old
Fort
Pt

Lake

Sandy
Pt

Vee
Bay

Thomason
Peninsula

Fleury
Pt

Niska
Channel

Niska
Lake

See Map 108

See Map 97

2.5km   0   5km

Scale 1:300,000

© Backroad Mapbooks

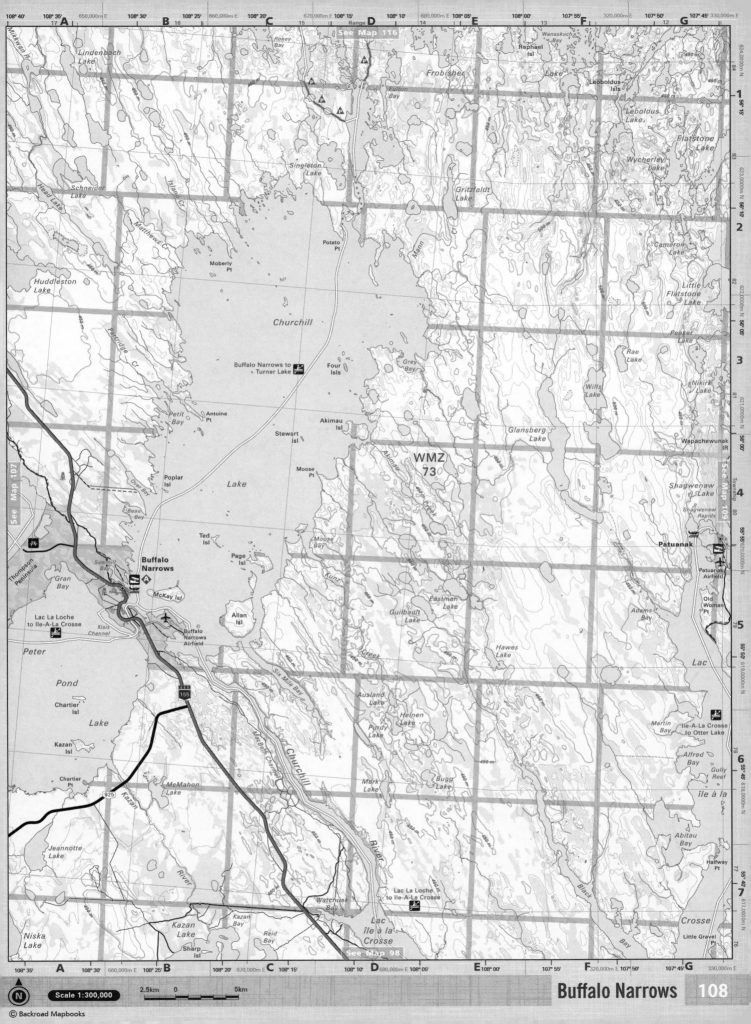

Lindenbach
Lake

Mikkwan R.

Roney
Pt

Frobisher
Lake

Raphael
Isl

Leoboldus
Isls

Leboldus
Lake,

Flatstone
Lake

Wanaskuchak
Bay

Fulton
Bay

Singleton
Lake

Gritzfeldt
Lake

Wycherley
Lake

Head Lake

Schneider
Lake

Matthews Cr

Island Cr

Cameron
Lake

Potato
Pt

Moberly
Pt

Churchill

Little
Flatstone
Lake

Huddleston
Lake

Peaker
Lake

Partridge Cr

Buffalo Narrows to
Turner Lake

Four
Isls

Grey
Bay

Rae
Lake

Wills
Lake

Nikirk
Lake

Antoine
Pt

Petit
Bay

Akimau
Isl

Glansberg
Lake

Wapachewunak
IR

Stewart
Isl

**WMZ
73**

Akimau
Creek

Shagwenaw
Lake

Poplar
Isl

Moose
Pt

Lake

Oxen Bay

Beau
Bay

Shagwenaw
Rapids

Patuanak

Moose
Bay

Ted
Isl

Patuanak
Airfield

Page
Isl

Kunz

Eastman
Lake

Old
Woman
Pt

Adams
Bay

Thompson
Peninsula

Sawmill
Bay

**Buffalo
Narrows**

McKay Isl

Allan
Isl

Guilbault
Lake

Gran
Bay

Lac La Loche
to Ile-A-La-Crosse

Kisis
Channel

Buffalo
Narrows
Airfield

Creek

Hawes
Lake

Lac

Martin
Bay

Ile-A-La Crosse
to Otter Lake

Peter

Six Mile Bay

Ausland
Lake

Heinen
Lake

Alfred
Bay

Pond

Chartier
Isl

Purdy
Lake

Gully
Reef

Kazan
Isl

MacBeth Channel

Merk
Lake

Bugg
Lake

Île à la

Lake

155

Churchill

Abitau
Bay

Chartier
Pt

McMahon
Lake

Halfway
Pt

925

Kazan

River

Jeannotte
Lake

Lac La Loche
to Ile-A-La Crosse

Black

Crosse

Watchusk
Bay

Niska
Lake

Kazan
Lake

Kazan Bay

Reid
Bay

Lac
île à la
Crosse

Little Gravel
Pt

Sharp
Isl

See Map 107

See Map 109

Range

Township

Scale 1:300,000

2.5km 0 5km

© Backroad Mapbooks

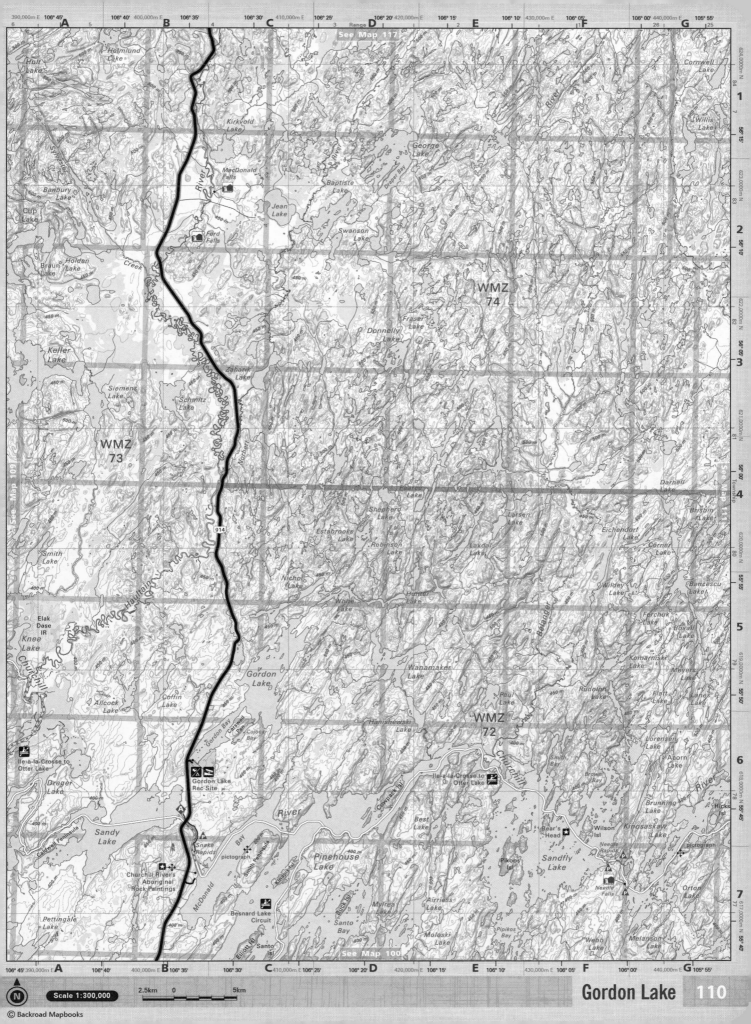

390,000m E 106° 45'   106° 40'   400,000m E   106° 35'   4   106° 30'   410,000m E   106° 25'   Range   106° 20'   420,000m E   106° 15'   106° 10'   430,000m E   106° 05'   106° 00'   440,000m E   26   105° 55'

6   A   5   B   4   C   D   2   E   1   F   G   25

Holt Lake

Holmlund Lake

Cornwell Lake

Willis Lake

Kirkvold Lake

Banbury Lake

MacDonald Falls

George Lake

Baptiste Lake

Dreger Bay

Cup Lake

Jean Lake

Ford Falls

Swanson Lake

Braun Lake

Holden Lake

Creek

WMZ 74

Keller Lake

Fraser Lake

Donnelly Lake

Zahark Lake

Siemens Lake

Schmitz Lake

WMZ 73

Norbet

Darnell Lake

Pearce Lake

914

Shepherd Lake

Larsen Lake

Brisbin Lake

Estabrooks Lake

Eichendorf Lake

Robinson Lake

Laxdal Lake

Corner Lake

Smith Lake

Nichol Lake

Hanneu Lake

Wildey Lake

Bancescu Lake

Wine Lake

Haultain

Ferchuk Lake

Boxall Lake

Elak Dase IR

Komarniski Lake

Knee Lake

Gordon Lake

Wanamaker Lake

Rudolph Lake

Paul Lake

Meyers Lake

Churchill

Platt Lake

Lanes Lake

Allcock Lake

Coffin Lake

WMZ 72

Hanishewski Lake

Lorensen Lake

Ile-a-la-Crosse to Otter Lake

Gordon Bay

Carswell

Cojocar Bay

Smith Bay

Acorn Lake

Dreger Lake

Ile-a-la-Crosse to Otter Lake

Brown Bay

Brunning Lake

Gordon Lake Rec Site

Cowpack Isl

Bear's Head

Wilson Isl

Kingsaskaw Lake

Hicks Isl

Snake Rapids

pictograph

Best Lake

Needle Rapids

Sandy Lake

Smith Peninsula

Pinehouse Lake

Pikoos Isl

Sandfly Lake

Caldwell Peninsula

Kimpinski

River

Airriess Lake

Needle Falls

Orton Lake

Churchill River's Aboriginal Rock Paintings

Santo Isl

pictograph

McDonald

Besnard Lake Circuit

Buck Isl

Myirea Lake

Pettingale Lake

Elliott

Santo Isl

Santo Bay

Moloski Lake

Pipikos Bay

Webb Lake

Melanson Lake

See Map 109

106° 45' 390,000m E   106° 40'   400,000m E   106° 35'   106° 30'   410,000m E   106° 25'   106° 20'   420,000m E   106° 15'   106° 10'   430,000m E   106° 05'   106° 00'   440,000m E   105° 55'

A   B   C   D   E   F   G

N

Scale 1:300,000   2.5km   0   5km

© Backroad Mapbooks

Gordon Lake   110

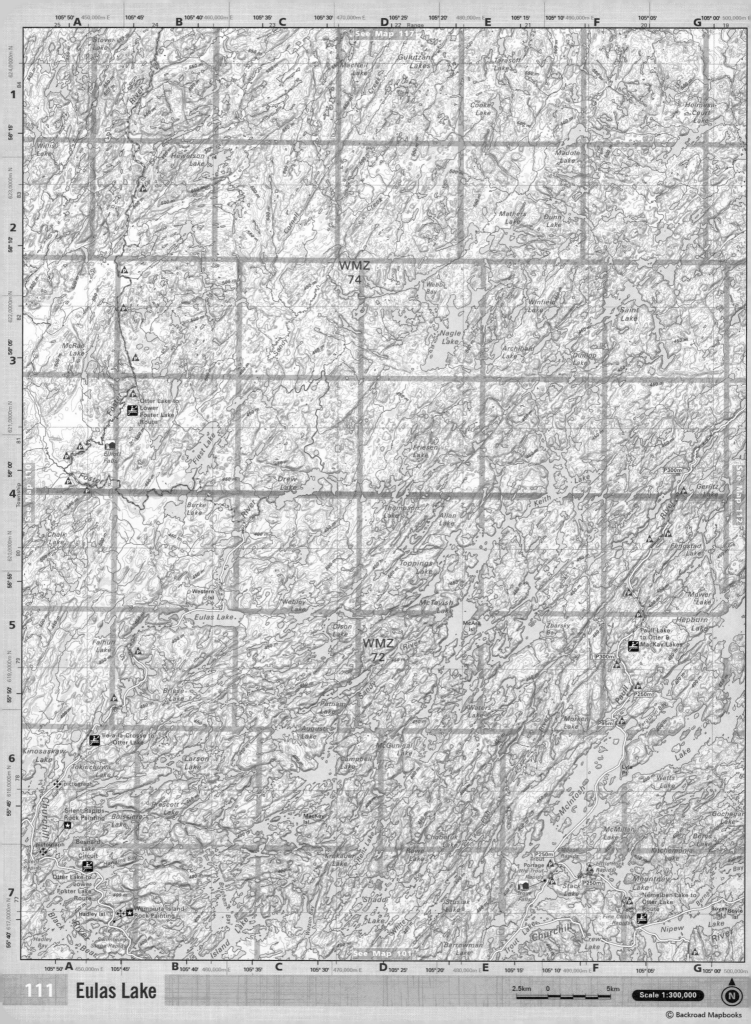

WMZ
74

WMZ
72

111 Eulas Lake

2.5km   0   5km

Scale 1:300,000

© Backroad Mapbooks

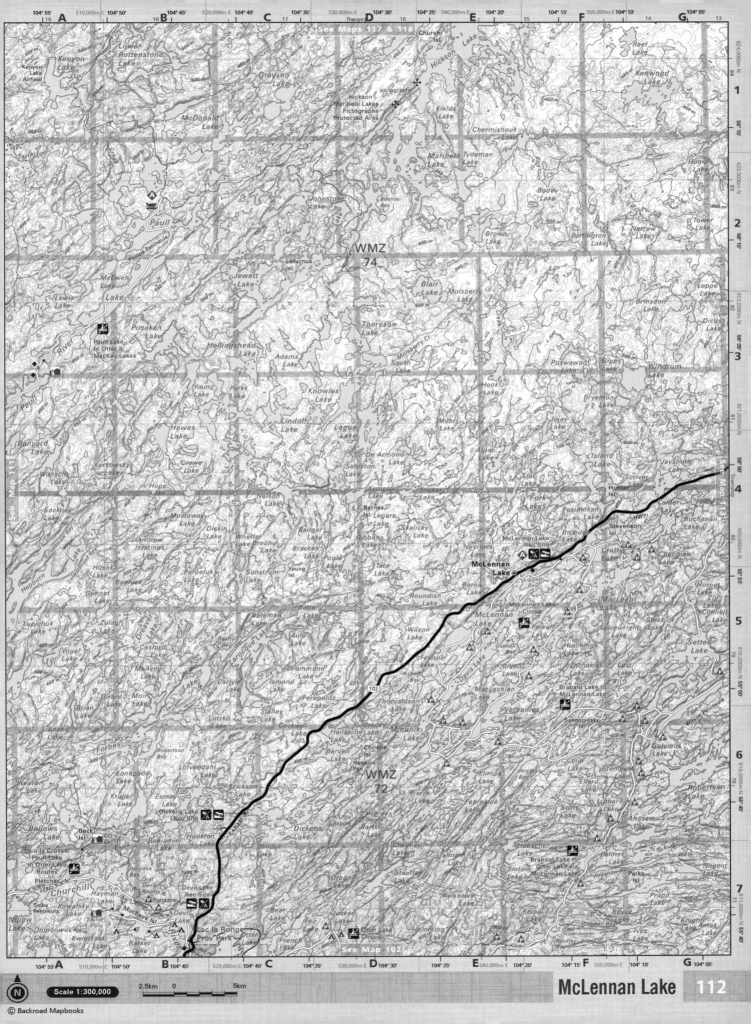

Scale 1:300,000

© Backroad Mapbooks

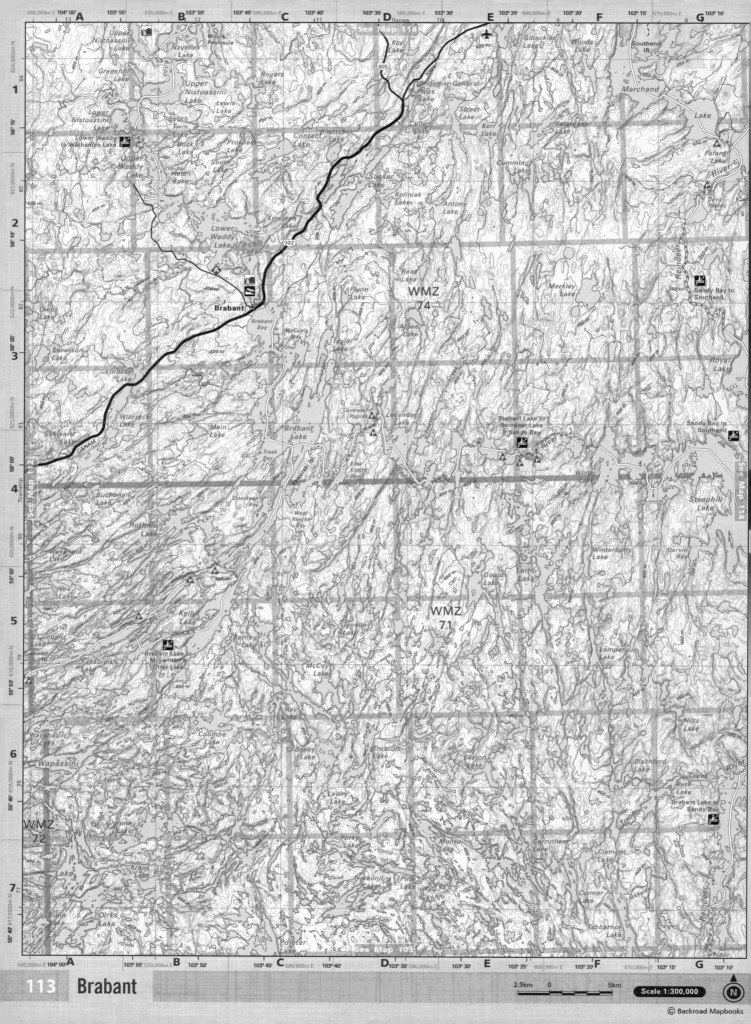

Scale 1:300,000

© Backroad Mapbooks

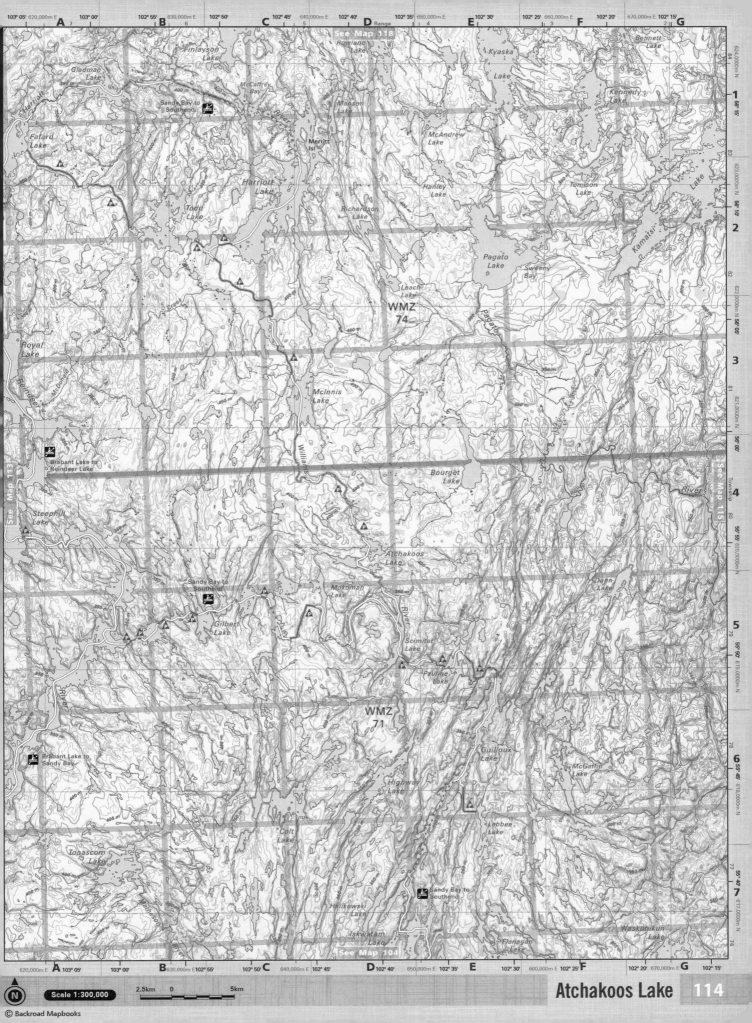

Finlayson
Lake

McCaffrey
Bay

Rowland
Lake

Kyaska
Lake

Bennett
Lake

Gladman
Lake

Harriott

Fafard
Lake

Kennedy
Lake

Sandy Bay to
Southend

Manson
Lake

Merritt
Isl

McAndrew
Lake

Harriott
Lake

Todd
Lake

Richardson
Lake

Hanley
Lake

Tomison
Lake

Kamatsi
Lake

Pagato
Lake

Sweeny
Bay

Leach
Lake

**WMZ
74**

Royal
Lake

Creek

McInnis
Lake

Pagato

McDonald

Reindeer

Brabant Lake to
Reindeer Lake

Williams

Bourget
Lake

River

Steephill
Lake

Atchakoos
Lake

Dunn
Lake

See Map 113

See Map 115

Sandy Bay to
Southend

Gilbert
Lake

Mokoman
Lake

River

Scimitar
Lake

Pauline
Lake

**WMZ
71**

River

Guilloux
Lake

McGaffin
Lake

Brabant Lake to
Sandy Bay

Tonascom
Lake

Highway
Lake

Labbee
Lake

Matheson

Colt
Lake

Sandy Bay to
Southend

Halikowski
Lake

Iskwatam
Lake

Flanagan
Lake

Waskuhikun
Lake

See Map 104

Range

Township

N

Scale 1:300,000

2.5km   0   5km

© Backroad Mapbooks

Atchakoos Lake 114

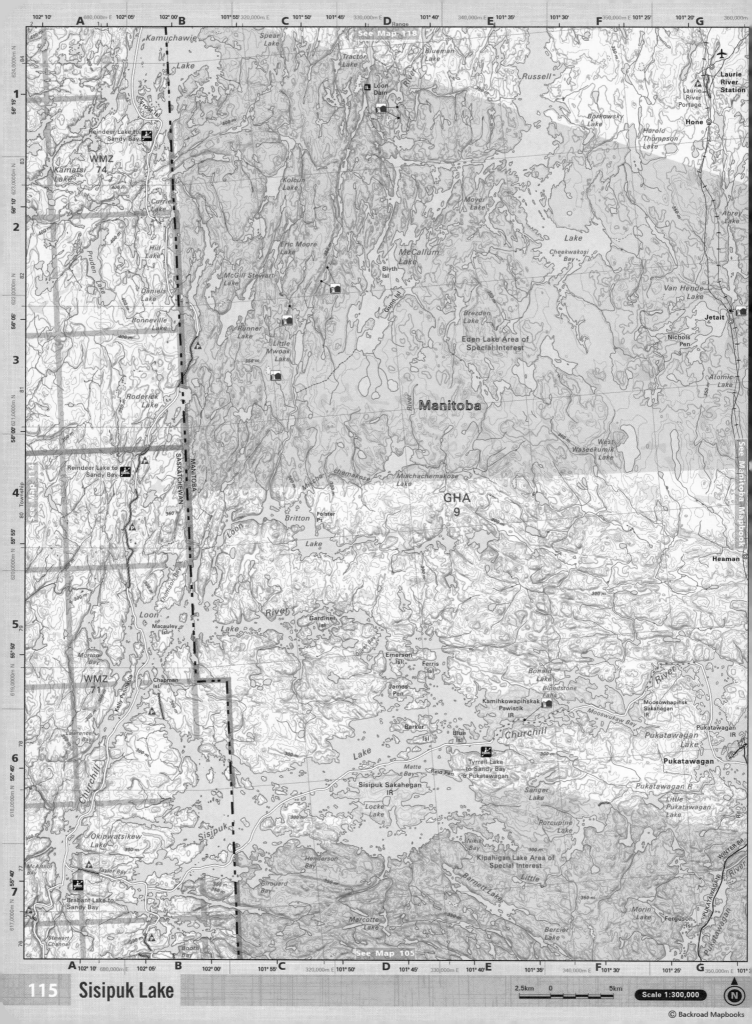

115 Sisipuk Lake

2.5km 0 5km

Scale 1:300,000

© Backroad Mapbooks

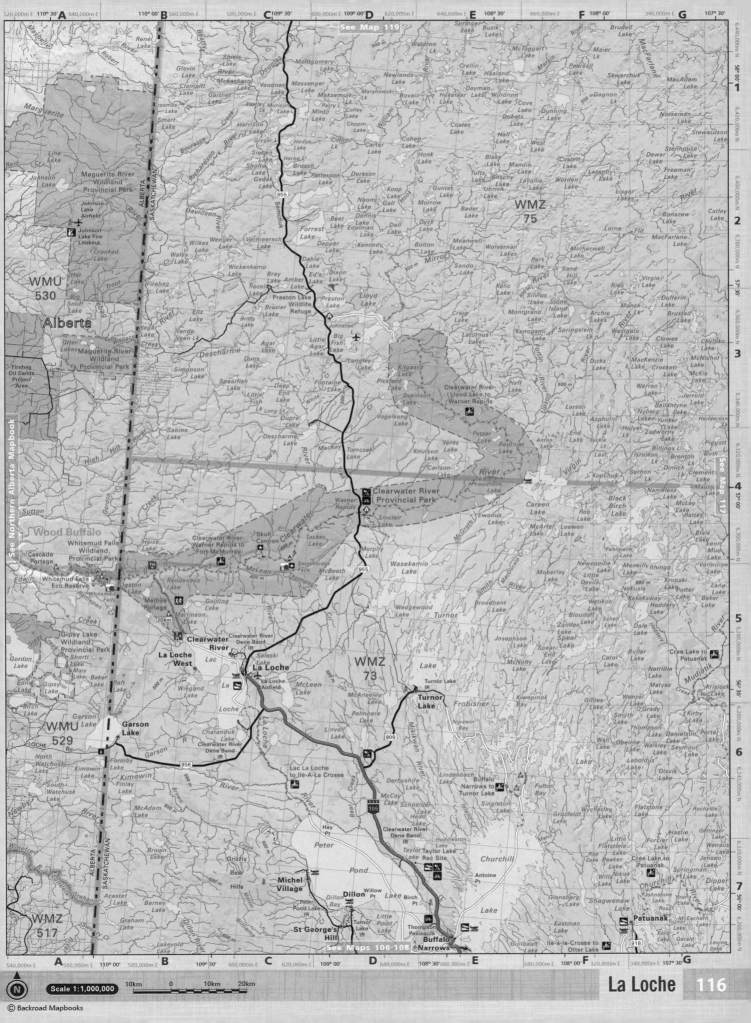

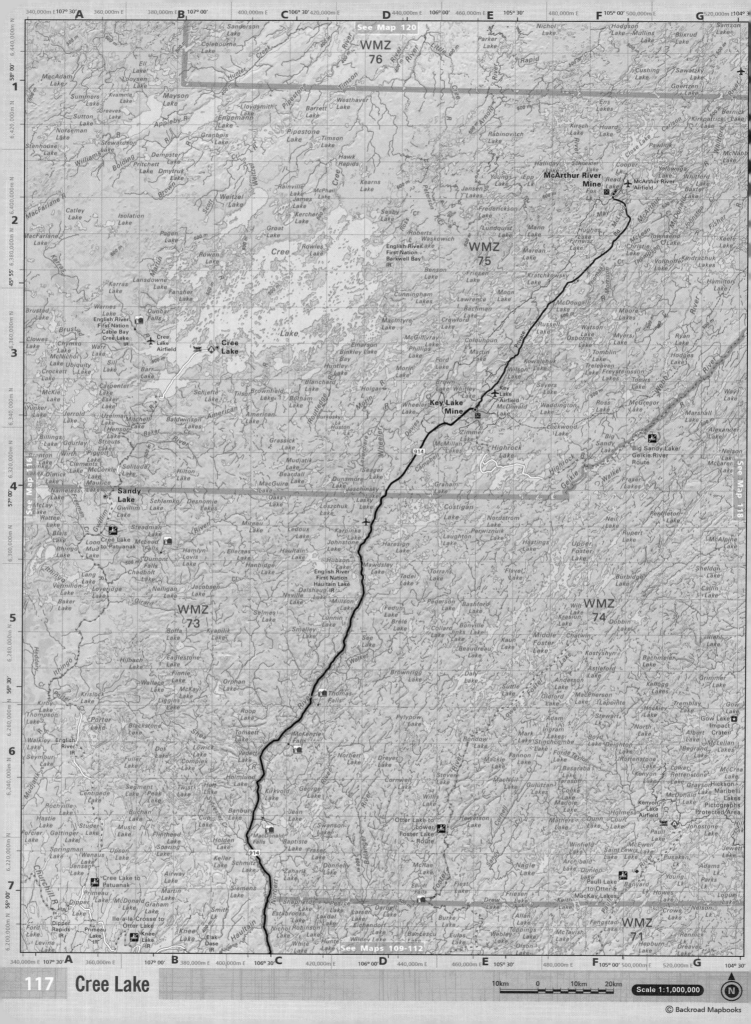

Scale 1:1,000,000

© Backroad Mapbooks

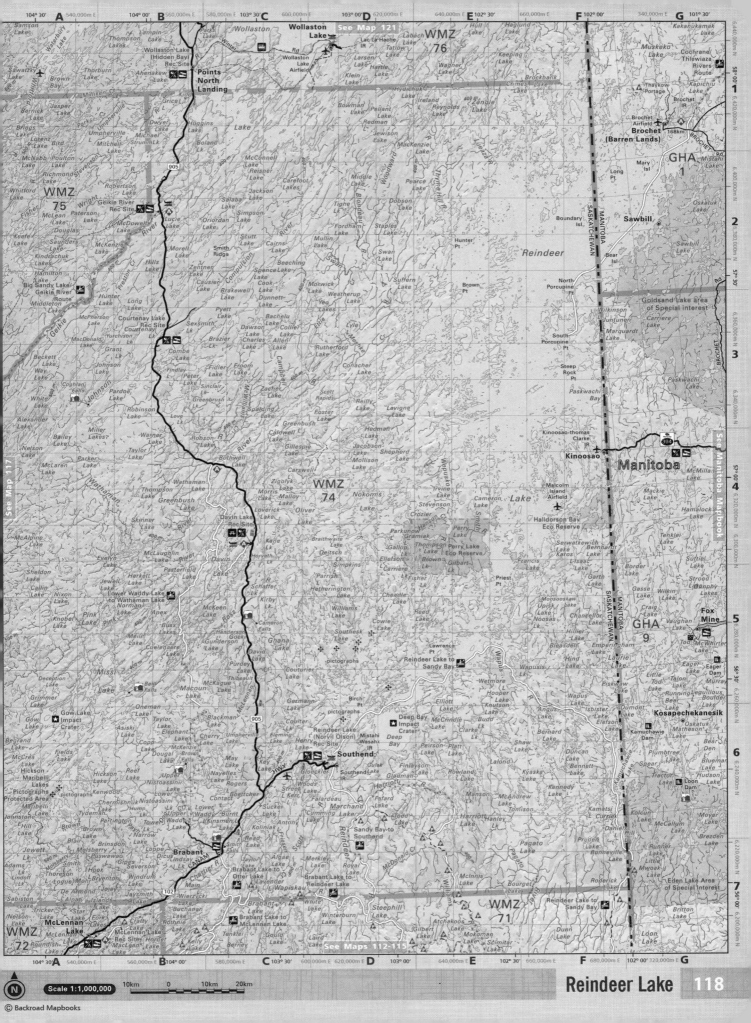

Scale 1:1,000,000
10km 0 10km 20km

© Backroad Mapbooks

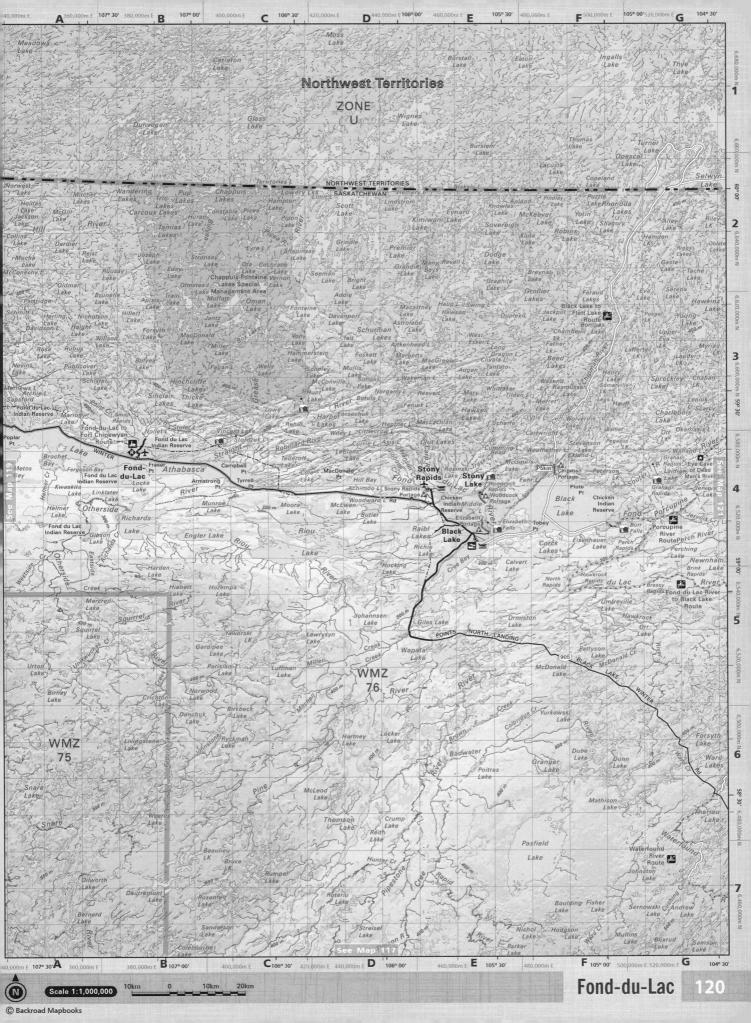

Fond-du-Lac

120

Scale 1:1,000,000

© Backroad Mapbooks

ADVENTURES

FISHING

HUNTING

PADDLING

BACKROAD

PARK

TRAIL

WINTER

ATV [OHV]

SNOWMOBILE

WILDLIFE

Get ready to get out and explore the beautiful province of Saskatchewan – over the following pages you will find everything you need to know about the best things to do and see in Saskatchewan, from long-distance paddling routes and secluded fishing hotspots to backroad attractions such as museums, geological features and historic sites. Whether you are looking to get away from it all and escape on a multi-day wilderness adventure, or prefer to stay in the comfort of your vehicle and within cell phone service, with a bit of searching you will find the adventure that is just right for you. From hunting to hiking, wildlife viewing, ATVing, snowmobiling and more, we have got you covered. As you are about to discover, Saskatchewan is a land of more than just prairies – sand dunes, mountains, rivers and lakes are yours to explore. Enjoy the views from the highest point of land between the Rockies and the Maritimes, discover ancient pictographs along a remote river system or visit a bird sanctuary – the choice is yours! In the following Adventure sections you will find detailed listings for virtually anything you could dream of doing in Saskatchewan's great outdoors, complete with map coordinates, directions, activity symbols, highlights, interesting facts and more. We have also included Adventure summaries at the beginning of each of the 11 sections to give you an overview of each activity. Once you decide on an adventure, find it on the map, make a plan, pack your bags and get out there!

East Block, Grasslands National Park, Saskatchewan
©Tourism Saskatchewan / Eric Lindberg

BACKROAD ADVENTURES

When people first think about Saskatchewan they only picture flat lands and farms, but there is much more to it than just the prairie landscape. When you take a closer look at the province you find an area with diverse and interesting land formations, steeped in Canadian history.

Some of the most intriguing landscapes are the sand hills and sand dunes. In the southern region, you can find the Great Sandhills; these vast mountains of sand resemble a desert landscape. Nearly 2,000 square kilometres (1,240 mi²) in area, these hills can get up to 90 metres (295 ft) high, truly resembling a great desert. Much further to the north you will find the Athabasca Sand Dunes. These dunes, found on the southern shore of Lake Athabasca, are the most northern of their kind in the world and, to add to the mystique, they are only accessible by air or boat.

Just as the sand hills and dunes of the north look like they belong in some foreign, distant land, so do the badlands that make up the south. These areas have had little influence from glaciation but have eroded to form spectacular landscapes. These areas hold many hidden gems, from Sam Kelly's Caves to fossil remains of the great Tyrannosaurus Rex.

Many of these landforms, whether they were formed by glaciation or other geological processes, left great landmarks for ancient peoples to orient their travels throughout the province.

Just like there are wonders of nature, there are also wonders of ancient art. There are some fine examples of First Nations petroglyphs found along the Churchill River and near St. Victor that date back thousands of years. More recent art can be found in several of the small towns and communities in the province in the form of murals painted on the side of buildings. These murals tell stories of western life from the ancient days to modern life.

More recent history can be found throughout the province. From the battlefields of the North West Rebellion of 1885 to the remains of North West Mounted Police forts and The Hudson Bay Company trading forts, much can be learned of the early days of the Province of Saskatchewan and Canada. Other historical landmarks show the struggles of the settlers as they came west to make a new life for themselves from eastern Canada and other parts of the world.

As you travel the highways and backroads of Saskatchewan, you will see for yourself that there is much more to this prairie province than you thought.

70 Mile Butte Lookout Point (Map 3/G5)

An easy walking trail leads to this lookout near the northwestern corner of Grasslands National Park. This is one of the highest points in the park and is famous for its spectacular sunsets – be sure to bring your camera.

Ambroz Blacksmith Shop (Map 17/B5)

The Ambroz Blacksmith Shop, a Provincial Heritage Property, in the town of Mossbank is the only original blacksmith shop in Saskatchewan. It was built in 1919 and is still found on its original site with original tools in working order.

Ancient Echoes Interpretive Centre (Map 47/C7)

Located in the village of Herschel, this centre provides ecotours of the surrounding area, an exhibit room that contains a natural history display, aboriginal artifacts, a painting collection and more. The centre is open seven days a week from May until August, and by request outside of that – call 306-377-2045 to book a tour. There is also a tea room that is open all year. Herschel is located just north of Highway 7.

Athabasca Sand Dunes (Map 119/D4–G4)

The Athabasca Sand Dunes located in northern Saskatchewan within Athabasca Sand Dunes Provincial Park are the most northern major sand dunes in the world. These dunes are nearly 100 km (620 mi) long and border the southern shore of Lake Athabasca. Those wishing to see these dunes will either need to fly or boat in. Those wanting to do some backcountry camping here (there are six designated primitive camping areas) will want to double check with the Saskatchewan Government on where camping is allowed in the park. Because the area is divided into three management zones, different guidelines govern both camping and day-visits. Visitors should remember that this area is fragile and precautions should be taken to protect the environment here.

Batoche National Historic Site of Canada (Map 60/E3)

The village of Batoche was the scene of the last battle of the Northwest Rebellion of 1885. Several buildings, including homes and a church, have been restored for the public to explore and view. The site is located 88 km northeast of Saskatoon and is open 7 days a week in July and August, seasonally in the spring and fall and closed during the winter months.

Battle of Tourond's Coulee / Fish Creek National Historic Site (Map 60/D5)

The Battle of Tourond's Coulee / Fish Creek was an important battle in the North West Rebellion. Occurring on April 24, 1885 the Métis forces were able to stop the Canadian North West Field Force from advancing on the headquarters of the Métis at Batoche. The site is located 17 km south of Rosthern along Highway 312; the battlefield is marked by a fence and a cairn that can be viewed from the road.

Bear's Head – Sandfly Lake (Map 110/F7)

This noticeable site is located along the Besnard Lake Circuit paddling route. Good fishing is found in the lake as well.

Beaver River Sand Cliffs (Map 88/B7)

Located just north of the Beaver River Bridge on the east side of Highway 903, the Beaver River Sand Cliffs offer great views and the chance to leap into the soft sand off the cliffs, if you are feeling spry.

Big Muddy Badlands (Maps 6, 7)

The Big Muddy area tells tales of cattle rustlers, horse thieves, whiskey runners, and road agents—it was the Wild West of the prairies. Besides its unique and colourful history, the area is also a contrast to the flat prairie visitors expect to see. Instead, there are scenic buttes, rock outcroppings and hoodoos. Natural grasses have reclaimed the area after early settlers eventually abandoned their dreams of farming.

This area was considered as Station Number 1 on Butch Cassidy's Outlaw Trail from Canada to Mexico. Other well-known Wild West outlaw names from the Big Muddy include the Jones-Nelson Gang, Dutch Henry and the Wild Bunch. Chief Sitting Bull, Crazy Horse and an estimated 700 followers camped in the high buttes of the Big Muddy in the late 1800s. Today, roads and access through the Big Muddy are limited due to much of the land being private property. However, tours (ranging from 3 to 8 hours) are available through the tourism association in the town of Coronach. Checkout the full tour details on their website, *www.townofcoronach.com/tours-badlands.html*

Big Muddy Nature Centre and Museum (Map 7/B6)

The Big Muddy Nature Centre and Museum is found in the community of Big Beaver. The collection is housed in a restored Missionary Alliance church and features artifacts and photos of the outlaws and the North West Mounted Police. It also provides information about the Big Muddy Badlands and their unique geological formation.

Big Rock Buffalo Rubbing Stone (Map 57/D4)

This large erratic (a rock left behind has a glacier retreats) was a landmark for early travelers of the region. Settlers and the North West Mounted Police would use this rock to navigate through the area. Buffalo would also visit here to rub their coats and rid themselves of parasites.

Brunyee Ridge (Map 25/E4)

Located in Saskatchewan Landing Provincial Park, you can find the Brunyee Ridge area on the south shore of the South Saskatchewan River, just west of Highway 4. There are no marked trails here but it is a fantastic area to explore on foot, with stunning views across the South Saskatchewan River Valley.

Buffalo Jump (Map 7/E5)

This is the largest of four Buffalo jump sites in the valley used by early Plains inhabitants. Buffalo were herded into a narrowing funnel towards the jump. Four separate rock lines are still situated on the rolling uplands above the prominent cliff, forming two drive lines, which extend at least 4 km (2.5 mi) east to cropland. The driving lines appear as small clumps of stones spaced about 1.5 metres (5 ft) apart. When used as part of the buffalo jump there were sticks propped into the rocks to herd the animals. There are approximately 7,000 of these stone configurations in this jump area. The red rock escarpment has a 10.7 metre (35 ft) drop. At the bottom of the cliff area there is also evidence that the area was used as a processing location. There is a large amount of fire-cracked rock from the fires, which you can see. Near the buffalo jump there is also a rock effigy of a buffalo. It is the only known buffalo effigy in Canada.

Canada's Dead Sea (Map 50/F7)

Little Manitou Lake, near Watrous, has a mineral density three times saltier than the ocean. The lake is free to float and you can not sink here, no matter how hard you try, but access to facilities requires visitors to purchase a day-pass from Manitou Springs Resort. The best time to visit the "Dead Sea" is between June and August.

Cannington Manor Provincial Historic Park (Map 22/A6)

An English gentleman, Captain Edward Pierce, established Cannington Manor in 1882 with the intent to create a British agricultural society on the prairies. Two original village buildings still exist along with several recreations. The key original building, the All Saints Anglican Church, built in 1884, is still used occasionally for services. A Visitor Centre provides historic information and is managed by costumed interpreters. Most of the village buildings are wheelchair accessible. The park is open from the May long weekend until June 30th daily except Sundays and from July 1st until the September long weekend daily except on Tuesdays.

Carlton House Historic Site (Map 60/B2)

Also known as Fort Carlton, this site was used as a Hudson's Bay Company fur trading post from the late 1700s until 1885. Later, it was rebuilt by the provincial government for use as a historic park, which opened in 1967. This was also the site of Big Bear's surrender in 1885, following his defeat at Steele Narrows. Carlton House is located about 65 km north of Saskatoon.

Castle Butte (Map 7/A5)

Castle Butte is a 70-metre-high (200 ft) sandstone and clay formation, with a circumference of about 402 metres (1,320 ft). This relic of the ice age is located a short drive north of the small community of Big Beaver. Its prominent position on the flat valley floor made it a landmark that was used for navigation by original inhabitants, early surveyors, North West Mounted Police patrols, outlaws and settlers alike. There are steep but climbable pathways to the top of the butte. There are also petrified trees at the top of the butte, although erosion and time are gradually destroying them.

Checkerboard Hill (Map 34/E7)

The view from Checkerboard Hill is considered to be one of the best in the province. From the top of the hill it is possible to view the South Saskatchewan River and the surrounding hills, offering fantastic views of changing colours in fall. Checkerboard Hill is located northwest of the town of Leader.

BACKROAD ADVENTURES

Chimney Coulee Provincial Historic Site (Map 2/D1)
This coulee is in the middle of the horseshoe area. There is a commemorative plaque here beside the remains of chimneys, which stood for many years to mark the sites of Métis cabins, trading posts and a police post. From the mid-1800s Métis hunters and traders regularly wintered here and a chapel was maintained for their use.

Churchill River's Aboriginal Rock Paintings (Maps 101, 102, 110–112, 118)
Found along the Churchill River waterway, these paintings, or petroglyphs, tell stories dating back thousands of years. There are nineteen known sites along the river from Pinehouse Lake to the border with Manitoba. The paintings show people, structures, thunderbirds, beavers, bears and other animals. Viewing the ancient art is best while canoeing along the river system. Those wanting more information on the paintings should track down a copy of the book The Aboriginal Rock Paintings of the Churchill River by Tim E H Jones.

Claybank Brick Plant National Historic Site (Map 18/A4)
The Claybank Brick Plant was stationed in an area rich in high-refractory clay required for face bricks, tiles, fire-resistant bricks and other products. The historic site still contains the original plant and equipment, as well as a historic bunkhouse and cookhouse. Admission to the site allows you to also access a hiking trail through the adjoining Massold Clay Canyons and clay pits where materials for bricks was excavated. The plant is open year round, but scheduled guided tours are only available at specific times between May and August. Additional details can be found at *www.claybank.sasktelwebsite.net*.

Cochin Lighthouse (Map 68/A5)
It might be hard to believe they would need a lighthouse on the prairies, but the Cochin Lighthouse, located on Pirot Hill, was built in 1988, and is a working lighthouse. At 11.6 metres (38 ft) high and 569 metres (1,867 ft) above sea level, a walk up 153 steps affords some great views out over the area.

Crooked Bush (Map 59/C3)
Located in the Redberry Lake Biosphere Reserve, this 1.2 hectare (3 acre) grove features trees totally twisted and bent upon themselves. The grove takes on an almost mythical quality as visitors wander along the boardwalk winding through the grove. The Crooked Bush is 14.5 km west of Hafford on Highway 40, where you turn north on Flint Road and travel 16 km before taking a 2.5 km jog to the left. Watch for the signs on Flint Road.

When travelling in the wilderness, remember that you are a guest in the home of many wild animals – give them the space and respect they require to behave naturally.

Cumberland Delta Lookout Point (Map 75/C2)
This scenic lookout can be found along Highway 9, about 7 km south of the intersection with Highway 55. As the name suggests, you will find sweeping views of the Cumberland Delta here.

Cumberland House Provincial Historic Park (Map 85/A4)
The first inland Hudson's Bay Company post and the oldest village in the province were built here. The only visible remnant of the post is the thick, stone-walled powder house, which was used for storing gunpowder. The Northcote, a steamboat used by the fur trade and at Batoche during the North West Resistance, is preserved in part here as well.

Cypress Hills Provincial Park (Map 12/B7)
Cypress Hills Provincial Park is an anomaly on the prairies, since it is the only portion that escaped being covered during the ice age. They were, as described by the Inuit word "nunataks," islands in the sea of ice. Today, the hills tower 600 metres (1,969 ft) over the flat prairies below. Here you can find fossils millennia old, but close to the surface since the land has not been shaved off or buried. Some of these include Rhinophynus (ancestors to the modern rhinoceros), Entelodonts (giant pigs), Leptomeryx (a type of deer), as well as crocodiles. If you explore the ravines that cut the prairie near the base of the hills, you will find a sudden change occurs in the type of fossils found. These Cretaceous clays and sediments, which are over 66 million years old, contain dinosaur fossils. Geological evidence collected in the soils tell the tale of the last 9,000 years of history in the area, showing first a warming trend, then a cooling trend in the last 4,600 years.

Deep Bay Impact Crater (Map 118/D6)
Located at the southwestern tip of Reindeer Lake, this conspicuously circular bay was formed by a meteor impact around 99 million years ago. At 220 metres (720 ft), it is also the deepest waterbody in Saskatchewan. Provincial Road 102 offers the closest road access to the bay, though there is no road access directly to it.

Douglas Provincial Park Sand Dunes (Map 38/E7)
Found on the eastern shore of Lake Diefenbaker along Highway 19, Douglas Park contains some impressive sand dunes in its northeast section. The dunes rise 30 metres (100 ft) and stretch for more than a kilometre and are accessed by a 5 km (3 mi) hike. An interpretive centre at the trailhead is worth stopping at.

Doukhobors at Veregin Historic Site (Map 43/G1)
Located in the community of Veregin, this site shows what life was like in the early 1900s in Doukhobor communities. The Doukhobor Prayer Home is the highlight to a visit here, but the site also shows smaller homes and their contents. These contents include brick ovens and bathhouses as well as smaller artifacts. Other buildings include barns and a blacksmith shop.

Duck Mountain Highlands Viewpoint (Map 44/D1)
You can find this viewpoint in the southeastern part of Duck Mountain Provincial Park, right on the Manitoba border. The viewpoint can be accessed on the way to the Duck Mountain Cross-Country Ski Area.

Eye Cave of Dead Man's River (Map 120/G4)
Not much is known about this unique geological formation on the banks of the "Dead Man's River" – you may just have to check it out for yourself to unlock its mystery. But be warned, this is a remote area that requires wilderness survival skills.

Foam Lake (Map 53/A7)
Foam Lake lies just to the west of Highway 310 and north of the town of the same name. This area has a unique history of Icelandic settlement, and you can find a monument to this end along the Vatnabyggd Trail near the lake's western shore. Other attractions on the lake include the Bertdale Site, which is found on a peninsula in the middle of the lake, the Johnson Site at the lake's north end, which features a viewing tower for birders and a boat launch, and the Lure Crop Site on the western shore, which is an example of a marshland conservation tactic where crops are planted in a specific area to attract waterfowl from other, more critical areas during damage season.

Forestry Farm Park and Zoo Historic Site (Map 49/D2)
Originally opened as a tree nursery in 1907, this is now the site of Saskatoon's municipal zoo. Between 1913 and 1966, 147 million trees were shipped from here. Some of the main attractions at this site, beyond the zoo itself, include the Forestry Farm House, fishing pond, zoo train, heritage rose garden and more.

Fort Battleford National Historic Site (Map 58/A3)
Fort Battleford was built in 1876 and was finally abandoned in 1924. It was just as important diplomatically as it was militarily, playing an important role in treaty negotiations. During the North West Rebellion, the fort also played a significant role and was one of the main bases of operation; it housed 200 soldiers and 107 horses. Today many of the original buildings still stand and have period furniture in them; the stockades and bastions have been reconstructed. The site is open Monday to Friday in May and June and seven days a week in July and August.

Fort Carlton Provincial Historic Park (Map 60/B2)
Fort Carlton was founded in 1810 and operated until 1885. While the original fort no longer stands, there is a reconstructed palisade, fur and provisions store, trade store, clerk's quarters and tepee encampment; much like they would have had in the late 1800s. Visitors can see, touch and smell artefacts such as buffalo hides, beaver pelts, war clubs, blankets, guns, twist tobacco, birch bark baskets and so much more. Interpretive staff are available to answer questions and lead visitors in activities like playing the spoons or packing furs. Outside the walls of the fort, a short trail leads down to the North Saskatchewan River. Visitors can also walk along a portion of the original Carlton Trail, where you can still see the ruts left by Red River carts. There is a campground here.

BACKROAD ADVENTURES

Fort Espérance National Historic Site (Map 33/D5)
The Fort Espérance National Historic Site monument is located west of the original Fort, near the town of Rocanville. The fort stood from 1785 to 1819 and was established by the North West Trading Company. Cellar depressions are all that remain at this historic site along with a picnic site and pit toilets.

Fort Livingstone National Historic Site (Map 55/A5)
Fort Livingstone, located near the border of Manitoba near the town of Pelly, is another of the significant forts of Canada. It was here in 1874 that this fort became the first post of the new North West Mounted Police and served as the headquarters of the police force till 1876. Also, Fort Livingstone held the territorial government of the North West Territories between 1876 and 1878 before it was moved to Battleford.

Fort Pelly National Historic Site (Map 54/G6)
Fort Pelly was constructed in 1856 and served as a fur trading post for the Hudson Bay Company until 1912. From 1871 until its closing in 1912 it was the headquarters for the Swan River District of the Hudson`s Bay Company. Today, there is not much left other than interpretive signs guiding visitors.

Fort Pitt Provincial Historic Park (Map 76/C7)
Fort Pitt was established on the north bank of the North Saskatchewan River in 1829. It was a Hudson's Bay Company fur trade post built halfway between Fort Carlton and Fort Edmonton. Fort Pitt played important roles in the fur trade, the signing of Treaty Six and in the North West Resistance of 1885. Today, the site consists of archaeological remains of two separate posts.

Fort Walsh National Historic Site (Maps 1/B1, 12/B7)
The North West Mounted Police established the fort after the 1873 Cypress Hills Massacre. This fort gets its name from Superintendent James Morrow Walsh of the NWMP, who maintained peaceful relations with Sitting Bull and his 5,000 Lakota followers. Its components include Farwell's Trading Post, the fort, a museum and theatre, the Fort Walsh Townsite hike, cemeteries, along with onsite bus tours and visitor amenities. The fort is open late May to early September and is located 55 km southwest of Maple Creek along Highway 271.

Fort Qu'Appelle Trading Post (Map 30/F3)
The Fort Qu'Appelle Trading Post was established by the Hudson Bay Trading Company in 1849 between Echo and Mission Lakes. After being moved several times the post's permanent home became the site of present day Fort Qu'Appelle. By 1870, the fort was both a relay point for furs and a pemmican supply post. In 1897, a new brick and stone Hudson's Bay Company general store was built on what is now the corner of Company Avenue and Broadway Street in Fort Qu'Appelle. The building, designated as a provincial heritage property, now houses private retail businesses. The Fort Qu'Appelle Museum is adjacent to the shuttered log building of the original 1865 Fort Qu'Appelle trading post. Visitors to the museum can view a collection of First Nations artifacts, Hudson's Bay Company items and displays related to the area's historic North West Mounted Police Post.

Frenchman Butte National Historic Site (Map 76/E7)
About 5 km east of the small community Frenchman Butte is a gently rising knoll where in May of 1885 First Nations, under the command of Kah-Paypamhchukwao (Wandering Spirit), and Canadian Forces commanded by General Strange clashed in a battle of the North West Rebellion. Today, visitors can walk the battlefield that has been left much the way as it would have looked in 1885; 98 defensive rifle pits dug by First Nation warriors are found here. Plan a stop at the Frenchman Butte Heritage Centre as well, which features an RV park for camping.

Gardner Dam (Map 38/A5)
Found along Highway 44 near the north end of Lake Diefenbaker, this is the largest earth-filled dam in Canada. A visitor's centre is found adjacent to the dam, featuring interpretive displays, souvenirs, food and more.

Good Spirit Sand Dunes (Map 43/B2)
These sand dunes are accessed via the Dune Discovery Interpretive Trail on the south shore of Good Spirit Lake. This is an easy 3 km (1.9 mi) trail that is wheelchair accessible. The dunes reach up to five stories tall and you can also enjoy sweeping vistas of Good Spirit Lake.

Goodwin House (Map 25/E4)
The Goodwin House is used as a Park Office and Visitor Centre for the Saskatchewan Landing Provincial Park. It is located right on Highway 4. Each stone was cut and squared by chisels and hammers in this century old home, which was built by an RCMP officer. It is mortared together with a mixture of lime, sand and horsehair, since cement was not available. The home was a haven for weary travelers and in 1926 also became the Post Office.

Government House Regina (Map 29/F6)
This historic site, located in Regina, was constructed between 1889 and 1891 and is still the location of the Office of the Lieutenant Governor (the Queen's representative to Saskatchewan). Government House looks much the same as it did 100 years ago and offers tour to the public. Plan your visit ahead of time by visiting www.governmenthouse.gov.sk.ca/about.

Gow Lake Impact Crater (Map 117/G6)
This crater measures 5 km (3 mi) in diameter and contains an island in its middle. Despite its size, this is still the smallest known crater in Canada with an uplift structure such as this. There is no road access to this remote location north of Lac La Ronge.

Great Sandhills (Map 24)
The Great Sandhills cover over 1,900 km^2 (730 mi^2) of land with high, rolling dunes. The land mass lies in the Chinook region and is subject to strong winds, predominantly from the west and northwest, which are shifting the dunes east. While some of the dunes are up to 30 metres (98 ft) high and composed of fine white sand, there is some native vegetation holding parts of it together. Besides prairie grasses, there are also some low bushes such as the rose, sage brush or chokecherry, along with small clumps of aspen, birch, and willow. Mule deer and sharp-tailed grouse are two of the most common wildlife you will see here.

The main viewing area for the Great Sandhills is reached south of the town of Sceptre on Highway 32. It is situated on private property that has been opened for the public. There is another private property viewing area that requires permission before entering found east of Highway 21 at Liebenthal. The Great Sandhills Museum can be found in Sceptre as well.

Great Sandhills Museum (Map 24/A1)
Located in the village of Sceptre, this museum features a variety of exhibits on the area's natural and cultural history, including the nearby Sandhills and the Empress Line Railway. While there are 11 rooms inside, outdoors you will find a historical village with a barn, church and antique machinery, as well as a flower garden.

Grey Owl's Cabin (Map 80/B2)
Found within Prince Albert National Park, Grey Owl's Cabin is located along the shore of the secluded Ajawaan Lake. Grey Owl was an early conservationist that was hired as a naturalist by the Dominion Parks Service in the 1930s; he built two cabins at Ajawaan Lake. There is no road access to these cabins and access is either by foot or by water. You can hike to the cabin along a 20 km (12.5 mi) trail (one-way) from the trailhead at the end of Kingsmere Road. By watercraft, you follow the Kingsmere River to the north end of Kingsmere Lake where a 3 km (1.9 mi) hike-in is possible. It is also possible to portage a canoe the 600 metres to Ajawaan Lake and paddle along the shore to the cabins. There is a backcountry campsite found at the northern end of Kingsmere Lake.

Highest Point in Saskatchewan (Map 1/A1)
Sitting at 1,392 metres (4,565 ft) above sea level, this unnamed elevation can be found just south of Cypress Hills Interprovincial Park on a branch off of South Benson Road.

Humboldt Historic Murals (Map 51/B2)
While driving through the area it is worthwhile to stop at Humboldt and check out the murals. Seven buildings have been painted with wall murals depicting different challenges of early pioneers and the creation of Humboldt.

Hunt Falls (Map 120/C3)
Formerly known as Lefty Falls, these are the largest falls in Saskatchewan at around 60 metres (180 ft) wide and 15 metres (50 ft) tall. Chances are that if you visit the falls you will have them all to yourself, as they are only accessible by float plane, landing on Eagle Rock just above the falls. The falls are located along the Grease River in Saskatchewan's northern reaches.

Jones Peak (Map 2/C2)
Found east of the community of the town of Eastend, access to this lookout is on a fairly rough road and a four-wheel drive vehicle is recommended. From the peak you will have a beautiful view of the Frenchman River Valley. Keep your eye out for foxes and prairie dogs, as well.

Keyhole Castle Historic Site (Map 71/A5)
Located in Prince Albert and dating back to 1913, this large home was built for businessman, mayor of Prince Albert and federal politician Sam McLeod. The building is named for its unique style of windows and even contains a ballroom on the top floor. Currently, the Keyhole Castle operates as a bed and breakfast.

Killdeer Badlands (Map 5/C6)
Located in the eastern block of the Grasslands National Park, these badlands escaped glaciation during the previous ice age, helping to create unique landforms of sand dunes and rocky canyons. The badlands are also home to some of the richest dinosaur fossil collections in Canada.

Holy Trinity Anglican Church (Map 102/D3)
The Holy Trinity Anglican Church, found near Stanley Mission, is the oldest standing building in Saskatchewan. The church was completed in 1860 after 6 years of building. At that time, the community of Stanley Mission was located around the church, however over time the community moved over to the other side of the river to be closer to transportation links. Today, the church basically stands alone on a point projecting out into the river, inviting visitors to explore this piece of history.

La Roche Percee Provincial Historic Site & Short Creek Cairn (Map 10/A6)
Located in the Souris Valley, these unusual rock formations have been eroded by wind and water. The rocks were once covered in First Nations symbolic animal carvings and later autographs of early explorers, NWMP and surveyors. There is a memorial cairn that recognizes the Short Creek Camp, which was used by the NWMP during the westward march in 1874.

Lacolle Falls Hydroelectric Dam (Map 71/F5)
This abandoned, partially completed dam is found on the North Saskatchewan River around 45 km east of Prince Albert. Construction on the dam was initially begun in 1909 and stopped four years later due to cost and technical difficulties – the $3 million project nearly bankrupted the town of Prince Albert. This site is difficult to access but grid roads do run close to it.

Lake Athabasca (Map 119)
This remote lake in Saskatchewan's northwestern corner offers some spectacular natural features for those who make it out here. Boat access sites on the lake's north shore include the sheer cliffs of Reed Bay and the Lodge Bay Cliffs. In Athabasca Sand Dunes Provincial Park on the lake's south shore you can find the Thomson Bay Exhumed Forest, which was buried by sand dunes and later unearthed as the constantly shifting sand moved further east. To the west of this, the William River flows into Lake Athabasca, creating a unique sand dune river delta.

Last Mountain House Historic Park (Map 29/E3)
Last Mountain House, near the town of Craven, was built at the south end of Last Mountain Lake at the end of the fur trade in 1869. Last Mountain House served briefly as a winter fur trade outpost of Fort Qu'Appelle. Designated a provincial heritage site, there are three reconstructed log buildings, a privy and an icehouse. The park is open from July 1 to the September long weekend with interpretive staff and has a voluntary admission fee.

Last Mounted Horse Patrol (Map 7/B7)
This is a commemorative marker situated along Highway 34, 6 km south of the Big Beaver access road. The plaque celebrates the last horse patrol used by the North West Mounted Police in 1939 to protect settlers and bring law to the areas along the Outlaw Trail.

Limestone Crevices of Amisk Lake (Map 95/B5)
These crevices drop abruptly to depths of 6-12 metres (20-40 ft) and it is possible to climb down and explore inside them. The limestone was formed by the remains of coral reef and mud from an ancient sea. You can find the crevices about 1 km north of Meridian Creek on Highway 167 (South Weir Road).

Little Manitou Lake (Map 50/F7)
Little Manitou Lake is found along Highway 365, about 115 km southeast of Saskatoon. This lake is fed by underground springs and its high mineral content allows swimmers to float, similar to the famous Dead Sea. Local First Nations have been using the lake for its healing properties for centuries. In addition to a regional park, there is a resort and spa located on the lake.

Little Swan River Viewpoint (Map 65/C6)
This viewpoint is found about 3.5 km east of the hamlet of Little Swan River on a branch road off of Highway 982. The Swan River runs through lush boreal forest and even offers the odd brook trout for anglers.

Lund Wildlife Exhibit (Map 71/A5)
Created by Frank Lund, a blacksmith turned taxidermist, this collection of stuffed wild animals has toured the prairies and the west coast and is now maintained by Frank's grandson. You can find it on 4th Street in Prince Albert, in between 8th and 9th Avenue.

Manitou Falls (Map 121/A5)
These falls located on the Fond du Lac River where the river goes through a narrow limestone gorge. These picturesque falls are often visited by adventurists canoe tripping down the Fond du Lac River.

Maple Creek Museums (Map 12/F4)
The town of Maple Creek offers a couple of fantastic historical sites to visit. On Jasper Street you can find the Oldtimers Museum, which is located in an old schoolhouse and contains two floors of exhibits. This space also hosts local art exhibits and other events. To the south, just west of the Cypress Hills Provincial Park Golf Course, you can find the Antique Tractor Museum and Frontier Village, a charming interpretive site that brings the history of prairie farming and homesteading to life.

> *Take care of the areas we love by packing out everything you pack in, and leaving behind only footprints.*

Marr Residence Historic Site (Map 49/C3)
Built in 1884, this building was a part of the area's earliest European settlement and even served as a field hospital during the North West Rebellion. This is the oldest building in Saskatoon that is still in its original site, at 326 11th Street East.

McNichol Lake Plaque (Map 102/C2)
McNichol Lake is found within Lac La Ronge Provincial Park and can be accessed along various canoe routes between MacKay and Otter Lake. The plaque is found on a small island in the middle of the lake.

Mennonite Heritage Village (Map 14/G1)
The Mennonite Heritage Village, located in Swift Current, shows visitors what life was like in Mennonite communities in Saskatchewan from 1880s to the 1920s. Attractions here include examples of homesteads, barns, churches and gardens of these settlers. Operating hours, special events and more can be found on the village website at *www.mennoniteheritagevillage.ca*.

Mistusinne Cairn (Map 38/C6)
More than 9,000 years ago the South Saskatchewan River Valley was a sacred site for the Plains people who roamed the prairie region. The Mistusinne, or "huge rock" in Cree, marked a gathering place and spot of religious importance. When Gardiner Dam was constructed and the plains were flooded by the South Saskatchewan River to create Lake Diefenbaker, a portion of the rock was moved to the Elbow Harbour Recreation Site. A cairn was erected to recognize the rock's importance to the early peoples.

Moose Bay Mound (Map 32/B4)
The Moose Bay Mound marks an ancient aboriginal burial ground at Crooked Lake Provincial Park and is around 1,000 years old. It is one of the most northern examples of burial mounds built throughout North America between 1000 B.C. and 1600 A.D. The site is significant for its relative isolation. It is comprised of a grassy dome or conical mound, 15 metres (19 ft) in diameter and 1.5 metres (5 ft) high, situated on a steep hill high above the Lower Qu'Appelle River. In 1968, an excavation of the Moose Bay site by archaeologists revealed a total of 8 burial units. Each consisted of bundled remains surrounded by mortuary offerings of decorated pottery vessels, birch bark containers, tubular stone pipes and bone tools.

Murals of Nipawin (Map 73/A3)
The city of Nipawin has created 13 murals depicting different aspects of life on the Saskatchewan Prairie. Visitors can walk the city streets on their own or take a guided tour for more insight into the artists and their work.

Murals of Whitewood (Map 32/F7)
The town of Whitewood has painted 5 murals on buildings; these murals show what life was like back in the west at the turn of the century when Saskatchewan was still sparsely populated.

National Doukhobor Heritage Village (Map 43/G1)
Located in the community of Veregin, this site shows what life was like in the early 1900s in Doukhobor communities. The Doukhobor Prayer Home is the highlight to a visit here, but the site also shows smaller homes and their contents. These contents include brick ovens and bathhouses as well as smaller artifacts. Other buildings include barns and a blacksmith shop. Additional information can be found online at *www.ndhv.ca*.

Natural Prairie Grasslands (Map 3/G5–5/C7)

The best place to see the prairie landscape how it looked before most of it was changed for agriculture is in Grasslands National Park. This area is an excellent location to view rare plants and animals. In the southern portion of the eastern block of the park you will be able to find grasslands that have had minimal impact by human hands. While Grasslands National Park is open year-round, the visitor centre is only open from mid-May to mid-October. How you discover the area is up to you, access can be as easy as a self-guided drive through the area to overnight backpacking adventures.

Ness Creek Site (Map 79/F5)

This campground and event facility is home to the Ness Creek Music Festival, among other events, as well as being a destination for ecotourism and outdoor education. The site is surrounded by boreal forest, wildlife and signs of early First Nations activity. There is a permaculture forest garden, forest interpretive centre, cabins for rent and more. You can find this site off of Highway 922 near Delaronde Lake – look for the sign to Nesslin Lake.

If you plan to travel through remote areas it is imperative that you leave a detailed itinerary with friends or family.

Next of Kin Memorial Avenue Historic Site (Map 49/C2)

This is the only intact example of the "Roads of Remembrance" that were built in various Canadian cities after WWI. Modeled after the country avenues of France and begun in 1922, this avenue is found in Saskatoon's Woodlawn Cemetery.

Nicolle Flats Homestead (Map 28/G5)

Located in Buffalo Pound Provincial Park, a short walk along the Nicolle Flats Trail brings you to this 1880s homestead, consisting of a stone house and barn.

Nipekamew Sand Cliffs (Map 91/G3)

The Nipekamew Sand Cliffs are found south of Provincial Road 165, about 3.7 km west of the junction with Highway 912. The cliffs were formed by 120 million year old sand deposits that were eroded by the Nipekamew River. Due to the fragile nature of these cliffs, the side road and trailhead to reach them are unmarked. Expect to hike just over a kilometre to reach the cliffs.

Nitenai Salt March (Map 75/B1)

The Nitenai Salt Marsh is found off of Highway 55, just west of the junction with Highway 9. The marsh is home to several rare species of plants.

Notukeu Heritage Museum (Map 15/B6)

The Notukeu Heritage Museum is located in the Centre Cultural Royal, Ponteix's centre of Western Canadian French social and cultural activities. Many of the artifacts in the museum come from the private collection of Henri Liboiron, a former resident of the town of Ponteix. The artifacts show the life in the area for the past 10,000 years. Visitors will learn about such things as medicine wheels, building a tipi, buffalo drives and making pemmican.

Parr Hill Springs (Map 65/C6)

These springs are located within the Par Hill Lake Recreation Site on the eastern shore of Par Hill Lake. The springs can be accessed by a side road off of Highway 982, just south of the hamlet of Little Swan River.

Percival Windmill (Map 32/D7)

The Percival Windmill is visible from the Trans-Canada Highway. Erected somewhere around a century ago, the windmill is a Monitor Vaneless, which was a popular type of windmill on the prairies as it could withstand the gusting strong winds. The windmill pumped water for livestock and farms for decades.

Popoff Tree (Map 59/F4)

Named after Samuel J. Popoff, this tree is over 160 years old and predates the province of Saskatchewan by about 50 years, making the province's oldest and largest tree. Standing 22 metres (72 ft) tall and 5 metres (16 ft) across, this is one of Saskatchewan's few remaining cottonwood trees. You can find the tree 17 km south of Blaine Lake along Highway 12 – look for a sign saying Tree Road.

Prince Albert Visitor Centre (Map 71 /A5)

Found at the intersection of 2nd Avenue and Marquis Road, this log building contains a gift shop that features locally produced art, food, clothing and jewelry, as well as friendly staff who can tell you all about the best things to see and do around Prince Albert.

Regina Floral Conservatory (Map 29/F6)

The Regina Garden Associates operates this indoor tropical garden. The garden is open from late summer to late spring (September until June) from 1:00-4:30 pm daily and offers residents and those passing through Regina a tropical paradise to escape too during the winter months. At the time of writing, this attraction is free of charge but visitors are encouraged to make a donation to the Regina Garden Associations. There is plenty of useful information on their website, *www.reginafloralconservatory.ca*.

Rice River Canyon (Map 74/G2)

The Rice River Canyon is a fairly remote area accessible from Highway 55, about 8 km east of the turnoff to Pakwaw Lake. From here, you can hike up the river for as far as you like, but be ready to get your feet wet as there are no defined trails and you will end up having to cross the river. It is about 7 km (4.5 mi) to the Rice River Canyon Forks. This area is known to contain many fossils.

Roan Mare Valley (Map 7/E5)

Roan Mare Valley was named during the outlaw era, when the Big Muddy was a hideout for notorious criminals. Since that was a much wetter period, the valley itself, which is now quite dry and called a coulee, was a muddy mess. The roan mare was left in the valley while rustlers rode off to do their work, before returning under the cover of darkness. They had discovered she would lead them safely across Big Muddy Lake to the south shore with the stolen animals when urged on with gunshots. Once they had traded for different animals to sell to the settlers, they had her lead them back over the water to the north side and left her there again. Legend has it that a young roan filly roamed the valley even after the outlaws disappeared.

Royal Saskatchewan Museum (Map 29/G6)

The Royal Saskatchewan Museum is located in the city of Regina. Its Earth Sciences Gallery showcases over two billion years of geological and fossil history from the province. The exhibits detail ancient volcanoes from the last days of the dinosaur's right to the great ice ages. Megamunch, a roaring robotic tyrannosaurus rex, is a hit with kids. The First Nations Gallery presents the history and culture of Saskatchewan's First people. For more information check out their website at *www.royalsaskmuseum.ca*.

Roche Percee Sandstone Caves & Hoodoos (Map 10/B6)

The Roche Percee Sandstone formations on the east side of the hamlet are a place of mystery and intrigue. Formed by past oceans and thrust to the surface, these sculpted stones and caves have been hiding places for many over the past few centuries. The US cavalry sheltered here, as well as rum runners of the 1930s. In addition to hoodoos, deep ravine ledges, pierced rocks, and pockmarked pillars, you will also find concretions or sandstone rocks formed like a pearl in an oyster—they can weigh up to 454 kg (10,000 pounds).

Sam Kelly's Caves (Map 7/D7)

Found in the Big Muddy region of Saskatchewan, these caves are well worth a visit when in the area. There are many caves in the Big Muddy region and many were used as hideouts for outlaws in the late 1800s and early 1900s. Sam Kelly (aka Charles "Red" Nelson) was one of these outlaws and co-leader of the Nelson-Jones Gang that specialized in horse and cattle rustling. His caves were strategically located near the border with Montana so that he could escape to the United States when the Canadian authorities were after him (or vice versa when the American authorities were looking for him). Sam Kelly used two caves, one for his horses and another for himself. Today, the caves are located on private land and tours are available.

Sandcastles (Map 26/B4)

The landforms here do resemble a sandcastle and are caused by the weathering of the soil and rock of the area. Aboriginals used the area, as is evident by teepee rings that have been found. Today, the area is home to prairie falcons and bull snakes. Marine fossils have also been found in the area, providing a clue to how the landscape would have been in prehistoric times. Plan to visit the magnesium sulphate lake as well, located approximately 32 km northwest of Beechy. Some of the sulphate, known as Epsom salt, is harvested yearly to be made into bath salts.

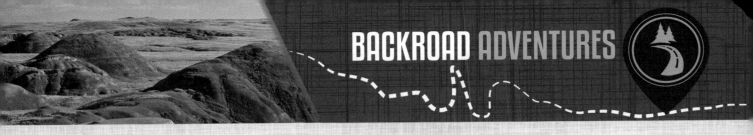

Saskatchewan Railway Museum (Map 49/B3)

Located off Highway 7, in the southwest side of Saskatoon, the museum features buildings, locomotives, streetcars, rolling stock and memorabilia relating to railway history. Opening hours, admission costs and more can be found on the museum website, *www.saskrailmuseum.org*.

Saskatchewan River Forks (Map 71/G5)

Located about 40 km east of Prince Albert, this is where the North and South Saskatchewan Rivers merge to create the Saskatchewan River. There is a scenic recreation site with a picnic area, washrooms and fire pits that overlooks the confluence. To reach this site, take Sask Forks Road north from Highway 302 just before you would cross the South Saskatchewan River.

Saskatchewan Science Centre (Map 29/F6)

The Saskatchewan Science Centre is open year round and features over 180 hands-on, interactive exhibits, an Imax theatre and education programs. Located in Regina, full details can be found on the centre's website, www.sasksciencecentre.com.

Saskatoon Forestry Farm & Zoo (Map 49/D3)

Located on the northeast side of Saskatoon, the zoo features a Red Panda and cougars (although this feature attraction changes yearly) in the PotashCorp Ark along with a pair of grizzly bears in the Kinsmen Bear Exhibit. There is also a petting zoo, the Forestry Farm and a fishing pond. The zoo is open from May to October and can be found at 1903 Forestry Farm Park Drive.

Short Creek Cairn (Map 10/B7)

This cairn is found just west of Roche Percee on old Highway 39. Near the cairn are some unusual rock formations that are covered with First Nations pictographs as well as the autographs of European explorers and surveyors.

Skytrail Pedestrian Bridge (Map 37/G2)

Overlooking the South Saskatchewan River, the Skytrail is home the longest pedestrian bridge in Canada, at over a kilometre wide and 48 metres (157 ft) tall. Part of the Trans Canada Trail, the bridge was a rail bridge from 1912 until the mid-1980s, lying dormant for years until it was donated for conversion to a pedestrian bridge in 2003. Needless to say, the views from the bridge are spectacular and it is very popular with birdwatchers.

Smoothrock Falls (Map 116/C5)

Most people visit Smoothrock Falls as part of a canoe or kayak trip down the Clearwater River. The falls are located 2 km downstream of the Gould Rapids and are one of the most iconic features of the river, plunging over a series of drops over a twisting and turning route. During high water, an overflow channel provides breathtaking views as well, and potholes worn into the rocks offer a chance to dip in and cool off on a hot day. A wilderness campsite can be found above the falls.

Steele Narrows Provincial Historic Park (Map 77/A3)

The last battle of the Northwest Rebellion was fought here on June 3, 1885. While there are no archaeological sites to be explored by visitors, there is interpretive signage, picnic tables and a boat launch. There is a short, steep climb up to a viewpoint over the area.

St. Victor Petroglyphs Historic Park (Map 6/B3)

These petroglyphs are found near the town of St. Victor in the Big Muddy Badlands area of south central Saskatchewan. Carved into horizontal sandstone at a top of a cliff, the age and author of the carvings here are not known. Some experts believe that the carvings here were made at different times and by different people as the images reflect different styles. Many of the pictures are of animal tracks and are believed to represent hunting mythology.

The best time to view the petroglyphs is on a clear day in the early morning or towards sunset when shadows are cast into the shallow grooves bringing up the outlines of the shapes. Wooden walkways have been built to help minimize human impact on the fragile sandstone site. Please respect these carvings by using the walkways when visiting here. The park also provides picnic tables and toilets, while the adjacent Sylvan Valley Regional Park offers camping.

Standing Rock (Map 24/F6)

On the east side of the Great Sandhills, near the town of Hazlet, you will find the Standing Rock. Approximately 14,000 years ago this rock was on the eastern half of the province, near the Hudson Bay area. It was moved by a huge glacier and dropped into its current location when the glacier stopped and melted away.

Sukanen Ship Pioneer Village & Museum (Map 17/E1)

Located south of Moose Jaw, this is really three different museums in one location. It features a Pioneer Village, a history of Tom Sukanen and his story of building a ship in the middle of the prairies, as well as a Fire Collection showcasing the history of firefighting. Additional details can be found on the museum website at *www.sukanenshipmuseum.ca*.

Sunken Hill (Map 26/B4)

Back in 1949, for some unknown reason the land here sank. John Muir drove his car through here back in 1949 to check cattle; several days later the cattle were checked again. The previous tire tracks could be seen appearing to drive right off a cliff then down on the now lower sunken hill. The tracks lined up perfectly with tire tracks on the opposite hill. Keep in mind that if you chose to hike or bike here, parts of the Sunken Hill Trail cannot be accessed during winter months or after a rainfall. In addition, visitors are asked to close all gates as they enter and leave the trail, as it is located on private land.

Swift Current Petroglyph Boulder (Map 14/G1)

Located on private property (Green Hectares Bed and Breakfast), this petroglyph shows aboriginal carvings that date back over 3,000 years. Make sure to get permission to cross the private land before going to view it.

Touchwood Hills Post Provincial Historic Park (Map 41/D4)

Touchwood Hills Post was built in 1879, the last Hudson's Bay Company trading post to be built in the area. It was built along the Carlton Trail, a short portion of which still remains. There is a commemorative plaque and concrete markers at this site.

Tunnels of Moose Jaw (Map 28/E7)

A series of tunnels connect numerous main street businesses in the city of Moose Jaw. Some of them are reputed to have been used by Al Capone in an illicit whiskey trade during Prohibition. This activity earned it the nickname of "Little Chicago" during the 1920s when it gained a reputation for rum running and prostitution. For more information on touring the tunnels you can visit *www.tunnelsofmoosejaw.com* or call (306) 693-5261.

Wanuskewin Heritage Park (Map 49/D2)

The Wanuskewin Heritage Park, located 5 km north of Saskatoon, depicts the lifestyle of Northern Plains First Nation culture. A variety of trails and interpretive programs show visitors different aspects of the First Nations culture and traditions. More information can be found on the park website at *www.wanuskewin.com*.

Waskwei River Shale Outcrops (Map 75/C3)

The Waskwei River can be found along Highway 9, about 19 km south of the intersection with Highway 55. Hiking up the river will lead you to some ancient layered rock walls, as well as the occasional fishing hole. Make sure to bring your bug spray, as this is prime mosquito habitat.

Wood Mountain Post Historic Park (Map 5/E4)

Wood Mountain Post housed a detachment of North West Mounted Police from 1874 to 1918. The detachment closely patrolled the area and border with the United States looking for horse and cattle rustlers as well as whisky smugglers. Today, two reconstructed buildings show what life was for the detachment. The park is open from the beginning of June until the middle of August. This park is only 4 km away from the Wood Mountain Regional Park, which is accessible by a walking trail.

World's Largest Coffee Pot (Map 39/B5)

While traveling Highway 11 between Regina and Saskatoon you might as well stop at the halfway point of Davidson and have some coffee. But you might not be able to finish the 150,000 cups that their coffee pot can hold – Davidson boasts the world's largest coffee pot. Standing 7.3 metres (24 ft) tall, this roadside attraction is worth a visit.

W.R. Motherwell Homestead National Historic Park (Map 31/C3)

The restored farm site of William Richard Motherwell, who was the Commissioner of Agriculture as well as Provincial Secretary in Saskatchewan's first government in 1905, is located 3 km south of the town of Abernethy off Highway 22. It is open from Victoria Day in May until Labour Day in September and managed by costumed guides.

Fly Fishing, Battle Creek, Saskatchewan
©Tourism Saskatchewan / Greg Huszar Photography

FISHING
ADVENTURES

Saskatchewan is isolated from oceans and due to this it is a very dry province. But, there are still plenty of waterbodies that an angler can fish. The southern portion of the province (basically from Saskatoon south) is the prairie region.

With its typical flat terrain and grasslands, lakes of this region are typically shallow and many waterbodies are dam-created reservoirs made for irrigation. Also, in this region there are many streams that do not drain towards an ocean, but have internal drainage systems where the waters flow into lakes. This can create saline lakes systems surrounded by white salt crusts, such as Chaplin Lake, Reed Lake, Old Wives Lake, Big and Little Quill Lakes. Lakes here are also susceptible to drought and it is not uncommon for smaller lakes to completely dry up; winter kill from freezing is also common. Both of these conditions can greatly affect fishing from year to year. It is best to look for bigger or stocked lakes in these areas.

As you go north, the flat plains of the prairies give way to rolling plains with scattered lakes and glacial kettles (the small pothole looking lakes on the maps). In this region, from Saskatoon to Lac la Ronge, you will find several large parks that offer some great fishing and recreation for the entire family. Lakes here are less susceptible to drought, but winter freezes can still create winter kill.

In the northern region, the terrain becomes more rolling and numerous lakes can be found, from small ponds to the huge lakes like Reindeer Lake and Lake Athabasca. Roads become less frequent and the use of float planes or canoes to get to the fishing waters becomes necessary. There are simply too many northern lakes holding lake trout, northern pike and walleye to mention. Instead, we have listed a good number to give you an idea what to expect in the area. We also recommended a few outfitters and fishing lodges to help you access this amazing fishery.

Fishing in Saskatchewan is regulated by the Ministry of Environment. It is important to always check regulations prior to fishing as regulations can change between seasons and within seasons. Regulations and license information can be found on the fishing section of the Ministry of Environment's website (*www.environment.gov.sk.ca/fishing*). The Saskatchewan Wildlife Federation (www.swf.sk.ca) and the ever-popular Saskatchewan Walleye Trail, or fishing tournaments, (*www.saskwalleyetrail.ca*) are a couple of other sites of interest to anglers in the province.

Fisherman holding a Northern Pike
©Shutterstock / Shaftinaction

Stocking Charts

Saskatchewan has an extensive fish stocking program that supplements sport fisheries in many of the province's lakes, rivers and streams. Trout are the most commonly stocked species, with brook, brown and rainbow trout stocked in numerous waterbodies. Northern pike, splake, walleye and yellow perch are also stocked, though to a lesser degree than the trout species.

Brook Trout Stocking

	MAP	BROOK TROUT	BROWN TROUT	LAKE TROUT	NORTHERN PIKE	RAINBOW TROUT	SPLAKE	TIGER TROUT	WALLEYE	YELLOW PERCH	OTHER
Amber Lake	116/C3	•	•								
Atchison Lake	88/C2	•				•	•				
Battle Creek - Battle Creek Rd	12/A7	•	•			•			•		
Battle Creek - Parc Historique National du Fort-Walsh	1/B1	•	•						•		
Battle Creek - Reesor Lake	12/B7	•	•			•			•		
Bear Creek - Hwy 724	13/B4	•	•								
Bear Creek - Piapot	13/B3	•	•								
Belanger Creek - Cypress Lake	1/F2	•	•			•					
Belanger Creek - Hwy 21	1/F2	•	•			•					
Buffalo Pound Trout Pond	28/F5	•	•			•					
Caddis Lake	92/A4	•	•								
Coal Pit-SPC-C	9/F6	•					•	•			
Diamond Lake	82/B2	•				•					
Dorothy Lake	82/C1	•				•					
Ed's Lake	116/C2	•				•					
Fir River	64/G1	•									
Greenbush River	64/E1	•									
Hay Meadow Creek - Fife Lake	6/A5	•	•	•						•	
Jackfish Creek - Hwy 794	67/G3	•									
Jackfish Creek - Minnehaha	67/F4	•									
Jackfish Creek - Sibbald Lake/Glaslyn	68/A3	•									
Jackfish Creek - Weyapanase Bay	67/G5	•									
Junction Lake	91/B3	•	•								
Lady Lake	54/B4	•					•	•			
Lussier Lake	102/B1	•									
Maistre Lake	81/F4	•									
McDougal Creek - Hwy 106	82/C2	•									
McDougal Creek - Hwy 120	82/D3	•									
McDougal Creek - Mossy River	83/C2	•									
Moose Mountain Trout Pond	21/E6	•				•					
Negan Lake	104/C6	•				•					
Nipawin Lake	82/C3	•									
Nipekamew Creek	82/B2	•									
Opal Lake	82/B2	•	•								
Oscar Lake	59/C1	•									
Pear Lake	80/G6	•				•					
Pine Cree Creek	2/E1	•									
Poplar Ridge Lake	78/G4	•				•					
Ridge Lake	81/G1	•									
Round Lake	76/F4	•							•		
Russell Creek	15/A4	•									
Sand Lake	82/A2	•									

Lake Fishing

Saskatchewan is a land of many lakes. From the popular and easy-to-access fishing lakes in the southern part of the province to the remote fly-in lakes of the north, there is a lake (or several) for every type of angler here. Whether you are looking for a casual day out with the family or a multiday getaway into virgin lake country, this landlocked province has no shortage of options.

Adams Lake (Map 12/B7)

Adams Lake, in Cypress Hills Interprovincial Park has rainbow and brown trout. Access is available only through the park. Walk-in camping is available nearby.

Admiral Reservoir (Map 14/D7)

The Admiral Reservoir is situated 6 km southwest of Admiral with grid road access. It is a small, 41 hectare (101 ac) waterbody with no boat launch. You can expect to pull stocked walleye and yellow perch, as well as sauger.

Aikenhead Lake (Map 102/A4)

Found north of Lac La Ronge, this medium sized lake is home to burbot and northern pike. And there are sources that say that walleye, whitefish and yellow perch can also be found here. A power boat will help you explore the lake fully, but a canoe will also get you to the fish. Access is found on the road to the Anglo-Rouyn Mine.

Alameda Reservoir (Map 10/F4)

The Alameda Dam is located 3 km east of the town of Alameda on Moose Mountain Creek. Don't be surprised to reel in a 9 kg (20 lb) northern pike. Also, expect to find walleye, sauger and yellow perch. Access is best at Moose Creek Regional Park. Here, there is a large fishing dock and a paved boat launch along with 84 campsites.

Alpine Lake (Map 81/E4)

Alpine Lake is found in between Candle Lake Provincial Park and Whiteswan Lake Game Preserve and is best accessed by ATV or snowmobile. Those who reach the lake can enjoy fishing for northern pike.

Alsask Lake (Map 34/D3)

Alsask Lake can be found southeast of the community of Alsask via a series of grid roads. Northern pike and yellow perch can be found the lake's waters.

Althouse Lake (Map 102/B2)

Located just outside of the western boundary of Lac La Ronge Provincial Park, Althouse Lake can be accessed via Provincial Road 102. Resident northern pike and splake are the main draw for anglers here.

Amyot Lake (Map 98/F4)

Amyot Lake is found close to the larger Lac Île-à-la-Crosse, on the opposite side of Highway 155 from the lake's southern arm. Amyot Lake offers good fishing for resident northern pike and walleye.

Anderson Lake (Map 43/F7)

Found along the Yellowhead Highway (Hwy 16) at the town of Saltcoats, this lake is home to a regional park with camping and a boat launch. Anglers will find northern pike in the waters. Check the regulations for special catch and release restrictions.

Anglin Lake (Map 80/G7)

Resting in Anglin Lake Recreation Site, next to Prince Albert National Park, anglers will find some great fishing opportunities for northern pike and stocked walleye. There are three campsites in the recreation site, including Anderson Point that features a boat launch and fish cleaning station. An elaborate trail system and channels to the nearby lakes help ambitious explores test the other lakes in the area.

Annie Laurie Lake (Map 54/A4)

Annie Laurie Lake offers some excellent fishing for northern pike and can be reached via 2nd street in Preeceville, just north of town.

Antelope Lake (Map 14/B1)

Antelope Lake is a key part of Antelope Lake Regional Park, which makes a good place to set up camp. The lake, which dries up on occasion, holds northern pike and was previously stocked with rainbow trout. More recently walleye have been stocked here. There is a stocked trout pond within the regional park for kids of all ages to try.

Amisk Lake (Map 94/A3–95/B6)
This large lake, found near the border with Manitoba, offers great fishing for northern pike, walleye and lake trout. Access is along Highway 167. A boat launch and campsite can be found just north of the town on Denare Beach at the Amisk Lake (Sawmill bay) Recreation Site. More camping and access can be found south of Denare Beach along Highway 167, while amenities can be found in town. Outfitters are also found around the lake. Check the regulations for special restrictions.

Atton Lake (Map 57/C1)
Atton Lake offers fishing for northern pike and walleye. Camping can be found at Atton's Lake Regional Park, on the southern shore, while groceries and other amenities can be found in the town of Cut Knife, to the southwest.

Attitti Lake (Map 104/F5)
This larger lake located east of Waskwei Lake can be a challenge to get too, but there is some good fishing for lake trout, northern pike and walleye. There are no nearby roads so the only practical ways into here are by air or canoeing and portaging.

Aubichon Lake (Map 88/F4)
Aubichon Lake is found next to Highway 155 about 9.5 km north of the Beatty Lake Recreation Site. Anglers can find resident northern pike here.

Avonlea Reservoir [Watson Reservoir] (Map 18/C4) 🐟
Avonlea Reservoir is a 243 hectare (600 ac) lake created in 1960 when the PFRA constructed a dam on Avonlea Creek. Local residents formed a regional park authority and purchased the land containing a petrified forest of 300 year old ash and maples. The park was named for a local physician, Dr. Dunnet and opened in 1967. It offers camping and a boat launch at the north end of the reservoir near the dam. Anglers can find stocked walleye along with northern pike and yellow perch. Amenities can be found in the park or the town of Avonlea.

Bad Carrot Lake (Map 94/C4)
Bad Carrot Lake lies to the west of the much larger Hanson Lake and can be reached via Beaver Drive, which branches to the southeast off of Highway 106. Bad Carrot Lake is known for its resident northern pike and walleye. Note that the lake is closed to fishing from March 1st to May 31st.

Baldy Lake (Map 82/C3) 🐟
This small lake located in Narrow Hills Provincial Park offers good fishing for northern pike, splake and walleye. The walleye are stocked on occasion. Access is off a secondary road from Highway 106. There are 6 rustic campsites and it is possible to launch small boats at the site.

The lakes and streams noted with the 🐟 symbol have been stocked.

Barker Lake (Map 112/B7)
Barker Lake is found along the Churchill River system. Canoers can paddle west from Devils Lake to reach Barker Lake. With lots of islands and bays to explore, anglers can spend a relaxing day paddling and fishing for the northern pike, walleye, whitefish, sauger and perch in the lake.

Bartlett Lake (Map 101/G2)
Bartlett Lake is found north of Mackay Lake and is accessed by paddling and portaging the Paull Lake to McKay Lake paddling route. Paddlers going through Bartlett can try their luck for northern pike, burbot and lake trout. Those not wanting to do the full route can make a long day trip by accessing the lake via McKay and the 500 metre portage.

Barrier Lake (Map 63/C5–D5) 🐟
Barrier Lake is an open water section of the Barrier River located west of Greenwater Lake Provincial Park. This lake offers fishing for northern pike and stocked walleye. Access is by grid roads; camping and a boat launch can be found northeast of Algrove.

Batka Lake (Map 44/D1)
Located in the southern portion of Duck Mountain Provincial Park, this lake makes a good option for fishing northern pike, walleye and perch. There is camping in the park as well as amenities further north.

Brook Trout Stocking

	MAP	BROOK TROUT	BROWN TROUT	LAKE TROUT	NORTHERN PIKE	RAINBOW TROUT	SPLAKE	TIGER TROUT	WALLEYE	YELLOW PERCH	OTHER
Sandy Creek	28/B6	•									
Scissors Creek	33/C6	•	•						•	•	
Sealey Lake	82/C1	•				•					
Sedge Lake	90/F6	•									
Shuard Creek	13/B5	•									
Snell Lake	79/F2	•					•				
Steep Creek	71/D5	•									
Suffern Lake	56/B3	•									
Swan River - Hwy 8	54/G4	•									
Swan River - Hwy 982	65/C6	•									
White Gull Creek - 106	82/C5	•									
White Gull Creek - Hwy 120	82/B5	•									
Wilson Lake	42/G4	•					•				
Wynyard Reservoir	52/C7	•	•				•				

Baxter and Dugout Lakes (Map 79/F2)
Located just west of Prince Albert National Park, these lakes can be accessed by a branch road off of Highway 922. Baxter is home to some decent size northern pike, while Dugout holds pike and walleye.

Bean Lake (Map 82/B1)
This remote lake in Narrow Hills Provincial Park offers fair fishing for northern pike and walleye. Access can be a challenge as you will need to hike in about 5 km from Little Bear Lake to the north. There is no camping at the lake.

Beaupré Lake (Map 89/D5)
Beaupré Lake, found along Highway 924, offers fishing for northern pike and walleye. The Beaupré Creek Recreation Site is found just off of the highway, on the eastern shore.

Beatty Lake (Map 88/F5) 🐟
This small lake found north of the town of Green Lake along Highway 155 is stocked with splake. A recreation site with boat launch can be found here. This lake is open all year.

Bentley Bay – Churchill River (Map 109/F6)
One of the countless waterbodies along this mighty river, this bay is attached to the sprawling Knee Lake. Those paddlers who bring along a fishing rod will find burbot, lake trout, lake whitefish, northern pike, walleye and yellow perch. The odd lunker is pulled from these waters.

Berna Lake (Map 112/E5) 🐟
This small lake found near McLennan Lake is stocked with rainbow trout. The hidden lake makes a nice alternative to the many pike and walleye lakes in the area. This lake is open all year.

Berven Lake (Map 112/D6)
This many armed lake can be found next to Provincial Road 102, about 21 km north from Lac La Ronge Provincial Park's northern boundary. Berven Lake contains burbot, lake trout and northern pike.

Besnard Lake (Map 100/F4–101/B2)
Besnard Lake is a larger lake located east of Pinehouse Lake. Access and camping is best from the Besnard Lake Recreation Site at the end of Provincial Road 910. Anglers here will find huge expanses of open water, many islands and large bays to explore while searching out burbot, lake trout, perch, pike, walleye and whitefish. Be mindful for big waves when the wind picks up and be wary when navigating this sometimes confusing lake. See the regulations for a closed section.

Big Arm Bay – Last Mountain Lake (Map 39/G6)
Big Arm Bay off Last Mountain Lake is a popular spot for northern pike, walleye, whitefish and yellow perch. There are special open and closed seasons; check the annual angler's regulations. Camping and boat launches can be found around the main part of Last Mountain Lake.

Big Whitemoose Lake (Map 102/F5)
This medium sized lake comprises part of the border with Lac La Ronge Provincial Park. Access is by air or canoeing and portaging from nearby lakes. Those that journey into this lake will find good populations of northern pike and walleye. Little Whitemoose Lake to the north offers a similar fishery.

Big Sandy Lake (Map 92/G6)
Big Sandy Lake lies south of Highway 106 and offers good fishing for northern pike, walleye and whitefish. There is a recreation site on the north shore offering camping and a boat launch, while Big Sandy Lake Outdoor Adventures offers more established camping and lodging, a boat launch, boat rentals and other amenities. Walleye retention is limited at one fish.

Birch Lake (Map 21/F6)
Birch Lake is found in Moose Mountain Provincial Park, which has a wide range of facilities available. The lake is accessed by trail and has no boat launch. While it is subject to periodic winterkill due to its shallow waters, yellow perch are native to its waters. Note the electric motor only restriction.

Bittern Lake (Map 81/A5)
Bittern Lake is found west of Candle Lake and offers some great walleye fishing, as well as fair numbers of northern pike and perch. Access is from a secondary road near the town of Montreal Lake. Many camping options can be found at nearby Candle Lake Provincial Park to the east. Watch for special walleye limits.

Black Lake (Map 120/F4)
This large remote northern lake is accessed primarily by air. Those that make their way up here will find fantastic fishing for arctic grayling, lake trout, northern pike and walleye. Camp Grayling operates an outfitters lodge from the shores of the lake.

Black Bear Island Lake (Map 101/A1–111/D7)
This complex lake is typically accessed by air or canoe. Those that make it into this lake will find good fishing for northern pike, walleye and lake trout. Good shoreline campsites can be found around the lake, but the lake can be confusing to navigate.

Blacker Lake (Map 12/F7)
This lake is accessed from Highway 21, near Cypress Hills Interprovincial Park. It is stocked with brown trout. Camping options can be found in the park.

Blackstrap Reservoir (Map 49/E6)
This reservoir is considered Saskatoon's fishing hot spot with good populations of walleye as well as northern pike, burbot and large perch. On the southeastern shore you will find the Blackstrap Provincial Park, which offers a boat launch and 50 camping sites. Check the regulations for special catch and release restrictions.

Blue Heron Lake [Fish Lake] (Map 70/B2)
Blue Heron Lake also known as Fish Lake on some maps and is found at the community of Blue Heron. A canoe or other small boat will help you get out and find the northern pike, walleye and perch that live in the waters.

Boire Lake (Map 88/C6)
Boire Lake is found next to Minnow Lake, just east of Meadow Lake Provincial Park. The lake is accessible by a branch road off of Highway 903 and contains northern pike and yellow perch.

Boundary Dam Reservoir (Map 9/G7)
The Boundary Dam Reservoir, southeast of Estevan, is the only location in Saskatchewan to find largemouth bass. In addition, there is northern pike, yellow perch and stocked walleye in the reservoir. There is camping and a boat launch available at the Boundary Dam site of Woodlawn Regional Park.

Brabant Lake (Map 118/C7)
Unlike many of the northern lakes, Brabant Lake is accessible by road (Provincial Road 102 north of La Ronge). However, like most of the lakes in the area, anglers will find northern pike, walleye and lake trout here.

Braddock Reservoir (Map 15/C3)
Situated in a very rural area, this waterbody is found south of Provincial Road 721, around 7 km west of the intersection with Highway 363. The reservoir offers fishing for stocked walleye. The nearby Baumann Reservoir offers stocked rainbow trout.

Bradwell Reservoir (Map 49/G5)
Just down the road from the town of Bradwell is the Bradwell Reservoir. Although having a small boat helps you get around, there are steady reports of hooking into the good-sized pike and stocked walleye from shore. Perch and whitefish are also found in the waters. Check the regulations for special catch and release restrictions.

Branch Lake (Map 76/F2)
Found west of the popular Makwa Lake area, this narrow lake offers visitors and locals a nice option for northern pike, walleye and perch. A boat ramp is found at the southeastern shore off Range Road 243.

Brightsand Lake (Map 67/D1–77/D7)
Brightsand Lake is found east of St. Walburg and offers fishing for stocked northern pike. There are also walleye, perch and whitefish in the lake. Brightsand Regional Park can be found on the northern shore off of Municipal Road 795. This park offers camping and cabin rentals, a boat launch, a fish cleaning station and a stocked trout pond.

> *Walleye – also known as pickerel, these fish will readily take spinners, jigs tipped with soft plastics, crankbaits, worms, minnows, leeches, bucktail, earthworms and crayfish. Look for them in the morning or evening, or on cloudy or overcast days, as these fish avoid light.*

Brightwater Reservoir (Map 38/D1)
Just a few kilometres west of Hanley is the Brightwater Reservoir. This shallow reservoir is best known for northern pike. There are reports of lake whitefish, pike and a few walleye in the waters. Check the regulations for special catch and release restrictions.

Broderick Reservoir (Map 38/A3)
Just south of the community of Broderick is its reservoir. Lake whitefish, perch and northern pike being found under the surface. The pike are the main attraction here. Trolling can be great for the pike. Shore fishing off the rocks on the eastern side can produce well with a red and white spoon. Ice fishing can be great at times. Check the regulations for special catch and release restrictions.

Bronson Lake (Map 76/D4)
This lake, just to the west of the Bronson Forest Recreation Site offers a good option for fishing in the area. Anglers here will have a chance to go after northern pike, walleye and yellow perch. Camping, cabin rentals, fuel and other amenities can be found in the recreation site.

Buffalo Pound Lake (Map 28/D3–G5)
Buffalo Pound Lake is a long narrow lake located northeast of Moose Jaw. Buffalo Pound Provincial Park is found on the southern and southwestern shores. The park offers a boat launch, fishing cleaning station and camping. Anglers here will find catfish, carp, perch, pike, sauger, whitefish and stocked walleye fishing. Recently rainbow, brown and brook trout have been stocked into the lake, while the Buffalo Pound Trout Pond is also stocked with rainbow. Note the perch limit on the big lake.

Bug Lake (Map 78/F5)
This small lake lies in the Porcupine Hills off the west side of Highway 945. Home to northern pike, whitefish and yellow perch, the Bug Lake Recreation Site offers day-use with a boat launch.

Bulbick Lake (Map 102/A4)
Found within the popular Lac La Ronge area, this lake is home to northern pike, lake white fish and yellow perch. Access can be found off Provincial Road 915 or by a narrow channel from Lac La Ronge.

Burton Lake (Map 51/B1)
Burton Lake is located directly north of Humboldt along Highway 20 and offers anglers the chance to reel in some stocked walleye.

Bushy Lake (Map 57/D1)
Northeast of Cut Knife, Bushy Lake is found east of Atton Lake and the regional park there. Bushy is stocked with walleye and also offers northern pike and yellow perch.

Caddis Lake (Map 92/A4)
Caddis Lake is found near Highway 912 approximately 10 km south of the junction of Provincial Road 165 and Highway 912. A trail leads to the lake. This small lake gets stocked with a 500 brown and brook trout each year. Despite being stocked, the fishing can be slow at times. Check the regulations for special trout retention and barbless hook requirements.

Camp 10 Lake (Map 80/G1)
Found just north of the junction of Highway 916 and 2, this smaller lake gets stocked heavily each year with rainbow trout. A recreation site is located at the lake making it a popular weekend destination. This lake is open all year.

Candle Lake (Map 81/D5–F6)
This large lake offers plenty of recreation for the entire family. Anglers coming here will find northern pike, walleye, burbot and whitefish. But, fishing can be spotty due to heavy use by boaters. There are plenty of camping options within the Candle Lake Provincial Park, with over 200 sites and several boat launches. Rentals, groceries, fuel and other amenities can be found in the town of Candle Lake, on the southern shore of the lake. Check the regulations for special restrictions.

Canoe Lake (Map 98/C5)
This northern lake found at the intersection of Provincial Road 903 and 965 offers fishing for walleye, pike and lake trout. Camping, lodging and amenities can be found around Cole Bay. Check the regulations for special retention limits and closed area.

Carter [Klein] Lake (Map 68/D3)
This small waterbody is found east of the community of Glaslyn, just north of Highway 3, and contains stocked northern pike and yellow perch.

Cedoux Reservoir (Map 19/F5)
The Cedoux Reservoir is 7 km north of the village of Cedoux. It has some native northern pike in its waters.

Ceylon Reservoir (Map 7/F3)
This small waterbody is only 8 hectares (20 ac) in area. There is a regional park here which has good camping facilities, a boat launch and floats. The lake is not suitable for large boats. Expect to find northern pike and yellow perch here.

Chachukew Lake (Map 104/B5)
Located west of Pelican Narrows, Chachukew Lake sits on a popular canoe route but has no easy road access. Like most northern lakes there are plenty of pike and walleye to look for.

Charron Lake (Map 62/F7)
Charron Lake is found to the east of Naicam and is accessed by a series of grid roads to the south of Highway 349. There is a boat launch on the northern side of the lake. Charron Lake is known to hold northern pike and walleye.

Cheeyas Lake (Map 90/F7)
This long, narrow lake is found to the south of Wayakwin Lake, not far off of Rock Lake Road. Road access to the lake is limited, but it is situated along some popular snowmobile routes, making this a popular ice fishing destination. Anglers can find lake whitefish and northern pike here.

Chitek Lake (Map 78/F6)
This lake, located in the Porcupine Hills area, offers some good fishing options. Anglers here should expect to find northern pike, walleye, perch and whitefish. There is a boat launch and dock as well as camping with both electric and basic sites. The nearby town of Chitek Lake offers many amenities. Access is from Highway 24. The current walleye limit is 3, while the Indian Bay area is closed to angling.

Chris Johnson [Miracle] Lake (Map 54/F5)
Found southwest of Norquay, this small lake contains stocked northern pike as well as stocked yellow perch.

Christopher Lake (Map 70/G1–71/A1)
This lake that is connected with Emma Lake is popular with all boaters. Anglers here will have to compete for space and will find the fishing here to be spotty. But, those that do come here to fish will be trying for northern pike, walleye, lake trout, perch and various trout species. Camping can be found at nearby Emma Lake and amenities can be found around the lake.

Churchill Lake (Map 108/B5–D2)
This northern lake offers those that prefer to drive to their northern fishing lake a great option. Anglers here will find great fishing for northern pike and walleye. Amenities can be found in the town of Buffalo Narrows on Highway 155; this town is located at the channel between Churchill and Peter Pond Lake. Tinker's Camp, on the southern Peter Pond Lake offers lodging and guiding. Watch for special walleye limits.

Brown Trout Stocking	MAP	BROOK TROUT	BROWN TROUT	LAKE TROUT	NORTHERN PIKE	RAINBOW TROUT	SPLAKE	TIGER TROUT	WALLEYE	YELLOW PERCH	OTHER
Amber Lake	116/C3	•	•								
Battle Creek - Battle Creek Rd	12/A7	•	•			•				•	
Battle Creek - Parc Historique National du Fort-Walsh	1/B1	•	•			•				•	
Battle Creek - Reesor Lake	12/B7	•	•			•				•	
Belanger Creek - Cypress Lake	1/F2	•	•			•					
Belanger Creek - Hwy 21	1/F2	•	•			•					
Blacker Lake	12/F7		•								
Bone Creek - Hwy 614	13/D6		•								
Bone Creek - Hwy 633	13/E5		•								
Bone Creek - Swift Current Creek	13/G5		•								
Buffalo Pound Trout Pond	28/F5	•	•			•					
Caddis Lake	92/A4	•	•								
Conglomerate Creek - Frenchman River	2/B2	•	•								
Conglomerate Creek - Hwy 614	2/D1	•	•								
Conglomerate Creek - Hwy 614N	13/C7	•	•								
Coteau Bay	38/A5				•	•	•	•	•	•	•
Diefenbaker Lake	38/C6				•	•	•	•	•	•	•
Fairwell Creek - Frenchman River	2/A2	•	•								
Fairwell Creek - Hwy 706	2/A1	•	•			•					
Hay Meadow Creek - Fife Lake	6/A5	•	•							•	
Jet Lake	79/E2		•								
Junction Lake	91/B3	•	•								
Little Raspberry Lake	87/E6		•					•	•		
Opal Lake	82/B2	•	•								
Picnic Lake	67/E5		•				•	•			
Piprell Lake	82/A2		•				•	•	•		
Shannon Lake	82/C4		•								
Wynyard Reservoir	52/C7	•	•			•					
Zeden Lake	82/C4		•				•	•	•	•	

Clam Lake (Map 101/B4)
This is a medium sized lake that has large spans of open water and many bays and islands to confuse anglers. Access into this remote lake is often by those canoeing through to Besnard Lake from Nemeiban Lake. Once here anglers will find northern pike and walleye.

Clarence Lake (Map 81/G1)
Surrounded by forest, Clarence Lake is found in the southeast corner of Clarence Steepbank Lakes Provincial Park, not far from Highway 927. Clarence Lake Road brushes the northern end of the lake, which contains northern pike and walleye.

Clarke Lakes (Map 89/F6)
Clarke Lakes is a series of three lakes joined by narrow channels. Found along Highway 922, it is possible to launch small boats near the highway. Pike are the main attraction here. Perch can also be found and there is the odd walleye found in the waters.

Clearwater Lake (Map 25/F2)
This spring-fed lake offers fishing for previously stocked brook trout, northern pike and rainbow trout. There are also native yellow perch here. Clearwater Lake Regional Park is located on the shores of the lake. This park offers camping, cabin rentals, a boat launch and supplies.

Codette Lake [Codette Reservoir] (Map 72/D4–73/A4)
Found just south of Nipawin, this reservoir is part of the Saskatchewan River. Boat launches can be found around the lake with Smits Beach and Wapti Regional Park also having filleting tables. Northern Pike and walleye are the main attractions here. Pike are mostly in the eastern part and the walleye can be found throughout. Goldeye, lake whitefish, sauger and yellow perch can also be found.

FISHING ADVENTURES

Cold Lake (Map 86/B4)
Cold Lake is a large lake that borders with Alberta. As it does share its border, either an Albertan or Saskatchewan angling license is required. Anglers will find good fishing for northern pike, walleye, whitefish and perch. Access to the Saskatchewan side of the lake is possible within Meadow Lake Provincial Park and the primitive 4 unit campsite found at the eastern shoreline just off of Highway 919. Check the regulations for special gear restrictions and limits.

Condie Reservoir (Map 29/E5)
Condie Reservoir is a small fishing hole 12 km northwest of Regina. It has a poor boat launch. Anglers pull northern pike, walleye, sauger and yellow perch from its waters. Condie Nature Refuge Recreation Site provides facilities. The current perch limit is 10 and no motors may be used.

Constance Lake (Map 69/E5)
This small lake near Emerald Lake is a good option for those wanting to fish something a bit different than the other nearby lakes. Splake is often stocked here and the fishing can be good at times. Camping can be found at Emerald Lake and full amenities are located nearby. Check the regulations for the no fishing restriction in April and early May.

Cookson Reservoir (Map 6/F7)
This reservoir is occasionally stocked with walleye and can be accessed from Highway 18 east of Coronach. The site is popular for ice fishing since it also holds northern pike, although caution is always advised at the beginning and end of the season.

Cora Lake (Map 82/D1)
Found just north east of Narrow Hills Provincial Park, Cora Lake is a small lake that gets stocked heavily each year with rainbow trout. Also, burbot can be found here. A 500 metre hike from Highway 106 is required to reach the lake and portaging in a small canoe will help you explore the lake. Open all year, shore fishing is also possible.

Corneille Lake [Carter Bay] (Map 94/D1–104/D7)
Corneille Lake is actually a bay off the much larger Mirond Lake, but it is of a fairly large size itself. Highway 135 runs past the lake, providing good access for anglers, who can try their luck for northern pike and walleye.

Coteau Bay – Lake Diefenbaker (Map 38/A5)
Located near the northern tip of Lake Diefenbaker, this bay contains stocked brown trout, rainbow trout and walleye, as well as resident populations of burbot and yellow perch.

Coulee Lake (Map 12/C7)
Coulee Lake is in the West Block of the Cypress Hills Interprovincial Park. Access is available through the park or on the grid road off of Highway 271. This small lake has been stocked with rainbow and brown trout in the past but not in recent years.

Always make sure you are aware of all fishing rules and regulations for your area.

Cowan Lake (Map 79/B2–E5)
This long narrow lake is found west of Prince Albert National Park and offers some good fishing for northern pike, walleye and perch. Big River Regional Park offers camping, a boat launch and dock. Fish are often caught right off the dock. Amenities can be found in the town of Big River, while an alternate camping location and boat launch can be found at the Cowan Dam on northern arm of the lake. Outfitters can also be found around the lake.

Craik Reservoir [Arm Lake] (Map 39/C7)
The Craik Reservoir, also known as Arm Lake, was created when a creek was dammed in the small scenic valley where the Craik Regional Park is located. There is a boat launch and docks to give motorboats access to the lake. This waterbody holds carp, northern pike, walleye and yellow perch. The perch and walleye are currently being stocked.

Crean Lake (Map 80/E3–E4)
One of the bigger lakes in Prince Albert National Park, Crean Lake can be accessed by canoe through Hanging Heart Lake. Anglers can expect lake trout, northern pike, perch, walleye and whitefish in the bigger lake, and pike and walleye in Hanging Heart Lake. Remember that you will need a special angling license and there are special restrictions for fishing within national parks.

Cree Lake (Map 117/B3–D2)
With tons of islands and bays to explore there is no shortage of fishing locations on this large northern lake. Anglers wanting to fish this lake will need to arrive by air. Northern pike, walleye, arctic grayling and lake trout inhabit these waters. Several outfitters are found around the lake.

Crooked Lake (Map 32/B5)
Crooked Lake is on the Qu'Appelle River, which crosses Southern Saskatchewan. Camping and a good boat launch are provided through Crooked Lake Provincial Park. Anglers should expect to find northern pike, walleye and perch.

Crystal Lake (Map 54/D5)
Crystal Lake is a resort community found west of Highway 9. The area has been used for recreation for over 100 years. A boat ramp is found on the western shores and there is a counter clockwise direction of travel for boaters. Walleye are stocked in heavy numbers each year. Northern pike and yellow perch can also be found in the waters.

Cub Lake (Map 82/D1)
Cub Lake is located east of Little Bear Lake and offers fishing for northern pike. Access is by a short trail to its southwestern bay from the secondary road off of Highway 106.

Cumberland Lake (Map 84/G3–85/B4)
Cumberland Lake is a large lake in northern Saskatchewan not for from the border with Manitoba. Anglers here will find good fishing for northern pike, walleye and whitefish. Access to the lake is best at the town of Cumberland House where there are nearby boat launches and a provincial park to provide camping.

Cutarm Creek Reservoir (Map 33/B3)
Found 14 km northeast of Esterhazy off Highway 80, this reservoir offers anglers a chance to find stocked walleye and sauger.

Cypress Lake (Map 1/E2)
Cypress Lake is found southeast of Cypress Hills Provincial Park and is home to northern pike, rainbow trout, walleye and yellow perch. This lake is easily accessed from the Cypress Lake Recreation Site west of Highway 21. The pike, perch and walleye get supplemented with stocking on occasion.

Damour Lake (Map 69/E7)
Found in the farming community of Damour this lake offers anglers the chance to go after northern pike, walleye and perch. Having a small boat will help you get out and explore the two main parts of the lake and the bays.

Davin Lake (Map 118/C5)
Davin Lake, found along Provincial Road 905, offers some great fishing for northern pike, walleye and lake trout. There is a recreation site at this lake as well as the Davin Lake Lodge.

De Balinhard Lake (Map 87/B5)
Known for its northern pike and walleye fishing, De Balinhard Lake is located within Meadow Lake Provincial Park and can be accessed along the Boreal Trail. A campsite is found along the lake's southern shore.

Deep Lake (Map 79/D4)
Located to the west of the larger Delaronde Lake, Deep Lake is accessed by a rough branch road off of Highway 55 and is known for its northern pike fishing.

Deer Lake (Map 76/D1)
Deer Lake is found next to Highway 21, not far from the Alberta border. The Deer Lake Trail accesses the northern end of the small lake, while a boat launch can be found near its eastern end. Northern pike and yellow perch can be found here.

Delaronde Lake (Map 79/D1–E5)
This large, long lake found west of Prince Albert National Park offers some fine fishing. Anglers here should find northern pike, walleye and perch. Camping, a boat launch and dock can be found at Delaronde Lake (Zig Zag Bay) Recreation Site. Other camping options can be found around the lake, as well as outfitters. Amenities can be found in the town of Phillips Beach. Watch for special walleye limits.

Dellwood Reservoir (Map 50/G6)
The Dellwood Reservoir is found southeast of the small community of Plunkett. Northern pike and walleye are found here. Trolling plugs is a good tactic but fishing from the shore is known to be very productive. Check the regulations for special catch and release restrictions.

Deschambault Lake (Map 93/D5–94/A1; 103/F7)
This large, northern lake is easily accessible by car off of Highways 106 or 911. The big lake offers some great fishing for northern pike, walleye and perch. Camping is possible on the South Arm, while Northern Lights Lodge operates on the lake. Check the regulations for special restrictions.

Deserter Lake (Map 68/F4)
This small lake south of Highway 3 offers fishing opportunities for stocked northern pike. Mainly accessed by snowmobile in winter, camping and other fishing opportunities can be found at nearby Meeting Lake.

Devil Lake (Map 102/B1–112/B7)
Devil Lake is another of the smaller lakes found along the Churchill River. Accessible from the Devil Lake Recreation Site found north of Missinippe on Highway 102, the lake holds populations of northern pike and walleye.

Dickens Lake (Map 112/C6)
Found just north of Lac La Ronge Provincial Park, this lake offers some good fishing for northern pike, lake trout, burbot, whitefish and perch. Access to the lake is by a recreation site found just off the highway. A canoe or small boat is best to get out and explore the lake. The recreation site has two campsites.

Dipper Lake (Map 109/C4)
This lake is part of the Churchill River and is usually accessed by canoe. You will find northern pike, walleye and lake trout here.

Doré Lake (Map 89/B1–E3)
Doré Lake is home to great fishing for northern pike and walleye. Outfitters can be found around the shores of the lake, while Doré Lake Recreation Site offers camping. Access is by Highway 924. Check the regulations for special restrictions.

Douglas Lake (Map 95/C3)
You can find Douglas Lake just southwest of Creighton along Highway 167. Anglers can also access the southern reaches of the lake via backroads. This is a non-motorized lake.

Dreger Lake (Map 109/G7–110/A6)
This relatively narrow lake makes up one of the many lakes along the Churchill River. Those that make it into this lake tend to do so via air or canoe. And those that do make the trip here will find northern pike and walleye.

Drinking Lake (Map 102/F3)
Drinking Lake, found along the Churchill River is primarily accessed either by air or canoe. Those that journey to this lake will find camping along the shore and good fishing for northern pike and walleye.

Drope Lake (Map 102/D3)
Drope Lake is a medium sized lake located east of the town of Stanley along the Churchill River. It is commonly accessed by those canoeing along the river. Those that do make it to this lake will find walleye, lake trout and northern pike.

Dupueis Lake (Map 92/D7)
This smaller lake located east of Little Bear Lake offers fair fishing for northern pike and perch. Access is by a short trail off of Highway 106. There is no camping at this lake.

Durocher Lake (Map 98/F7)
This long, sectioned lake contains many bays and narrow sections and stretches parallel to Highway 155 south of the community of Beauval. Northern pike are known to swim the lake's waters.

Eagle Lake (Map 62/C4)
This out-of-the-way lake can be found northwest of the community of Pleasantdale and is accessible by a branch road off of Highway 6. Anglers will find stocked walleye here, as well as resident yellow perch.

Eastend Reservoir (Map 2/D2)
This reservoir covers about 112 hectares (277 ac) and is easily accessed from the town of Eastend. The reservoir is home to northern pike, yellow perch and stocked walleye. In addition to a decent open water fishery, the reservoir is also a popular ice fishing destination during winter months.

East Trout Lake (Map 91/F7–G7)
East Trout Lake is located east of Montreal Lake. Anglers here will find good fishing for lake trout, northern pike, walleye and whitefish. Camping, a boat launch and dock are found on the southeastern shore at the East Trout-Nipekamew Lakes Recreational Site, while outfitters can also be found on this lake. Check the regulations for special retention limits.

Echo Lake (Map 30/F3)
Echo Lake is popular for its beaches and its fishing, although water levels fluctuate through the year and from year to year. The total area of the lake is about 1,044 hectares (2,580 ac). Access and camping are available through the Echo Valley Provincial Park, while supplies are also available at the B-Say-Tah store along the south side of Echo Lake, about 3 km from the park. Echo is popular for its walleye, burbot, northern pike, whitefish and perch.

Elaine Lake (Map 90/C6)
Found just off of Highway 916, this lake offers fishing for northern pike, walleye, whitefish and perch. Elaine Lake Recreation Site is found on the southern shore.

Elbow Lake (Map 65/G5)
This lake makes one of several lakes that make up the Woody River Recreation Site in the Porcupine Hills area. Anglers here will find stocked walleye, as well as naturally reproducing northern pike and perch. The lake is almost 20 metres (65 ft) deep in one spot, while the pothole lake across the highway known as Stark Lake also holds fish. There is no camping here, but nearby Townsend Lake has camping.

> *When first scouting a lake, try to locate the shoals or humps in the bottom of the lake that attract insects and baitfish.*

Eldredge Lake (Map 64/G6)
Located west of McBride Lake on Highway 983, anglers will find pike, perch and walleye here. There are no campsites or services at this lake.

Emerald Lake (Map 69/E5)
This small lake is found southeast of the town of Shell Lake and offers a good fishing option. Anglers here will find northern pike and stocked walleye. Emerald Lake Regional Park offers camping and has a boat launch, fish cleaning station and boat/canoe rentals.

Emma Lake (Map 70/F1–G1)
Emma Lake is a heavy use outdoor recreation lake that offers fair fishing for anglers. Those that come here to fish will find northern pike, walleye, lake trout, perch and various trout species. As this lake is so popular with boaters, the fishing here is spotty and you will need to be prepared to go where the other boaters are not. Camping can be found at Emma Lake (Murray Point) Recreation Site, while other amenities can be found around the lake.

Fafard Lake (Map 118/D6)
This remote lake is located along a popular canoe route, with Reindeer Lake to the west and Royal Lake to the south. Provincial Road 102 accesses the put-in and campsite on Reindeer Lake. Fafard Lake offers excellent fishing for several species of fish, including burbot, northern pike, sauger, walleye and yellow perch.

Fairview Reservoir (Map 36/B6)
This reservoir is located in a rural farming area close to the hamlets of Plato and Wartime. The reservoir is accessed via grid roads that connect with Highway 342 to the west and Highway 44 to the north.

Fairy Glen Lake (Map 82/B3)
This small and narrow lake in Narrow Hills Provincial Park offers good fishing for northern pike and walleye. Access is by Highway 912; there is no camping or boat launch.

Fern and Atchison Lakes (Map 88/C2)
These small lakes are found northeast of Meadow Lake Provincial Park and offer fishing for stocked trout. Fern Lake is stocked with rainbow and splake. Atchinson is stocked with rainbow and brook trout. Both lakes are open all year, but have special limits on the trout. Access is found on secondary roads found to the east of Highway 903.

Fife Lake (Map 6/B5)
Rockin Beach on Fife Lake has a long history as a popular local recreational destination. Fife Lake can be easily accessed through Rockin Beach Regional Park, just north of Highway 18. While the lake did refill again, fluctuating water levels have caused winterkill in the past, but the lake has recovered by being restocked with pike and perch.

Rainbow Trout Stocking

	MAP	BROOK TROUT	BROWN TROUT	LAKE TROUT	NORTHERN PIKE	RAINBOW TROUT	SPLAKE	TIGER TROUT	WALLEYE	YELLOW PERCH	OTHER
Atchison Lake	88/C2	•				•	•				
Battle Creek - Battle Creek Rd	12/A7	•	•			•			•		
Battle Creek - Parc Historique National Du Fort-Walsh	1/B1	•	•			•			•		
Battle Creek - Reesor Lake	12/B7	•	•			•			•		
Baumann Reservoir	15/C3					•					
Belanger Creek - Cypress Lake	1/F2	•	•			•					
Belanger Creek - Hwy 21	1/F2	•	•			•					
Bell Pond	46/A2					•					
Berna Lake	112/F5					•					
Biggar Pond	47/F3					•					
Bill's Lake	65/B6					•					
Buffalo Pound Trout Pond	28/F5	•	•			•					
Camp 10 Lake	80/G1					•					
Cora Lake	82/D1					•					
Coteau Bay	38/A5			•	•	•			•	•	•
Cutknife Pond	57/B2					•					
David Laird Pond	58/B3					•					
Deer Lake	79/B6					•	•	•			
Denzil Pond	45/F1					•					
Diefenbaker Lake	38/C6			•	•	•			•	•	•
Doghide River Trail (Tisdale Park) Trout Pond	63/A2					•					
Dog Lake	90/F6					•					
Dorothy Lake	82/C1	•				•					
Downton Lake	101/E6					•					
Dr. Mainprize Pond	9/B4					•					
Eagle Creek - Eagle Creek Regional Park	48/D2				•	•			•		•
Ed's Lake	116/C2	•				•					
Etomami River - Bertwell	64/F4					•					
Etomami River - Etomami Lake	54/B1					•					
Etomami River - Hwy 983	64/F6					•					
Etomami River - Hwy 9N	65/A4					•					
Etomami River - Red Deer River	65/A2					•					
Etomami River - Reserve - Thomson Ave	64/F5					•					
Etomami River - Shand Creek	64/E4					•					
Exner Lake	77/B3					•		•			
Feldspar Lake	112/D5					•					
Fern Lake	88/C2	•				•	•				
Five Mile Dam	14/A3					•					
Fontaine Lake	116/D3					•		•			
Hudson Bay Borrow Pit	65/A2					•					
Jade Lake	82/B2					•	•				
Kerrobert Reservoir	46/C4					•					
Kipling Reservoir	21/C3					•					
Kit Lake	81/G1					•					
Lady Lake	54/B4	•				•		•			
Lake Lenore Reservoir	61/G7					•					
Leader Trout Pond	23/F1					•					
Lisieux Pond	6/A5					•					
Little Jade Lake	82/B2					•					
Lloydminster Trout Pond	66/C4					•					

Fifth Lake (Map 87/F5)

This is a small lake located in Meadow Lake Provincial Park. There is no easy road access to the lake but those who make the trek can enjoy fishing for northern pike and walleye.

Fishing Lake [Big Fishing Lake] (Map 53/B6)

Fishing Lake is a popular recreation lake with several parks found around its shores. Anglers will find northern pike and perch along with stocked walleye in the waters. A boat ramp is found at Leslie Beach and a boat is a definite asset here. Check the regulations for special catch and release restrictions.

Five Fingers Lake (Map 102/A3)

Five Fingers Lake is found just west of Lac La Ronge Provincial Park. Accessible by a short hike, this lake offers anglers a chance to go after northern pike, walleye, whitefish and perch. Getting a canoe into here would help to explore the lake and find the fish.

Flotten Lake (Map 87/G4–88/A4)

Flotten Lake is a medium sized lake within Meadow Lake Provincial Park. This lake offer great fishing for northern pike as well as good fishing for walleye and other smaller game fish. Camping and a boat launch can be found on the eastern shore off of Highway 904. The current walleye limit is 3.

Fowler and Hoffman Lakes (Map 76/G3)

Off Provincial Road 699, these lakes rest just northeast of the Bronson Forest Recreation Site. There is a small undeveloped recreation site on Fowler and fishing for northern pike and walleye on both lakes. There are plenty of camping options, along with cabin rentals, fuel and other amenities in the area.

French Lake (Map 102/C1)

French Lake is located along the Otter Lake Circuit canoe route, connecting with Otter Lake to the west and the Stewart River to the north. There are several backcountry campsites found on the lake and anglers can find northern pike and walleye in these waters.

Frobisher Lake (Map 116/E6)

This large lake is located close to the community of Turnor Lake, from where an access road reaches the lake. There are many islands on this lake, providing plenty of cover for northern pike, walleye and yellow perch that live here.

Fur Lakes (Map 69/F4)

Fur Lakes are a series of lakes joined by narrow channels. These lakes are found a short distance away from the community of Shell Lake. A recreation site is found here and makes a great base to base day trips to the lakes. It is possible to launch small boats to make it easier to find the northern pike, walleye and whitefish that live here.

Galletly Lake (Map 76/E4)

This lake is found within the Bronson Forest Recreation Site, accessed via Highway 21 north of Lloydminster. There is no direct road access to the lake itself, but an ATV trail does reach the lake's southern shore, allowing access to the lake whitefish, northern pike, walleye and yellow perch that inhabit the lake.

Gaudry Lake (Map 88/C6)

Situated north of the city of Meadow Lake, Gaudry Lake is found to the east of Highway 903. Anglers can cast in this small lake for northern pike, walleye and yellow perch.

Good Spirit Lake (Map 43/B2)

This is a prime recreation lake that supports good populations of northern pike, walleye and yellow perch. Good Spirit Lake Provincial Park can be found on the western and southern shores. The park provides a good boat launch and has 3 campgrounds with 214 sites.

Gouverneur Reservoir (Map 15/A6)

This large reservoir has a rustic boat launch found about 6 km northeast of Cadillac. The water has native northern pike, yellow perch and stocked walleye.

Granite Lake (Map 94/F1)

This medium sized lake in northern Saskatchewan offers the feeling of fishing a remote lake, but is still accessible by road. Granite Lake Recreation Site is located along the southern bay's shoreline and is reached by a secondary road north of Highway 106. Paddlers on canoe trips within the region also visit the lake on their way to other nearby lakes. Regardless of the mode of transportation into this lake, anglers will find good fishing for lake trout, northern pike and walleye.

Green Lake (Map 78/F1–G3)
Found at the small community of Green Lake, this long narrow lake offers some great fishing. Northern Pike and walleye are the main gamefish here. Burbot and yellow perch are also found. A lodge is located here offering cabins and camping sites. A boat is needed to fully explore this lake.

Greenwater Lake (Map 63/F5)
The signature lake within the boundaries of Greenwater Provincial Park, this lake offers good fishing for stocked walleye as well as northern pike. The park has a boat launch and 4 campgrounds with 186 sites along with rentals for power boats, canoes and cabins.

Greig Lake (Map 87/F5)
Greig Lake is a medium sized lake located within Meadow Lake Provincial Park. This lake offers good fishing for northern pike and walleyes that can get up to 3 kg (6 lbs) as well as other smaller game fish. There is plenty of camping here with space for nearly 150 units plus group camping; as well as many amenities including showers, laundry and ice to name a few. The campsite as well as the boat ramp is located on the eastern shore of the lake from the access road off of Highway 224. The current walleye limit is 3.

Grenfell Reservoir (Map 31/G7)
The tiny Grenfell Reservoir is 5 km southwest of the town of Grenfell. It has native walleye and yellow perch.

Gromnicki Lake (Map 100/F2)
This remote lake is found along an access road to the north of Besnard Lake Recreation Site. The lake contains lake whitefish, northern pike, walleye and yellow perch.

Gow Lake (Map 118/A6)
This remote lake created by a meteor impact in northern Saskatchewan offers some great fishing for lake trout, northern pike and walleye. Anglers wanting to fish this lake will need to fly-in and stay at the Northern Reflections Lodge. Check the regulations for special catch and release restrictions.

Gull Lake (Map 101/A3)
This small lake between Besnard Lake and Morning Lake is typically visited by those on canoe trips in the region. Those that do make it here will find northern pike and walleye.

Hackett Lake (Map 79/F3)
Found along Highway 922 this lake offers anglers a nice easy access option. Northern pike and walleye fishing here can be great at times. Also, burbot and yellow perch can be found here. Try fishing the southeastern section in and around the island. A recreation site with a campground and boat launch is found in the northeastern corner of the lake. Watch for special walleye limits.

Halkett Lake [Sandy Lake] (Map 70/E1–80/E7)
This lake is located within Prince Albert National Park, so special angling regulations and licenses are applicable. Highway 263 provides easy access to this fair sized lake, which offers lake trout, northern pike and walleye. There is a campsite and boat launch on the lake.

Hanging Heart Lake (Map 80/D4)
Home to a popular canoe route in Prince Albert National Park, Hanging Heart Lake offers trippers a chance to test their luck for northern pike and walleye. Remember that you will need a special angling license and there are special restrictions for fishing within national parks.

Hanson Lake (Map 94/C3)
Hanson Lake offers many bays and islands to explore for northern pike and walleye. Accessed off a secondary road from Highway 106, the Hanson Lake Recreation Site is located on the southwestern shore offering a campsite and boat launch. See the regulations for special restrictions.

Harris Reservoir (Map 12/F5)
The Harris Reservoir, 10 km south of Maple Creek, is fairly small at 171 hectares (423 ac). Access is only by trail. Anglers pull northern pike and yellow perch from the reservoir. The pike are supplemented with a stocking program.

Hasbala Lake (Map 121/F2)
Hasbala Lake is at the extreme northeast corner of the province where the borders of Saskatchewan, Manitoba, Nunavut and Northwest Territories meet up. Anglers that come to this lake (via air) will find great fishing for northern pike, lake trout and arctic grayling. Hasbala Lake Lodge provides accommodations. Check the regulations for special catch and release restrictions.

Rainbow Trout Stocking	MAP	Brook Trout	Brown Trout	Lake Trout	Northern Pike	Rainbow Trout	Splake	Tiger Trout	Walleye	Yellow Perch	Other
Loch Leven	12/E7	•				•					•
Luseland Trout Pond	46/B3					•					
Mackie Lake	82/D4					•	•				
Macklin Borrow Pit	45/D1					•					
Macklin Regional Park Pond	56/A6					•					
Maidstone Pond	66/G6					•					
McLaren Lake	23/C7				•	•			•		
McRobbie Lake	95/D4				•	•					
Melfort Memorial Pond	62/C2					•					
Mid Lake	94/E2					•					
Moise Lake	104/C6					•					
Moose Mountain Trout Pond	21/E6	•				•					
Musker Pond	81/D6					•					
Negan Lake	104/C6	•				•					
Nesland Lake	69/F4					•		•			
Nisbet Pond	70/G5					•					
Nistum Lake	95/B6					•					
Olson Lake 2	69/B2					•					
Pear Lake	80/G6	•				•					
Picnic Lake	67/E5			•		•		•	•		
Pine Lake	82/C4					•	•				
Piprell Lake	82/A2			•		•	•	•			
Poplar Ridge Lake	78/G4	•									
Redberry Pond	59/C3					•					
Reserve Reservoir	64/F6					•					
Road Lake	92/E7					•					
Sandy Lake	21/D6					•					
Sandy Lake	98/F6					•					
Saskatoon Trout Pond	49/D2					•					
Scott Reservoir	57/D6					•					
Sealey Lake	82/C1	•									
Shirley Lake	89/C5					•					
Singh Lake	91/G7					•					
Steep Creek	71/D5	•									
Steiestol Lake	63/F5					•					
Suffern Lake	56/B3	•				•			•		
Swift Current Creek - Hwy 738	26/A4					•	•		•	•	•
Swift Current Creek - Reid Lake Reservoir	14/D3					•	•		•	•	•
Swift Current Pond	14/E1					•					
Ted's Lake	79/F1					•					
Terra Lake	79/F2					•					
Vivian Lake	87/D6					•					
Waldheim Pond	60/A4					•					
Weekes Reservoir	64/D5					•					
White Bear Reservoir	25/C1					•					
Wilson Lake	42/G4	•				•					
Wynyard Reservoir	52/C7	•	•			•					
Yonker Lake	56/C3					•					
Yorkton SWF Trout Pond	43/D5					•					
Zeden Lake	82/C4				•	•	•	•	•		

FISHING ADVENTURES

Hatchet Lake (Map 121/C6)
This fly-in lake is home to the Hatchet Lake Lodge. Anglers that make their way up here will find great fishing for northern pike, lake trout, walleye and arctic grayling. Check the regulations for special catch and release restrictions.

Hayes Lake (Map 81/G1)
Hayes Lake is found next to Clarence Lake on the southeast boundary of Clarence-Steepbank Lakes Provincial Park and is easily accessed from Highway 927. Anglers can find northern pike and yellow perch here.

Hayman Lake (Map 112/B7)
Hayman Lake is one of many lakes found along the Churchill River. This small lake holds populations of northern pike and walleye. Access is mainly by canoe since it is possible to paddle upstream from nearby Devil Lake.

Head Lake (Map 101/C4)
Head Lake is a relatively small lake located west of Nemeiben Lake that is often accessed by those canoeing and portaging through to lakes further west. Those that do make it into this remote lake will find northern pike and walleye. Check the regulations for special catch and release restrictions.

Heart Lake (Map 92/D7)
Reached by trail, anglers can get to Heart Lake from Little Bear Lake or a 2.5 km trail from Highway 106. The reward is good fishing for northern pike and whitefish.

Hebden Lake (Map 102/B3)
Another small lake located within in Lac La Ronge Provincial Park that is often visited by those canoeing the lakes and rivers of the area. Access is also possible via an access road off of Provincial Road 102. Anglers that find their way here will find northern pike and walleye.

Helene Lake (Map 68/B1)
Helene Lake is found north east of the community of Glaslyn at the end of Township Road 530 where a boat ramp can be found. Walleye have been stocked in the past but the lake is known to suffer from winterkill.

Herbert Reservoir (Map 26/E6)
This small reservoir west of the town of Herbert has northern pike, walleye, sauger and yellow perch. Camping can be found nearby. The walleye here are supplemented with stocking.

Heritage Lake (Map 81/F5)
This small lake is found northeast of Candle Lake and is a good option for northern pike and walleye fishing. A recreation site with camping and a boat launch can be found at the lake.

> *Life jackets and personal flotation devices are known to save lives; they only work when they are worn and fitted correctly.*

Highfield Reservoir (Map 15/C1)
This reservoir east of Swift Current offers fishing for northern pike. Access is best on grid roads from Highway 363 from the south or via the Trans-Canada Highway and grid roads from the north.

Hirtz Lake (Map 86/D5)
Hirtz Lake is a relatively small road-access lake located within Meadow Lake Provincial Park. Access to this lake is via a secondary road off of Highway 919, west of the Sandy Beach Campsite. Anglers will find a small rustic campsite here, where it is possible to launch cartop boats and search out northern pike, whitefish and stocked walleye. Watch for special restrictions on walleye.

Humboldt Lake (Map 51/B3)
Just south of the town of Humboldt is Humboldt Lake. Walleye get stocked into the lake and there are reports of a few northern pike and perch here as well.

Humphrey Lake (Map 86/E5)
Accessed by the Boreal Trail, Humphrey Lake is found just south of Pierce Lake within Meadow Lake Provincial Park. The smaller lake contains several islands and bays which provide good cover for the northern pike and walleye that live in it.

Hunt Lake (Map 102/C3)
Visitors to this lake usually reach it by canoe and portage from either Stroud or Mountain Lake. Those that do visit this lake will find northern pike and walleye.

Ingebright Lake (Map 23/G6–24/A6)
Ingebright Lake is found 10 km southeast of Fox Valley to the west of Highway 21 off the Saskatchewan Minerals Road. Anglers pull walleye, sauger and yellow perch from here.

Iroquois Lake (Map 69/D5)
This lake south of the town of Shell Lake offers fishing for northern pike, but its best known as a good walleye lake. Whitefish are also present but their limit is set at 4. Camping and amenities can be found at the two towns on the lake's shore, Pelican Cove and Pebble Baye.

Isbister Lake (Map 65/F5)
Isbister Lake, found along Highway 980, makes up part of the Woody River Recreation Site in the Porcupine Hills area. This lake has some good pike fishing. There are also some walleye and yellow perch here. The lake offers a small, quiet campsite with boat launch, dock, picnic tables, bathrooms and a fish cleaning table.

Iskwatikan Lake (Map 102/E4)
This lake has lake trout, northern pike, walleye and whitefish. Access to this lake is either by air or by canoe and portage from nearby lakes; this lake is often visited by those on canoe trips heading towards or away from the Churchill River. Iskwatikan Lake Lodge is located on Hickson Island and offers lodging and guiding. Check the regulations for special catch and release restrictions.

Island Lake (Map 78/F4)
Island Lake is found to the north of the intersection of Highways 945 and 943, southeast of the town of Meadow Lake. There is a recreation site on the lake's south end, and anglers can enjoy casting for northern pike and yellow perch here.

Ispuchaw Lake (Map 82/C4)
Ispuchaw Lake, in Narrow Hills Provincial Park, offers good fishing for northern pike and walleye. Access is by a short secondary road from Highway 106. There is a small, rustic 5 unit campsite with a boat launch located here.

Jackfish Lake (Map 55/D7)
Jackfish Lake is a small lake near Madge Lake in Duck Mountain Provincial Park. This lake was previously stocked with various species of trout but reports now say that the trout are all but gone; fishing here now is primarily for perch. There is no shortage of camping nearby with 7 campgrounds and 466 separate sites.

Jackfish Lake (Map 67/G6–68/A6)
This large lake is found along Highway 4 and offers some good recreational fishing opportunities. Home to northern pike, walleye, perch and whitefish, a commercial fishery for whitefish takes place here each winter. Camping can be found at the Battlefords Provincial Park where there are 3 campgrounds with over 300 campsites. Boat rentals and fishing supplies are available within the park.

Jade Lakes (Map 82/B2)
Jade Lakes are two small lakes found amongst a series of other small lakes just north of Highway 913, in the northwest corner of Narrow Hills Provincial Park. Jade Lake is accessible by a short walk from the road, where Little Jade Lake is accessible by paddling through a narrow channel. Anglers here can expect to find stocked rainbow, splake and tiger trout. Open all year, there is an electric motor only restriction.

Jan Lake (Map 94/B2–104/B7)
This large northern lake is accessible by car from Highway 135. Anglers coming here will find northern pike and walleye along with rustic camping at the Jan Lake Recreation Site. There is also a lodge found north of the recreation site that offers a few more amenities and creature comforts. Check the regulations for a closed section.

Jarvis Lake (Map 88/B6)
Sandwiched between Waterhen lake and Highway 903, Jarvis Lake offers good fishing for lake whitefish, northern pike and yellow perch. To the east of the highway, Gaudry, Boire and Minnow are nearby lakes offering a similar fishery.

Jasper Lake (Map 81/G1)
This small lake is found between Clarence Lake and Steepbank Lake in Clarence-Steepbank Lakes Provincial Park and can be accessed via Clarence Lake Road. Northern pike are the main sportfish here.

Jay-Jay Lake (Map 92/F5)
Jay-Jay Lake is found along Provincial Road 165, northeast of the larger Big Sandy Lake. A recreation site can be found on the lake, which offers northern pike and yellow perch for anglers.

Jeannette Lake (Map 87/G4) 🛶
Like many of the lakes within Meadow Lake Provincial Park, Jeannette offers some good fishing for northern pike and stocked walleye. A boat ramp can be found at the southern end at the end of a secondary road off of Highway 904. The current walleye limit is 3.

Johnston Lake (Map 86/G5) 🛶
Found just north of the much larger Lac des Illes in Meadow Lake Provincial Park, this small lake contains stocked walleye and resident northern pike, and is easily accessible from Highway 950.

> *Take along extra clothing in a waterproof bag in case you get wet.*

Jumbo Lake (Map 77/A3)
Jumbo Lake is found in Makwa Provincial Park and offers northern pike, walleye, yellow perch and whitefish. Other nearby options include Little Goose and Tullibee Lakes, both offering pike, perch and walleye. There are 3 campgrounds, with a total of 305 sites, located around the various lakes in the provincial park. Each campground has a boat launch.

Jumping Lake (Map 61/D2) 🛶
Found northwest of the small community of Crystal Springs, Jumping Lake is easily accessible via the Waitville Grid Road and offers anglers stocked walleye.

Junction Reservoir (Map 12/E4) 🛶
Junction Reservoir is located 6 km north of Maple Creek with grid road access. The water holds stocked walleye and yellow perch. Camping and amenities can be found in and around the town of Maple Creek to the south.

Kakinagimak Lake (Map 104/G5)
Kakinagimak Lake is a long but relatively narrow lake located in northern Saskatchewan not too far from the Manitoba border. Getting into this lake to fish the numerous northern pike and walleye and more elusive lake trout can pose a challenge. Nearly all visitors to this lake will do so by air or while on canoe trips.

Katepwa Lake (Map 30/G3–31/A4)
Katepwa Lake is found in the Qu'Appelle Valley and offers fishing for walleye, burbot, northern pike and rockfish. The resort villages of Katepwa Beach and Sandy Beach are found on the north shores of Lake Katepwa, while a boat launch can be found at Katepwa Point Provincial Park.

Kazan Lake (Map 98/B1)
This is a large, remote lake that is located to the northwest of the village of Île-à-la-Crosse. The limited access offers those who manage to reach it excellent fishing for burbot, northern pike, walleye and yellow perch.

Keeley lake (Map 88/C1)
This keyhole-shaped lake is found west of Highway 903, off the Keeley Lake Access Road. Anglers can enjoy fishing for burbot, northern pike, walleye (limit of three) and yellow perch.

Keg Lake (Map 69/E1)
Located west of Highway 55, a series of branch roads access this long, narrow lake that contains numerous bays, narrow sections and islands. Visitors can find good fishing for northern pike.

Keg Lake (Map 102/G3–103/B3)
Keg Lake is a relatively small lake along the Churchill River. This remote lake is best accessed by air or canoe and portages. Once here you will find camping spots along the shore and fishing for northern pike and walleye.

Kenosee Lake (Map 21/F6) 🛶
Kenosee Lake is in the beautiful Moose Mountain Provincial Park, which is highland area forest, unlike the plains that surround it. The park provides great camping and a good boat launch. You can expect to pull northern pike, yellow perch and stocked walleye.

Keskuchow Lake (Map 88/B6)
Keskuchow Lake is found just to the east of Highway 903, about 27 km north of Meadow Lake. Northern pike can be found in this lake.

Kimball Lake (Map 87/E6) 🛶
Kimball Lake is another of the many good choices of lakes to fish within Meadow Lake Provincial Park. This lake offers fair fishing for northern pike and smaller stocked walleye. Access can be found along Highway 224 off of a short secondary road. There is a 200+ unit campsite with amenities including showers and groceries as well as a boat launch found here. Watch for special walleye limits.

Kingsmere Lake (Map 80/C3)
Found in the heart of Prince Albert National Park, anglers and paddlers will find good fishing for lake trout, northern pike, perch, walleye and whitefish. Remember that you will need a special angling license and there are special restrictions for fishing within national parks. The numerous smaller lakes in the area also hold pike and walleye.

Kipabiskau Lake (Map 62/F5–63/G5) 🛶
This long narrow lake east of Pleasantdale offers plenty of recreation for the entire family. Anglers will find stocked walleye as well as northern pike and perch. Camping can be found at the regional park near the town of Kipabiskau.

Kinosaskaw Lake (Map 110/F7–111/A6)
This medium sized lake is part of the Churchill River just east of Sandfly Lake and is typically accessed by air or by those canoeing the river system. Those that make it here will find northern pike and walleye.

Knee Lake (Map 109/E6–110/A5)
This large lake is one of the many lakes found along the Churchill River. Knee Lake, along with Bentley Bay, is home to burbot, lake trout, lake whitefish, northern pike, walleye and yellow perch. Visitors to this lake tend to come in via air or while on canoe trips on the river system. Watch for wind and waves on the open stretches of this lake.

Konuto Lake (Map 95/B4)
Konuto Lake borders the Amiskosakahikan Indian Reserve No. 210 and can be accessed by branch roads off of Highway 167 and Maraiche Road. This is one of the rare lakes in Saskatchewan that offers fishing for smallmouth bass.

Kornitski Lake (Map 42/F2) 🛶
This small lake is accessed by taking a grid road directly east from Insinger and features stocked yellow perch.

Lac des Iles (Map 86/F5–87/A5)
This large lake located within Meadow Lake Provincial Park offers good fishing for northern pike, walleye, perch and whitefish. Camping, lodging and a boat ramp can be found at the western end of Highway 954 on the southern shore of the lake. Camping and a boat ramp are also available on the northern shore just off of Highway 950 at the Murray Doell Campsite. Watch for special walleye limits.

Lac Eauclair (Map 78/F5)
This lake, located to the northeast of Chitek Lake, is a good fishing option in the Porcupine Hills. Lac Eauclair was previously stocked with lake trout but has not seen any recent stockings. Also, whitefish can be found here. Access is by a secondary road from Highway 945 and there is basic camping, a boat launch and boat dock located here. Check the regulations for special retention limits on lake trout.

Lac Huard (Map 78/G6)
Located within the Porcupine Hills to the east of Highway 945, anglers can try their luck for northern pike and perch. There is a natural boat launch and dock at the north end, while camping options can be found at nearby Chitek Lake and Shell Lake. Amenities can be found in the town of Chitek Lake.

Lac Ile-a-la-Crosse (Map 98/F5–109/A6)
This large lake is part of the Churchill River, with numerous access points from Highway 155 and surrounding roads. This lake is often visited by those on canoe trips as they paddle through the area; there are numerous sandy beaches with good natural campsites along the lake shore. Canoeists and all boaters should be careful of waves when the wind picks up. Those fishing will find good populations of northern pike, walleye and lake trout. Watch for special walleye limits.

Lac la Loche (Map 116/C5)
This northern lake at the end of Highway 155 is home to some great northern pike and walleye fishing. There are also a few yellow perch here. Amenities can be found in the town of La Loche.

Splake Stocking

	MAP	BROOK TROUT	BROWN TROUT	LAKE TROUT	NORTHERN PIKE	RAINBOW TROUT	SPLAKE	TIGER TROUT	WALLEYE	YELLOW PERCH	OTHER
Beatty Creek	88/E5						•				
Beatty Lake	88/E5						•				
Burtlein Lake	82/C1						•	•			
Coal Pit-SPC-C	9/F6	•					•	•			
Constance Lake	69/E5					•	•			•	
Deer Lake	79/B6					•	•	•			
Diamond Lake	82/B2	•					•				
Fern Lake	88/C2					•	•				
Fontaine Lake	116/D4					•	•				
Jade Lake	82/B2					•	•	•			
Little Raspberry Lake	87/E6		•			•	•				
Mackie Lake	82/D4					•	•				
Mullock Lake	102/A2					•	•				
Pine Lake	82/C4					•	•				
Piprell Lake	82/A2		•			•	•	•			
Ranger Lake	81/F4						•				
Round Lake	76/F4	•		•			•				
Sapphire Lake	82/B2						•				
Snell Lake	79/F2	•					•				

Lac la Peche (Map 59/D1)
Lac la Peche can be found north of 786 Road, west of its intersection with Highway 12 to the northwest of Blaine Lake. The popular fishing lake offers good fishing for stocked walleye.

Lac La Ronge (Map 91/F1–102/D5)
Lac La Ronge is a large lake within the borders of Lac La Ronge Provincial Park that contains good populations of northern pike, walleye and lake trout. There is good access to the lake from Highways 2 and 912. The town on La Ronge, located along Highway 2, offers all amenities and there are plenty of camping options nearby. Watch for wind and waves, especially in small boats, as the wind can really pick up on this lake.

Lac Pelletier (Map 14/F4)
Lac Pelletier is easily accessed through Lac Pelletier Regional Park south of Highway 343. This busy park offers excellent facilities, including a good boat launch. The lake itself is 6 km (4 mi) long and home to northern pike, walleye, burbot, whitefish and yellow perch. The walleye are supplemented with a stocking program.

Lady Lake (Map 54/B4)
This small lake near the town of Lady Lake is often stocked with brook, rainbow and tiger trout. Open year-round, trout up to 5.5 kg (12 lbs) have been caught here. Lady Lake Regional Park offers camping and a boat launch.

Lake Athabasca (Map 119/A5–120/D4)
This massive northern lake also flows into Alberta. Flying in is the only real option to get to this lake, but those that do make their way there will find fishing for trophy lake trout and northern pike. Goldeye, lake whitefish and walleye are also present, while the rivers that flow in and out of the big lake hold arctic grayling.

Lake Diefenbaker (Maps 24, 25, 26, 27, 38)
Lake Diefenbaker is considered a world-class fishery. However, the lake is part of the South Saskatchewan River system and the normal range of water fluctuation is 7.5 metres (25 ft). The lake supports healthy populations of a variety of fish including: brown trout, burbot, goldeye, lake trout, northern pike, rainbow trout, sturgeon, walleye and whitefish. Currently, the brown trout, rainbow and walleye populations are being supplemented by stocking. There is no shortage of camping and amenities along the shores here. Check the regulations for closed sections.

Lake of the Prairies (Map 44/C4–F7)
Also known as the Shellmouth Reservoir due to the dam at its south end, Lake of the Prairies runs 48 km into Manitoba. Since most of the reservoir is found in that province, the lake is managed under Manitoba's fishing regulations. The lake is considered one of the better northern pike fisheries in the area and also produces lots of walleye and some large perch. Other species to look for include burbot, carp, goldeye, rainbow trout, smallmouth and largemouth bass, rockfish and sauger. Check the regulations for special restrictions.

Larsen Lake (Map 69/B4)
Larsen lake is located to the southeast of Spiritwood, next to the Spiritwood Golf Club. This small lake contains stocked walleye as well as resident northern pike.

Larsen Reservoir (Map 8/B2)
Larsen Reservoir is found northeast of the town of Radville. The lake is currently being stocked with pike and perch. Walleye and rainbow were stocked in the past. There is an older boat launch and camping is available nearby.

Last Mountain Lake (Map 29/D3–40/A4)
Last Mountain Lake is considered one of the premier places to fish in Southern Saskatchewan. It is easily accessed from Regina Beach Recreation Site west of Highway 54 and just north of the town of Lumsden. You may also get to the lake through Rowan's Ravine Provincial Park. The lake boasts trophy walleye and pike fishing, as well as jumbo perch and burbot. Walleye routinely top the scales at 5.5 kg (12 lbs) or more and northern pike have been known to grow larger than 13.6 kg (30 lbs). There's also a little known carp fishery here. Ice fishing is very popular on this lake.

Lavallée Lake (Map 80/B1–90/B7)
Located near the north end of Prince Albert National Park, this lake sits along a popular canoe route and is accessible via portage from a couple of smaller lakes, as well as by trail. The lake contains lake whitefish, northern pike and walleye, but be aware that special regulations and licensing applies for angling in national parks.

Lawrence Lake (Map 79/E1)
This lake is located close to Highway 922 but does not have direct road access. If you make your way to the lake you can find good fishing for northern pike.

Lawson Lake (Map 102/F5)
Lawson Lake is a medium sized lake located fully within the boundaries of Lac La Ronge Provincial Park. This remote lake is best accessed by those on canoe and portage trips within the park. Those that make it into this remote lake will find a few rough campsites along the shore and good fishing for northern pike and walleye.

Lenore Lake (Map 61/G6–62/A5)
Lenore Lake is best known for its walleye fishery, which are stocked on occasion. Anglers will have great success in the weeds of the lake. Also, northern pike, whitefish and yellow perch are found in the waters. The western side of the lake is best for pike. Ice fishing is popular here and a derby is held. The nearby reservoir offers a chance to go after stocked rainbow trout.

Lepine Lake (Map 86/F5)
This long narrow lake is part of the Cold River and is located fully within the boundaries of Meadow Lake Provincial Park. Access is possible along Highway 950 and small boats can navigate from Pierce Lake. Camping is possible at the nearby Howe Bay site on Pierce Lake or a few nice backcountry sites along the northern shore. Anglers will find good fishing for northern pike, walleye, perch and whitefish. Watch for special walleye limits.

Limestone Lake (Map 93/G5–94/A4)
Limestone Lake is accessed by Highway 106 to the east of Deschambault Lake. Limestone offers good fishing for northern pike, walleye and perch. The recreation site offers rustic camping and a boat launch on the northern shore, not far from the highway.

Lindstrom Lake (Map 103/E3)
Lindstrom Lake is a medium sized lake located adjacent to the Churchill River. With no road access, it is best to access this lake by air or canoe. Those that do get to this lake will find good fishing for northern pike and walleye.

Listen Lake (Map 89/G7–90/A7)
Located just outside of the northern boundary of Prince Albert National Park, Listen Lake has no road access but offers good fishing for lake whitefish, northern pike and walleye.

Little Amyot Lake (Map 98/F5)
Little Amyot Lake is found west of Beauval, along Highway 155, and features a recreation site with camping and a boat launch. Anglers will find stocked walleye and resident northern pike in this lake.

Little Bear Lake (Map 82/C1–92/C7)
Little Bear Lake, north of Narrow Hills Provincial Park, offers good fishing for lake trout, northern pike, walleye and whitefish. Access is off of Highway 106 on a 4 km secondary road that ends at the lake. There is plenty of camping and a boat launch here.

Little Crooked Lake (Map 101/D2)
This smaller lake is typically accessed by those canoeing tripping from Nemeiben Lake on the way to the Churchill River. Those that do make it to this remote lake will find good fishing for northern pike and walleye.

Little Fishing Lake (Map 76/F4)
This is one of the main recreation lakes located within the Bronson Forest Recreation Site. Anglers here will find good fishing for northern pike, walleye and perch. There are also lake whitefish here. Amenities and cabin rentals can be found in the nearby town of Little Fishing Lake, while a campsite, boat launch and sandy beach provide access to the lake.

Little Lake (Map 88/A4)
Found in Meadow Lake Provincial Park, to the east of Flotten Lake and to the north of Nesootao Lake, this lake is indeed small but offers good fishing for northern pike and yellow perch.

Little Loon Lake (Map 68/B3)
Found to the east of Glaslyn along Highway 3, Little Loon Lake offers stocked walleye along with resident northern pike. A regional park provides access and camping.

Little Phillion Lake (Map 90/B5)
Little Phillion Lake is not too much smaller than Phillion Lake – both lakes are found not far off of Highway 916. Little Phillion Lake contains northern pike and yellow perch.

Little Shell Lake (Map 69/D4)
Little Shell Lake is found north of Shell Lake, just west of Highway 12, and offers anglers the chance to catch some northern pike and walleye.

Little Raspberry Lake (Map 87/E6)
This small lake is located within in Meadow Lake Provincial Park and is often stocked with splake, tiger and brown trout. It has also been stocked with cutthroat trout in the past. Access to this lake is by a secondary road off of Highway 224 by Kimball Lake. Anglers can launch small boats along the shore with camping available at nearby Kimball Lake. This lake is open year round.

> *Practicing catch and release will greatly help ensure the future viability of sport fisheries.*

Lloyd Lake (Map 116/D3)
Although this lake is near Provincial Road 955, flying in is the only real option here. This lake holds good populations of northern pike, walleye and arctic grayling with many bays, river mouths and islands to sample. Anglers coming to this lake will want to check out Lloyd Lake Lodge for accommodations and guiding. Check the regulations for special catch and release restrictions.

Loch Leven (Map 12/E7)
Loch Leven is a tiny 10 hectare (25 ac) pond near the entrance to the West Block of Cypress Hills Interprovincial Park. It is on the park's main paved road. Anglers will find stocked rainbow as well as brook and cutthroat trout. Check the regulations for special regulations.

Loch Lomond (Map 54/A4)
Loch Lomond offers some excellent fishing for northern pike and can easily be accessed from Highway 49 west of Princeville.

Lorenz Lake (Map 81/G3)
This smaller lake located near Whiteswan Lakes offers good fishing for northern pike, along with a few walleye and yellow perch. Access is by secondary roads from Highway 913.

Lost Echo Lake (Map 82/B3)
This small lake in Narrow Hills Provincial Park offers good fishing for northern pike, whitefish and walleye. Access is by secondary roads and a trail from Highway 912. Wilderness camping is possible at this lake, but there are no amenities.

Lovering Lake (Map 28/E2)
Lovering Lake is a small pond southwest of Chamberlain, which is on Highway 11. There is gravel road access and a rustic boat launch, with access through Lovering Lake Recreation Site. Expect to catch burbot, northern pike and stocked walleye.

Lower Fishing Lake (Map 82/C3)
Lower Fishing Lake is the recreation centre of Narrow Hills Provincial Park. This lake offers nearly 100 campsites, lodging, boat rentals and many other amenities. Fishing here is good for northern pike and walleye. Access is found about 3 km from Highway 106.

Lower Foster Lake (Map 117/F5–E6)
A fly-in only lake, Lower Foster Lake sees limited fishing pressure so there is some great fishing here for northern pike and lake trout. Anglers wanting to fish here will want to contact Beaver Lodge Fly-inn for accommodations. Check the regulations for special catch and release restrictions.

Lowther Lake (Map 78/E2)
Located to the west of Green Lake, Lowther Lake can be reached by a series of bush roads south of Highway 55 and offers northern pike, walleye and yellow perch.

Lucien Lake (Map 61/E6)
Found just west of the community of Middle Lake, Lucien Lake is a popular recreation and resort lake. Residents and visitors will find lake trout, northern pike, walleye and perch in the lake. Public access can be found along the eastern shore.

Lussier Lake (Map 102/B1)
Lussier Lake is located near the northwestern corner of Lac La Ronge Provincial Park, just outside of the park boundary and across Provincial Road 102 from the Otter Lake airstrip. Anglers will find stocked brook trout in this small lake. The lake gets stocked with 3,000 to 4,000 brook trout each year.

Lynx Lake (Map 101/G4–102/A5)
This small lake is located in Lac La Ronge Provincial Park and is accessible from either Provincial Road 102 or 915. Canoeists also pass through this lake while on longer trips. Walleye are stocked and northern pike are also found here.

MacKay Lake (Map 102/A3)
Found just west of Provincial Road 102 along a canoe route that explores Lac La Ronge Provincial Park, MacKay Lake offers burbot, lake trout and northern pike. There is a recreation site that offers camping and a boat launch on the lake.

Macklin Lake (Map 56/A6)
Macklin Lake is found just south of the town of Macklin, within Macklin Regional Park, and is stocked with yellow perch.

Madge Lake (Map 55/C7)
This is the main lake in Duck Mountain Provincial Park and is primary destination for anglers. This lake offers fishing for northern pike, walleye, yellow perch and burbot. Within the park there are 7 campgrounds with 466 separate sites. Amenities can be found through the park. There is a walleye restriction and no barbed hooks allowed.

Maligne Lake (Map 94/E2)
This smaller lake is part of the Sturgeon-Weir River and is easily accessible from Highway 106. Anglers here will find good fishing for northern pike and walleye. Those wishing to camp can do so at the Leaf Rapids Recreation Site.

Makawa Lake (Map 77/A2–B3)
Makawa Lake offers some great fishing year round. Anglers here will find northern pike, walleye, rainbow and tiger trout along with perch and whitefish for the kids to go after. There are 3 campgrounds, with a total of 305 sites, located around the various lakes in the provincial park. Each campground has a boat launch.

Maraiche Lake (Map 95/C5)
Found in the popular Amisk Lake Recreation Area, Maraiche Lake offers anglers another option in the area. Northern pike, walleye, yellow perch and burbot can all be found here. A boat launch can be found in the northeastern corner of the lake.

Marean Lake (Map 63/E5)
This lake, located within Greenwater Provincial Park, is a good option for those looking to do some fishing. Anglers here will find northern pike and walleye. The park has a boat launch and 4 campgrounds with 186 sites as well as rentals for power boats, canoes and cabins.

Margo Lake (Map 53/C6)
Located just southwest of the village of Margo, Margo Lake contains northern pike and walleye.

Martins Lake (Map 69/E7)
This smaller lake offers fishing for northern pike and walleye. There is full service camping, a boat launch and dock at the regional park found at the lake.

Matheson Lake (Map 87/D6)
Matheson Lake is a small lake within Meadow Lake Provincial Park along Highway 224. This lake offers fishing for northern pike, walleye and whitefish. Anglers will find a 42 unit campsite with a boat launch.

McBride Lake (Map 64/G6–65/A6)
McBride Lake is located in the Porcupine Hills area and offers some good fishing opportunities. Anglers will find northern pike, perch and stocked walleye here. There is a campsite as well as a boat launch and dock. An ice fishing derby takes place here at the end of March.

> *Keep your lures polished and shiny by using whitening toothpaste and a toothbrush.*

McComb Lake (Map 102/B2)
Located not far from Provincial Road 102 north of the Lac La Ronge area, this lake is another of the great fishing lakes of the area. Lake trout, northern pike and whitefish can be found in the waters. Getting a small canoe into the lake will help you explore the bays and corners of the lake.

McLaren Lake (Map 23/B7)
Found south of Burstall near the Alberta border, this lake is readily accessible through McLaren Lake Regional Park. Although water levels fluctuate, the fishing remains fair. There are stocked northern pike and rainbow trout. In the past walleye and yellow perch have been stocked. The lake is open year-round.

McLennan Lake (Map 112/E5)
McLennan Lake is found along Provincial Road 102 and provides northern fishing opportunities for those that prefer to drive to the northern lakes. Anglers that make their way up here will find excellent fishing for northern pike, walleye and lake trout. In the nearby lakes and rivers rainbow trout and arctic grayling can be found. Bear's Camp offers year round cabins and boat rentals; there is a cafe, store, fuel and tire repair services here. Ice fishing is also possible.

McNichol Lake (Map 102/C2)
Another of the relatively small lakes of Lac La Ronge Provincial Park, getting to McNichol Lake can be a bit of a challenge as there are no nearby roads. Fishing here is primarily for northern pike and walleye.

McPhee Lake (Map 80/F5)
Located just outside Prince Albert National Park this lake offers northern pike and stocked walleye. Getting a boat onto the lake will help you reach the far corners, but where you can reach the shoreline you should have some success.

Meeting Lake (Map 68/F5)
Meeting Lake, to the north of Highway 378, offers fishing for stocked walleye and holds northern pike and perch. Camping can be found at the regional park as well as, a boat launch and a marina.

Melville Reservoir (Map 32/A1)
The Melville Reservoir is located south of the town of Melville. This small reservoir has a poor boat launch on gravel road access. The reservoir holds stocked walleye and yellow perch. The perch limit is 10, but the reservoir is only open to electric motors.

Memorial Lake (Map 69/D4)
This lake, located at the town of Shell Lake, offers some good fishing. Northern pike, perch and walleye can be caught here. The regional park offers a large campsite and cement boat launch, along with other amenities, for anglers.

Miko Lake (Map 78/F5)
This small lake in the Porcupine Hills offers a good fishing option for anglers. Expect to find northern pike and walleye here. This day-use lake has a boat launch and a dock. Camping can be found to the south at Lac Eauclair.

Milton Lake (Map 121/B3)
Milton Lake is a remote fly-in lake in the northern region. Anglers heading to this lake will almost surely stay at the Milton Lake Lodge and find great fishing for northern pike and lake trout.

Ministikwan Lake (Map 76/E3)
This large lake that partially borders the Bronson Forest Recreation Site offers some good fishing for northern pike, walleye and perch. Camping, cabin rentals, fuel and other amenities can be found in the recreation site. Check the regulations for special retention limits and closed sections.

Minnow Lake (Map 88/D6)
Minnow Lake can be found east of Highway 903 close to Meadow Lake Provincial Park. Northern pike and yellow perch can be found here.

Mirasty Lake (Map 89/D6)
This fair-sized lake is found along the short stretch of Highway 916 that bridges Highways 922 and 924. Northern pike can be found here.

Mirond Lake (Map 104/C5–D7)
This large lake, located along Highway 135 near Pelican Narrows, offers great fishing for northern pike and walleye, along with lake trout and yellow perch. Silence of the North operates an outfitters service on the lake and offers campsites, cabins, groceries, a boat launch, boat/canoe rentals and fuel.

Mission Lake (Map 30/G3)
Mission Lake is the smallest of the Calling Lakes in the Qu'Appelle Valley chain. The area's annual catch-and-release Walleye Cup draws participants from across North America and is the fourth in a series of regional walleye tournaments on the Walleye Trail. You can also expect to find burbot, northern pike, whitefish and perch. Mission Lake is easily accessed from the boat launch at Haffner Beach in the village of Lebret.

Mistawasis Lake (Map 69/C6)
Mistawasis Lake is found between Highway 12 and Provincial Road 686, south of Shell Lake. A boat launch and sandy beach can be found at the south end of this lake, which offers good fishing for northern pike, walleye and yellow perch.

Mistohay Lake (Map 87/C5)
This medium sized lake located within Meadow Lake Provincial Park offers fair to good fishing for northern pike, whitefish and stocked walleye up to 1.5 kg (3 lbs). A 20 unit campsite and boat launch can be found on the southern shore along Highway 224. Check the regulations before fishing.

Moise Lake (Map 104/C6)
Located just north of the Jan Lake Ecological Reserve, this small lake can be accessed from Highway 135 and contains stocked rainbow trout.

Montmartre Reservoir (Map 20/C2)
Found southeast of the town of Montmartre, this reservoir is located just off of 606 Road and is stocked with walleye.

Montreal Lake (Map 81/A3–91/C5)
Montreal Lake is a very large lake north of Prince Albert. This lake offers great fishing for huge northern pike and walleye along with burbot. There are also other sportfish like perch and whitefish. The best access is from the towns of Montreal Lake or Timber Bay in the southern part of the lake. The current walleye limit is 1.

Moose Mountain Lake (Map 20/F5)
Moose Mountain Lake is found north of Stoughton to the west of Highway 47. The lake, like the stream, is home to northern pike and yellow perch.

Moosomin Lake Reservoir (Map 22/D3)
The Moosomin Lake Reservoir can be accessed through Moosomin & District Regional Park where there is a good boat launch and fish cleaning station. Camping can also be found in the regional park. You will find northern pike, walleye, sauger and yellow perch. The walleye here are supplemented with stocking. Check the regulations for special catch and release restrictions.

Morin Lake (Map 69/E2)
Morin Lake is best accessed from Morin Lake Regional Park, found where Provincial Road 695 turns into 793. Visitors will find stocked walleye along with northern pike here.

Morning Lake (Map 100/G4–101/A4)
Morning Lake is a medium sized lake located east of Besnard Lake. Access is possible to the southern shore of the lake by secondary roads off of Provincial Road 910. This lake also sees many visitors on canoe trips going towards Besnard Lake. Those that make it to this lake will find good fishing for northern pike, walleye and yellow perch.

Mosher Lake (Map 95/B3)
Located at Denare Beach, Mosher Lake offers anglers a medium sized lake to explore and fish. Northern pike, perch, walleye and whitefish can all be found in the waters. A boat is needed to get out and fully explore the bays of the lake.

Mountain Lake (Map 102/D3–E1)
Mountain Lake is a long lake that borders Lac La Ronge Provincial Park. Unlike many lakes in the area, this lake is easily accessible by road from Provincial Road 915 and the town of Stanley. Anglers here will find shoreline camping and fishing for lake trout, northern pike and walleye. Check the regulations for special restrictions.

Mountney Lake (Map 111/F7)
Mountney Lake is a small lake that is often accessed by those canoeing the Churchill River system. Once here you will find populations of northern pike and walleye.

Murray Lake (Map 68/A6)
This lake is located next to Jackfish Lake and offers fair fishing for northern pike, walleye and whitefish. Camping can be found on Jackfish Lake at The Battlefords Provincial Park, where there are 3 campgrounds with 317 campsites. Boat rentals and fishing supplies are available within the park.

Mustus Lakes (Map 87/D5–E5)
This series of 4 lakes located within Meadow Lake Provincial Park offers fair fishing for northern pike, walleye and yellow perch. The first lake can be accessed by a secondary road off Highway 224, across from the turnoff to Kimball Lake. The second lake can be accessed by a short secondary road to a picnic site off of Highway 224. And from the second lake it is possible to do a short portage to the third lake. The fourth lake is a bit further way and is a bit more difficult to access. The current walleye limit is 3 on each lake.

Nagle Lake (Map 111/E3)
This remote northern lake has no road access but offers excellent fishing for lake trout, northern pike and walleye.

Namew Lake (Map 85/C2–E1)
This large lake in northern Saskatchewan borders partially with Manitoba. Anglers here will find good fishing for lake trout, northern pike, walleye and whitefish. There are also a few burbot here. Amenities and lake access can be found at the southern end of Highway 967 at the town of Sturgeon Landing.

Narrow Lake (Map 92/E6)
Just as the name implies, this lake is narrow. Located northeast of Little Bear Lake there is good fishing here for northern pike and stocked walleye. Access is from Highway 106 along a secondary road that leads to a primitive boat launch.

Nelson Lake (Map 54/A4)
Nelson Lake contains stocked walleye as well as resident northern pike and yellow perch. You can find this lake along grid roads directly east of the tiny hamlet of Ketchen.

Nemeiben Lake (Map 101/C5–D3)
Nemeiben Lake is a large lake that partially borders Lac La Ronge Provincial Park. Access to this lake is easiest at the provincially run campground. Anglers and boaters will find many bays to explore and search for the big lake trout northern pike and walleye. There are also burbot, lake whitefish and yellow perch in the lake. The bays and islands can be confusing to navigate and the lake is prone to high winds and waves. Check the regulations for special catch and release restrictions.

Ness Lake (Map 79/G5)
Located north east of Big River, Ness Lake is a great day or weekend destination. Northern pike, perch, whitefish and stocked walleye can be found here. Access can be found at the northwest corner of the lake where a small campground is located. It is possible to launch boats at the campground.

Nesslin Lake (Map 79/G4)
Found a little further down the road from Ness Lake is Nesslin Lake. Here, another campground and boat launch can be found. Anglers can find northern pike, walleye, whitefish and the odd lake trout in the lake. There are plenty of nearby options with pike and/or perch including Little Nesslin, Lostman's, and Swede Lakes.

Northern Pike Stocking	MAP	BROOK TROUT	BROWN TROUT	LAKE TROUT	LAKE WHITEFISH	NORTHERN PIKE	RAINBOW TROUT	SAUGER	WALLEYE	YELLOW PERCH	OTHER
Arm River - South Arm Lake	39/C7					•			•	•	•
Brightstand Lake	77/D7					•				•	
Cater (Klein) Lake	68/D3					•				•	
Chris Johnson (Miracle) Lake	54/F5					•					
Cypress Lake	1/E2					•			•	•	
Deserter Lake	68/F4					•					
Harris Reservoir	12/F5					•					
Larsen Reservoir	8/B3					•			•		
McLaren Lake	23/C7					•					

Yellow Perch Stocking	MAP	BROOK TROUT	BROWN TROUT	LAKE TROUT	LAKE WHITEFISH	NORTHERN PIKE	RAINBOW TROUT	SAUGER	WALLEYE	YELLOW PERCH	OTHER
Admiral Reservoir	14/D7					•			•	•	•
Cater (Klein) Lake	68/D3					•				•	
Ceylon Reservoir	7/G3					•				•	
Chris Johnson (Miracle) Lake	54/F5					•				•	
Condie Reservoir	29/F5					•				•	
Craik Reservoir [Arm Lake]	39/C6					•			•	•	•
Cypress Lake	1/E2					•	•		•	•	
Junction Reservoir	12/F4					•				•	
Kenosee Lake	21/F6				•					•	
Kornitski Lake	42/F2					•				•	
Larsen Reservoir	8/B3					•			•		
Macklin Lake	56/A6					•				•	
Oungre Reservoir	8/G6					•				•	
Oyama Reservoir	19/C1					•				•	
Round Lake (NW of Prince Albert)	70/F4					•				•	
Smuts Lake	60/E6								•	•	
Strands Lake	7/E2							•		•	

Newburn Lake (Map 53/D7)
Found along Chain-of-Lakes School Road in between Invermay and Sheho, this small lake offers anglers northern pike and walleye.

Nickle Lake (Map 8/G1)
Nickle Lake is found southeast of Weyburn off Highway 39 and is most often accessed through the Nickle Lake Regional Park, which has a good boat dock and a couple boat launches. The park also offers camping and boat/canoe rentals. Anglers pull northern pike, walleye, sauger and yellow perch from its waters. The walleye in this lake are supplemented with stocking.

Nikik Lake (Map 80/G4–81/A4)
Found along a quiet backroad south of Montreal Lake and Highway 930, Nikik Lake offers some excellent northern pike fishing.

Nipekamew Lake (Map 91/G6–92/A7)
This lake offers good fishing for northern pike and walleye. Access is by Highways 912 or 927. Camping and a boat launch are found on nearby East Trout Lake. The current northern pike limit is 4.

Nipew Lake [Dead Lake] (Map 101/G1–112/A7)
Nipew Lake, also known as Dead Lake, is a medium sized lake found along the Churchill River system. Access is best by air, by canoeing downstream on the Churchill River or paddling upstream from Devil Lake. Those that come to this lake will find northern pike and walleye.

Niska Lake (Map 97/G1–107/G7)
Connected by a narrow channel to Peter Pond Lake in the north, Niska Lake can be accessed from Provincial Road 925 and offers good fishing for northern pike and walleye.

Nistowiak Lake (Map 102/E3)
Nistowiak Lake is one of many lakes located along the Churchill River. This medium sized lake is often visited by those canoeing the Churchill River, as there is no road access. Those that make it into this lake will find camping options along the shore and good populations of northern pike, walleye and lake trout.

Nistum Lake (Map 95/B6)
This smaller lake rests near the southeast end of Amisk Lake and offers fishing for stocked rainbow year-round. Camping and more fishing opportunities can be found at Amisk Lake.

Nokomis Lake (Map 118/D4)
Accessed by canoe from Oliver Lake and the outfitters there, Nokomis Lake offers some great fishing for northern pike. Check the regulations for special catch and release restrictions.

North Lake (Map 92/E7)
Located north of Narrow Hills Provincial Park, North Lake can be reached via Cub Lake Road from Highway 106. This lake offers fair fishing for northern pike and walleye.

Nunn Lake (Map 102/E5)
Nunn Lake is a good sized lake located within the boundaries of Lac La Ronge Provincial Park. Access is mainly by canoe and portaging from nearby lakes. Those that do make it into this lake will find good shoreline camping and plenty of northern pike, lake trout and walleye. Check the regulations for special catch and release restrictions.

Odell Lake [Falling Horse Lake] (Map 82/D4)
This 148 hectare (366 ac) lake is found in the southeastern corner of Narrow Hills Provincial Park. Accessible by Esker Road, anglers here can expect to find northern pike.

Oliver Lake (Map 118/C4)
Oliver Lake is found east of Provincial Road 102 and the Davin Lake Airfield. Oliver has many bays and islands to test your luck for lake trout and northern pike. Oliver Lake Wilderness Lodge offers fly-in outfitter services. Check the regulations for special catch and release restrictions.

Oscar Lake (Map 59/C1)
This small lake northwest of Highway 40 and the town of Blaine Lake is often stocked with brook trout. Access is off Range Road 92.

Osimisk Lake (Map 79/F4)
Osimisk Lake is sandwiched between Delaronde Lake and Prince Albert National Park and can be accessed by the Big River ATV Trails. Northern pike, walleye and yellow perch can be found in this lake, and there is camping available. Little Osimisk, to the northwest, also offers pike and perch.

Otter Lake [Big River] (Map 79/B5)
Otter Lake is a long, narrow lake with lots of channels and bays that can be accessed by a branch road off of Highway 946. Anglers can find lake whitefish and northern pike here.

Otter Lake (Map 102/B1–D2)
This medium sized lake makes up park of the Churchill River system. It is easily accessible from Missinipe on Provincial Road 102, where last second supplies can be found. There are good populations of northern pike, walleye and lake trout in Otter. Paddlers often visit this lake while exploring the Churchill River System. Check the regulations for a closed section.

Oungre Reservoir (Map 8/F6)
This very small reservoir northwest of the town of Oungre can be accessed through the Oungre Regional Park. There is a rough boat launch here for anglers looking for northern pike and yellow perch.

Oyama Reservoir (Map 19/C1)
This small reservoir, northeast of Kronau has a healthy northern pike population. Most of the pike are small, averaging 0.5 kg (1 lb), but there are a few topping 4.5 kg (10 lbs). There is a rustic gravel boat launch and small dock. The current perch limit is 10.

Pagan Lake (Map 88/B7)
Pagan Lake can be found just off of Highway 903, around 19 km north of the town of Meadow Lake. Anglers will find northern pike, walleye and yellow perch here. In fact, the provincial record yellow perch was pulled from this lake in 1991. A recreation site provides a boat launch and camping.

Pancake Lake (Map 79/F3)
Pancake Lake is located to the east of the much larger Delaronde Lake and can be accessed by a branch road off of Highway 922, as well as by the Big River ATV Trails. Pancake Lake offers good fishing for stocked walleye.

Parr Hill Lake (Map 65/C6)
Also known as Ranch Lake, this scenic lake rests in the Porcupine Hills area, not far from Highway 982. The lake is a good option for those wanting to find some northern pike, walleye and yellow perch. Camping, a boat launch and dock are available at the recreation site here.

Pasqua Lake (Map 30/D3–E3)
Pasqua Lake is in the Qu'Appelle Valley chain, which is really one body of water divided by alluvial fans created when fast-flowing tributaries enter the Qu'Appelle River and drop sediment on the valley floor. Pasqua is popular for its northern pike and walleye, and also holds burbot, whitefish and yellow perch. Camping and a good boat launch are available at Echo Valley Provincial Park, which is built on a delta between Pasqua Lake and Echo Lake. A boat launch for bigger boats is also found on the east side of the bridge.

Peck Lake (Map 76/E4)
Located within the Bronson Forest Recreation Site this lake makes a good destination for not only angling, but for the entire family. Anglers here will find northern pike, perch and stocked walleye. There is a boat launch and a campsite, while other amenities and cabin rentals can be found nearby within the recreation site. Check the regulations for special retention limits and closed sections.

Peitahigan Lake (Map 87/D5)
Located within Meadow Lake Provincial Park, just to the west of Third Mustus Lake and to the north of Highway 224, this lake is stocked with walleye.

Pepaw Lake (Map 65/B6)
Pepaw Lake, located in the Porcupine Hills, is a good recreation destination. Anglers here will find northern pike and walleye. There is a day-use only recreation site with a boat launch and dock. Camping can be found to the south at nearby Parr Hill Lake.

Perch Lake (Map 76/F7)
Found north of the town of Paradise Hill along Highway 21, Perch Lake offers anglers northern pike, walleye and, as the name suggests, yellow perch.

Peter Pond Lake [Big and Little Peter Pond Lake] (Map 107/D2–108/A6)
Peter Pond Lakes, referred to locally as Big and Little Peter Pond Lake, are separated by the narrows created by the Thompson Peninsula. Accessed from the town of Buffalo Narrows, anglers here will find excellent fishing for northern pike and walleye. The main access is by Highway 155 with secondary roads gaining access around the lake. Tinker's Camp, at the Niska Channel on Little Peter, offers cabins, boat rentals, a boat launch as well as other amenities. The town of Buffalo Narrows has groceries, fuel and other amenities. Check the regulations for special restrictions.

Peyasew Lake (Map 79/G4)
Peyasew Lake can be found in between Highway 922 and Prince Albert National Park, close to the Delaronde Lake Recreation Site. Anglers will find northern pike, walleye and yellow perch here.

Phelps Lake (Map 121/C4)
This remote fly-in lake is home of Wolf Bay Lodge. Anglers coming to fish these waters will find lake trout, northern pike and walleye in good numbers.

Philion Lake (Map 90/A4)
Found next to the much larger Smoothstone Lake, Philion Lake can be reached by a branch road off of Highway 916 and offers lake whitefish, northern pike and walleye. Nearby Little Philion offers northern pike and yellow perch.

Picnic Lake (Map 67/E4)
Picnic Lake is found east of town of Edam to the north of Provincial Road 769. Anglers here can expect to find brown and rainbow trout that are stocked regularly, along with tiger trout.

Pierce Lake (Map 86/E5)
Pierce Lake is located within Meadow Lake Provincial Park and has good access from Highway 919. Howe Bay in the southeastern portion of the lake offers camping, lodging, boat ramp and other amenities. Further west, at Sandy Beach, you will find camping and a boat ramp. Angling here is excellent for northern pike, walleye, lake trout, perch and whitefish. Anglers using small boats will want to keep in mind this is a large lake that sees heavy use by many different water recreation sports; watch out for windy weather and fast boaters. Also, watch for special restrictions on walleye and lake trout.

FISHING ADVENTURES

Pike Lake (Map 49/B5)
Pike Lake is home to Pike Lake Provincial Park and can be found south of Saskatoon along Highway 60. As you may have guessed, pike are the main draw here.

Pinehouse Lake (Map 100/A4–110/C6)
Pinehouse Lake is a very large lake found along the Churchill River. This lake is home to northern pike, walleye and lake trout. Access can be found at the town or Pinehouse Lake, by those canoeing the Churchill River and by air. It is highly advisable to have a good chart of the lake and a compass as there are numerous islands and bays that make navigation a challenge. You will also want to watch out for waves when the wind picks up. Contact the Kamkota Lodge for guiding and accommodations. Check the regulations for special restrictions.

Piprell Lake (Map 82/A2)
Piprell Lake, just west of Narrow Hills Provincial Park, offers good fishing for stocked rainbow and brown trout. Open all year, access to this lake is off a short access road from Highway 913. There is a recreation site on the lake.

Pitch Lake (Map 69/B3)
Pitch Lake can be found north of Highway 3 and east of Highway 24, not far from the community of Spiritwood. Northern pike and yellow perch can be caught in this lake.

Pointer Lake (Map 103/C1–113/C7)
This remote fly-in lake northwest of Lac La Ronge offers excellent angling for lake trout and northern pike.

Pratt [Jimmy] Lake (Map 69/F5)
This lake is accessed by grid roads south of Highway 3, near the small hamlet of Mont Nebo and the Mistawasis First Nation. Anglers can find stocked walleye and resident northern pike here.

Primeau Lake (Map 109/D4)
Primeau Lake is one of the many lakes that make up the Churchill River system. Access to this lake is typically by canoe trips along the river. This lake is home to northern pike, walleye and lake trout.

Rachkewich Lake (Map 101/D1)
Rachkewich Lake is a smaller lake south of the Churchill River. Those that make their way to this lake often do so while canoeing from the river on their way to Nemeiben Lake. Those that pass by here will find northern pike and walleye.

Rafferty Reservoir (Map 9/B4–F6)
The Rafferty Reservoir, west of the city of Estevan, holds northern pike, sauger and walleye. The reservoir, which runs roughly 57 km in length and is rarely over 2 km wide, is readily accessed by boat launches in the Mainprize Regional Park and the dam west of Estevan. Check for special retention limits here.

Randall Lake (Map 90/D5)
This lake is located to the northwest of Weyakwin Lake and can be accessed by a branch off of Highway 916. Northern pike is the main species of sportfish in this lake.

Reid Lake Reservoir (Map 14/C4–D3)
The reservoir holds northern pike, walleye and yellow perch that can be caught during the open water and ice fishing seasons. Although there are many roads and a few campsites that surround the three arms of the reservoir, one of the best access points is from the boat launch found on Ferguson Bay. Watch for special restrictions here.

Reindeer Lake (Map 118/D6–G1)
Reindeer Lake is an impressive inland waterway. With 5,000 islands and 92 river inlets, there is plenty of structure to work. And there is no shortage of trophy fish to go after. Arctic grayling, lake trout, lake whitefish, northern pike and walleye inhabit the lake and adjacent rivers. And there is no shortage of outfitters found around the lake to help land those big fish. Although it is possible to drive to this lake, flying in is the better alternative. Check the regulations for special catch and release restrictions.

Rhona Lake (Map 61/E4)
This long, narrow lake is located in between Highway 41 and Basin Lake, just south of the small community of Yellow Creek. The lake contains stocked walleye and resident northern pike.

Rock Island Lake (Map 77/C1)
This lake is located in between Highway 26 and Highway 55 in the middle of farm country. The lake offers anglers the chance to reel in some northern pike or yellow perch.

Roughbark Reservoir (Map 8/G2)
This horseshoe shaped water body south of Nickle Lake can be accessed off of the grid roads in the area. Anglers here can expect to find walleye here.

Round Lake (Map 32/E5)
Round Lake is situated on the Qu'Appelle River and has burbot, northern pike, smallmouth and largemouth bass, walleye, whitefish, yellow perch, channel catfish, common carp and rockfish. With all these different species you can expect heavy pressure during fishing season. Occasionally the walleye get supplemented with stocking. A private campground is available, along with an older boat launch.

Round Lake (Map 63/F7)
Round Lake, south of Greenwater Provincial Park, offers fishing for walleye. Anglers will find a recreation site here with limited camping opportunities and a boat launch.

Northern Pike - begin your search for northern pike in the quiet, vegetated waters. Larger pike will inhabit calm areas leading into bays. They will also hang around rocky points, shoals, islands and other places with larger fish to feed on.

Round Lake (Map 70/F4)
Found northwest of Prince Albert, this Round Lake can be accessed via Briarlea Road. The lake offers stocked yellow perch and resident northern pike.

Round Lake (Map 76/F4)
This small lake located within the Bronson Forest Recreation Site offers some good fishing for stocked brook trout and splake. There is no camping immediately at this lake, but there are several camping options not far to the north and south of here. Cabin rentals, fuel and other services can be found within the recreation site. Note the fishing closure in April.

Rusty Lake (Map 87/E6)
Located within Meadow Lake Provincial Park and alongside Highway 224, this lake is best known for its northern pike, but walleye and yellow perch are also found there. Watch for special walleye limits.

Saginas Lake (Map 65/B5)
Located in the Porcupine Hills, this lake and its nearby neighbours offer some good recreation fishing destinations. Anglers should expect to pull northern pike and stocked walleye here, especially near the dam. The recreation site at the lake offers camping as well as a boat launch and dock.

Sandfly Lake (Map 110/F7)
This larger lake is one of many lakes along the Churchill River that is home to northern pike, walleye and lake trout. There are many islands and bays that can make navigation challenging, but fishing quite productive. Access is by air or canoe.

Sandy Lake (Map 21/D6)
Sandy Lake, located within Moose Mountain Provincial Park, can easily be accessed from the road that goes through the centre of the park in a west/east direction. Anglers here can expect to find stocked rainbow trout.

Sandy Lake (Map 98/F6)
This small lake can be found southwest of Beauval, in between Highways 965 and 155. Anglers can enjoy stocked rainbow trout in this lake.

Sandy Lake (Map 110/B6)
This is another one of the many lakes that make up the Churchill River and its many paddling routes. Provincial Road 914 does come very close to the lake and it is possible to portage a canoe in from there. Once on the lake, the lake lives up to its name and you will find numerous sandy beaches and campsites. The lake holds northern pike and walleye.

Sealey Lake (Map 82/C1)
Sealey Lake is easy accessible off of Highway 106 at the northern end of Narrow Hills Provincial Park. There is a day-use area with a boat launch and dock, and good fishing for stocked rainbow and brook trout. This lake is open all year.

Selwyn Lake (Map 120/G2–121/A1)
Selwyn Lake is found along the Northwest Territories border and offers some great fishing for arctic grayling, lake trout northern pike, walleye and whitefish. This fly-in lake is home to the Selwyn Lake Lodge.

FISHING ADVENTURES

Walleye Stocking

	MAP	BROOK TROUT	BROWN TROUT	LAKE TROUT	LAKE WHITEFISH	NORTHERN PIKE	RAINBOW TROUT	SAUGER	WALLEYE	YELLOW PERCH	OTHER
Adams Lake	12/B7		•				•		•		
Admiral Reservoir	14/D7					•			•	•	
Allen Lake	65/D5								•		
Anglin Lake	80/G7					•			•	•	
Antelope Lake	14/B1					•	•		•		
Arm River - Chamberlain	28/E2					•			•		•
Arm River - Hwy 11	28/G3					•			•		•
Arm River - Hwy 2	28/F2					•			•		•
Arm River - Hwy 354	29/A3					•			•		•
Arm River - Hwy 732	39/D7					•			•		•
Arm River - Hwy 747	39/C5					•			•		•
Arm River - Little Arm Bay	29/C3					•			•		•
Arm River - North Arm Lake	39/C6					•			•		•
Arm River - Reservoir	28/E2					•			•		•
Arm River - South Arm Lake	39/C7					•			•		•
Arm River - Vanzance Lake	39/B3					•			•		•
Assiniboia Reservoir	6/C1								•		
Avonlea Creek	18/C4					•			•	•	
Avonlea [Watson] Reservoir	18/C4					•			•	•	
Baldy Lake	82/C3					•			•	•	
Barrier Lake	63/C5					•			•		
Batka Lake	44/D1					•			•	•	
Battle Creek - Battle Creek Rd	12/A7	•	•			•	•				
Battle Creek - Parc Historique National Du Fort-Walsh	1/B1	•	•			•	•				
Battle Creek - Reesor Lake	12/B7	•	•				•				
Blue Heron (Fish) Lake	70/B2					•			•		
Boundary Dam Reservoir	9/G7					•			•		•
Braddock Reservoir	15/C3								•		
Bradwell Reservoir	49/G5				•	•			•		
Buffalo Pound Lake	28/F4				•	•		•	•	•	
Burton Lake	51/B1					•			•		
Bushy Lake	57/D1					•			•		
Cabri Reservoir	25/A4							•	•		
Christopher Lake	71/A1					•			•		
Cookson Reservoir	6/F7					•			•		
Coronach Reservoir	6/E6								•		
Coteau Bay	38/A5			•	•	•		•	•	•	
Craik Reservoir [Arm Lake]	39/C6					•			•	•	
Crystal Lake	54/D5					•			•	•	
Cutarm Creek - Bredenbury/ Cutarm Lake	32/G1							•	•		
Cutarm Creek - Hwy 22/Gerald	33/C4							•	•		
Cutarm Creek - Hwy 637	32/G2							•	•		
Cutarm Creek - Hwy 8	33/C4							•	•		
Cutarm Creek - Hwy 80	33/B3							•	•		
Cutarm Creek - Qu'Appelle River	33/D5					•		•	•		
Cutarm Creek - Reservoir	33/B4							•	•		
Cypress Lake	1/E2					•			•		
Diefenbaker Lake	38/C6			•	•	•	•	•	•	•	
Eagle Lake	62/C4					•			•	•	
Eastend Reservoir	2/D2								•	•	

• *Sauger also stocked*

Settee Lake (Map 112/G5)
Settee Lake is a remote lake located northeast of Lac La Ronge and south of Provincial Road 102. There is no road access to the lake but a canoe route does run through it, and anglers can find lake trout, northern pike and walleye here.

Shadd Lake (Map 111/D7)
This is a remote lake with no road access, located north of Lac La Ronge. Anglers can find pike and walleye here.

Shagwenaw Lake (Map 109/A5)
This medium sized lake holds lake trout, northern pike and walleye, along with burbot and lake whitefish. It can be accessed at the northern end of Provincial Road 918 at the town of Patuanak and is home to many backcountry campsites.

Shannon Lake (Map 61/D4)
Shannon Lake is found just off of Highway 41 in between Wakaw Lake and Basin Lake. A boat launch can be found near the south end of the lake, which offers fishing for stocked walleye.

Sheasby [Pebble] Lake (Map 76/C2)
Featuring burbot, northern pike and walleye, this lake is found in a forested area south of Cold Lake, in between Highway 21 and the Alberta border.

Shell Lake [Big Shell Lake] (Map 69/D5)
Found south west of the community of Shell Lake, anglers will find a recreation site that offers camping and a boat launch. This makes the lake a great day destination for locals, or a stop over for travellers coming through the area. Northern pike, walleye and the odd burbot can be found in the waters. Pike and walleye are also found in nearby Little Shell Lake.

Shell Lake (Map 78/G5)
This small lake in the Porcupine Hills offers some good fishing options. Those that come here to fish will find northern pike and perch. There is basic camping, a boat launch and dock found here at the Shell Lake Recreation Site. Access is by a short secondary road from Highway 945. Amenities and more camping can be found at nearby Chitek Lake.

Shirley Lake (Map 89/C5)
This small lake near Doré Lake offers fishing for stocked rainbow along with a recreation site. Other fishing and camping options can be found nearby. The lake is open year-round.

Shutte Lake (Map 53/F2)
Found along Township Road 372, this small lake offers anglers a nice option for walleye. A stocking program here helps to maintain the walleye population. The best access is found along the eastern side of the lake.

Sim Lake (Map 102/B3)
Sim Lake, located in Lac La Ronge Provincial Park, is one of the many small lakes that make up this area. As there are no roads nearby access is best by canoeing and portaging from nearby lakes and rivers. Those that make it into this lake will find northern pike and walleye.

Sled Lake (Map 89/B6)
This large lake is located south of Dore Lake. Northern pike, walleye and perch can be found here, but a boat is recommended to get out and explore the lake. There are recreation sites and camping found in the area.

Smallfish Lake (Map 65/G6)
This lake rests along Highway 980 and the Woody River Recreation Site in the Porcupine Hills area. You should expect to find northern pike and perch here. There are 6 campsites for RVs plus a good grassy area for tents. There is a boat launch, dock and fish cleaning building here too.

Smith-Jones Lake (Map 100/F2)
Found north of Besnard Lake, Smith-Jones Lake offers anglers a wilderness fishing opportunity without having to paddle or hike into. A rough road leads to the lake. Anglers will find northern pike, walleye and whitefish. A canoe or small boat will help you reach all the bays on the lake.

Smoothstone Lake (Map 89/F4–90/A3)
This lake, located near Doré Lake, offers fishing for northern pike and walleye. Access is from a secondary road off Highway 916 through Smoothstone Lake Recreation Site. The current walleye limit is 1.

Smuts Lake (Map 60/E5)
This small lake west of Highway 41 along Township Road 410 offers fishing for stocked walleye. There is a speed limit of 25 km/hr on the lake.

FISHING ADVENTURES

Snowfield Lakes (Map 81/D3)
This pair of small lakes are found off of Highway 926, north of Candle Lake. Lake whitefish and northern pike can be found here.

South Lake (Map 33/C4)
South Lake is a man-made lake in Carlton Trail Regional Park. This lake was previously stocked with walleye for catch and release fishing. Nearby From Lake also offers fishing for stocked walleye. Canoes and paddling are allowed on the lakes.

Spirit Lake (Map 65/G5)
Located in the Porcupine Hills and within the boundaries of the Woody River Recreation Site, Spirit Lake makes a great angling getaway lake. This lake offers great walleye fishing and also produces northern pike and yellow perch. There is camping at this lake as well as a boat launch, dock, bathrooms and a fish cleaning building. ATV trails lead east to Armit Lake in Manitoba.

Spruce Lake (Map 67/B1)
Spruce Lake is found adjacent to Highway 3, just north of the community of Spruce Lake, and offers anglers northern pike and yellow perch.

Steepbank Lake (Map 81/F1)
Found in the heart of Clarence-Steepbank Lakes Provincial Park, this long and narrow lake offers anglers some excellent fishing for lake trout, northern pike and walleye.

Steistol Lake (Map 63/F5)
This small lake in Greenwater Provincial Park is a good option for those wanting to go after something different. The lake is stocked with rainbow trout and there are reports of some big fish coming out of this lake. This lake is best fished from a small boat and canoe rentals are available. The park also offers four campgrounds and cabins rentals. Open year-round, no motor boats are allowed on the lake.

Stickley Lake (Map 82/C3)
Stickley Lake is a small lake located within Narrow Hills Provincial Park. Anglers that come here will find northern pike. Access is by a secondary road off of Highway 106.

Strands Lake (Map 7/D2)
Strands Lake is a small, 20 hectare (50 ac) lake, 6 km southeast of Ogema. It has had rainbow trout introduced, but check with locals to make sure winter kill has not affected the population.

Stroud Lake (Map 102/B4)
This small lake located in Lac La Ronge Provincial Park holds good populations of northern pike and walleye. Access to this lake is typically by canoe and portage from Hunt Lake or Leckie Lake.

Struthers Lake (Map 61/E2)
Struthers Lake is found in between the Waterhen Marsh and Dickson Lake, accessible via Valley Drive to the southwest of Kinistino. Stocked walleye is the main draw for anglers here.

Stuart Lake (Map 82/A1)
This lake, located west of Narrow Hills Provincial Park, offers fishing for northern pike. There is no camping, but there is a primitive boat launch. Access is off of Highway 912 and a short trail.

Sturgeon Lake (Map 70/E3)
Offering stocked walleye and resident northern pike, Sturgeon Lake is really a widening of the Sturgeon River. The waterbody is easily accessed along Provincial Roads 693 and 778 and has a regional park providing camping and a boat launch.

Suffern Lake (Map 56/B3)
Found south of Highway 40 and Marsden, Suffern Lake is stocked with brook and rainbow trout, offering a fine early season trout fishery. Suffern Lake Regional Park can be found along the northern shore of the lake. The lake is open year-round.

Sulphide Lake (Map 102/A4)
Sulphide Lake is one of many smaller lakes located within Lac La Ronge Provincial Park. Access to this lake is typically by canoe and portage from other nearby lakes. Those that do make it here will find good populations of northern pike and walleye.

Summercove Reservoir (Map 4/F4)
Summercove is a small reservoir south of Mankota. It has gravel road access and a deteriorated boat launch. Stocked walleye and native sauger can be pulled from the reservoir.

Walleye Stocking

	MAP	BROOK TROUT	BROWN TROUT	LAKE TROUT	LAKE WHITEFISH	NORTHERN PIKE	RAINBOW TROUT	SAUGER	WALLEYE	YELLOW PERCH	OTHER
Echo Lake	30/F3	•		•					•	•	•
Elbow Lake	65/F5						•		•		
Emerald Lake	69/E5						•		•		
Fairy Glen Lake	82/B3						•		•		
Fishing Lake (Big)	53/B6						•		•		
Fishing Lake (Little)	53/A6						•		•		
From Lake	33/D4								•		
Gordon Lake	56/A3								•		
Gouverneur Reservoir	15/A6						•		•		
Greenwater Lake	63/F5						•		•		
Grenfell Reservoir	31/G7								•		
Herbert Reservoir	26/D6			•			•	•	•		
Hirtz Lake	86/D5	•	•						•		
Humboldt Lake	51/B3								•		
Iroquois Lake	69/E5						•		•		
Jeannette Lake	87/G5						•		•		
Johnston Lake	116/D3								•		
Johnston Lake	86/G5								•		
Jumping Lake	61/D2								•		
Junction Reservoir	12/F4								•	•	
Kamsack Town Reservoir	44/A1								•		
Kenosee Lake	21/F6					•			•	•	
Kimball Lake	87/E6						•		•		
Kipabiskau Lake	62/G5								•	•	
Lac Des Iles	86/G5	•	•						•		
Lac La Peche	59/D1								•		
Lac Pelletier	14/E4						•		•	•	•
Larsen Lake	69/B4						•		•		
Lenore Lake - Big	61/G6	•	•						•		
Lenore Lake - South	61/G6	•	•						•		
Little Amyot Lake	98/F5						•		•		
Little Loon Lake	68/B3						•		•		
Lost Echo Lake	82/B3						•		•		
Lovering Lake	28/E2						•		•		
Lucien Lake	61/E6	•							•		
Lynx Lake	101/G4						•		•		
McBride Lake	64/G6						•		•	•	
McPhee Lake	80/F5						•		•		
Meeting Lake	68/G5								•	•	
Melville Reservoir	32/A1								•		
Memorial Lake	69/E4						•		•		
Mission Lake	30/G3	•	•						•	•	
Mistohay Lake	87/C5	•	•						•		
Montmartre Reservoir	20/C2								•		
Moosomin Lake Reservoir	22/D3							•	•		
Morin Lake	69/E2								•		
Narrow Lake	92/E6								•		
Nelson Lake	54/A4								•		
Ness Lake	79/G5	•	•						•		
Nickle Lake	8/G1								•	•	
Pancake Lake	79/F3						•		•		
Pasqua Lake	30/E3	•	•						•	•	

Walleye Stocking

	MAP	BROOK TROUT	BROWN TROUT	LAKE TROUT	LAKE WHITEFISH	NORTHERN PIKE	RAINBOW TROUT	SAUGER	WALLEYE	YELLOW PERCH	OTHER
Peck Lake	76/E4					•			•	•	
Peitahigan Lake	87/D5								•		
Pinkney Lake	81/G3			•			•		•		
Pratt (Jimmy) Lake	69/F5					•			•		
Rhona Lake	61/E4					•			•	•	
Roughbark Creek	8/G2					•		•	•	•	
Roughbark Reservoir	8/G2					•					
Round Lake	32/E5			•	•				•	•	•
Round Lake	63/F7					•			•		
Saginas Lake	65/B5					•			•		
Shannon Lake	61/D4								•		
Shutte Lake	53/F2								•		
Smuts Lake	60/E6								•	•	
Struthers Lake	61/E2								•		
Sturgeon Lake	70/E3					•			•	•	
Summercove Reservoir	4/F3							•	•		
Summit Lake	82/B2				•	•			•	•	
Theodore Reservoir	42/G3					•			•	•	
Thomson Lake	16/C6					•			•	•	
Top Lake	79/F4								•		
Townsend Lake	65/F5					•			•		
White Bear [Carlyle] Lake	21/F6							•	•		
Whitesand Lake	53/C6								•		
Willows [Assiniboia] Reservoir	6/B1					•	•		•	•	
Wolseley Reservoir	31/D7					•			•	•	
Wood River - Gravelbourg	16/D5					•			•		
Wood River - Shamrock Regional Park	16/D3					•			•		
Zelma Reservoir	50/C6			•		•			•	•	

• Sauger also stocked

Summit Lake (Map 82/B2)
Summit Lake is located within Narrow Hills Provincial Park and offers good fishing for northern pike, walleye and whitefish. Access is off of Highway 913. There is no camping, but there is a boat launch.

Swede Lake (Map 79/G4)
Swede Lake is a small lake found just south of Nesslin Lake, accessed via Nesslin Lake Road, that offers some fine fishing for northern pike.

Table Lake (Map 95/C4)
Found southeast of Denare Beach in the Amisk Lake area, Table Lake offers anglers a fun lake to explore. Northern pike, walleye and yellow perch are found in the waters here. Getting a canoe into the lake is helpful to explore all the bays and island on the lake.

Taggart Lake (Map 79/C2)
This fish-shaped lake is found not too far off of Highway 55, north of the community of Big River. Lake whitefish, northern pike and walleye can be found in this lake.

Theodore Reservoir (Map 42/G2)
Part of the Whitesand River system, this reservoir boasts some impressive sized fish. Angling records indicate pike recorded in the 9 kg (20 lb) range and perch nearing 1 kg (2 lb). Walleye are stocked in the reservoir. Camping and a boat launch can be found at Whitesands Regional Park, which is accessed off Grid Road 651 north of Theodore and Highway 16.

Thomson Lake (Map 16/C6)
Thomson Lake is easily accessed through Thomson Lake Regional Park, which offers visitors a marina with a boat launch, filleting station and camping facilities. The park was the first regional park established in Saskatchewan. The lake is stocked annually with walleye, while northern pike and yellow perch rely on natural reproduction.

Tibiska Lake (Map 80/E1)
Tibiska Lake is located in Prince Albert National Park and contains northern pike and walleye. This remote lake can be accessed by a bush road heading south from Highway 916.

Tobin Lake (Map 73/B3–83/F7)
This large man-made lake was formed by the damming of the Saskatchewan River in 1963 northeast of Nipawin. Home to some world class northern pike and walleye fishing, there are also large lake sturgeon and a host of other species here. There are numerous camping and outfitter options around the 74 km long lake, while amenities can be found in the nearby towns of Nipawin, Tobin Lake and Squaw Rapids. Check the regulations for special restrictions.

Top Lake (Map 79/F4)
Top Lake is easily accessed by Highway 922, just across from Delaronde Lake Recreation Site. The abnormally shaped lake offers stocked rainbow trout.

Townsend Lake (Map 65/F5)
Townsend Lake is one of the core lakes of the Woody River Recreation Site on Highway 980 in the Porcupine Hills area. This lake offers pike, perch, white sucker and stocked walleye. Anglers will also find one of the larger campsites in the area, a boat launch, dock and fish cleaning station. There are ATV trails in the area, along with Moose Range Lodge for those that prefer a bed.

Trade Lake (Map 103/C3–D4)
Trade Lake is a large lake located along the Churchill River. As there are no nearby roads it is best to access this lake by air or canoe and portaging along the Churchill River. Those that do make their way here will find good shoreline camping and great fishing for northern pike, walleye and lake trout.

Trent Lake (Map 104/F7)
This smaller, remote lake west of Wildnest Lake sees most of its visits by those on canoe trips within the region. Those that do make it into here will find fishing for northern pike and walleye.

Triveet Lake (Map 101/B3)
This long, narrow lake is often visited by those on canoe trips towards Besnard Lake. Anglers that make it to this remote lake will find northern pike and walleye. Lake whitefish and burbot are also available.

Trout Lake (Map 101/E1)
This medium sized lake is home to northern pike, walleye and lake trout. Access to this lake is best done by air or by those paddling the Churchill River system either downstream or upstream from Devil Lake. Although not an overly large lake, there are numerous islands and bays that could make navigation challenging.

Tullibee Lake (Map 77/A3)
This lake is really a branch off of Makawa Lake, separated by a narrow channel over which passes Provincial Road 699. It holds the usual northern Saskatchewan species of pike, perch and walleye.

Turnor Lake (Map 116/E5)
This road accessible lake in the north offers good fishing for northern pike and walleye. Access is from Provincial Road 909.

Turtle Lake (Map 67/F1–77/F7)
Turtle Lake offers fishing for northern pike, walleye and whitefish. There are several towns around the lake offering amenities, while camping and access can be found at Turtle Lake Recreation Site.

Twin Lakes (Map 57/F2)
This pair of small lakes are connected by a narrow channel and are home to yellow perch. Located in farm country northwest of North Battleford, Twin Lakes Road leads to the lakes from Highway 16.

Tyrrell Lake (Map 95/B1)
Tyrell Lake is found just off of Highway 106, northwest of Flin Flon, Manitoba. A recreation site is found on the south shore of the lake and anglers can expect some good fishing for northern pike and yellow perch here.

Uchuk Lake (Map 82/D1)
Uchuk Lake is a small lake northeast of Narrow Hills Provincial Park that offers fair fishing for perch. Access is from a secondary road off of Highway 106.

Upper Fishing Lake (Map 82/C3)
This small lake in Narrow Hills Provincial Park offers good fishing for northern pike and walleye. Access is from Highway 106. There is a primitive boat launch here and there are many camping options nearby.

Utikumak [White Fish] Lake (Map 88/C2)
This lake is found close to the larger Keeley Lake, just off of Highway 903. Expect to find northern pike here, as well as the namesake whitefish.

Vivian Lake (Map 87/D6)
Vivian Lake is a small, quiet lake located within Meadow Lake Provincial Park. Open all year, anglers will find fair fishing for stocked rainbow, but the lake suffers from doldrums in warmer weather. A small, rustic 9-unit campsite where it is possible to launch small boat can be found off of Highway 224.

Wakaw Lake (Map 61/B4)
This long narrow lake sees heavy recreational boating pressure and only provides fair fishing during peak recreation times for northern pike and walleye. Wakaw Lake Regional Park has camping and a boat launch.

Wapata Lake (Map 120/E5)
This fly-in only lake offers great fishing for lake trout, northern pike and walleye. Cree River Lodge operates out of this lake and offers guiding and day trips to the many smaller lakes in the area.

Wapawekka Lake (Map 92/B1–93/A1)
This very large lake near Lac La Ronge offers great fishing for northern pike, walleye and perch. Direct access to the lake can be found at the western end via access roads from Highway 912, while a well-established outfitter is located on Churchman Island in the eastern part of the lake. Check the regulations for special restrictions.

Waskesiu Lake (Map 80/C4–E5)
Forming the hub of Prince Albert National Park, Waskesiu Lake offers good fishing for lake trout, northern pike, perch, walleye and whitefish. Remember that you will need a special angling license and there are special restrictions for fishing within national parks.

Waskwei Lake (Map 104/E6)
Waskwei Lake is a medium sized lake located east of Pelican Narrows and Mirond Lake. Those wanting to fish this lake for the ample northern pike and walleye must either do so by air or canoeing and portaging.

Wassegam Lake (Map 80/D1)
Wassegam Lake is found toward the northern boundary of Prince Albert National Park and can be accessed by portage from the neighbouring lakes or by a series of bush roads that run south from Highway 916. Lake trout, northern pike and walleye can be found in this lake, which is subject to special regulations and licensing due to being in a national park.

Waterhen Lake (Map 87/G5–88/B5)
This large lake located within Meadow Lake Provincial Park offers some great fishing for northern pike, walleye and other smaller game fish. Camping, a boat launch and many other amenities can be found on the southwestern shore on the access road off of Highway 904. Watch for special walleye limits.

Welwyn Reservoir (Map 33/E7)
Welwyn Reservoir is situated in the Welwyn Centennial Regional Park. There is a good boat launch and paved road access. Native species in the reservoir are northern pike, yellow perch and walleye. Camping is available in this park.

Weyakwin Lake (Map 90/F5–G6)
This lake, found west of the town of Weyakwin on Highway 2, has fishing for northern pike, walleye, trout and whitefish. Camping and a couple of boat launches can be found at the Wayakwin Lake Recreation Site on the southern shore. The current walleye limit is 3.

White Bear Lake [Carlyle Lake] (Map 21/F6)
White Bear Lake is just outside the Moose Mountain Provincial Park, which is a great place to set up your camping gear. This relatively large lake has stocked walleye and sauger. There is a rustic boat launch here. The White Bear Lake Resort is also located near the shores of the lake.

White Gull Lake (Map 81/F5)
White Gull Lake, near Candle Lake, offers some good fishing for northern pike and walleye. This lake is also suspected to hold brook trout. There are plenty of camping options at nearby Candle Lake Provincial Park, as well as at the Heritage Lake Recreation Site.

Whitesand Lake (Map 53/C6)
Whitesand Lake is found south of the community of Margo, right next to Usinneskaw Lake. The main draw to this lake for anglers is the stocked walleye.

Whiteswan and Pinkney Lakes (Map 81/F3)
These lakes can be accessed through Whiteswan Lake (Whelan Bay) Recreation Site and offer good fishing for stocked lake trout and naturally reproducing northern pike. Pinkney also holds walleye that get stocked on occasion. At Whiteswan, there is lodging, camping, a boat launch and dock, while Pinkney offers a rustic boat launch at the end of the short access road from Highway 913. Check the regulations for special restrictions.

Wildnest Lake (Map 104/G7–105/A6)
Wildnest Lake is a larger lake with considerable open water. It is best to work the many islands and bays to find the lake trout, northern pike and walleye that reside here. This lake is commonly visited by those on canoe trips or by flying in.

Willows Dam Reservoir [Assiniboia Reservoir] (Map 6/C1)
This reservoir is best accessed through the Assiniboia Regional Park, which offers a boat launch. The lake was previously stocked with rainbow trout that are best caught during the spring and fall when the water temperatures are cooler. Walleye fishing is now supplemented with stocking. Native fish in the reservoir include northern pike, walleye and yellow perch. Ice fishing is popular here.

Wilson Lake (Map 42/G4)
Wilson Lake is a small lake found to the west of the community of Springside, accessible via a series of grid roads. Anglers will find stocked brook and rainbow trout here.

Wolf Lake (Map 92/E7)
Wolf Lake is a small lake east of Little Bear Lake that offers fishing for walleye and pike. Access is by a 4.5 km trail from Highway 106 or a 500 metre trail from North Lake. There is no camping at this lake.

Wollaston Lake (Map 118/C1–121/C7)
This large northern lake is home to several outfitters. Flying is the fastest way to reach the lake, but those wishing to drive can do so via Provincial Roads 102 and 905. Anglers will find good fishing for arctic grayling, lake trout, lake whitefish, northern pike and walleye. Check the regulations for special catch and release restrictions.

Wolseley Reservoir (Map 31/D7)
Wolseley Reservoir is found south of the scenic small town of Wolseley. This reservoir is subject to winterkill, but usually has a population of northern pike, walleye and yellow perch.

Wood Lake (Map 103/F4–G5)
This large lake remote lake holds good populations of walleye, lake trout and northern pike. Being that there are no nearby roads, access is best by air or canoe.

Woody Lake (Map 65/G5)
This day-use only lake within the Woody River Recreation Site makes an attractive option for those wanting to go after walleye. Pike are also available at the lake, which also offers a boat launch/dock and fish cleaning station. Camping can be found at nearby Townsend Lake or Spirit Lake.

Worthington Lake (Map 76/E3)
Located within the Bronson Forest Recreation Site, this is a good option for those wanting to try some fishing. Anglers here will find northern pike, walleye and perch. This is a day-use only lake that can be accessed off Highway 21.

Zapfe Lake (Map 65/G5)
East of Woody Lake, this fairly remote lake is connected to the Woody River and Townsend Lake. Anglers will find ATV trails in the area along with fishing for walleye, pike and perch.

Zelma Reservoir (Map 50/C6)
Not far from the tiny community of Zelma is the Zelma Reservoir. This good-sized reservoir sees some impressive releases of walleye occasionally. Anglers will also find northern pike, perch and whitefish. Shore fishing is popular here, but it is possible to launch boats. Check the regulations for special catch and release restrictions.

Zeden Lake (Map 82/C4)
This small lake in Narrow Hills Provincial Park offers good fishing for stocked rainbow, brown and tiger trout and also holds splake. Access is by a short access road from Highway 106. There is a 13 unit campsite, with a boat launch and dock.

River & Stream Fishing

Saskatchewan has no shortage of creeks and rivers with both stocked and resident fish populations. Although walleye and northern pike are the most common catches, there is a good selection of brook trout streams along with a few that hold arctic grayling and rainbow trout. Perch is another popular sportfish, while burbot, carp, lake trout and whitefish also roam the various streams. And while many waterbodies in the south suffer from drought and winterkill, the more remote northern regions offer consistently incredible angling.

Arm River (Map 39/B2–29/C3)
With its headwaters up in the Allan Hills and flowing south, this river is found in the south central portion of the province. The river flows into Last Mountain Lake and is one of the few spawning rivers supporting the important Last Mountain Lake fishery. Expect to find stocked walleye, wild carp and northern pike in the river. Access is available through the Arm River Recreation Site, although Highway 11 and countless grid roads provide decent access along its entire length.

Assiniboine River (Map 54/B4–44/D4)
Beginning near the town of Preeceville, the Assiniboine River runs generally in a southeastern direction. It meets Lake of the Prairies at the Manitoba border and eventually spills into the Red River. This Assiniboine is home to many sportfish including northern pike, walleye, burbot and perch. Anglers can find good access as it passes through the province, especially near the town of Kamsack. One of the better places to try is found near the border with Manitoba where the river opens up into a reservoir known as the Shellmouth Reservoir or Lake of the Prairies.

Avonlea Creek (Map 18/C3–E6)
Avonlea Creek was dammed in 1960 resulting in a 243 hectare (600 ac) reservoir in the naturally treed valley. Most anglers ply the waters of the lake in search of stocked walleye as well as perch and northern pike. A boat launch and camping is available in Dunnet Regional Park. However, where the creek flows into the confluence with the Moose Jaw River, perch, northern pike and carp can also be caught. The Blue Hills are nearby and hold 70 million-year-old rock exposures, which are part of the Bearpaw formation.

Barrier River (Map 62/D6–63/D4)
Draining Kipabiskau Lake and flowing eastward, this river can be accessed at many bridge crossings between Highways 6 and 35 and Provincial Road 773. Barrier River also flows into and out of Barrier Lake. Both lakes are home to stocked walleye and also hold northern pike and perch, all of which are known to roam the river.

Battle Creek (Map 12/B7)
Battle Creek flows through Cypress Hills Provincial Park providing ideal trout habitat. Rainbow trout and brown trout are currently being stocked. Brookies and walleye can also be found throughout the length of the creek. Road and trail access along with wilderness camping is available throughout the provincial park.

> *Be sure to check the stocking charts in the lake section for those streams that are stocked.*

Battle River (Map 56/A1–58/A3)
The Battle River's source water is located in Alberta at Battle Lake. The river makes its way eastward into Saskatchewan and eventually into the North Saskatchewan River at the town of Battleford. Anglers that make their way to the banks of this river can expect to find northern pike, walleye, yellow perch and burbot.

Bear Creek (Map 13/B3–B6)
Bear Creek runs south of Piapot and is accessed through private property or by trail in some spots. It was first stocked with brown trout in the 1920s (no longer stocked), and has been managed for brook trout since the 1950s. The creek is on the north facing slope of the Cypress Hills and some stretches are heavily overgrown and hard to reach.

Bear River (Map 92/C6–93/C4)
The Bear River flows east into Deschambault Lake and can be accessed from Provincial Road 165. This river also connects with Ballantyne Creek, which flows south to Big Sandy Lake. Anglers should find good fishing for northern pike, walleye and yellow perch.

Beaver River (Maps 77, 86, 87, 88, 98, 99)
Draining Beaver Lake in Alberta and flowing in a generally easterly direction into Saskatchewan, this river connects with the Green River where it turns and flows north into the Churchill River system at Lac Ile-a-la-Crosse. The Beaver River is a text book stream with lots of meandering bends as it flows across the province. Anglers can find plenty of access points from the bridges that cross the river and the roads that run alongside it. Expect to find northern pike, walleye, burbot, whitefish, perch and, in the deeper lakes, lake trout.

Belanger Creek (Map 1/F2–12/F7)
Belanger Creek flows from the Cypress Hills area into the Frenchman River. Currently the creek is being stocked with rainbow, brook and brown trout, but not all three species are stocked each year. Because brown trout prefer slow moving water you will find them predominately in the lower reaches of the creek. Brook trout are in the faster moving upper portions, with the rainbow in the central reaches. The creek is easily accessed off of Highway 21 south of the town of Maple Creek.

Boggy Creek (Map 29/E5)
Boggy Creek is limited to shore fishing for access, although anglers on its reservoir, Condie Reservoir, often prefer canoes. Expect to pull northern pike, walleye and yellow perch.

Bone Creek (Map 13/D6–G5)
Bone Creek has been called southern Saskatchewan's best brown trout stream. It is a long creek that runs 45 km from the Cypress Hills into the Swift Current River northeast of Eastend. Access is available from a variety of backroads in the area. The creek was originally stocked with brown trout in 1928 from Banff, and is still managed for that species with regular stocking since 1971. These trout range from 1–4 kilograms (2–10 pounds) and are easily the largest trout in the region. They are only found in the upper reaches, which is often deep, swift and all but unapproachable through willow bushes along the banks. The water is crystal clear and pristine in quality. Other native species found in the creek include mountain sucker, creek chub and minnows.

Carrot River (Maps 72, 73, 74, 75, 85)
Beginning near Waterhen Marsh and flowing in a north-easterly direction, the Carrot eventually flows into Manitoba alongside Highway 9. This river offers fishing for northern pike, walleye, burbot and perch. There are several access points from bridges. Pasquia Regional Park, just south of the town of Carrot River on Highway 23, offers camping and a launch boat for those wanting to explore fishing the river by canoe.

Churchill River (Maps 101-105, 108-112, 115)
With its origin at Churchill Lake, this historic and long river makes its way in a generally easterly direction into Manitoba and eventually flowing into Hudson Bay. This river is really a long series of lakes with river sections in between. There are many access points and many portions of this system can only be accessed by float plane or canoe. In fact, paddling this river is a very popular activity with many different routes utilizing the system. Popular access points include Lac Ile-a-la-Crosse, Pinehouse, Besnard, Otter and Mountain Lakes along with Sandy Bay. Those that find their way along the river can expect to find northern pike, walleye, yellow perch, and in the larger lakes that make of the system, lake trout and lake whitefish.

Clearwater River (Map 116/D3–A4)
Clearwater River is an unpolluted river in the north that offers some great fishing for arctic grayling as well as for northern pike and walleye. Access is by Provincial Road 955 and camping is possible within the Clearwater River Provincial Park. A canoe route links Lloyd Lake with Warner Rapids and continues west past the Alberta border towards Fort McMurray.

Cold River (Map 86/D4–87/B5)
This river flows out of Cold Lake in an easterly direction and quickly empties into Pierce Lake and makes a short reappearance before finally draining into Lac des Iles. Although short lived (roughly 35 km long), anglers can expect to find northern pike, walleye, yellow perch and, closer to the lakes, lake trout and whitefish. A canoe route links the lake, while Meadow Lake Provincial Park offers camping and other services. Check the regulations for special restrictions.

Conglomerate Creek (Map 2/B2–13/C7)
This creek is often called Little Frenchman's Creek, since it flows out of Cypress Hills, through open pasture lands and into the Frenchman River. The creek is stocked with brown trout and has been stocked in the past with brook trout. Although it is easy to access, it does flow through private property and permission is required from landowners before dropping your hook. The creek is reached from Provincial Road 614 north of the town of Eastend.

Cowan River (Map 79/B1–88/F6)

Draining Cowan Lake and flowing into the Beaver River, this short river offers anglers a decent fishery for northern pike and walleye. Perch are present as well for those wanting some light tackle fun. Several branch roads off of Highway 55 and Highway 924 access the lake. Check the regulations for special restrictions.

Cutarm Creek (Map 32/G1–33/D5)

Cutarm Creek has fluctuating levels of water, so the best fishing is usually around the reservoir, which is 14 km northeast of Esterhazy. Anglers here will find stocked walleye and sauger. Another popular location is near its confluence with the Qu'Appelle River, which adds northern pike and perch to the mix.

Davis Creek (Map 1/G2–12/G6)

Davis Creek flows into the Frenchman River from the Cypress Hills. Access is readily available near the village of Belanger. At the last sampling, the waters only contained brook stickleback so anglers are advised to try nearby streams like Belanger, Weaver or the Frenchman.

Dillon River (Map 107/B6–E4)

Dillon River flows from Dillon Lake into Peter Pond Lake at the town of Dillon. The lower reaches closer to town have easier access. More adventurous anglers can try the upper reaches. Northern pike and walleye are found in the river and the current walleye limit is 3.

Eagle Creek (Map 47/B6–59/A7)

Eagle Creek drains Opuntia Lake and flows southeast, meandering its way back north and into the North Saskatchewan River. Anglers here can expect to find northern pike, walleye and burbot. Recently, rainbow trout have been stocked into the system. Much of the river is shallow and weedy, but where you can find a deeper pool there are some fish in the 0.5–2 kg (1 lb–4 lb) range. Try looking for beaver dams where the water would be a bit deeper. Eagle Creek Regional Park can be found on the creek, northeast of the town of Perdue, offering camping and a launch point for small boats/canoes.

East Poplar River (Map 6/E5–F7)

The East Poplar River flows into Cookson Reservoir, which was created by the Morrison Dam in 1976. The Morrison Dam was built to provide cooling water for the 600-megawatt Coronach Power Generating Station. The reservoir has been stocked with walleye that have made their way upstream to provide a decent fishery along with the native perch. The last sampling of the Lower East Poplar, taken near the US border, showed only lake chub, fathead minnow, brook stickleback and Iowa darter...not exactly the most popular of sportfish.

Etomami River (Map 54/A2–65/A2)

The Etomami River runs primarily on the western side of Highway 9, north and south of the junction with Highway 983. The river eventually meets the Red Deer River south of the town of Hudson Bay. Anglers will find stocked rainbow trout on the Etomami.

Fairwell Creek (Map 2/A2–13/B7)

Fairwell Creek drains into the Frenchman River from the Cypress Hills. Sections of this creek are only accessible through private property, so please obtain permission before fishing. The main sportfish in the creek are rainbow and brook trout along with stocked brown trout. The rainbow were stocked in the past. There is also a number of non-sportfish species in the creek.

Fir River (Map 74/F5–65/A2)

Running southeast from Wildcat Hill Provincial Park through the town of Hudson Bay to meet the Red Deer, the Fir River is stocked with brook trout. Fir River Road runs parallel to the river, offering several places to drop a line as well as a recreation site.

Fond du Lac River (Map 120/D4–121/C6)

Fond du Lac River is a remote northern river flowing through Black Lake that offers some great arctic grayling fishing. There are also walleye and pike, while the lake offers lake trout as well. Access is primarily by air, although the Athabasca Seasonal Winter Road and a canoe route do run through the upper reaches. Check the regulations for special catch and release restrictions.

Frenchman River (Maps 1, 2, 3, 4)

The Frenchman River has a variety of different access points as it intercepts public Highways 21, 13, 37, and 4. It is the major watershed in southwest Saskatchewan, running from Cypress Hills through the Grasslands National Park, and finally into Montana. South of Val Marie it is commonly referred to as the Lower Frenchman River. This section of river is often murky and is quite shallow. Although a variety of fish are found in the river, most of the angling attention is concentrated around the middle sections of the river where brook trout can be found, or the lower section where yellow perch and the odd brook trout reside. You will also find burbot, northern pike, walleye and sauger along its length.

Hay Meadow Creek (Map 5/G5–6/A5)

Feeding Fife Lake, Hay Meadow Creek can be accessed from Highway 2, just south of Lisieux. The creek is stocked with brook trout, while the lake has been stocked with northern pike and perch. Stocked trout limit is 2.

Jewel Creek (Map 8/C2–9/A3)

Jewel Creek is one of three streams flowing into the Rafferty Dam/Reservoir project. While water levels fluctuate, you will often pull northern pike, yellow perch and walleye from this river, particularly close to Rafferty. Access is available through Mainprize Regional Park, where the Jewel, Roughbark and Souris meet.

Lightning Creek (Map 11/D4–22/B5)

Lightning Creek runs along Highway 8, near the town of Redvers allowing for fairly easy access. The creek has some native yellow perch in its waters, particularly near the dam, which is 2 km north of Redvers.

Lilian River (Map 54/B2–C4)

Draining tiny Lilian Lake, this river flows into the Assiniboine River near the town of Sturgis. Access can be found from many roads that cross the river and along the train tracks that go along it for most of its length. Anglers can find northern pike in the system.

Lodge Creek (Map 1/A4–C6)

This creek flows from Alberta to the US border through southwest Saskatchewan. The creek is home to northern pike and is readily accessed from Highway 13 in the north and Highway 21 to the southeast.

Long Creek (Map 8/A1–9/F7)

A major tributary of the Souris River, Long Creek flows past the town of Radville and the Radville-Laurier Regional Park, which is a nice spot to drop a hook from. Anglers pull northern pike and perch from shore. Long Creek has one major impoundment on it: the Boundary Reservoir south of Estevan, which is home to the only bass fishery in Saskatchewan. There are also pike, perch and walleye in the reservoir.

Meeyomoot River (Map 91/E5–F2)

Draining Meeyomoot Lake north into Lac la Ronge, the lower reaches of the river are the easiest to access. Near the crossing of Provincial Road 165 a secondary road follows the river for a most of the length into Lac la Ronge. Anglers can expect to find northern pike and possibly some brook trout.

McCusker River (Map 97/F4–G1)

This river drains the lake that shares its name and flows into Niska Lake just south of Peter Pond Lake. The easiest access is where Highway 903 crosses the river. Northern pike and walleye are found here. The river is closed to fishing March 1st to June 30th.

McDougal Creek (Map 82/C2–83/C2)

McDougal Creek marks a good portion of the eastern border of Narrow Hills Provincial Park before flowing east into the Mossy River. The two main access points are from Highway 106 on a 2.5 km secondary road, and where Highway 120 intersects the creek. Anglers will find good fishing for stocked brook trout (that were first stocked back in 1934) and wilderness style camping along the creek.

Mistohay Creek (Map 87/B5)

Found within Meadow Lake Provincial Park, Mistohay Creek connects de Balinhard Lake and Mistohay Lake with the Waterhen River to the south. Anglers can find northern pike and walleye in the system. The current walleye limit is 3.

Montreal River (Map 91/A5–101/E6)

The Montreal River flows north from Montreal Lake before meeting Sikachu Lake, where it branches east into Lac la Ronge after passing through Sikachu, Egg and Bigstone Lakes. Access can be found off Highway 2 or Provincial Road 165. Anglers will find northern pike, walleye and yellow perch in the system.

Moose Jaw River (Maps 17, 18, 19, 28, 29)

The Moose Jaw River is a tributary of the Qu'Appelle River system starting in the prairie northwest of Weyburn. Perch, northern pike and carp can be found at different points of the river. However, water levels can be very low and steep banks with a lack of vegetation restrict a lot of the river access. All of these factors can make fishing certain stretches of the river rather difficult. Access is found south of Highway 39 as well as off Highway 2 and north of the Trans-Canada near Moose Jaw.

Moose Mountain Creek (Map 10/G5–20/D2)
Moose Mountain Creek drains run-off from the Moose Mountains, a natural plateau, then joins with the Souris River and eventually ends up in Lake Winnipeg before it reaches Hudson Bay. The creek flows into and out of Alamada Reservoir near the appropriately named town of Oxbow, 60 km east of Estevan. Anglers will find northern pike and yellow perch in the creek, while the reservoir also offers walleye and sauger. Further upstream, Moose Mountain Lake also offers pike and perch. Check the regulations for special restrictions.

Morgan Creek (Map 5/C7)
Morgan Creek runs through the Grasslands National Park. At the last sampling eight species were found in its waters. However, none of these species are considered sportfish. Check at the park office and Visitor Information Centre located in the village of Val Marie for the latest information on the creek.

Mossy River (Map 82/F1–84/G3)
With its headwaters east of Little Bear Lake and flowing eastward into Cumberland Lake, this river offers some fine fishing for eastern brook trout. Brook trout were introduced to the river system back in 1979 and they were able to take hold and make a nice fishery. The best access is on the secondary roads that lead east of Cub Lake off the Hanson Lake Road (Highway 106). Closer to Cumberland Lake, anglers should also find northern pike and walleye.

Nine Mile Creek (Map 12/A7)
Nine Mile Creek flows from Alberta through Cypress Hills Interprovincial Park and then merges with Battle Creek. You can expect to find brook trout, longnose dace and mountain sucker. Access is easiest from within the park.

Nipekamew River (Map 82/A1–B2)
Located just west of Narrow Hills Provincial Park, this small stream offers some good trout fishing. Several thousand brook trout are released into the creek each year. Access can be found where the river parallels Piprell Whiteswan Road and where it crosses Highway 912.

Notekeu Creek (Map 15/A6–16/D5)
Notekeu Creek is dammed at Gouverneur Reservoir, while nearby Notekeu Regional Park offers camping and another good access point. The creek is shallow during drought years, so shore fishing is best near the dam. Look for native northern pike, walleye, sauger and yellow perch. The Notekeu eventually joins Wood River, which also suffers from water issues at times, near Gravelbourg.

North Saskatchewan River (Maps 57-60, 66, 67, 70, 71, 76)
Beginning far off in the meltwaters of the Saskatchewan Glacier in the Rocky Mountains, this large river makes its way eastward across Alberta and into Saskatchewan. Flowing in a generally easterly direction, the river continues through the city of Prince Albert before eventually converging with the South Saskatchewan River to form the Saskatchewan River. There are many places where anglers can gain access to the river with parks, recreation sites and highways lining the shores or crossing over the river. Anglers can expect to pull out sturgeon, northern pike, walleye and burbot. Other species include sauger, the close relative to walleye, goldeye, mooneye, yellow perch and suckers. Being a larger river, a jet boat is a good way to work the river, but a canoe also works.

Pine Cree Creek (Map 2/E1–13/E7)
Pine Cree Creek runs through the Pine Cree Regional Park and into Swift Current Creek, 13 km northeast of Eastend. Provincial Road 633 provides good access for anglers wanting to test their luck for stocked brook trout.

Pipestone Creek (Map 20/G1–22/F4)
Pipestone Creek is often very shallow, depending on annual snowfall and rainfall. The best fishing along the creek is at the Moosomin Lake Reservoir, 8 km southwest of Moosomin. Here you will find the Moosomin Regional Park with a good boat launch and a chance to catch northern pike, walleye, sauger and yellow perch.

Porcupine River (Map 120/G3–121/A2)
East of Black Lake, this remote, northern river offers great fishing for arctic grayling. Access is usually by air to Milton Lake (and the lodge there) and then down the East Porcupine River. Northern pike and lake trout are found in the bigger lakes on the system.

Poplar River (Map 5/F5–6/C7)
The Poplar River is a tributary of the Missouri River, flowing 269 km (167 mi) through Saskatchewan and Montana. Only a short stretch of the river is found in southern Saskatchewan and is readily accessed south off Highway 2/18 near Rockglen. Anglers will find perch, northern pike and carp.

Qu'Appelle River (Maps 27–33)
The Qu'Appelle River originates at the outlet of the Qu'Appelle Dam on Lake Diefenbaker and flows east for approximately 400 km (248 mi) before meeting with the Assiniboine River in Manitoba. The river flows through the Qu'Appelle Valley, which was created when glacial thaws gouged out a channel 2 km wide and 30-150 m (100–490 ft) deep. The Qu'Appelle River water depth fluctuates greatly throughout the summer season, so fishing is normally best near lake areas along its length or at the dam. Expect to find burbot, northern pike, walleye, whitefish and yellow perch. You will also find channel catfish and rock bass around the areas of Round Lake and Crooked Lake.

Red Deer River (Map 34/C7)
The Red Deer River is a mainly Alberta river, which flows from the Rocky Mountains into the South Saskatchewan River at the Red Deer Forks just over the Saskatchewan border. On the Alberta side, the Red River Valley is home to one of the world's premier locations of cretaceous dinosaur bones. Even during drought years in Alberta, which results in a decline in the Red Deer's water flow, the river usually offers up good goldeye, lake sturgeon, northern pike, sauger, walleye and yellow perch.

Red Deer River (Map 63/D5–75/G7)
Not nearly as popular as its southern brother, this Red Deer River flows out of central Saskatchewan, past Hudson Bay, the town, and into Manitoba. The river eventually flows through Red Deer Lake and Lake Winnipegosis. There are reports of walleye near the Manitoba lakes, but no confirmed reports if these popular fish have made their way into Saskatchewan.

Reindeer River (Map 103/G1–113/F1; 118/D6–D7)
Linking Reindeer Lake with the Churchill River, the Reindeer River looks more like a lake than a river for most of its length. The river is a popular paddling destination, with routes that connect to many parts of the region. Anglers can expect to find lake trout, northern pike, walleye and yellow perch in the system. Check the regulations for a closed section.

Roughbark Creek (Map 8/C2–9/A3)
Roughbark Creek meets Jewel Creek and the Souris River in a confluence south of Weyburn, where the Jewel Creek Nature Conservancy has been created. Further south, the Rafferty Reservoir is home to the Mainprize Regional Park and a boat launch. Walleye and yellow perch are native to the creek, with higher populations around the reservoir. The reservoir also holds northern pike and sauger.

Rushlake Creek (Map 15/A2–26/C7)
Rushlake Creek was dammed to create Highfield Reservoir. Although the creek is very low in drought years, some northern pike usually make their way into the stream. Access is found off grid roads between the Trans-Canada Highway in the north and Highway 363 in the south.

Russell Creek (Map 14/G4–15/D5)
This small creek running by the town of Neville holds stocked brook trout. It is a popular fishing spot after spring runoff. Access can be found along Highway 43 and grid roads leading south.

Sandy Creek (Map 28/A6–B6)
This creek runs alongside the grid road running east out of Mortlach. The creek is stocked with small brook trout that are best caught with a worm and hook. Camping is available at the Besant Recreation Site.

Saskatchewan River (Maps 71, 72, 73, 83, 84, 85)
The Saskatchewan River begins where the North and South Saskatchewan Rivers meet just east of Prince Albert. From here the river flows easterly into Manitoba eventually draining into Lake Winnipeg. Angling access points along the river are many and the fish species include burbot, goldeye, lake sturgeon, lake whitefish, northern pike, rainbow trout, sauger, walleye and yellow perch. Tobin Lake is a big, man-made waterbody that interrupts the river east of Nipiwan. The big lake offers world class northern pike and walleye fishing. Northeast of the lake, Highway 123 skirts the south side of the river all the way to Cumberland House. Alternatively, it is possible to run a jet boat or even canoe to access some of the more remote holes. The river's name is derived from the Cree word kis-is-ska-tche-wan, meaning swift current.

Scissors Creek (Map 33/C6)
A tributary of the Qu'Appelle River, Scissors Creek was stocked with brook trout and brown trout in the past, but is susceptible to winterkill. A few walleye, pike and perch may also be found near the junction with the Qu'Appelle.

FISHING ADVENTURES

Shell Brook River (Map 69/D5–70/G5)
This meandering river runs predominantly west to east north of Highway 3 and the town of Shellbrook. Flowing into the North Saskatchewan River west of Prince Albert, this tributary makes for some nice small to medium sized river fishing for northern pike and walleye. Access can be found over much of its length from Township and Range Roads.

Smoothstone River (Map 80/B2–89/G5; 89/G3–100/B4)
With its headwaters in northern Prince Albert National Park and meandering generally northward into Pinehouse Lake, this river is longer than many would think. It flows through several large and small lakes and anglers will find northern pike and walleye. Access can be found along its length where several major roads cross the river, including Provincial Road 165. Check the regulations for a closed section.

> *We have included most major systems and a collection of smaller creeks and rivers. However, especially up north, the feeder streams to lakes and rivers that are fish-bearing can, and often do, hold the same species.*

Souris River (Maps 8-11, 19)
The Souris River originates in southern Saskatchewan, passes through the state of North Dakota, and then crosses into Manitoba before joining the Assiniboine River. Its total length is approximately 700 km (435 mi). Large reservoirs have been constructed and include Boundary, Rafferty and Alameda Reservoirs in Saskatchewan. Northwest of Weyburn, the river is characterized by low banks and a poorly defined valley. South of Weyburn, the valley becomes more defined, with a slightly steeper slope. Downstream from Estevan, the Souris flows east, parallel to the international boundary, with denser tree cover along the banks. The Souris is entirely dependent on run-off and rainfall and water levels fluctuate widely, which leads to periodic winterkill of fish. Anglers pull bullhead, northern pike, walleye, sauger and yellow perch from its waters. Access is readily available from grid roads and at Highways 47, 39 and 9.

South Saskatchewan River
(Maps 23-27, 34, 35, 37, 38, 49, 60, 71)
The South Saskatchewan River originates in Alberta at the confluence of the Bow and Oldman Rivers and winds into Lake Diefenbaker. From Lake Diefenbaker, the South Saskatchewan heads north, where it joins the North Saskatchewan to become the Saskatchewan River, then flows east across Manitoba into Lake Winnipeg. The South Saskatchewan itself winds for 890 km (550 mi) across the province. Access to the river is provided through various parks, grid roads and highways. Anglers can find a variety of native fish species including burbot, goldeye, lake sturgeon mooneye, northern pike, sauger, walleye, whitefish and yellow perch.

Southwest of Lake Diefenbaker, Saskatchewan Landing Provincial Park as well as Lemsford Ferry and Eston Riverside Regional Park offer facilities and access. North of Lake Diefenbaker, the river flows past Outlook and Saskatoon where parks and/or good road access is possible. Continuing north and east the river runs near Prince Albert where Highways 2, 3 and 302 all cross the river before it joins the North Saskatchewan. Parts of the river valley are very steep-sided and have canyon walls, although the scenery is rich with a variety of plants and numerous animals.

Sucker Creek (Map 1/F1–12/E7)
Sucker Creek flows south into the Frenchman River, after originating in the higher elevations of the Cypress Hills in Sucker Creek Valley. This scenic valley was formed by glacial water run-off as the glaciers melted. The creek dries up in drought years, but even then lush vegetation marks its course. The creek can be accessed from Highway 21 near Cypress Lake. Brook and brown trout were stocked in the past and are known to grow to good sizes. Many of the bigger trout are found in the section south of the junction with Weaver Creek. There are also reports of burbot here.

Sturgeon-Weir River (Map 95/B6–E7)
Sturgeon-Weir River is a short but challenging paddling river that drains Amisk Lake into Namew Lake. Paddlers exploring this river can expect to find northern pike, walleye and perch. Those not wanting to paddle the river can reach the ends easily enough via good roads. Check the regulations for a closed section.

Swan River (Map 55/G3–65/D4)
Flowing from the Porcupine Hills south and then east into Manitoba where it eventually drains into Swan Lake, most of the river in Saskatchewan offers good habitat for stocked brook trout. Access in the northern reaches, south and north of Highway 982, is more difficult along bush roads. Further south, Highway 8 and the many grid roads in that area provide decent access.

Swift Current Creek (Maps 2, 13, 14, 25, 26)
Locally known as Pine Cree Creek, this long creek flows from Pine Cree Regional Park, through a scenic valley and the city of Swift Current, eventually draining into Lake Diefenbaker east of Saskatchewan Landing Provincial Park. Since most of the angling pressure occurs around Pine Cree Park, the creek was previously stocked with brook trout to help maintain the fishery. Outside of the park, a lot of the creek flows through private property so permission of landowners is required. Northern pike, sauger, walleye and yellow perch are pulled along the length of Swift Current Creek. Further upstream, the Reid Lake Reservoir was created by a dam formed in 1913. The reservoir is home to burbot, perch, pike, rainbow trout and walleye. The rainbow are stocked on occasion.

Torch River (Maps 72, 73, 81-84)
Draining Candle Lake and eventually flowing into the Saskatchewan River much further east, this river offers fishing for northern pike, walleye, yellow perch, lake whitefish, goldeye and burbot. One of the more popular fishing spots is at the bridge on Highway 913 near the beginning of the river and Candle Lake. The remote sections northeast of Tobin Lake near the Saskatchewan River confluence are rarely fished. The Torch is a dam-controlled river, but water levels are still too high to fish in early spring. By July the river is usually quite low, so anglers and paddlers are best to visit in late spring.

Wascana Creek (Map 19/G4–29/D4)
Beginning north of Weyburn, this stream meanders northwest through Regina and then into the Qu'Appelle River near Lumsden. The lower reaches of the river are more popular for fishing. Here, anglers will find northern pike and carp. It should be noted that angling is prohibited in Wascana Lake and the creek is subject to winterkill.

Waterhen River (Map 87/B5–88/F4)
Draining Lac des Iles and flowing through Meadow Lake Provincial Park and into and out of Waterhen Lake, this river eventually joins the Beaver River some 112 km later. The Waterhen offers angling opportunities for lake trout, northern pike, walleye, whitefish and yellow perch. There are several access points in the park as well as camping and other facilities. A recreation site can also be found at its eastern end along Highway 155 just west of where the river ends. The river is a popular paddling destination and most paddlers come armed with fishing gear. Note that the current walleye limit is 3 and the lake trout limit is 2.

West Poplar River (Map 5/E6–7)
The West Poplar River is a fork of the Poplar River, which is a tributary of the Missouri River. West Poplar flows into Montana through the portal of West Poplar and offers perch, northern pike and carp. Although Highway 2 and a few backroads access the river, there are long stretches that see few anglers.

Whitesand River (Map 44/A1–53/D6)
The Whitesand River begins just south of the town of Margo at Whitesand Lake and makes its way towards the Assiniboine River near the town of Kamsack. As with most rivers and creeks in the area, anglers can expect to find northern pike, walleye and perch. Angling records near the Theodore Reservoir (found on the river) have pike recorded in the 9 kg (20 lb) range and perch nearing 1 kg (2 lb). Walleye and perch are stocked in the reservoir. Camping and a boat launch can be found at the reservoir at the Whitesands Regional Park, found northeast of the town of Theodore.

Wood River (Map 4/D3–16/G3)
The Wood River runs through a mainly agricultural area from just south of Mankota, north past Lafleche and Gravelbourg, eventually emptying into the salt flats of Old Wives Lake. The Wood River had suffered from poor water quality in the past, but recent reports say that northern pike and walleye are being caught in the river. Camping, trail and canoe access is available through Shamrock Regional Park. Further south, Thomson Lake also intercepts the river and is home to a regional park with camping, boat launch and fishing for pike, perch and stocked walleye.

Hunting, Ceylon, Saskatchewan
©Tourism Saskatchewan / Greg Huszar Photography

HUNTING ADVENTURES

Saskatchewan offers a wide range of wildlife for hunters. There are seventy-two species of wild mammals presently found in the province of Saskatchewan but, hands down, the province is best known for producing world-class white-tailed deer. There are virtually no areas without some population of white-tailed deer and each area offers its own hunting experience.

Saskatchewan is divided into 12 biomes or ecoregions. The prairie region in the south has temperate grasslands, savannas and shrublands with moderate rainfall. Grasses, herbs and shrubs, rather than trees, are the dominant vegetation type with ungulates such as elk and mule and white-tailed deer roaming the expansive region. In the central part of the province you will find aspen parkland, consisting of groves of aspen poplars and spruce, interspersed with areas of prairie grasslands and large stream or river valleys lined with dense shrubbery. In the northern region, it is all boreal forest characterized by coniferous forests. Typical examples of conifers include cedar, fir, pine, hemlock, redwood, spruce and yew. This region is home to a number of large herbivorous mammals, such as black bear, caribou, elk, moose and white-tails.

Saskatchewan also offers excellent bird hunting over marsh and lake areas, as well as in harvested grain fields. Saskatchewan sits on one of the continent's major waterfowl flyways; a flyway that ducks, geese and other migrating birds take on their yearly migrations. Waterfowl are abundant in the southern areas, as well as in major flyway patterns and stopovers including the Quill Lakes area, the Qu'Appelle Valley region and Lake Diefenbaker. Upland game birds including the Hungarian partridge, sharp-tailed, ruffed and spruce grouse, pheasant and ptarmigan populate the province as well, usually hanging out in the dense underbrush or in the wheat fields of southern Saskatchewan.

As a general rule, the season opens September 1st, but there are some restrictions. Be sure to check the annual regulations for open season dates. For more information on all regulations regarding licenses, big game draws, and hunting, visit the Government of Saskatchewan website: *www.environment.gov.sk.ca/hunting*. If you notice any fishing, wildlife or environmental resource violations, contact the TIP Service at 1-800-667-7561 or Sasktel cell #5555.

Remember, the information given here is a guide only, as regulations in each zone may change annually. Hunters are also reminded to ask permission before hunting on or crossing any privately owned land.

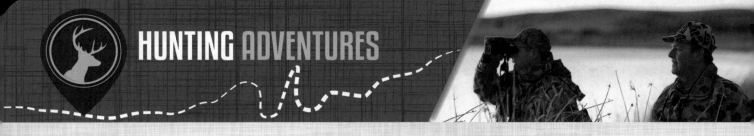

Big Game Species

Saskatchewan is home to many big game species, including black bear, caribou, moose, elk and even antelope. However, the province is most famous for its white-tailed deer hunt – the world record typical white-tailed deer was shot in southwestern Saskatchewan in 1993. While deer can be found everywhere, travelling by boat or ATV into remote areas is a preferred strategy for finding bigger game such as moose and bear. For visitors to the province, hiring a local outfitter is a good idea. A comprehensive list of hunting outfitters in Saskatchewan can be found online at www.soa.ca.

Black Bear

Black bear can live in a variety of habitats, but prefer the dense woods of the boreal forest. They are omnivorous and opportunistic hunters, eating leaves, berries, roots, fish, mice, young deer, ants, grubs, honey, carrion and garbage. They require a large amount of food, especially in the autumn when they are building up their fat reserves to survive the long hibernation. Black bear have excellent eyesight, are highly dexterous and can reach running speeds of 40–50 km/h (25–30 mph). The skulls of black bear are broad, with narrow muzzles and large jaw hinges. Actually, calling them black bear can be misleading as the bear's long fur ranges from a deep black to a light blonde. Females tend to have slenderer faces that are pointier than males'. Their claws are typically black or grayish brown. The claws are short and rounded, being thick at the base and tapering to a point. Black bear range in weight from 100 to 200 kg (220 to 440 lbs) for an adult male and from 45 to 140 kg (100 to 310 lbs) for females.

Black bear have an amazing sense of smell, so make sure every effort is made to mask your scent. This practice will bring more bear into your target zone.

Caribou

Caribou are a moderately large, deer-like ungulate found across Saskatchewan. Bulls weigh about 250 kg (551 lbs) and cows about 150 kg (330 lbs). Both sexes are covered with brown to grey coloured hair with a lighter coloured mane on the neck that is much more pronounced on bulls. Both sexes grow antlers, although the female antlers are much smaller than those of a mature male. In profile the main beam of caribou antlers resembles a forward facing "C" shape often with small palms and clusters of points at the two ends. These animals feed on grasses and annual plants in summer but in winter they feed heavily on terrestrial and arboreal lichens found in older forests. They are usually found in small groups of 6-10 animals. Bulls often form bachelor groups except in the October rut when a dominant bull will gather his harem of cows.

Cougar

Also known as the mountain lion, the cougar is the largest wild cat found in North America. Adult males average from 60 to 70 kg (130 to 160 lbs) and females weigh from 40 to 50 kg (90 to 110 lbs). From nose to tip of tail, a large cougar may be as long as 3 metres (10 ft). A third of that total length is the cougar's long tail. Cougar are predators and feed primarily on deer, but they will often hunt other large game animals, as well as rodents, hares and birds. Cougars are very secretive and are rarely seen. They usually hunt at night and rarely stray from the cover of dense trees. On rare occasions, people have been attacked by cougars. Conflicts usually happen in late spring and summer, when young cougars begin searching for their own territory.

Coyote

Coyote are usually considered more of a pest than a popular species for hunting and residents of Saskatchewan may hunt coyote without a license throughout the year on land to which they have the right of access. Despite the often-aggressive attempts to destroy as many coyote as possible by landowners, coyote still survive and thrive. Coyote are larger than foxes, but smaller than a wolf. An adult coyote weighs between 10 and 23 kg (22 to 50 lbs). They are usually grey or reddish grey, with black markings on the back and tail and lighter colouration underneath. The ears are long and the muzzle is slender and pointed. The busy tail is usually carried low and close to the hind legs.

Elk

Elk are one of the most distinguished members of the deer family, especially the bulls, with their large, sweeping antlers. Elk are also known as wapiti, and, while they are smaller than moose, they are much larger than the other members of the deer family in Alberta, with bulls weighing up to 450 kg (1,000 lbs) and cows up to 270 kg (600 lbs). Elk are mainly found in the foothills and mountains in areas of woodland mixed with grassland such as around the edges of forests and in mountain meadows. They forage on forbs and grasses in the summer and aspen bark and twigs in the winter when food is scarce. They migrate from high summer ranges to winter ranges in lower mountain valleys and foothills.

When scouting for moose habitat, look for droppings, rubs, tracks, wallows and beds. Moose, if undisturbed, will use the same bedding areas each season.

Moose

Moose are one of the most prized animals to hunt in Saskatchewan. They are the largest member of the deer family and the largest ungulate in North America. Because of their size, they have few predators. Moose are quite distinctive looking (some would say downright ugly). They have long legs, a large, drooping snout and a flap of skin in the shape of a bell under their throats. The have broad hooves and are usually dark brown to black. Male moose have large, broad antlers that are extremely prized among hunters. A full sized bull moose can stand 2.7 metres (9 ft) tall. Moose are common in the prairies and parkland and prefer to live in muskegs, brushy meadows and groves of aspen or coniferous trees, especially where there are nearby lakes, ponds or streams. In spite of their large size, moose can move through the underbrush quickly and quietly. Moose cannot see very well, but they have an acute sense of smell and hearing. When frightened, they will trot away with long smooth strides, threading their way through bush and trees that you would not think they would be able to navigate.

Mule Deer

There are two species of deer found in Alberta, mule deer and white-tailed deer. Mule deer take their name from a distinctive feature, in this case, their large mule-like ears. In addition to the big ears, mule deer can be identified by their thin, black-tipped tail and their large antlers that divide into two equal tines. Like white-tails, mule deer are greyish brown in winter and reddish-brown in summer. They are slightly larger than white-tailed deer, with bucks averaging about 100 kg (220 lbs) and does about 70 kg (155 lbs). Mule deer have an excellent sense of smell, sight and hearing, but mulies are often much more curious and will stop even when fleeing to have one last look. This is usually their downfall. They like to hang out in mixed-wood forests, hilly areas and the edges of coniferous forests.

Pronghorn become skittish during periods of high winds – wait for calmer weather when trying for an antelope.

Pronghorn Antelope

Pronghorns are roamers and like to feed off of the grasses and other shrubbery they live near. Pronghorns are very adapted to life in the grasslands and the sandy colours of their bodies provide camouflage among the barren landscape of the flat lands. Due to the odd shapes of their horns (they face forward), this southern Saskatchewan nomad gets its name. Male horns are bigger than females and in the late fall the horns will break off to make room for the new buds already starting to grow in. Pronghorns have large protruding eyes located further back in their head, giving them a wide range of vision so they can see when a predator coming (up to 6 km or 3.7 mi away). With long, skinny legs that let them take larger strides and a large heart and lungs that allow them more oxygen, pronghorns are excellent long distance runners. Pronghorns are mainly found in the southern part of Saskatchewan.

White-Tailed Deer

There are two species of deer found in Saskatchewan, mule deer and white-tailed deer. Of the two, white-tails are the most common. In fact, they are Saskatchewan's most abundant cloven-hoofed animals. They are named after their notable white tail. When the deer run, their tails are held erect, exposing the white underside, hence the name "white-tail." White-tails have no rump patch and are usually a grayish brown in winter and a reddish brown in summer. They are smaller than mule deer, with white-tailed bucks averaging 90 kg (200 lb), while does average about 60 kg (130 lb). Their antlers have un-branched tines extending up from single beams.

White-tails possess excellent senses of sight, smell and hearing and bound away gracefully when frightened. They are found in along the transition areas of forests or in open brush feeding on buds, twigs, saplings and evergreen needles in the winter, and on grass, fruit and leaves in the summer. They are frequently found in wooded river flats or in aspen groves. Their range is expanding westward into the foothills and they are becoming more common in the boreal forests of the north, too, where they browse on forbs, chokecherry, Saskatoon and other shrubs. In addition to food, brushy patches also provide good cover. The best hunting times are usually in the early morning and late evening, but deer can be bagged at any time of the day, especially around the November rut. Depending on location, hunting seasons can start as early as August and end as late as November.

Do not hunt in the same area on consecutive days. You will have more success switching up your hunting zone and returning once the previous area has settled down.

Game Birds

Saskatchewan has excellent game bird hunting, particularly in the south of the province where many migratory birds make a stop-over. The best areas to hunt waterfowl are marshes, lakes and fields. Game birds such as grouse, partridges and pheasants can be found along fence-lines, rural roads and abandoned farm yards. If you are visiting from out of province, consider hiring a local outfitter to help your chances of success – you can find a list of hunting outfitters in Saskatchewan online at www.soa.ca.

Ducks

There are, broadly speaking, two types of ducks, dabbling and diving. Dabbling ducks are typically found in fresh, shallow marshes and rivers rather than large lakes and bays. They are good divers, but usually feed by dabbling or tipping, rather than diving underwater, thus the name. The speculum, or coloured wing patch, is generally iridescent and bright and often a telltale field mark. Dabbling ducks include black, mallard and green-winged teal and are most commonly found in open wetlands and lakes.

Diving ducks get their name from their feeding habits as well, diving deep below the surface of the water to find food. They feed on fish and aquatic plants. Diving ducks include canvasback, redhead, ring-necked duck and greater and lesser scaup. Since their wings are smaller in proportion to the size and weight of their bodies, they have a more rapid wing beat than dabbling ducks. Diving ducks are sometimes found in small marshes (especially ring-necks), but are more frequently found in larger lakes. They favour deeper open water areas where there is a good growth of underwater vegetation.

Saskatchewan offers excellent waterfowl hunting throughout the province, over marsh and lake areas, as well as in harvested grain fields. Some of the best opportunities for bird hunting are in the southern part of the province, where migratory birds often stop along their journey.

Decoys are essential to a successful duck hunt. When hunting over water, plan to set out around two dozen decoys. When hunting over land, use about twice as many.

Geese

There are four species of geese hunted in Saskatchewan: snow geese, Canada geese, white-fronted geese and Ross' geese. Canadian geese are one of the most popular waterfowl and the most common species of goose in the province. In the early season, they can be found in agricultural areas, especially where there are lakes and wetlands nearby. Hunting geese in a field is like hunting dabbling ducks. Find an area, put out decoys and get under cover, either with camouflage gear or with netting. Geese like to land near where other geese are feeding, so set your decoys up so that you lead the birds to where you want them. The more decoys you use, the more likely geese are to land, as they find security in numbers. Feeding geese tend to make lots of noise, especially when they see competition approaching, so a goose call usually helps.

Grouse

There are three game species of grouse found in Saskatchewan; ruffed grouse, spruce grouse and sharp-tailed grouse. Not known for being the most cunning bird on the block, grouse are still a popular bird to hunt. What they lack in brains they make up for in colouring. You can nearly step on one of these birds before they take off in a chaotic explosion of feathers. On a still autumn morning, whilst sneaking through the forest watching and listening for the slightest hint of movement, this burst of activity can get the heart racing and the hands shaking. Once in the air, grouse are quick and often fly a random pattern through the forest, making them hard to hit. In fact, that's grouse hunting in a nutshell: go walk through the woods until you flush a grouse, and then try and shoot it down in the two second (at most) window you have. More often than not, grouse hunters will walk for hours without success. Grouse like to hang out in dense young forest or along transition zones near the edge or streams. Because they are often found in the thick brush, they are even harder to flush and the thick woods will often block your shot. A dog will often help tree grouse, which makes them easier to get.

Hungarian [Grey] Partridge

Grey partridge are small birds. A good sized cock is only 30 cm (12 in) long. Both sexes are nearly identical, but the adult male has a distinct, horseshoe-shaped, chestnut patch on its breast, while the breast patches of females and immature males are broken and less distinct. When they are flying their chestnut tail feathers can be seen. If you have ever been walking outdoors in spring and heard what sounds like a rusty gate creaking, chances are it is a male gray partridge trying to attract a hen. The hen builds a nest in grass or low bushes and lay up to twenty olive-colored eggs, which hatch in about 25 days. The hen and her chicks remain together throughout the summer, feeding on grain, seeds, leaves and berries. Mortality is high and usually only about one in eight chicks will survive to the fall. At this time coveys of 10 to 20 birds are formed. The coveys remain together all winter, dispersing in spring as the birds pair off and mate. The gray partridge is well suited to Saskatchewan's winters, using windbreaks and straw piles for shelter and grains and other seeds for food.

During dry or hot weather, look for pheasants near water sources such as streams, ponds, irrigation canals and watering equipment.

Ring-Necked Pheasant

While not native to the province, the male pheasant is one of the most identifiable of all the upland game birds in Saskatchewan. It has bright colours and a long, tapered tail. The hens, on the other hand, are a mottled brown and are more easily confused with other birds like spruce grouse. They tend to hide near the dense cover around irrigation ditches and in bluffs of trees near where food is plentiful such as grain fields. In the fall, the pheasants are found near stubble fields and other food sources. Focus your energy towards these areas.

Despite their bright colours and large sizes (cocks can get to 90 cm or 36 in), roosters can be irritatingly hard to find during hunting season. Remember to be quiet from the moment you arrive in an area; even a slammed car door can ruin a hunt as the birds tend to go to ground when they hear loud noises. Pheasants will often run away through tall grass and thick brush rather than fly, which can make them frustrating to hunt. If you can push them back towards water, they will eventually have to fly. Similar to grouse, a well-trained dog will help tree them or point them to make them easier to get. Because pheasants tend to be found in farmlands, make sure you ask permission before hunting on private land.

Wildlife Management Zones

Saskatchewan is divided into 76 Wildlife Management Zones, or WMZs, each with its own unique species, seasons and regulations. Generally, the further you get from civilization, the better your chances of success will be, so different zones vary greatly in productivity. WMZs in the south can be more productive for waterfowl and smaller ungulates, while accessing the remote zones of the north can lead to better success for large game such as bear and moose. Below you will find detailed listings for each WMZ in Saskatchewan.

WMZ 1 (Maps 5, 6, 7, 16)
Situated in south Saskatchewan, this management zone sits on the border of Montana with Wood Mountain to the west and the town of Minton to the east. The main features of this area are the lakes, Willow Bunch and Fife, where you can find many species of migrating waterfowl. As a main source of fresh drinking water, there is a high concentration of mule and white-tailed deer in the area with the odd elk roaming in the extreme western portion of this area.

WMZ 2 (Maps 2–5, 13–15)
With the Frenchman River flowing through the centre of this region, the hunting is excellent for both big game and migrating ducks and geese. Grasslands National Park occupies a small portion of this zone and there are several no hunting areas to be cognisant of. There is a large amount of mule and white-tailed deer in this area, with pronghorn antelope in the south roaming the expansive grassland region. Hunting in the eastern portion for elk can be a worthwhile challenge. Look for ross, snow and white-fronted geese in the spring and fall and mallard ducks amongst the lakes, rivers and wetlands.

WMZ 3 (Maps 1, 2, 3)
Located in the extreme southwest corner of the province, this area of land consists mainly of grassland, sagebrush plains and croplands. With such a wide range of land, hunters will find excellent mule and white-tail deer hunting in the area. This area also is home to a number of migrating ducks and geese in the spring and the fall. If you are looking to bag a trophy pronghorn, look no further. This region of Saskatchewan has the highest population of pronghorn antelope in the province.

The Saskatchewan Association for Firearm Education offers online courses for hunting safety – they can be found at www.saskhuntered.ca.

WMZ 4 (Maps 4–6, 15–17)
There are numerous lakes, streams and creeks which support many types of waterfowl and big game in this zone. Wood River meanders its way through the centre of this region, splitting between the towns of Kincaid to the west and Lafleche to the east. Mule deer run rampant here and there is a high concentration of white-tails as well. Ring-necked pheasants and sharp-tailed grouse can be flushed out in the tree-lined coulees, but watch out as you can practically step on one before they explode in a flurry of wings and feathers.

WMZ 5, 6 (Maps 1–3, 12–15, 25, 26)
If you want to hunt waterfowl, look no further than these zones. There is reported to be outstanding geese hunting around the town of Morse, located along the Trans Canada Highway northeast of Reed Lake. Within the vast grasslands and shrubbery of the prairie tundra you will also find upland game birds such as the sharp-tailed grouse and ring-necked pheasant. In the southern part of WMZ 6, look for big game such as mule and white-tailed deer, moose and elk stopping for water along the Frenchman River.

WMZ 7, 8 (Maps 1, 12, 23)
There are many lakes throughout these zones, with the most popular being Bitter Lake in WMZ 8 and Cypress Lake in WMZ 7. These lakes provide watering holes for a variety of big game animals, with mule and white-tailed deer being the most prevalent. Pronghorn roam the highlands in the northern part of the area, while elk and moose pick their way through the temperate grasslands, savannas and shrublands in central WMZ 7. If you are looking for game birds, there are ring-necked pheasants, Hungarian partridge and several species of grouse hiding in the underbrush.

WMZ 9, 10, 11 (Maps 12–14, 23–25)
Starting in Swift Current and travelling west towards Fox Valley, north to Burstall, west to Abbey, then south to Maple Creek you will find hundreds of small lakes, creeks, rivers and wetlands providing homes to thriving numbers of game birds and waterfowl. Saskatchewan sits on one of the continent's major waterfowl flyways; a flyway that ducks, geese, cranes and other migrating birds take on their yearly migrations. With kilometres of freshwater this area is also renowned for its large mule deer and, to a lesser extent, white-tails. Be sure to ask ranchers permission before hunting on private land.

WMZ 12, 13 (Maps 14, 23–27, 34, 35)
These zones are completely bordered on the northern side by the Saskatchewan River, from the towns of Leader and Cabri through on to Riverhurst. To the south is the major city of Swift Current. The best hunting is found along the river to the north where you will find a number of big game animals including the elusive mule and white-tailed deer, the swift and agile pronghorn antelope and, to a lesser extent, the prized elk.

WMZ 14 (Maps 23–27, 34–37)
This zone follows the north shores of the Saskatchewan River from the Alberta border to its eastern border on Highway 42. As this mighty river winds its way through this region, it brings fresh drinking water for numerous big game species. Mule and white-tailed deer are the most popular game in these parts, but there are a number of elk and pronghorn antelope roaming the eastern region of this zone. Inland, look for both ruffed and spruce grouse, ring-necked pheasant, and the Hungarian partridge in hayfields and pastures around Beachy and White Bear.

WMZ 15 (Maps 7–9, 19)
Bordered nicely to the south by Montana and North Dakota, the west by Highway 6, the north by Highway 13 and the east by the Souris River, this zone is notorious for its big game mule and white-tailed deer hunting. The wetlands are home to a variety of ducks, geese and upland game birds. Getting permission to hunt in this area is not that easy, but to the persistent hunter go the spoils of some trophy sized deer.

WMZ 16 (Maps 8–10, 19–21)
An unspectacular but practical zone, there are many small lakes, streams and rivers where the migratory waterfowl gather in the spring and fall. Upland game birds such as the Hungarian partridge and sharp-tailed grouse can also be found in the shrubbery and pastures of the many farms in the area.

WMZ 17, 18 (Maps 6–8, 17–20, 29–31)
Combined in the southeast portion of Saskatchewan, this area is prime pickings for mule and white-tailed deer, as well as pronghorned antelope. These zones boast hundreds of lakes; from the Chapleau Lakes in the northern sector to Gooseberry and Rock Lake to the southeast, plus the many smaller rivers and creeks along the way. In the spring and fall, these wetlands are home to thousands of migrating geese and ducks. With the bigger city of Regina just to the northwest, hunters do not have to stray very far for some good hunting. There is no hunting permitted on the Assiniboine Indian Reserve in WMZ 17.

WMZ 19 (Maps 16, 17, 26-28)
The main feature of this zone is the expansive Missouri Coteau covering much of the region. The Coteau is a narrow band of prairie upland that stretches from southern Saskatchewan into South Dakota. Approximately 15 to 40 km wide in places, the Coteau is home to a diverse community of wildlife. Each spring, snowmelt brings thousands of ponds to life, providing homes to great numbers of migrating geese and ducks and drinking water to the big game animals like mule and white-tailed deer.

WMZ 20 (Maps 17–19, 28–30)
This zone is known as the Regina – Moose Jaw WMZ and can only be hunted using shotguns and bows; no rifles. With its proximity to both major cities, the hunting is nothing spectacular, but you will find mule deer and white-tails feeding in the outskirts and upland game birds in the fields of wheatgrass.

WMZ 21, 22 (Maps 28, 29, 38–40, 50, 51)
Along with a healthy deer population, there is excellent moose and elk hunting in these zones. Highway 2 separates these regions, while Last Mountain Lake to the east is a mecca for migrating snow and white-fronted geese. This area is on the central flyway and there are numerous creeks and rivers that flow through the region and provide good habitat for migratory birds. Several species of grouse also call the areas home for the hunter vying for upland game birds.

HUNTING ADVENTURES

WMZ 23, 24 (Maps 25–28, 36–39)

As the Saskatchewan River runs directly along the border of these zones, hunters can have the opportunity to bag a variety of big and small game including mule deer and white-tails, elk and, to a lesser extent, moose. For the intrepid waterfowl hunter, the Qu'Appelle Valley, Luck Lake and the Gordon McKenzie Arm all have excellent duck and goose hunting since this region is on a major flyway and acts as stopover for migrating birds. This area is also known for its upland game bird hunting with ring-necked pheasant, Hungarian partridge and sharp-tailed grouse in abundance, especially moving west into WMZ 24.

WMZ 25 (Maps 25, 35, 36, 46, 47)

This area of Saskatchewan is barren, but that does not mean the hunting is poor. White-tails and mulies are in extreme abundance in these parts, and in the southern sector you may find the sure-footed pronghorn antelope. Whitebear Lake is east of Mondou and is the best place to try your luck for waterfowl. There are many farmlands in the area; make sure you are not on private land without permission when stalking your trophy buck.

WMZ 26 (Maps 34, 35, 45, 46, 56)

This zone is bordered on the west by Alberta and shares many of the same geographical traits. Described as aspen parkland, this area is along the transitional zone between the prairie region in the south and the boreal forest to the north. Here you will find the area overrun with mule and white-tailed deer, plus the impressive pronghorn antelope in the southern region. The Macklin Game Reserve sits in the extreme north of this zone.

WMZ 27 (Maps 45, 46, 47, 56, 57)

Located in the central western portion of Saskatchewan, this area is known for its excellent white-tailed deer hunting, as there is a large population within a relatively small area. Early morning and around dusk are generally the best times for hunting white-tails. This zone is pretty well your last chance for pronghorn since there are fewer and fewer as you head north form here. As always, check the regulations before heading out.

WMZ 28 (Maps 46, 47, 57)

Although small in comparison to some of the other areas, this zone has a lot to offer. Migratory birds along the western side of this zone are what most hunters come for. Lakes host the majority of waterfowl, but do not rule out the fields and farmlands for upland game birds. Between the towns of Ruthilda and Dodsland you will also find good mule and white-tailed deer populations.

WMZ 29 (Maps 36–38, 47–49)

Located south of Saskatoon, this zone features the Saskatchewan River running south to north in the eastern sector where you will find mule deer, white-tails and elk stopping along the banks for a refreshing drink. Migrating white-fronted and Ross' geese can be found in the spring and autumn seasons as well as partridge and grouse. This is prime country for the pesky coyote as well. Two major game preserves; Crystal Beach Lake and Outlook straddle the Saskatchewan River.

WMZ 30 (Maps 38, 39, 48–50, 58–60)

This zone is completely engulfed by the bigger city of Saskatoon. Around the city limits it is a shotgun, archery and muzzleloader area only zone. Further afield, the Saskatchewan River runs directly through the centre of the area and acts as a stopover for big game, waterfowl and upland game birds, especially further north.

WMZ 31, 32 (Maps 9–11, 21)

These zones are bordered on the south by North Dakota and to the east by Manitoba. The Souris River meanders along the south end of WMZ 31, bringing with it an abundance of white-tailed deer. Both zones are heavily populated so be on the lookout for predators like black bear and cougar as well as scavenging coyotes. This region is also great for migratory waterfowl and upland game birds.

WMZ 33 (Maps 10, 11, 20–22)

The main feature of this zone is Moose Mountain Provincial Park. Sandwiched between the towns of Stoughton and Carlyle, the park covers approximately 388 km² (240 mi²) of land; 80% is aspen poplar and balsam poplar forest. Here you will find a large population of white-tails and, to a lesser extent, mule deer, moose and elk. Adding to the mix are a variety of upland game birds like the sharp-tailed and ruffed grouse.

WMZ 34 (Maps 11, 20, 21, 22, 31–33)

Bordered on the north by the Trans-Canada Highway and to the east by the Manitoba border, the hunting in this area is focused around the hundreds of lakes, rivers, and creeks criss-crossing through this region. The area acts as a major stopover for migrating geese and ducks and is a hunter's dream for bagging that trophy buck or flushing out grouse, pheasants and partridge. Although low in numbers in this area, be on the lookout for the omnivorous black bear.

WMZ 35, 36 (Maps 21, 22, 29–33)

Winding its way through these two zones is the Qu'Appelle River, starting at the eastern border of Saskatchewan and stretching all the way west through Crooked Lake, Katepwa Point and Echo Valley Provincial Parks. Along the way you will find high populations of white-tailed deer, a small number of moose and elk around the town of Whitewood and black bear combing the river for a number of different prey. The area's marshes and lakes, as well as harvested grain fields, offer excellent waterfowl hunting where migratory birds often stop along their journey.

For a list of outfitters offering guided hunts contact the Saskatchewan Outfitters Association at (306) 763-5434 or visit them online at www.soa.ca.

WMZ 37 (Maps 31–33, 42–44, 54, 55)

Formed in the shape of a left facing boot, this zone is one of the largest in the southern province, bordered on the east by Manitoba, the south by Highway 22, the west by numerous lakes and rivers, and the north by the game bird district border. However, the main species here is white-tailed deer, which roam freely throughout the region. Make sure you are hunting on acceptable land as there are many provincial parks and private farmlands in this region.

WMZ 38, 39, 40 (Maps 29–31, 40–43, 51–54, 62, 63)

As the prairies creep closer to the aspen parkland in central Saskatchewan, wheat fields and grasslands slowly transition to aspen poplars and spruce-lined river valleys. Hundreds and hundreds of lakes and rivers are strewn amongst these zones from the Little Black Bear, Star Blanket, Okanese and Peepeekissis Indian Reserves in the south (no hunting without permission by the Chief or Band Council) to the beautiful and serene Quill Lakes in the north. The most common animal here is the white-tailed deer, but you can also find the odd moose and black bear lurking about. These areas make for great upland game bird hunting with species such as the sharp-tailed grouse and Hungarian partridge. The marshes and lakes offer some fantastic duck and goose hunting. Be sure to remember your binoculars so you can observe from a distance or see better in the thicker shrubbery of central Saskatchewan.

WMZ 41, 42 (Maps 50, 51, 60–63, 71)

From Colonsay and Lanigan in the south to Wakaw and St. Brieux in the northern sector, these zones offer fantastic white-tailed deer hunting. In fact, some of the biggest bucks can be found in this region along the shores of lakes and rivers. This is the largest boreal-grassland transition zone in the world, and is a zone of constant competition and tension as prairie and woodlands struggle to overtake each other within the aspen parkland. In WMZ 42, there are many wildlife refuges, bird sanctuaries and game preserves so make sure you are hunting within the appropriate area.

WMZ 43 (Maps 61–63, 71–73, 83)

Sandwiched between the flat, lonely prairies and the lush, green boreal forests of northern Saskatchewan, this transitional zone provides a hunter's paradise with the best of both worlds. There is an abundance of big mule and white-tailed deer roaming this area along with large herbivores like elk and moose being pursued by carnivorous predators such as cougar, black bear and wolf. Around where the Carrot River winds its way through the area, upland game bird hunting is very good with species of grouse, pheasant and, to a lesser extent, the northern ptarmigan.

WMZ 44 (Maps 58–60)

This tiny zone is bordered on the south, west and east by the fast flowing Saskatchewan River and to the north by Highway 40 and the north/south game bird districts. The Redberry Lake Wildlife Refuge and Bird Sanctuary sits in the northeast, so make sure you are not within these limits. White-tails and mulies roam in great numbers in the southern regions along the river. Also, look for moose, elk and black bear as this area slowly turns from aspen parkland to boreal forests.

HUNTING ADVENTURES

WMZ 45, 46 (Maps 47, 48, 56–58, 66, 67, 76)
Bordering along the Alberta border, this zone boasts good hunting where the prairie grasslands region meets the boreal forest transitional zone. Mule and white-tailed deer mingle with moose and elk, while various species of upland game birds such as grouse, pheasant and partridge inhabit the area. Around Manitoba Lake, in WMZ 46, is the best place to hunt as the big game species need to drink large amounts of freshwater. Predators like black bear and cougar roam the foothills looking to hunt as well.

WMZ 47 (Maps 57, 58, 66–68, 76, 77)
You will find all shapes and sizes of waterfowl the closer to the lakes you go, while white-tailed deer and black bear are the predominant big game animals. The deer population thins out as you move north, but there is plenty of upland bird hunting along the way as the coniferous forests of cedar, pine and fir make for great coverage as you move closer to moose country. Jackfish Lake is a watering hole for many mammals, but be cautious as the Murray Lake Bird Sanctuary sits on its southwest banks.

> *Be sure to check the annual hunters and trappers regulations guide for the area you are hunting in. It is available online through the Government of Saskatchewan's website.*

WMZ 48 (Maps 53–55, 63, 64)
This zone rests along the northern border of the north/south game bird districts offering up sharp-tailed, ruffed and spruce grouse. It is a perfect spot to find huge mule deer and white-tails and, to a lesser extent, elk. Black bear and cougars stalk this region in search of prey so be aware of your surroundings at all times. To the north is where the provincial forest WMZ's begin. This is the preferred habitat of the majestic moose, which can be seen striding through the stands of cedar, pine and hemlock.

WMZ 49 (Maps 63–65, 73–75, 83)
Horseshoed around Wildcat Hill Provincial Park, this zone has some great white-tailed deer hunting around the town of Porcupine Plain and Horsehide Lake. Moose, elk and black bear roam through this transitional region of coniferous forests and dense shrubbery. To the north, the Carrot River provides more of the same as big game stop for refreshing drinks along the banks.

WMZ 50, 51, 52 (Maps 59–61, 70–73, 81–83)
Sitting along the shores of the Saskatchewan River, these zones includes the towns of White Fox, Smeaton, Meath Park and the bigger city of Prince Albert. One would think the hunting would only be mediocre being so close to the city limits, but not so, as many trophy sized bucks have been taken down in this region. With the many farmlands interspersed with coniferous forests and dense shrubbery, this is prime country to hunt ruffed, spruce and sharp-tailed grouse. The moose and elk populations also starts to increase in size the further north you go as forests of cedar and pine loom ominously in the distance.

WMZ 53 (Maps 68–71, 78–80)
The Sturgeon River nips the northeast corner of this smaller zone located west of Prince Albert. In the northwest region, moose and black bear are starting to become more visible as the forests get thicker (Makwa Lake Provincial Park sits just north of Leoville,) and the land a little more remote. White-tails are a big attraction between Debden and Spiritwood in the central region of this zone. Prince Albert National Park occupies the northern quadrant of this zone and there is no hunting allowed in the park.

WMZ 54 (Maps 58–60, 68–70)
The Saskatchewan River runs up the eastern side of this mid-sized zone. While the mule deer population tends to decrease in this region, the white-tails thrive. In the north, moose and elk roam the expansive coniferous tree stands of spruce, fir and redwood. Ruffed and spruce grouse also attract game bird hunters in this mid-boreal upland biome.

WMZ 55 (Maps 76–78, 86–88)
This jagged zone sits between Meadow Lake and Makwa Lake Provincial Parks. There is quite a healthy population of trophy sized white-tailed bucks in the area as Beaver Lake rests in the northern region. Where there is water, there are deer. You may also find the odd moose skirting the edges of the parks, but they tend to retreat into deeper forested areas. Late September is a fine time to try calling in the more aggressive rutting bulls.

WMZ 56, 57 (Maps 53–55, 63–65)
Literally thousands of lakes dot these provincial forest zones, making for some of the best white-tailed deer, elk and moose hunting in the province without getting on a plane. Bordered to the east by Manitoba, this mid-boreal upland biome features a varied landscape that includes steeply sloping and eroded escarpments, hilly glacial till plains and level plateaus. Loamy, gray soils produce tall trees such as aspen, white spruce, jack pine, black spruce and tamarack making great hiding spots for tracking these big game herbivores.

WMZ 58 (Maps 65, 75, 85)
Bordered to the east by Manitoba and the south and west by the tall coniferous trees of the mid-boreal uplands, this zone is unique in the fact that it sits in a lowlands region of east-central Saskatchewan. This area is dominated by wetlands making for great waterfowl hunting, but also is a prime region for hunting black bear, moose and woodland caribou. These big game species can often be seen roaming through the large white spruce, balsam, poplar and aspen forests or amid the well-drained levees of the Saskatchewan River floodplain.

WMZ 59 (Maps 63–65, 73–75, 85)
Surrounding Wildcat Hill Provincial Park and covering 21, 772 hectares (53,799 ac), this zone features the Carrot River on the northern border and lowlands to the east as you travel closer to the Manitoba border. Characterized by fast flowing rivers, dense coniferous forests and some extremely rugged terrain, the area makes for great hunting as white-tailed deer, moose, black bear and, in the western sector, elk navigate their way through stands of aspen, spruce and pine.

WMZ 60, 61, 62 (Maps 72–75, 82–85, 95)
These three zones feature hundreds of lakes both big and small, plus the many rivers and creeks which flow in, out and around these bodies of water. This makes a virtual hunter's paradise with healthy populations of moose, black bear, elk and caribou weaving their way from lake to lake. The biggest lake by far in this region is Cumberland Lake in the extreme northern area, while Egg, Big and Highbank Lakes are not too shabby size-wise in the south and east either.

WMZ 63, 64, 65 (Maps 70–72, 80–82, 91, 92)
There are three big provincial parks within these three regions; Narrow Hills, Candle Lake and Clarence-Steepbank Lakes, respectively. Outside of these there are thousands of hectares with hundreds of drinking holes for some excellent big game hunting. This region is renowned for its white-tailed deer hunting with high populations of black bear, moose and elk. Look for spruce grouse lying motionless on the forest floor, using its camouflage to escape predators but causing them to be vulnerable to the keen-eyed hunter.

WMZ 66 (Maps 78–81, 88–91)
With Prince Albert National Park occupying its south-eastern quarter (no hunting allowed), there are three main areas for good big game hunting. Dore and Smoothstone Lakes in the north and Delaronde Lake to the south offer tall coniferous stands of aspen, jack pine, white and black spruce and tamarack that provide cover for moose, white-tails and black bear picking their way through the dense shrubbery. Be on the lookout for spruce grouse as well, as they sometimes will be metres away without being noticed. In order to improve your chances of spotting game birds and animals, wear natural colours and unscented clothing. Be sure to stay downwind and keep your movements to a minimum.

WMZ 67 (Maps 67–69, 77–79)
Scattered throughout the eastern region of this zone are numerous lakes, with Chitek Lake being the foremost in the south and Eyapawutik and Little Pelican Lakes on its northern shoulder. Here you are reaching the northern limits for white-tailed deer hunting, as their populations dwindle the further north you travel. However, this is prime hunting for black bear, moose and elk. Woodland caribou start to make an appearance in these parts as well.

WMZ 68S, 68N (Maps 76, 77, 86, 87)

These two small zones are stacked on top of each other. They are unique in the fact that 68S is within the Saskatchewan Provincial Forest range while its northern cousin is not. The Beaver River runs along the northern border of 68N all the way to the Alberta border to the west, while the southern regions provide landscapes of both boreal transition and mid-boreal upland. The boundary between these varying eco-regions seems to attract mule deer and white-tails in great numbers. In the low-lying farmlands you can find good upland game bird and waterfowl hunting.

WMZ 69 (Maps 77, 86–88, 98)

The majority of this zone is sandwiched between the Primrose Lake Air Weapons Range to the north and Meadow Lake Provincial Park to the south. This region is known as boreal transition since this is where Saskatchewan's agricultural land ends and the forests begin. The hunting here is good, with large populations of white-tailed deer, moose, elk and black bear roaming the diverse tundra. The hilly upland areas in this zone support tall stands of aspen, but white spruce and jack pine trees start to decrease the further north you go.

WMZ 70, 71 72 (Maps 82–85, 92–95, 100–105, 110–115, 117, 118)

Featuring the Churchill River flowing through much of Wildlife Management Zones 71 and 72, this area is bordered on the eastern side by Manitoba and provides thousands and thousands of hectares of prime hunting destinations. The landscape is rugged Precambrian Shield, with lakes and connecting rivers, streams and creeks accounting for 40% of the area. Amidst the low stands of black spruce and jack pine, you will find high populations of black bear, moose and woodland caribou. In the dense forest underbrush, look for the camouflaged spruce grouse to explode in a flurry of feathers when disturbed.

WMZ 73 (Maps 88–91, 96–101, 106–110, 116, 117)

Starting in the south near the town of Beauval and travelling north up through Ile-a-la-Crosse, Buffalo Narrows and La Loche, you will find tall stands of aspen and white spruce dispersed amongst the hundreds of lakes and rivers perfect for hunting big game such as black bear, moose, mule and white-tailed deer and woodland caribou. This large management zone is intersected by Highway 914 in the eastern quadrant, but other than that, the area is remote with many fly-in only locations.

WMZ 74 (Maps 110–118)

In the northeast of this zone, along the Manitoba border, sits the second largest lake in Saskatchewan, Reindeer Lake. Among the many indented shorelines and small islands, this lake draws a lot of big game as it is a major watering hole. High populations of moose, woodland caribou, black bear and timber wolf are reported to inhabit this region as the low stands of jack pine and black spruce mix with a scattering of white spruce and aspen. Both spruce grouse and ptarmigan share the dense forest floors. Southend is a small village resting on the southern shores of Reindeer Lake. With a population of approximately 700, the village makes a good base since it is found at the end of Highway 102.

WMZ 75 (Maps 116–120)

This rugged, remote region sits along the Alberta border and stretches across the province as far as Cree Lake in central Saskatchewan. The lake itself is 80 km (50 mi) long and 67.5 km (42 mi) wide with over 500 picturesque islands dotting the clear waters. The most common big game animal here is the woodland caribou, with lesser populations of moose and black bear. To the west is the Clearwater River flowing westward with forest cover along the shoreline of mainly jack pine. Many places along the shore are covered entirely with moss, making great sightlines for stalking game.

WMZ 76 (Maps 117–121)

This zone is the biggest in Saskatchewan, starting in the extreme north along the Alberta border and continuing east until Manitoba. There are two distinct biomes in this region. The Athabasca Plains and its spectacular sand dune area are found on the south shore of Lake Athabasca. These dunes are the most northerly, active sand dune region in the world with dunes reaching 30 metres (100 ft) high and stretching for over 100 km (60 mi). Populations of big game are scarce in this region with small pockets of migratory barren-ground caribou and the odd moose.

To the north of Lake Athabasca is the unique Tazin Lake Upland region with ancient Precambrian rocks towering 100 metres (325 ft) above the surrounding terrain of white spruce. The upper slopes are treeless, with a scattering of black spruce and jack pine found lower on these massive rocks. Moose and black bear are the most prevalent species here, but you can find small herds of migratory barren-ground caribou amongst bigger lakes in the eastern region like Black Lake and Wollaston Lake.

HUNTING TIPS FROM THE PROS

Be Scent Free
Wild animals are very sensitive to human smells. Take a scent-free shower before heading out and avoid using deodorant and scented lotions. Keep your hunting clothes sealed in a bag with leaves and dirt until you are in the bush and make sure to set up your stand downwind of your shooting area. Also consider using odour eliminating sprays.

Get There Early
Plan on leaving for your scouting position well before the first or last hours of daylight. Most animals are more active at daybreak and twilight and you want to be as still as possible during these times.

Bring the Right Gear
While a gun or bow and hunting knife are essential, you would be surprised how many people forget to bring rope or a tarp with them on a hunting trip. Make a list of items before heading out and go over it with your hunting buddy.

Mark Your Map
Go on scouting missions ahead of your hunt and use a topographic map or satellite imagery to mark exit and entry lanes, potential ambush spots, campsites, routes for bringing out the animal, etc.

Dress Appropriately
Because you will likely be outdoors through the fluctuating temperatures of early morning or late evening, it is best to wear layers so you can adjust your clothing accordingly.

Quality Glass
High quality optics are crucial for scouting. Binoculars with a minimum of 10x42 magnification are a good idea, while a tripod will add stability. If possible, be sure to add a spotting scope to your inventory to help calculate distances.

Know Your Weapon
Make sure to get plenty of practice with your weapon of choice before the start of hunting season. Being unfamiliar with your weapon will limit your chances of success and might cause your target to suffer more than it has to.

Canoeing on the Churchill River, Saskatchewan
©Tourism Saskatchewan / Chris Hendrickson Photography

PADDLING ADVENTURES

For folks interested in paddling, Saskatchewan offers two vastly different landscapes. Southern Saskatchewan is largely a dry land area with mixed grasslands. It is rare to find a river that is deep enough to float a boat, and many of the ones that are deep enough are best done as multi-day floats. Varying amounts of rainfall also affect the quality of both lakes and rivers throughout the whole region. Generally, rivers run to the sea, but that is not the case in much of Southern Saskatchewan where the drainage is internal. Run-off within these internal drainage systems can create saline lakes surrounded by white salt crusts, such as Chaplin Lake, Reed Lake, and Old Wives Lake.

But as you move north, the number of waterbodies increases drastically. Past Prince Albert, the prairie landscape has completely transformed into a land dominated by lakes and rivers. Paddling is not just possible; it is almost a necessity to get around up here, with fewer and fewer roads as you venture north. Air and water become the only means of travelling, making northern Saskatchewan a paddler's paradise.

Even in the north, water levels and canoeing conditions vary from month to month and year to year. New hazards appear, old ones disappear, and water levels might make paddling more difficult or even impossible. Paddlers always need to be alert.

Thrill-seekers interested in big water often run the waterways during the early spring when the winter run-off is at its peak. More casual canoeists can run these routes in the calmer waters of summer or pick routes that are more about the scenery and the wildlife. We have included the put-in and take-out locations for the most popular runs on that river. Also included are short descriptions highlighting the route along with a modified version of the international scale to grade rivers. The grade of a run tells you how difficult overall a stretch of river is. Class rates individual rapids, chutes and other features. In most cases, portages have been established to allow less experienced paddlers a chance to avoid the difficult features of any run.

Note that these descriptions given in this book are limited, and may not contain enough detail to navigate certain routes safely, especially rivers with higher ratings. We recommend that you check the current conditions with local canoeists or outdoor stores and always scout ahead. More details on some of these routes can be found online on the Canoe Saskatchewan website at *canoesaskatchewan.rkc.ca*.

Lac La Ronge Provincial Park, Saskatchewan
©Tourism Saskatchewan / Paul Austring

PADDLING ADVENTURES

Alameda Reservoir (Map 10/F4)
The Alameda Dam is located 3 km east of the town of Alameda on Moose Mountain Creek. Moose Creek Regional Park, one of the newest in Saskatchewan, provides access with two floating docks and a concrete boat launch on the eastern shore. The reservoir is 23 km (14 mi) long, allowing for a good day trip.

Amisk Lake to Cumberland House (Map 95/B6–85/G4)
This canoe trip follows a historic trade route linking the Churchill and Saskatchewan River systems. While the specs on this trip might look promising to novice paddlers—the trip is only 80 km (50 mi) long and can be completed in three or four days with a maximum of three portages, totalling approximately 440 metres (1,445 ft) – this is not a great route for beginners. There are many rapids that do not have developed portage trails. The trip starts at the outlet of Amisk Lake at the Sand Beach Recreation Site and follows Sturgeon-Weir River to Namew Lake. From Namew Lake to Cumberland House, the series of medium sized or large waterbodies, including Cross Bay and Cross Lake, are mostly shallow, weedy and unprotected. During strong winds, these lakes can become extremely rough. To shorten the trip, end at Sturgeon Landing, which can be accessed by vehicle from Highway 10 in Manitoba.

Amisk Lake: Missi Island Loop (Map 95/A3)
This 48 km (30 mi) paddle can be done in a couple or three days and is a good option for novice paddlers interested in a northern paddle. There are no portages along the main route, but there is the possibility of strong winds and a chance of getting lost amidst the many smaller islands and reefs around the big island. If the weather is good at the start of the trip, it is best to travel clockwise around the island, as this gets the most exposed portion of the trip out of the way first. The route is basically a circumnavigation of Missi Island, but people often explore side routes such as paddling up Neagle Creek and into Grassy and Wolverine Lakes. The put-in and take-out is at the community of Denare Beach.

Antelope Lake (Map 14/A1)
Antelope Lake has a fluctuating water level that changes the look of the lake from time to time. The lake is also open to motorized boats, personal watercraft and other forms of lake recreation that can affect paddling quality. The Antelope Lake Regional Park found east of Highway 37 provides access.

Bagwa Canoe Route (Map 80/B3)
One of the easiest places to paddle in Prince Albert National Park, the Bagwa Canoe Route begins on Kingsmere Lake, northwest of Waskesiu. The route can be done in a day but works best as an overnight trip. The route starts from a parking lot at the end of Kingsmere Road. From here you paddle 400 metres (1,300 ft) and then immediately take-out and carry your canoe for 1 km (0.6 mi). Fortunately, there is a rail cart here. Once back in the water, a bit of route finding is needed as the river is extremely shallow until you get to Kingsmere Lake. Stay left along the western shore of the large lake. If the weather is nice, head to Pease Point, turning west into the protected waters of Bagwa Channel, which leads into Bagwa Lake and through a channel into Lily Lake. There is a 200 metre (655 ft) portage into Claire Lake, and a second portage of about the same length brings you back to Kingsmere Lake and the return home.

> *Proper planning of your canoe trip is essential. In general, over 4 to 6 hours of travel time you should be able to cover between 10 and 15 km (6 and 9 mi).*

Besnard Lake Circuit (Map 100/F3–111/A7)
Besnard Lake is found west of La Ronge off of the gravel Highway 910. The starting point for this loop trip is either the bridge at the central narrows of Besnard Lake or the recreation site found northeast of the bridge. The 180 km (112 mi) route should take about a week to paddle and has 8 or 9 portages. The route is moderately difficulty, involving travel on several large lakes, including Neale, Bar, Pinehouse, Sandfly and Black Bear Island Lakes, which can become quite rough. The longest portage is 1.5 km (1 mi) long, but the portages are not always easy to find. Even though much of the route is on big lakes, there are sections of travel that involve some shallow, narrow, overgrown channels and streams that may have to be lined. There are no dangerous rapids that cannot be portaged, but no matter which way paddlers travel, portions of the route involve paddling or lining upstream. While the route can be travelled in either direction, clockwise is probably easier.

Big Sandy Lake and the Geikie River (Map 117/F4–118/B2)
From Big Sandy Lake, this route is around 80 to 100 km long (50 to 60 mi), depending on the route taken. The trip can last up to a week, although most people do it in less time than that. There are only four portages along the route, which is extremely isolated. The only access to Big Sandy Lake is by air, and there are many long and dangerous rapids to navigate. Portage trails that do exist are in poor shape. Many times, paddlers are forced to run tricky rapids or incorporate strenuous wading and portaging. Needless to say, this one should be left for experienced paddlers. The trip ends at the Highway 905 Bridge over the Geikie River at the recreation site. Another alternative is to paddle to Wollaston Post, where there is no road access, but there is regular air service.

Black Lake to Flett Lake, NWT (Map 120/D5–G1)
At 169 km (105 mi) long, most people take at least a week to paddle this route. Black Lake is just about as far north as you can drive in the province (the road terminates 20 km/12.5 mi farther on at Stony Rapids), although many people actually fly in to the lake, as it is 1,000 kilometres and 20 hours north of Saskatoon by road. The route leading north via Chipman Lake, Bompas Lake and Selwyn Lake was originally explored in 1893, however, that party had two canoes overturn and one member died from exposure. This is not a place for people who are not experienced and extremely fit. This is as remote a canoe trip as can be done in the province with long, rough portages – the first of twelve portages is 5 km (3 mi) long.

Bladebone Canoe Route (Map 80/C4–79/G2)
The Bladebone Canoe Route is a rigorous four-or five-day trip featuring some long, steep portages. Some have even called this a portage route, rather than a paddling route. The route starts on Kingsmere Lake, which can be quite busy. Once you leave the big, sometimes windy lake, the route is much more remote on small lakes and it is common to have the route to yourself. From the northwest end of Kingsmere Lake, the route heads through a number of small and mid-sized lakes, including Mikisew, Bladebone, Mitawanga, Heming, Osten, Purvis and Nova Lakes. From Nova Lake, it is possible to head southwest and out of the park and connect up with a road there, saving yourself the need to carry your canoe back along the many portages.

Brabant Lake to McLennan Lake (Map 113/C3–112/E5)
This route passes through several lakes, with 12 portages, but is only 86 km (53 mi) long, which is a sign that none of the lakes are very big. The launching point is on Brabant Lake, across the highway from the tiny community of the same name. The paddling is fairly easy with no dangerous rapids (the rapids that do exist are mostly shallow and need to be portaged) and some good fishing is to be found in the lakes. The most difficult part of the drip is passing out of Doerksen Bay through a reedy channel, where a small, nearly hidden stream enters the main channel from the left side; the route continues this way and not along the main channel. The portages are all relatively short, the longest being about 400 metres (1,300 ft), and the whole trip should take between 4 or 5 days.

Brabant Lake to Otter Lake (Map 113/C3–102/B1)
The put-in for this 125 km (78 mi) paddle is Brabant Bay, about 90 km north of the Churchill River on the Canam Highway (Hwy 102). Like many routes in the area, it was historically used by first nations and later, fur traders travelling between Stanley Mission and the Wathaman Lake area. The route should take less than a week to paddle and has 14 portages to maneuver around rapids mostly. Paddlers need to pay attention leaving Doerksen Bay, as the main channel is not the canoe route; instead, there is a slight thinning of the reeds on the left bank to mark the entrance of a small stream. The route continues through Kakabigish Lake, Kemp Lake, and Mountain Lake to Otter Lake and the take-out at the Devils Lake or Missinipe Recreation Sites, also on Highway 102. There is good fishing for walleye and, in the larger lakes, lake trout. The entire trip should take most paddlers between five or six days.

Brabant Lake to Reindeer Lake (Map 113/C3–F1; 118/D6)
From Brabant Lake to the town of Southend on Reindeer Lake, this trip is 112 km (70 mi) long and will take the better part of a week to do. The Wapiaskau River is quite a difficult river with many rapids and portages, so this route is best left to more experienced paddlers. There are 15 (or 16) portages along this route, with the longest being 425 metres (1,395 ft). The later portions of the route through Steephill Lake and the Reindeer River are much easier to travel.

Brabant Lake to Sandy Bay (Map 113/C3–104/G2)
This 225 km (140 mi) route starts at Brabant Lake and is a long, demanding trip with many rapids and portages. It will take most paddlers the better part of two weeks to complete this route along the Wapiskau River, Steephill Lake, the Reindeer River and the Churchill River. There are between 21 to 25 portages, many of them short, but the longest is 990 metres (3,250 ft). There is good fishing along the route. The easiest section is the middle, along the Reindeer River, where there are no rapids and only a few portages.

Bright Sand Lake (Map 67/D1–77/D7)
This lake, 27 km east of St. Walburg, offers a nice area to canoe or sail. As such, wind can be an issue here at times. Access is via the Bright Sand Lake Regional Park where there are also 28 km (17.5 mi) of hiking trails.

Buffalo Narrows to Turnor Lake (Map 116/E7–E6)
From Buffalo Narrows, this northern route leads some 100 km (60 mi) north to Turnor Lake. The trip starts with a long crossing of the exposed Churchill Lake where wind can pose a problem. From here the route cuts through Fulton Bay on its way to Frobisher Lake and its many nooks and crannies. Make your way over to Nipawin Bay and the end Highway 909, which is the common take-out point. It is possible to work your way north into Turnor Lake and take out at the community of the same name.

Buffalo Pound Lake (Map 28/D3–G5)
This 35 km (22 mi) long and 2 km (1.2 mi) wide lake follows the valley of a ravine corridor. The lake gets its name from the historic spot where bison were once driven over the valley edge in what was called buffalo pounding. You can enter the lake in Buffalo Pound Provincial Park or further north at Sand Point Beach. Full facilities are available in the provincial park.

Chief Whitecap Waterway (Map 38/A4–49/C3)
Starting from the Gardiner Dam, this 120.5 km (75 mi) paddling journey takes you through the remote and beautiful South Saskatchewan River landscape all the way to the city of Saskatoon. With multiple access points, you can make this journey as short or long as you like, and with multiple established campsites along the way it is easy to turn this into a multi-day adventure. Campsites can be found near the Gardiner Dam at the beginning of your journey, at Outlook 32 km (20 mi) in, at Big Pipe around 55 km (34 mi) in and at the Dakota Dunes around 90 km (56 mi) in. Other points of interest along the route include the Wolf Willow Winery and the Beaver Creek Conservation Area. One popular take-out point in Saskatoon is found at the CP railway bridge near 33rd Street; however, there is a portage required to get around the 2 metre (6 ft) weir above the take-out. This route is part of the Trans Canada Trail.

Clearwater River: Lloyd Lake to Warner Rapids (Map 116/D3–D4)
Most paddlers take a week to paddle from the put-in at the end of a 3 km road that is found off Highway 955, 122 km north of La Loche. This road is only passible in fair weather and it may be necessary to carry canoes down the road. There are only three portages along this stretch of the Clearwater River, but there are a half-dozen more rapids that paddlers might prefer to walk around. Many of the rapids are shallow and rocky, and best done in early summer. This is a remote trip and should only be done by experienced trippers. Anglers can find arctic grayling, pike and walleye. A note to paddlers: Highway 955 is a coarse, cut rock gravel road and two spare tires are recommended.

Clearwater River: Warner Rapids to Fort McMurray (Map 116/D4–A4)
Leading from the campground on the Clearwater River, 55 km northeast of La Loche, to Fort McMurray, Alberta, this 210 km (131 mi) trip will take experienced paddlers at least a week to do. There are seven to 13 portages along the route, with a number of them over 1,000 metres (3,280 ft), and the paddling can be challenging. The Clearwater was a key link during the height of the fur trade period. Peter Pond was the first European to cross the Methye Portage in 1778 and the Clearwater River became a prime exploration and trade route between the Hudson Bay and Arctic watersheds for over 100 years.

Cold River: Pierce Lake to Lac Des Iles (Map 86/E5–87/B5)
This short paddle through Meadow Lake Provincial Park incorporates sections of lake and river travel along the Cold River. There are some rapids along the river, but nothing that will need to be portaged. The 35 km (22 mi) paddle, with no portages, from Howe Bay on the southeast shore of Pierce Lake to Highway 26 Bridge over the Waterhen River east of Lac Des Iles can be done in one day, but is best done as an overnight trip. Experienced paddlers might continue on down the Waterhen River to connect with the Waterhen-Beaver River Canoe Route, although this stretch of water is not recommended for novice paddlers since there are no portage trails. Some rapids may be lined.

Crean Lake (Map 80/E3)
This trip starts from the Hanging Heart Lakes Marina and passes through the Hanging Heart Lakes (three small lakes) before passing into the large Crean Lake. There are a number of interesting destinations around the lake, including the old Chipewyan Portage on the western shores of the lake, which connected Crean Lake to Kingsmere Lake. Paddlers should not get too excited as the portage trail, if it still existed, would be 15 km (9 mi) one-way, with only a couple small lakes to break up the carry. Along the eastern shores, paddlers can paddle to Jackfish Bay and Lost Lake or all the way to Moose Bay in the northwest corner of the lake. Big Island is a popular destination, but paddlers need to be wary if the wind picks up. There are four wilderness campgrounds with 2-3 campsites each that come equipped with a bear cache and firewood.

Cree Lake to Patuanak (Map 117/C3–116/G6)
Access to the start of this trip is by air. From Leavitt Bay on Cree Lake, it is about 257 km (160 mi) to Patuanak, which will take at least a week to paddle. The trip is best left to experienced paddlers confident in their wilderness abilities. The route, which runs through the Brustad River, Gwillim River, Mudjatik River, Churchill River and Shagwenaw Lake, has a number of rapids to navigate. The most challenging sections have portages, of which there are 12 total. The longest is 2 km (1.2 km) and a second is just under half that. Also, travel is upstream on the Churchill, which means taking all portages and lining up most of the Drum Rapids. There is also a section of upstream paddling on the Brustad River; the rest of the river travel is downstream along some relatively swift moving rivers, making travelling this route in reverse difficult. There are a number of other canoe routes that connect to this one, making a trip of a few weeks or even a few months possible.

Crooked Lake (Map 32/B4)
Crooked Lake is a natural lake created by the Qu'Appelle River as it flows through a series of low hills near the city of Melville. Crooked Lake Provincial Park provides great access to both the lake and Qu'Appelle River system. Canoe rentals are available near the park.

Cypress Lake (Map 1/E2)
Cypress Lake is a dammed body of water created for irrigation projects. Today, the reservoir is being utilized more and more for recreational purposes. Access is available from the Cypress Recreation Site west of Highway 21. The lake is 11 km (7 mi) long and 3 km wide, and does allow motorboat access. Heglund Island, a bird sanctuary, is located on the lake and visitors are asked to give it a wide berth.

Deschambault Lake to Maligne Lake (Map 93/E4–94/E2)
This 150 km (93 mi) paddle starts at Mile 146 of the Hanson Lake Road (Highway 106), which passes close to Ballantyne Bay on Deschambault Lake. This is not a good place to leave a vehicle so it is recommended to find a shuttle or ask to park at the nearby resort/fishing camp. The route to Maligne Lake via Pelican Narrows, Mirond Lake and the Sturgeon-Weir River features lots of big lake travel, so be wary of the weather and build in a couple days to wait out the wind. If the weather is in your favour, it will take less than a week to complete. The route has four or five portages and can be travelled in either direction.

Deschambault Lake to Sandy Bay – Northeast Route
(Map 93/E4–104/G2)
It is just less than 200 km (120 mi) from the campground at the south end of the southeast arm of Deschambault Lake to Sandy Bay. To cut this trip by 65 km (40 mi), more experienced paddlers could choose to put-in at Pelican Narrows. Since the first section of the trip on the many bays and arms of Deschambault Lake is very sheltered with no rapids to speak of, inexperienced wilderness travellers might choose to end at Pelican Narrows. Past Pelican Narrows, the route calls for more portaging and navigational challenges, especially along the Nemei River, which has some tough portages, 18 in total, with the longest being 650 metres (2,130 ft). The route also incorporates Wunehikun Bay on Mirond Lake, Attitti, Kakinagimak and Nemei Lakes, to name a few.

Deschambault Lake to Sandy Bay – Northwest Route
(Map 93/E4–104/G2)
Weighing in at 170 km (105 mi) and just under a week's paddle, there are 15 portages, with the longest being 100 metres (330 ft), along this alternate route from Deschambault Lake to Sandy Bay. The first section of the trip is easy paddling with few challenges but some nice scenery and great fishing. Past Pelican Narrows, the route becomes much more challenging as it crosses through via Mirond Lake and Wunehikun Bay, Attitti Lake, Belcher Lake, Mukoman Lake, Ohoo Lake, Mukoman River and Sokatisewin Lake.

PADDLING ADVENTURES

Eagle Creek (Map 48/D2–59/A7)
Eagle Creek does not get paddled much since the stream is only navigable in early spring during run-off, when the water is bitterly cold. The 23 km (14 mi) route north from Eagle Creek Regional Park to the Ed and May Scissions Environmental Centre on Grid Road 784 West of Martensville offers plenty of easy rapids. Anglers can find northern pike, walleye and burbot.

Echo Lake (Map 30/F3)
Echo Lake is popular for its beaches, although water levels do fluctuate. Access and camping are available through the Echo Valley Provincial Park, while supplies are available at the B-Say-Tah store along the south side of Echo Lake, about 3 km from the park. Echo is one of the central lakes of the Calling Lakes chain in the Qu'Appelle Valley, nestled between Pasqua and Mission. All of the lakes are connected by the Qu'Appelle River, which provides the opportunity to continue paddling for several days.

Fife Lake (Map 6/B5)
While this lake is affected by drought conditions, it is big enough to offer people a chance to get out on the lake in a canoe or kayak. The peaceful area is quite scenic as it is surrounded by trees. Access to the lake is through Rockin Beach Regional Park north of Highway 18.

Remember that river conditions are always changing and advanced scouting is essential.

Frenchman River (Map 3/G5–4/B6)
The Frenchman River enters Grasslands National Park below the village of Val Marie, which is also where the park office and Information Centre are located. Rich in historical and fishing opportunities, the area also abounds with birds and wildlife. Water levels can get very low, even in the spring, and wading is required. Bring rubber boots and hiking shoes. The river is murky brown, and, although the banks are low, bush often impedes the view. The access point is found about 6.5 km south of Val Marie on Highway 4. Look for Butte Road leading east to the bridge crossing. This is a drop-point only, so vehicles may not be left. An alternate put-in is found at the Trottier House, about 1.6 km (1 mi) downstream. The take-out is found at Belza Bridge, which is accessed east of Val Marie on a dirt road that leads south from Highway 18. Wilderness camping is allowed in the park by permit. For more information and water conditions call 306-298-2257.

Garden River (Map 71/E5)
To get to the Garden River, head northeast from Prince Albert on Highway 55. Turn east onto the Cycil Ferry Road (Grid Road 780) and drive for 11 km. Watch for a pair of bridges over the river. The put-in is up the hill, then right onto the first grid road, which becomes a dirt track that is impassable in wet weather. The river can only be run when the water is high in the spring. There are many sweepers and this short section is better left to strong paddlers. The run south to the North Saskatchewan River is only 6.5 km (4 mi) long. Look for the take-out at the gravel bar on this bigger river's left. As the river drops 27 metres (90 ft) in its short run, it is not recommended for novice paddlers.

Grey Owl's Cabin (Map 80/B2)
This is not such much as a paddling route as it is a pilgrimage. The story of Grey Owl is legend in Canada and around the world – an Englishman who dressed as a native, a trapper who became one of the world's first conservationists. The cabins (there are actually two) can be accessed by hiking trail or by watercraft. Most of this trip is on the large, often windy Kingsmere Lake, although there is a short section along the Kingsmere River that requires a fair bit of portaging to navigate. A final 600 metre (1,970 ft) portage leads to Ajawaan Lake where the cabins can be found along the western shore.

Heart Lakes Canoe Route (Map 80/E4)
From the Hanging Heart Lakes Marina, this trip takes about five hours to paddle, passing through the three Heart Lakes to Crean Lake, where there is a campground called Crean Kitchen. The 18 km (11 mi) route can easily be done in a day, but many people do it as a lazy overnighter. There are three campsites and a shared kitchen shelter, along with a bear cache and firewood at the Crean Kitchen campground. It is also possible to explore Crean Lake further. Along the eastern shores, paddlers can paddle to Jackfish Bay and Lost Lake or all the way to Moose Bay in the northwest corner of the lake. Big Island is a popular destination, but paddlers need to be wary if the wind picks up.

Ile-a-la-Crosse to Otter Lake via the Churchill River (Map 98/F2–111/A7–102/B1)
This is one of the longer canoe routes in the province, weighing in at 386 km (240 mi), and will take up to two weeks to paddle. There are about 13 portages, with at least two over 1,000 metres (3,280 ft), that everyone will need to do and another seven or so that can be run by more experienced paddlers. Paddlers can start at the village of Ile-a-la-Crosse, although starting from the community of Patuanak shortens this trip by approximately 65 km (40 mi) and two to three days. There are a few sections of this long, remote trip that are challenging, and it is best left to experienced wilderness paddlers. There are a number of big lakes including Lac Ile-a-la-Crosse, Knee, Pinehouse, Sandfly, Black Bear Island and McIntosh where the wind can pick up, and a number of tough rapids. Most paddlers will choose to head downstream, as paddling upstream on the Churchill is challenging. It can be done, and it was how the voyageurs crossed this area, but it is hard work. The take-out is on Otter Lake at the Devils Lake or Missinipe Recreation Sites.

Jewel Creek (Map 9/A3)
Jewel Creek is one of three streams flowing into the Rafferty Dam/Reservoir project. The Jewel has potential for paddling in the early spring season or around the reservoir during the summer. The Jewel meets with the Souris River and Roughbark Creek at Mainprize Regional Park, which is the area's main paddling access point.

Katepwa Lake (Map 30/G3–31/A4)
Katepwa Lake is the easternmost of the four Qu'Appelle or Calling Lakes in the Qu'Appelle Valley. The Qu'Appelle River connects the four lakes, allowing paddlers to venture further northwest. The resort villages of Katepwa Beach and Sandy Beach on the north shores of Lake Katepwa offer supplies. Katepwa Point Provincial Park has a boat launch and other facilities, including canoe rentals.

Kenosee Lake (Map 21/F6)
Kenosee Lake is an ideal spot for paddling since motorized boats are not allowed on the popular Moose Mountain Park lake. A boat launch is located on Manitoba Street in the resort village of Kenosee Lake. Paddlers are advised to watch for hidden rocks in the shallow areas of the lake.

Lac La Loche to Ile-A-La-Crosse (Map 116/C5–98/F2)
From the community of La Loche, this challenging week-long plus trip follows an historic fur trade route and has a fair amount of travel on big, potentially windy lakes. As a result, ample time should be given for wind delays when planning. The 208 km (130 mi) paddle, which leads through the La Loche River, Peter Pond Lake, Buffalo Narrows, the Churchill River and the Aubichon Arm on Lac Ile-A-La-Crosse, has only one portage, and there is an optional side trip via the Methye Portage.

Lac Pelletier (Map 14/E4)
This lake is only 25 km south of the Trans-Canada Highway at Swift Current and is a popular destination. The area is situated within a well treed, scenic valley. The lake is naturally fed by springs that drain into Swift Current Creek and water levels are predictable. Access is available through Lac Pelletier Regional Park.

Lake Charron (Map 62/F6)
Located near Naicam, the lake can be accessed from the Lake Charron Regional Park and has a few small islands whose shorelines can be explored by canoe or kayak.

Lake Diefenbaker (Maps 25, 26, 27, 38)
Fed by the South Saskatchewan and Qu'Appelle Rivers, Lake Diefenbaker is a large waterbody that offers endless coves and bays to explore. However, the size of the lake can create difficulties such as afternoon wind, while boat traffic can be heavy. The many parks and recreation sites that line the lake offer good access points, camping or other facilities. These include Cabri Regional Park, which provides access to the northwest loop of the lake, and Douglas Provincial Park, which provides access to the eastern tip of the lake and 20 km (12 mi) of natural sandy shoreline. It is possible to put-in at Elbow Harbour Recreation Site and Palliser Regional Park for some nice paddling, but be aware that these are popular boat launches as well. Herbert Ferry Regional Park offers some excellent sheltered paddling along a natural cove, and Prairie Lake Regional Park is another good option for finding some sheltered routes. Paddlers can also try putting in at Riverhurst Ferry Recreation Site and Saskatchewan Landing Provincial Park – wherever you choose to paddle, gorgeous scenery abounds.

La Ronge to Deschambault Lake – Southern Route (Map 101/E6–93/E4)
This 169 km (105 mi) paddling trip should take a week or so to complete, but time needs to be built into schedules for rough weather, as there are three big lakes along this route. It is not a trip for beginners, as there are plenty of rapids and some long portages up to 1.5 km (0.9 mi) long, as well. There are also some extremely remote sections along this trip, requiring paddlers to be self-sufficient. The main waterbodies along this route are Lac La Ronge, Wapawekka Lake, Deschambualt River and Deschambault Lake. The take-out is located on Ballantyne Bay at the resort near Mile 146 of the Hanson Lake Road (Highway 106).

La Ronge to Deschambault Lake – Northern Route (Map 101/E6–93/E4)
Like all the routes that start on Lac La Ronge, there are a number of options of where to put-in. Most people start at La Ronge itself, but English Bay and Wadin Bay are also alternatives. This paddle is about 454 km (282 mi) and will take anywhere from a week to ten days to complete. There are 13 to 14 portages depending on the route taken. Much of the route is exposed on big lakes (Lac La Ronge, Hale, Iskwatikan, Nistowiak, Drinking, Keg, Trade, Wood, Pelican and Deschambault Lakes); ample time should be given for wind delays. This route incorporates the Churchill River to Pelican Narrows, part of the historic Canadian Northwest trade route. The scenery is gorgeous and campsites are ample. The take-out is located on Ballantyne Bay at the resort near Mile 146 of the Hanson Lake Road (Highway 106).

La Ronge to Jan Lake (Map 101/E6–94/C1)
Incorporating Lac La Ronge, Iskatikan Lake, the Churchill River and Pelican Narrows before heading onto Jan Lake, this route is about 250 km (155 mi) long. The trip takes around a week and incorporates 12 to 15 portages, the longest being 100 metres (330 ft), depending on the route chosen. The route starts on Lac La Ronge, at the town of La Ronge, English Bay or Wadin Bay. Most of the route is along open, exposed lakes and paddlers should give themselves enough time for bad weather. This route incorporates the Churchill River to Pelican Narrows, which is one of the most famous sections of water in the province, with plenty of scenery and camping spots. There is little current on the river sections of this route, so it can be done in either direction or as an out-and-back route. Doupe Bay is at the east end of Jan Lake, where paddlers will find a campground and the community of Jan Lake, which has road access to Highway 135.

La Ronge to Maligne Lake (Map 101/E6–94/E2)
Starting on Lac La Ronge, this route passes through Iskwatikan Lake, along the Churchill River to Pelican Narrows, through Mirond Lake and along the Sturgeon-Weir River to Maligne Lake. Depending on the route you take and your put-in, this trip is between 245 and 270 km (152-168 mi) long with 15-18 portages. Paddlers can put-in at La Ronge, English Bay or Wadin Bay and head across the lake, but this is not recommended except in calm weather. There are also a few optional portages at Nut Point, English Bay and from Wadin Bay to Ore Bay on Lac La Ronge. It should take most paddlers seven to 10 days to complete the route, but time needs to be set aside for bad weather. The Churchill River section includes a famous section of water that was paddled by the voyageurs as well as passing by Nistowiak Falls. The river sections of this route are very slow and can be paddled in either direction, but be wary of rapids and falls.

La Ronge to Otter Lake (Map 101/E6–102/B1)
This 92 km (57 mi) paddle has 15 portages (some that are optional, depending on skill level), all relatively short, and it will take most groups four or five days to complete. The paddle starts on Lac La Ronge and most people put-in at the town of La Ronge, but some people will put-in at English Bay or Wadin Bay. The take-out is at Otter Lake at the Devils Lake or Missinipe Recreation Sites on Highway 102. The large, often windy lake can be avoided entirely by launching at Lynx Lake. While the first section of the paddle is very exposed on the big lake, the route then travels a series of protected lakes and rivers. Because the rivers along this route are so slow moving, it is possible to do the route in reverse, or to double the length of the trip by turning around and heading back to La Ronge once you reach Otter Lake.

La Ronge to Stanley Mission via Fred Lake Circle Route
(Map 101/E6–102/C2–102/D5)
Stretching for 193 km (120 mi), this loop trip will take a week to ten days to complete. Paddlers can start at La Ronge, English Bay or Wadin Bay before passing through Lynx, Sulphide, Freda, McNichol, Otter, Mountain, Drope, Nistowiak and Iskwatikan Lakes (to name a few) and back into Lac la Ronge. There are a few sections of river travel with some current, but not enough to prevent paddlers from traveling this route in the reverse direction. There are

between 18 to 23 portages, depending on start and end points and paddler experience, the longest being 1,000 metres (3,280 ft). While the big Lac La Ronge is very exposed, the other lakes and streams are sheltered, until passing onto the lakes along the Churchill River system between Otter Lake and Nistowiak Falls. This section is one of the most historic waterways in the province, passing by the Stanley Mission Church.

La Ronge to Stanley Mission via Hunt Lake Circle Route
(Map 101/E6–102/C3)
Starting on Lac La Ronge, this route passes through Stroud, Hunt, Mountain, Drope, Nistowiak and Iskwatikan Lakes before returning to Lac La Ronge. The 170 km (106 mi) route can be started from La Ronge, English Bay or Wadin Bay. The route has 18 to 23 portages, depending on the start and end points chosen and individual skill and comfort levels, with the longest being 1,100 metres (3,610 ft). Along the way, it passes the historic community of Stanley Mission, site of the oldest church in Saskatchewan, Nistowiak Falls and the famous four portages route. The route can be done in either direction, and, in an emergency, it would be possible to take-out at Stanley Mission.

Last Mountain Lake (Map 29/D3–40/A4)
Last Mountain Lake is 80 km (50 mi) long and 2 to 3 km (1.2-1.9 mi) wide, and is easily accessed from Regina Beach Recreation Site west of Highway 54 and just north of the town of Lumsden, or Rowan's Ravine Provincial Park. However, it is rated one of the best fishing lakes in southern Saskatchewan, so expect a lot of motorboats during peak periods. Waterskiing is also popular due to the size of the lake. Canoe rentals are available and the lake is large enough for sea kayaks. The Last Mountain Lake Bird Sanctuary and National Wildlife Area is located at the north end of the lake.

Loch Leven (Map 12/E6)
Situated in the Cypress Hills Provincial Park this tiny shimmering body of water is surrounded by Lodgepole pines and other trees. It is one of the most scenic areas in the province and is a delight to canoe. Canoes and paddleboats are available to rent by the hour here.

Long Creek (Map 8/B3–9/G6)
Long Creek, a major tributary of the Souris River, flows past the town of Radville and the Radville-Laurier Regional Park. The park is a good spot to put-in or take-out during early spring. While water levels fluctuate on the creek, paddling is also an option around the Boundary Dam Reservoir, which is part of the creek south of Estevan. The reservoir holds smallmouth bass, while the creek also offers pike and perch.

Lower Waddy Lake to Wathaman Lake (Map 118/B6–C4)
This week-long, 145 km (90 mi) paddle starts at Lower Waddy Lake, just northwest of Brabant Lake and Highway 102. The route to Wathaman Lake takes you through Upper Waddy Lake, Nistoassini Lake, Nayelles Lake, Elephant Lake, Macoun Lake, Buss Lake and Davin Lake and features a number of longer, more challenging portages that should scare away inexperienced paddlers. But, while the portages are tough, the paddling is mostly easy. Macoun Lake is large and prone to wind, but the rest of the route offers mostly sheltered paddling. The majority of the 23 portages are short, with a few over 500 metres (1,640 ft) in length. Those looking to sample an easier portion of this trip, can paddle to the north end of McKenzie Lake and return, a distance of about 80 km (50 mi).

Lynx Lake Circuit (Map 101/G4–102/A3)
This 53 km (33 mi) route offers easy paddling, but some long portages, so paddlers should travel as light as they can. If they travel light enough, this route can be done in two days, although most people do it in three or four. There are 19 portages, but no rapids to speak of. However, the longest portage is over 1,000 metres (3,280 ft). Starting at Lynx Lake, the route leads through Sulphide Lake, Freda Lake, Freestone Lake, Hebden Lake, Contact Lake and back to Sulphide Lake. It is a good next step for people who have just cut their teeth on overnight canoe trips.

Lynx Lake to MacKay Lake (Map 101/G4–102/A3)
This 21 km (13 mi) route features 7 portages and typically takes 2 to 3 days to complete. The trip put-in is at the Lynx Lake Picnic Area north of La Ronge on Highway 102, and take-out is the Mackay Lake Recreation Site. The route runs through Sulphide, Contact and Kuskawo Lakes and offers some great wildlife viewing as well as fishing. The lakes are all fairly small and sheltered and there are no rapids to speak of. Although rough in sections, the longest portages are less than 500 metres (1,640 ft) long, while the islands offer some good campsites for overnight trips.

Makwa River (Map 77/E1)

Found west of Meadow Lake, the Makwa is a fun and challenging whitewater river. The put-in for this short 5 km (3 mi) run is found 14 km west of Highway 4 on the grid road leading to the small community of Compass. Many people start the run by shooting the culvert under the road! The river has lots of great whitewater features and stretches of Class II rapids as it makes its way north towards the Beaver River. Look for the take-out about 4.5 km along the winding road that leads north along the west side of the river from the put-in. Water levels are important, if the water is too low, paddlers will spend lots of time walking over the rocks, while when the water is too high, the features are underwater. The best time is typically May.

Maligne Lake to Amisk Lake (Map 94/E2–95/B4)

This 85 km (53 mi) paddle is a nice way for novice paddlers to get some multi-day tripping experience (preferably under the leadership of an experienced paddler), as it should take most groups three or four days. There are two to five portages, depending on the route chosen. The put-in is near the bridge at Maligne Lake (km 275 of the Hanson Lake Road/Highway 106), but most park at nearby Leaf Rapids Recreation Site if doing a multi-day trip. The route follows the historic thoroughfare for trappers, traders and explorers down the Sturgeon-Weir River to the community of Denare Beach on Amisk Lake. While the current on the Sturgeon-Weir River is not very strong, most people prefer travelling downstream.

McLennan Lake Circuit (Map 112/F4)

This 41 to 48 km (25-30 mi) trip is too long to do in a day, but can be done in two or possibly three, making it a great weekend outing. There are eight portages along the way, although none are too long making it is a nice, easy trip for beginners. The put-in is at the recreation site on the western shores of McLennan Lake. There are no rapids to run, nor any large expanse of unprotected water to cross. The loop, which includes MacLean, Davis and Versailles Lakes, can be travelled in either direction.

McLennan Lake to Otter Lake (Map 112/F4–102/B1)

From the recreation site at McLennan Lake, this 110 km (68 mi) trip will take paddlers five or six days to complete. There are lots of portages along the way (18 or 19), although most of them are short and easy. However, south of Kemp Lake is a 550 metre (1,800 ft) section that must be lined. Both Mountain Lake and Otter Lake are big and prone to being windy. Other notable lakes on the route include Davis Lake, Versailles Lake and Settee Lake. The take-out on Otter Lake is at the Devils Lake or Missinipe Recreation Sites on Highway 102.

Mission Lake (Map 30/G3)

Mission Lake is one of the central lakes of the Calling Lakes in the Qu'Appelle Valley chain, situated between Echo and Katepwa. Mission Lake is easily accessed from the boat launch at Haffner Beach in the village of Lebret. Camping facilities are available at nearby Echo Valley Provincial Park.

Montreal River (Map 91/B3–A2)

From the Highway 2 Bridge north to the take-out at the Highway 165 Bridge, this river route is only about 20 km (12 mi) long. The river is best paddled when the water is fairly high, typically May to June. There are a bunch of rapids on the river, mostly Class I, but a couple that qualify as Class II.

Moose Mountain Creek (Map 10/G4)

The Moose Mountain Creek is one of the main tributaries of the Souris River. Since water levels fluctuate through the year, most only paddle along the creek near the Alamada Reservoir. Access is found through Moose Creek Regional Park.

Moosomin Reservoir (Map 22/D3)

Moosomin Reservoir resides on Pipestone Creek and is 554 hectares (1,369 ac) in size. It can be accessed through Moosomin & District Regional Park, where there is a good boat launch and camping facilities.

Nemeiben Lake to Otter Lake – Option 1 (Map 101/D5–102/B1)

One of the shorter canoe routes in the Lac La Ronge area, this 105 km (65 mi) paddle is easily accomplishable in a week. There is a campground and put-in on Nemeiben Lake. The popular route leads through Six Portages, Trout Lake and the Churchill River and is well-travelled, so portages are in good conditions. However, there are 13 to 14 portages with the majority in the 300-500 metre (985-1,640 ft) length range, with a couple over 1,000 metres (3,280 ft). Parts of this route are on exposed water, and the possibility of being blown out exists. Travellers need to have time to weather out the wind.

Nemeiben Lake to Otter Lake – Option 2 (Map 101/D5–A2–102/B1)

This 156 km (97 mi), week-long circuit offers great scenery, good fishing, and plenty of great spots to camp. The trip has between 18-20 portages with a couple over 1,000 metres (3,280 ft). The route leads west from Nemeiben Lake to Besnard Lake then north to Black Bear Island Lake and the Churchill River system, which takes you past Six Portages and over to the take-out at the Devils Lake or Missinipe Recreation Sites on Highway 102.

Nemeiben Lake to Otter Lake – Option 3 (Map 101/D5–A2–102/B1)

This week-long trip from Nemeiben Lake to Otter Lake is the longer of the three routes, measuring in at 170 km (106 mi), and will take about a week to do. The put-in is at the campground on Nemeiben Lake and from here paddlers head west to Besnard Lake, north to Black Bear Island Lake and then follow the Churchill River over to Otter Lake. Paddlers have two choices leaving Nemeiben Lake; stay north of Stewart Peninsula and paddle through to Head Lake, or follow the south side of the Peninsula and portage across, which is a slightly shorter and less exposed route. There are sections of this route that are on open water and wind is always a factor. There are 19-22 portages, with a couple over 1,000 metres (3,280 ft). It is possible to paddle this route from Otter Lake. There is some upstream paddling, but not enough to really put off a determined group. There is also road access at Besnard Lake, which allows for a shorter version of this trip.

Newton Lake (Map 3/F4)

While this lake is popular with anglers, its small size and the fact it is home to the Val Marie Migratory Bird Sanctuary make it a nice spot for a paddle. The lake is accessed from a forest access road, 10 km north of Val Marie.

Nickle Lake (Map 8/G2)

Nickle Lake is 11 km southeast of Weyburn off Highway 39. It is a 245 hectare (605 ac) reservoir created on the Souris River. Access is available through the Nickle Lake Regional Park, which has a good boat dock and camping facilities.

North Saskatchewan River (Maps 57–60, 66, 67, 69, 70, 76)

There are 600 km (370 mi) of river to paddle, float or sail from the Alberta boundary to Codette Lake, the man-made reservoir that marks the end of the North Saskatchewan's natural course. Technically, Codette Lake is on the Saskatchewan River, as the North and South Saskatchewan join forces a few dozen kilometres upstream.

Most people paddle from bridge to bridge: Highway 17 to the Highway 1 bridge in North Battleford, for instance, or from there to Prince Albert. But there are many other places you can access the river between these points, making it possible to spend a few hours or a week on the river. The paddling is easy with very few issues other than picking the right channel to travel around an island. There are vast stretches with no sign of humans and plenty of wildlife, too. There are a few sites along the way and a number of historical sites including Fort Pitt and Fort Carlton.

Oro Lake (Map 17/G6)

Oro Lake has been adversely affected by drought, so water levels may be low. Regardless, the area is quite scenic and well treed. Access is available at the boat launch in Oro Lake Regional Park.

Otter Lake Circuit (Map 102/B1)

This 35 km (22 mi) paddle is a short, easy loop that can be done in a day or two. It is a great route for new paddlers as there are only three short portages leading into French and Ducker Lakes. The only real trouble is wind on Otter Lake. The put-in and take-out is typically the Missinipe Recreation Site, but an alternate put-in is found below the rapids at the campsite at Otter Rapids.

Otter Lake to Lower Foster Lake (Map 102/A1–111/B1; 117/D7–E5)

At 270 km (168 mi), this is one of the longer Saskatchewan canoe routes. And with a minimum of 27 portages and up to 32, it is also one of the routes where you will do the most walking. For all that, it can be done in about a week and a half. Lower Foster Lake is accessible by air from Missinipe, which is where this trip ends. The first half of the trip west from Otter Lake past Black Bear Island Lake is nearly all river travel along the Churchill, with only a couple of lakes to break up the paddling. There are a number of challenging rapids on the way, although most are easily scouted.

Otter Lake to La Ronge – Option 1 (Map 102/B1–D3–101/E6)

One of a series of interconnected and overlapping routes that pass by the Stanley Mission Church, this route is 130 km (81 mi) long and will take about a week to paddle. The put-in is the Missinipe Recreation Site on Otter Lake, but an alternate put-in is found at Devils Lake Recreation Site below Otter Rapids. The route follows historic fur trade routes and passes the oldest church in Saskatchewan at Stanley Mission, and there are several fishing camps along the route in case of emergency. Speaking of fishing, northern pike and walleye occur in all waters and lake trout are found in the larger lakes. Care must be taken on the open waters of the big lakes. The route, which leads east from Otter Lake to Stanley Mission, south through Iskwatikan and Thomas Lakes and into Hunter Bay before heading west on Lac la Ronge, can be followed in either direction. The trip has 7 portages, with the longest being 1,000 metres (3,280 ft).

Otter Lake to La Ronge – Option 2 (Map 102/A1–C3–101/E6)

Another variation taking paddlers from Otter Lake to La Ronge or vice versa, this one passes through Hunt Lake and Stroud Lake, as well as Mountain Lake. This route covers between 100 and 125 km (62 and 78 mi), again depending on where you put-in on Otter Lake and how you get across Lac La Ronge. There are between 6 and 9 portages, with the longest being 800 metres (2,625 ft). Most people can complete this trip in under a week, although you can take as long as you like. As with all the routes in this area, it is possible to do this route from either end, or return along the same route (or a different route; there are a half dozen or so in the area). This route does not take you directly to Stanley Mission, a must-see in the area, but an 8 km (5 mi) side trip will take you to there. While this is a mostly easy paddle, the open waters of Lac La Ronge are prone to wind and waves.

Otter Lake to La Ronge – Option 3 (Map 102/A1–E4–101/E6)

It is 120 to 145 km (75 to 90 mi) from Otter Lake to La Ronge via this alternate route. The 25 km difference is mostly dependant on the route taken across Lac La Ronge, but also depends on where you launch from on Otter Lake. The route passes by the Stanley Mission on its way through to Iskwatikan Lake, Hale Lake and Lac La Ronge. There are between 5 and 8 portages depending on the route taken. This is a land where people have been canoeing for thousands of years, and the voyageurs used this route during the fur trade. As a result, there are a number of interconnected routes here. It will take 5 to 7 days to do this route one-way, but the route can be done in either direction.

Otter Lake to Pelican Narrows (Map 102/A1–104/B5)

From the recreation site at Missinipe, it is about 160 km (99 mi) to Pelican Narrows, which will take most paddlers about a week to do. It is possible to launch below the rapids and the campground at Otter Rapids, which cuts a few kilometres of the trip. The route passes the Stanley Mission, as well as Stanley, where you will find a general store for supplies. There are 13 portages, all of reasonable length. The historic fur trade route continues past the picturesque Nistowiak Falls and the Frog Portage, which takes canoeists from the Churchill River system into the Saskatchewan River system and on to Pelican Narrows.

Otter Lake to Sandy Bay via the Churchill River (Map 102/A1–104/G2)

From the Missinipe Recreation Site on Highway 102 north of La Ronge, this 222 km (138 mi) paddle will take most groups at least ten days, and up to 12 to complete. There are anywhere from 14 to 19 portages depending on water levels and comfort levels of the group. The route follows old fur trade routes along the Churchill River to the Frog Portage, passing by the historic Stanley Mission and the picturesque Nistowiak Falls. Continuing east past the portage and Reindeer River, the Churchill leads into Sokatisewin Lake and Sandy Bay. There are some fairly big lakes on the route and wind is always a possibility.

Pasqua Lake (Map 30/D3–E3)

Pasqua Lake is the most westerly of the Qu'Appelle Valley or Calling Lakes chain, which are really one body of water divided by alluvial fans created when fast-flowing tributaries entered the Qu'Appelle River. Echo Valley Provincial Park provides a boat launch, camping facilities and supplies at the east end of the lake. There is also a boat launch in the community of Pasqua Lake.

Paull Lake to MacKay Lake (Map 112/B2–Map 102/A2)

Paull Lake is a fly-in lake about 60 km northwest of Missinipe. The route to MacKay Lake via the Paull River, Churchill River, Kavanagh Lake, Bassett Lake and Bartlett Lake is about 100 km (60 mi), depending on where you get dropped off. Expect this route to take close to a week and be prepared for at least 20 portages, some of which are quite long, including a 2 km (1.2 mi) carry from Thornton Lake to Bartlett Lake. There are a couple big lakes which can become rough when windy, and in late summer, the Paull River can be quite low, so plan to do this one earlier in the year.

Paull Lake to Otter Lake (Map 112/B2–101/A1)

Another alternative from Paull Lake is to paddle to Otter Lake, which is a bit further north on Highway 102 than MacKay Lake. The route to Otter Lake via the Paull River and Churchill River is about 100 km (60 mi), depending on which end of Paull Lake the pilot drops you at. The trip will take nearly a week, with 16 or 17 portages along the way, and although most are relatively short there are a couple at 800 and 1,000 metres (2,625 and 3,280 ft). There are a few larger lakes where the wind can pick up on, and in late summer, the Paull River can be quite low, so plan to do this one earlier in the year.

Pelican Narrows to Mile 190 Bridge (Map 104/B5–94/F2)

This 120 km (75 mi) paddle takes under a week for paddlers who are comfortable in a canoe. It is not a difficult trip, and has some pretty scenery and excellent fishing along the way. There are 15 well defined portages that link the Sturgeon-Weir River via Mirond Lake, Waskwei Lake, Attitti Lake, Kakinagimak Lake, Wildnest Lake and Granite Lake. Most are fairly short, with the longest portage being 500 metres (1,640 ft). The put-in is at the dock at Pelican Narrows, while the take-out is at the bridge over the Sturgeon-Weir River at Mile 190 on Highway 106 near Leaf Rapids Recreation Site. Paddlers should be aware of the wind when paddling along the north end of Mirond Lake. The paddle can be done from either end, as there is not a lot of current along the way. It is also possible to continue south on the river into Amisk Lake and Denare Beach.

Always bring dry clothing along in waterproof bags or containers – especially in spring and fall when air and water temperatures are usually cooler.

Pelican Narrows to Sandy Bay via the Churchill River (Map 104/B5–103/E3–104/G2)

From the community of Pelican Narrows, this 176 km (109 mi) trip will take experienced paddlers at least a week to travel. There are 11 portages that need to be made and another five that are optional, which slows the trip down considerably, but the longest is only 320 metres (1,050 ft). The first section of the trip is easy as you head west through Wood Lake to the river, but paddlers shouldn't be fooled, as the Churchill gets progressively more demanding.

Porcupine River (Map 121/A2–120/F4)

This 190 km (118 mi) river paddle takes approximately 10 days to complete. This remote river in northern Saskatchewan is rarely travelled. This is a fly-in and fly-out trip with the put-in at Selwyn Lake and the take-out where Fond-du-Lac River empties into Black Lake. An alternative take-out is to paddle across black Lake and exit at Stoney Rapids. There are 9 portages on the route with four waterfalls and rapids that can be large depending on water level.

Qu'Appelle River (Map 27/E1–33/F5)

From the outlet of the Qu'Appelle Valley Dam on Lake Diefenbaker, the Qu'Appelle River flows east for approximately 400 km (248 mi), meeting with the Assiniboine River in Manitoba. The water fluctuates throughout the season and early spring paddling is advised. Later in the year, paddling between the connecting lakes is the best alternative. Access is found at most road crossings as well as various parks and communities.

The first lake after the dam is Eyebrow Lake, which has limited access. Buffalo Pound Lake is next on the river, with easy access through Buffalo Pound Provincial Park. Further east, the section from Lumsden to the Fishing/Calling Lakes, which are made up of Pasqua, Echo, Mission and Katepwa Lakes, is part of the Trans Canada Trail waterway. Access to these lakes is provided at two provincial parks: Echo Lake and Katepwa Point as well as the various community boat launches. Crooked Lake and Round Lake are on the lower reaches of the Qu'Appelle River, and both have plenty of access points.

Rafferty Reservoir (Map 9/B4)

The Rafferty Reservoir is 12 km west of the city of Estevan on the Souris River. The reservoir is readily accessed by boat launches in the Mainprize Regional Park, one of the newest parks in the regional system. There is also a boat launch west of the dam site at Estevan for putting in or taking out. The waterbody is 57 km (35 mi) in length, running northwest to southeast, and rarely exceeds 2 km (1.2 mi) in width. Waves are rarely a problem, making it a nice paddling spot.

PADDLING ADVENTURES

Redberry Lake (Map 59/C3)
Home to the Redberry Lake Biosphere Reserve, one of only 16 biosphere reserves in Canada, this important bird migration sanctuary can be explored by foot and by canoe. Canoe rentals are available at the Research and Education Centre.

Red Deer River (Map 65/B2)
The best time to run the Red Deer is May, when the water levels are highest. There are few rapids to speak of, making this a good river for novice paddlers. The 27 km (18 mi) section from Hudson Bay Regional Park to the Highway 3 Bridge will take the better part of a day to paddle.

Reid Lake Reservoir (Map 14/C4–D3)
Also known as Duncairn Reservoir, Reid Lake Reservoir is home to the Duncairn Reservoir National Migratory Bird Sanctuary. Visitors are asked not to disturb the birds nesting in the sanctuary. The lake banks are steep, rocky and sandy but access is readily found through the sixteen public roads and three campsites that surround the three arms of the reservoir.

If there are portages on your trip, a lightweight Kevlar canoe and quality backpacks that properly fit you will make a big difference for your comfort and endurance levels.

Reindeer Lake to Sandy Bay (Map 118/D6–104/G2)
This 200 km (120 mi) paddle features some technical sections along the Churchill River and is not recommended for inexperienced paddlers. The first part of the trip is easy and may lull paddlers into thinking it is not as challenging as it is. However, the Churchill is a big, pushy river with lots of rapids and portages. It will take at least a week; more likely closer to 12 days to paddle this section of river with 9 to 13 portages, with the longest at 1,000 metres (3,280 ft). The put-in is near the town of Southend at the south end of the sprawling Reindeer Lake. From here you link to the Churchill system, which leads south to eventually meet Sandy Bay on Wasawakasik Lake.

Roughbark Creek (Map 9/A3)
The Roughbark meets with the Souris River and Jewel Creek at Mainprize Regional Park, located on the northwest shoreline of the Rafferty Reservoir. This is a good spot to put-in or take-out, and to base your paddling explorations of the area. The Roughbark has potential for paddling in the early spring season or around the reservoir during the summer.

Sandy Bay to Pukatawagan, Manitoba (Map 104/G2–115/G6)
This 107 km (67 mi) trip will take at least half a week to complete, although it could easily be extended simply by paddling around Sisipuk Lake. There are five portages along the route, which incorporates some big river travel and big lake travel that includes the Churchill River, Wasawakasik Lake, Loon Lake, Sisipuk Lake and Bonald Lake. While the trip does incorporate portions of the Churchill River, it avoids many of the roughest sections and is a possible route for intermediate canoeists looking to stretch themselves. Expert paddlers might elect to run some of the rapids. The fishing is excellent along the route, but both a Saskatchewan and Manitoba fishing license is required.

Sandy Bay to Southend (Map 104/G2–113/F1; 118/D6)
The town of Sandy Bay is about as far north as a vehicle can go in northeastern Saskatchewan, 72 km north of Pelican Narrows. The bay is on a reservoir created by the damming of the Churchill River. The 187 km (116 mi) paddle from Sandy Bay to Southend can be shortened by putting in at Sokatisewin Lake. The route has 21 portages, the longest being 1,200 metres (3,940 ft) in length. The route, which also incorporates Reeds, Ilskwatam, Guilloux, Pauline, Scimitar, Mokoman, Gilbert, Steephill, Royal and Marchand Lakes and the Reindeer River, can be done from either end. While there are no difficult rapids, there are many long, hard portages and sections of upstream travel. People doing this route need to be ready to paddle hard to get where they want to go. The route is not well travelled and it can sometimes be difficult to navigate. For the truly adventurous, it is possible to return to Sandy Bay via the Reindeer River (see Reindeer Lake to Sandy Bay), for nearly 400 km (240 mi) of paddling.

Saskatchewan River: E.B. Campbell Dam to Cumberland House (Map 83/F7–85/A4)
Beyond Nipiwan, the Saskatchewan River is dammed and Tobin Lake is a paddler's nightmare. The big lake is navigable, but only just, with deadheads and log jams. Many people elect to shuttle from Nipiwan to the D. Gerbrandt Recreational Site and the E.B. Campbell Dam and continue northeast to Cumberland House. This is a long, easy multi-day trip that can be done in as little as two days. There are no rapids along this stretch of water, although there are a number of channels to get lost (temporarily) in. It is 113 km (70 mi) to Cumberland House on Cumberland Lake, which can get windy at times. Also note that the river levels can fluctuate considerably and it is advised to camp well away from the river. The trip offers the opportunity to see coyotes, bear and moose and while there is some good fishing, consumption should be limited due to traces of mercury contamination. Cumberland House is the oldest continuously settled community in Saskatchewan.

Saskatchewan River: Cumberland House to the Pas (Map 85/A4–G3)
From Cumberland House to The Pas, Manitoba it is a two or three day paddle down the Saskatchewan River covering 133 km (83 mi). There are no portages to speak of unless paddlers chose to put-in above the Bigstone Cutoff above the ferry. Most start at the ferry. At low water, the banks of the river can be muddy, making finding a camping spot difficult. This is a good, easy trip for novice paddlers, and moose sightings are common. Many include this section as part of a much longer run along the Saskatchewan River into Manitoba.

Souris River (Maps 8–11, 19)
The Souris River flows for approximately 700 km (435 mi), from northwest of Weyburn into North Dakota, then back into Canada until it joins the Red River in Manitoba. While water levels fluctuate there is a potential to paddle the river early in the spring and through the season around the reservoirs built along its path. The Souris has a reputation as a lazy, meandering river, so is a good beginner's destination when water levels are high enough.

The Tatagwa Parkway, a 73 hectare (198 ac) conservation area along the banks of the Souris, provides good access in the city of Weyburn. Other access points include the various reservoirs along the river. These include Nickle Lake, with access from the regional park, and Rafferty Reservoir, with access through Mainprize Regional Park. Further east, the various recreation sites and/or highway crossings are often utilized as access points.

South Saskatchewan River: Alberta to Lake Diefenbaker (Map 34/B7–25/E4)
The South Saskatchewan River originates in Alberta at the confluence of the Bow and Oldman Rivers and winds into Lake Diefenbaker. The river valley is often steep, creating deep canyons, and is not readily accessed except at ferries or provincial parks. Water levels fluctuate through the year, and navigation can be difficult in the spring. There are a variety of points to access the river in Saskatchewan for short day trips. These include Estuary Ferry just east of the Alberta border, Lemsford Ferry and Eston Riverside Regional Parks and Saskatchewan Landing Provincial Park, near the west side of Lake Diefenbaker.

South Saskatchewan River: Lake Diefenbaker to Saskatoon (Map 37/G4–49/C3)
See Chief Whitecap Waterway

South Saskatchewan River: Saskatoon to Nipawin (Map 49/C3–73/A3)
Stretching for 335 km (208 mi), this is one of the longer documented canoe routes in the province. It can be done in under a week, as there are no portages to speak of, and the river moves at a fairly good pace. The best launching point is on the west bank of the river below the CP railway bridge near 33rd Street in Saskatoon. The route leads north into the Saskatchewan River proper (after the North and South branches join) and there are a number of take-out points in the Nipiwan area with the most popular being before the Francois Findlay Dam.

The river valley provides a wilderness feel with only a few signs of civilization. Historical sites such as the site of the Riel Rebellion and Batoche can also be seen. The route is best travelled in early summer, before the water gets too shallow, but drinking the river water is not recommended, even if boiled. Paddlers should also be wary of a couple of partial rock dams that can sneak up on unaware paddlers.

PADDLING ADVENTURES

South Saskatchewan River: Saskatoon Area Day Trips (Map 49/C3–C5)
There are a number of great daytrips on the South Saskatchewan River heading south out of Saskatoon. With numerous access points, you can pick and choose the length of your trip. Take-outs can be found in Saskatoon at Gabriel Dumont Park, the Victoria Boathouse and Rotary Park. An 11 km (7 mi) trip can be started at the Poplar Bluffs Conservation Area, but be wary of a steep bank to the put in. The Fred Heel Canoe Launch offers a 20 km (12.5 mi) trip and can be found by hanging a right off of Lorne Avenue just past Beaver Creek (heading south). From the clothing-optional Paradise Beach, you can embark on a 25 km (15.5 mi) paddle, or head upstream and explore the sandbars. For a 42 km (26 mi) trip, put in at the Pike Lake Pumping Station, but be careful of the unmaintained launch site. There are also many small chunks of river that can be paddled from the Gardiner Dam all the way to the old Birch Hills Ferry Crossing. Visit *meewasin.com* for more information.

Thomson Lake (Map 16/C6)
This lake was formed when the PFRA dammed Wood Mountain River in 1958 to provide a guaranteed supply of water to local towns. Thomson Lake Regional Park offers a marina, boat launch and camping facilities. Natural grasslands and trees surround the lake.

Torch River (Map 72/F1–73/A2)
The Torch River is a dam-controlled river flowing out of Candle Lake. In early spring the river is usually too high for paddling and by July the river is typically too low. This is not a hard and fast rule; as long as the flow rate is 25–30 cubic metres per second, the paddling should be good. The 25 km (15 mi) section between the access site off Township Road 542 north of Love and the White Fox Bridge on Highway 55 will take about eight hours to paddle. This is an easy whitewater river and a great place for novice paddlers to hone their skills. There are long stretches of easy Class 1 rapids that become rocks and beaver dams when the water is too low.

Tyrrell Lake to Pukatawagan, Manitoba (Map 95/A1–115/G7)
This 189 km (117 mi) route takes paddlers from Tyrell Lake Recreation Site into Manitoba. There are 13 portages along the route, most relatively short, with the longest being just over 400 metres (1,300 ft). The majority of the paddling is along flat water and so the route can be done from either direction. Pukatawagan, Manitoba is accessible by Via Rail leaving The Pas. There is enough upstream paddling that most people will want to travel from Tyrrell Lake north. Some of the bigger waterbodies crossed include Little Mari and Mari Lake, Kipahigan Lake, Sisipuk Lake, the Churchill River and Bonald Lake. The biggest hazard on this trip is getting lost, as there are many channels, islands, bays and other features. Most of the rapids are not run-able but are easily portaged. Anglers should note that they are passing into another province along the way and a Manitoba Fishing licence is needed.

Tyrrell Lake to Sandy Bay (Map 95/A1–104/G1)
This 228 km (142 mi) trip will take the better part of a week and a half to paddle. It is a challenging route and good route finding skills are essential. As well, there are a number of large exposed lakes and a few rapids that paddlers might decide to run. The trip starts at the recreation site at the south end of Tyrrell Lake and leads through Mari Lake, Kipahigan Lake, Sisipuk Lake, the Churchill River, Loon Lake, Okipwatsikew Lake and Wasawakasik Lake and a host of others. There are 14 portages along the route, most relatively short, with the longest being just over 400 metres (1,300 ft). Paddlers planning on fishing should note that the eastern reaches of this trip are in Manitoba and a separate licence is needed to fish those waters.

Wadin Bay Circuit (Map 101/F4–102/F4)
This round trip starts and ends at Wadin Bay on Lac la Ronge, although you could just as easily start from English Bay or La Ronge. The trip is about 186 km (116 mi) long and will take most paddlers just over a week. After crossing through Hunter Bay, Nunn Lake and Big Whitemoose Lake, the Whitemoose River section is a fairly small river, with some rapids and small, protected lakes. The route also passes Nistowiak Falls and the rapids below the dam at the outlet of Iskwatikan Lake, which leads south back to Lac La Ronge. While the Whitemoose River is not a fast river, and it is possible to paddle upstream, most people travel down. In low water, the river can be too shallow to navigate, adding to the 14 to 17 necessary portages, two of which are 1,000 metres (3,280 ft) long.

Waskesiu Lake (Map 80/E5)
One of the central lakes in Prince Albert National Park, Waskesiu is a big, long lake. It is possible just to paddle up and down the lake in front of the townsite at the east end of the lake or paddle to the west end of the lake, a distance of over 100 km (62 mi) return. A common destination is the Narrows, over halfway down the lake, where a jut of land just about divides the lake into two. Strong paddlers can make it to the narrows in a long day's paddle from the Waskesiu townsite.

Waterfound River – Fond du Lac River – Black Lake (Map 121/A7–120/F4)
The 262 km (164 mi) trip from Waterbury Lake (fly-in required from Points North Landing) to Black Lake takes approximately 12-14 days, with around five days on the Waterfound River and an additional nine on the Fond du Lac River. There are numerous rapids on the route, some between 750 and 1,600 metres (2,460-3,280 ft) in length. Paddlers can also shorten the trip by flying out where Fond du Lac meets the Porcupine River but some of the best scenery, including the waterfalls around Burr Island, is in this section of the river.

> *When packing a canoe, secure cargo low down and as close to the center as possible. The same goes for passengers. If you must move around inside of the canoe, maintain three points of contact at all times, and stay low*

Waterhen River (Map 87/B5–88/F4)
There are a number of take-out points along this route, which can be done as an overnight trip to the Highway 4 Bridge north of Dorintosh, a distance of 37 km (23 mi), as a two day trip to the west side of Waterhen Lake, a distance of 54 km (34 mi), or as a half-week trip to the junction of the Waterhen and Beaver Rivers, a distance of 112 km (70 mi). The Waterhen River is best accessed northeast of Golden Ridge at the Highway 26 Bridge or 8 km further downstream, although experienced paddlers can also run the section from Lac Des Iles. There are no rapids on the first part of the river, but the lower Waterhen does have some relatively easy rapids. The first section can be paddled by anyone, while the lower reaches should be left to more experienced paddlers. Waterhen Lake can be prone to wind. The best time to paddle the river is in May, when the water level is high.

White Fox River (Map 72/E3–73/A2)
The 34 km (21 mi) section of the White Fox River between the bridge found south of Garrick and the White Fox Bridge on Highway 55 is best run in mid to late May. The river is only navigable for a few weeks after the peak run-off, after which the water gets too low. While there are not many rapids, the current can be pushy and there are often lots of strainers to be wary of. The river is an important wildlife corridor and spotting wildlife is nearly a given.

Wood River (Map 16/D3–G3)
This river provides an opportunity for a leisurely paddle towards the marshy Old Wives Lake. Paddlers will find there are frequently shallow areas that can cause difficulty even in spring. Access is available through the Shamrock Regional Park. Check with park officials for conditions during the season.

DID YOU KNOW?

Our Saskatchewan GPS Maps have over 6,600 km of canoe & kayak routes, including paddling route access points with descriptions & portage locations. New for version 7 (2017), we also display lake bathymetry depth contours for close to 300 lakes, rivers and streams.

Grasslands National Park, Saskatchewan
©Tourism Saskatchewan / Chris Hendrickson Photography

PARK ADVENTURES

Saskatchewan has a long history of preserving some of its most scenic areas as parks. Whether you are watching a stunning sunset, angling for that prize fish or camping with the family, Saskatchewan has an abundant variety of parks to choose from.

Many of the provincial parks have fantastic opportunities for fishing in one of the 100,000 lakes, various reservoirs or streams. Outdoor enthusiasts can make reservations or find additional information on each park at *www.saskparks.net* or by calling 1-855-737-7275. Many of these parks offer the best of both worlds, allowing you to soak in Saskatchewan's natural treasures without leaving behind the creature comforts of home such as showers, flush toilets and laundry facilities. Some parks even offer services such as swimming lessons with an online reservation.

There are also recreation sites that are mainly managed under the provincial park system, but also have private operators. These sites can be found throughout the province, with some located near urban centres and others in remote parts of the province. We have done our best to list the more developed sites, but there are many more informal sites that can be used to access a lake or to simply get back in touch with nature.

The vibrant regional park system in Saskatchewan provides even more recreational opportunities. The Regional Parks Act was passed in 1960, helping develop partnerships between communities and government to establish and operate areas dedicated to outdoor recreation. A Regional Park Pass is required to use any facilities in a regional park, but can be purchased for a nominal fee for either the season or a day. This pass allows access to any of Saskatchewan's more than 100 regional parks. Most park seasons run from May 15th to September 15th and fees may be applicable. For more information and to find contact numbers and e-mail addresses for campsite or golf reservations visit *www.saskregionalparks.ca*.

Saskatchewan is home to two national parks, Prince Albert and Grasslands National Park. Both protect large areas of natural and historical significance, such as untouched prairie grasses that provide habitat for rare bird species. The province also has a number of national historic sites as well. These areas are all managed by the Government of Canada and often have different, stricter rules than provincial parks.

Whether it is backcountry adventuring, fishing, camping or sightseeing with the family, the elaborate park system provides an abundant variety of recreation opportunities for any outdoor enthusiast.

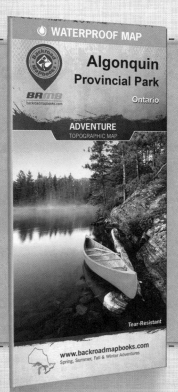

PARK ADVENTURES

Amisk Lake Recreation Site (Map 95/B3)
Found near the town of Creighton (which is just across the boundary from Flin Flon, Manitoba), this 410 hectare (1,015 ac) park allows for public access to Amisk Lake at Sawmill Bay. The recreation site, with 39 campsites, is divided into two parts: Sawmill Bay with 10 reservable, electrical sites and 17 regular, and Sand Beach with 12 sites. Amenities include a boat launch, beach and washrooms. Reservations are available at *www.saskparks.net*, or by calling 1-800-772-4064.

Antelope Lake Regional Park (Map 14/A1)
This regional park is situated 18 km northeast of the Trans-Canada Highway, to the east of Highway 37. It is set in a flat prairie area with an adjacent scenic hillside. There are 52 campsites with electric hook-ups, a picnic area and playground, washrooms with showers, a beach, concession, golf course, ball diamond, horseshoe pitch, swimming pond as well as a boat launch. The lake is stocked with rainbow trout.

Arm River Recreation Site (Map 28/F2)
This is a day-use site with washroom facilities that provides access to the Arm River. Look for the site east of Highway 2, just north of Highway 11.

Armit River Recreation Site (Map 65/F2)
This 60 hectare (150 ac) site, established in 1986, can be found off of Highway 3, just west of the Manitoba Border. Look for a branch road heading north about 6.5 km east of the intersection with Highway 980.

Assiniboia Regional Park (Map 6/B1)
This regional park operates from three locations: a 9-hole golf course, a family park facility and Willows Dam, all around the town of Assiniboia. The 17 site camping area near the aquatic centre has been developed so there are mature elms and cottonwoods to provide private sites. Amenities include electric hook-ups, washrooms with showers, laundry services, a picnic area and playground. The outdoor pool has a lifeguard and offers swimming lessons. Willows Dam Reservoir is found east of town off Highway 13 and offers a boat launch for canoes and other non-motorized watercraft to fish for walleye or perch. It is also a popular ice-fishing site in the winter.

Athabasca Sand Dunes Provincial Park (Map 119/E4)
The Athabasca Sand Dunes are one of the most unusual and remote features of northern Saskatchewan. They are Canada's largest active sand surfaces, one of the northernmost series of dunes in the world and the tallest in North America. Found along the southern shores of Lake Athabasca, the dunes are only accessible by float plane or by canoe. It is possible to hike along the dunes, but care must be taken as this is a fragile environment. There are six designated rustic backcountry campgrounds – be sure to pack out what you pack in.

Atton's Lake Regional Park (Map 57/C1)
Like many regional parks in Saskatchewan, this park, located near Cutknife, is built around a lake. That means watersports are the most popular activity here, however, motorboats are prohibited on Saturdays and Sundays, with fishing, boating or just laying on one of the sandy beaches being quite popular. There is more to do here than just play on or around the water, with a golf course, ball diamond, horseshoe pits and 100 campsites, 60 with power and water. Other amenities include washrooms with showers, laundry services, sani-dump station, picnic shelter, concession stand and grocery store. There is even cross-country skiing in the winter.

Battlefords Provincial Park (Map 68/A6)
Battlefords Provincial Park is found on the shores of Jackfish Lake and offers 317 campsites (208 with electric hook-ups). Amenities include washrooms with showers, group camping, equipment rentals, a boat launch, picnic area, lodge and convention centre and sani-dump station. Swimming, paddling and fishing are popular, while a couple of short hiking trails and a 4 km mountain bike trail explore the upland area. Golf and mini-golf are available also.

Beatty Lake Recreation Site (Map 88/E5)
This small recreation area is found north of Green Lake along Highway 155. The campground has 12 sites and a fish cleaning station and sandy beach.

Beaupre Creek Recreation Site (Map 89/C5)
This 20 hectare (50 ac) site, established in 1986, is located on the shores of Christie Bay on Beaupre Lake's west end. The site is easily accessible from Highway 924 and provides good access to the various lake activities.

Beaver River Recreation Site (Map 87/F7)
This recreation site is found northwest of Meadow Lake along Highway 4, approximately 16 km north of the junction with Highway 55. You can easily spot the site where the Highway crosses the Beaver River.

Beaver/Cowan Rivers Recreation Site (Map 88/F6)
Found north of Green Lake, this popular destination for anglers is found along Highway 155. There is a small campground with 11 sites and a day-use area.

Bengough & District Regional Park (Map 7/B3)
The town of Bengough is a gateway to the Big Muddy region of Southwest Saskatchewan. An inviting campground located on the outskirts of town has sites that are spacious and well-treed with ash and poplar. There are 24 campsites with full service and another 5 with water and electric hook-ups, group campsites, a picnic shelter and playground, washrooms with showers, beach volleyball, ball fields and horseshoe pitch. The swimming pool, wading pool and jacuzzi are east of the campground and are part of Community Recreation Centre on Main Street and there is a 9-hole golf course within walking distance of the campsite.

Besant Trans-Canada Campground (Map 28/A6)
You can find this site 33 km west of Moose Jaw or 7 km east of Mortlach along Highway 1. The campground has 61 sites with power, 3 with power and water and a number of unserviced sites. Showers, flush toilets and laundry can be found on site, as well as a playground, concession, changerooms and more. Group camping is also an option and tents and barbecues are available for rent. Located in a mixed forest, most campsites have good tree cover. This is an excellent spot to fish or birdwatch. The campground is open from May to mid-September.

Besnard Lake Recreation Site (Map 100/F3)
There are 39 sites and a boat launch at this recreation site, found 140 km west of La Ronge. Lodging and supplies are also found in the area. The lake is a popular fishing and paddling destination and sees its highest usage in spring.

Bethune Recreation Site (Map 29/A3)
Bethune Recreation Site provides picnic tables and washrooms for travellers stopping on Highway 11 northwest of Regina.

Big River Regional Park (Map 79/E5)
Located in the town of Big River, this park has two campgrounds: the Cowan Lake Campground with 12 electrical sites and the Community Centre Campground with 36 electrical sites, totalling over 50 campsites between the two. Amenities include group sites, washrooms with showers and laundry services, a ball diamond, horseshoe pitch, playground and sani-dump station. There is a private 9-hole golf course across the street from the campground, while fishing for walleye, pike and perch is possible off the dock at the end of Main Street. Reservations are available by calling (306) 469-2232 or emailing *bigriverregpk@sasktel.net*.

Big Sandy Lake Recreation Site (Map 92/G6)
This site is found 10 km from the 135 km mark on the Hanson Lake Road (Highway 106). The 430 hectare (1,060 ac) site was set aside to be used as a camping area, as well as to provide public access to the lake. The campground has 13 sites, 5 with electricity, accessible washrooms with showers, laundry services and a fish cleaning station.

Big Shell Lake Recreation Site (Map 69/D5)
Found south of the community of Shell Lake, this recreation site provides public access to Big Shell Lake via a boat launch, as well as a picnic area and a campground with 7 sites that have electricity and pit toilets.

Bigstone Cutoff Recreation Site (Map 84/G4)
This small site provides access to the Saskatchewan River. Mainly used by locals, there is a rough, natural boat launch and a place to pitch a tent if you are so inclined.

Birchbark Lake Recreation Site (Map 71/F2)
As the name suggests, you can find this recreation site on the shores of Birchbark Lake. The site is located on the lake's south end and can be reached via grid roads north of Highway 55.

Bird's Point Recreation Site (Map 32/E5)
This small recreation site is found on Round Lake in the Qu'Appelle Valley. The site is operated by the village of Bird's Point. There is a picnic area here, as well as a beach, boat launch and hiking trails.

Bittern Lake Recreation Site (Map 81/A5) 🏕️🚻⛵🚤

This 123 hectare (304 ac) recreation site is found on the south end of Bittern Lake and is accessible by a branch road heading south from Highway 930 near Montreal Lake. The recreation site is primarily used by anglers, as Bittern Lake offers excellent fishing opportunities.

Blackstrap Provincial Park (Map 49/E6)
🏕️🏔️🚻⛵🚤🎿🏃🚴🛶🚤🚤🛖♿

"Mount" Blackstrap was built as a venue for the 1971 Canada Winter Games and to give Saskatoon skiers a place to go downhill skiing. In 2008, the ski hill closed, but the provincial park that bears its name remains and the site is still a popular destination in both summer and winter. Winter visitors come for the cross-country ski trails and some may even make their way to the top of the mountain to ski down. More popular in summer, the park features some of the best mountain bike trails in Saskatchewan and Blackstrap Lake is a popular fishing and watersport destination. There are three campgrounds: Blackstrap with 20 sites, Kevin Misfeldt with 58 sites (10 with electricity and 4 walk-in tenting) and Sunset Ridge with 62 sites all with electrical. Amenities include accessible washrooms with showers, two playgrounds and a sani-dump station.

Borden Bridge Recreation Site (Map 59/D7) 🚻🚻🏃🚤🚤

Located just off of Highway 16 on the North Saskatchewan River, this is a popular recreation site with anglers, as well as those looking to stretch their legs and walk to the old railway bridge located near the site. This 15 hectare (37 ac) site was established in 1962.

Boundary Dam Reservoir Recreation Site (Map 9/G7) 🚻⛵🚤🚤

This day-use site provides access to the reservoir and is the main access onto the lake. Offering one of the few warm water fisheries in the province for small mouth bass, the water does not typically freeze in winter. Amenities include a beach with volleyball courts, a boat launch and playground.

Brightsand Lake Regional Park (Map 77/C7)
🏕️🏠🚻⛵🚤🎿🏃🚴🛶🚤🚤🏃

Found east of St. Walburg, this regional park is situated at the north end of the pretty Brightsand Lake. Sporting a mile-long sand beach, there are 102 campsites here, 25 with electricity and 12 with electricity and water, plus a pair of cabins to rent. Amenities include accessible washrooms, laundry services, a picnic shelter, fish cleaning station, concession and grocery store and sani-dump station. There is a 9-hole golf course and, of course, the lake itself, which is popular for both its beach and its fishing. In addition to the main lake, there is a trout pond on-site for the kids.

Broadview Recreation Site (Map 32/C7) 🚻

This is a basic road stop near Broadview on The Trans-Canada Highway (Hwy 1). There are picnic tables and non-flush washrooms.

Bronson Forest Recreation Site (Map 76/D5)
🏕️🚻⛵🚤🚤🎿🚤🚤🏃

Bronson Forest is 15,240 hectares (37,645 ac) in size and is home to multiple small lakes, most of which are home to healthy populations of fish. The fish are mostly walleye and pike, but there are rainbow trout in North Lake and splake in Round Lake. There are sandy beaches at Peck and Little Fishing Lakes where visitors will find 86 campsites between the two sites, 42 at Peck Lake and 44 at Bronson Forest. Amenities include a boat launch, camp kitchen, fish cleaning station, playground, washrooms and sani-dump station.

Buffalo Pound Provincial Park (Map 28/G5–29/A5)
🏕️🚻⛵🚤🚤🎿🚤🏃🚤🛖♿🚤

Situated next to the 35 km long and 2 km wide reservoir in the Qu'Appelle Valley, this park is a popular destination for swimming, boating, fishing and nature hikes. The full-service park includes a swimming pool along with food concessions, golf course, park store, playgrounds and special events. Wheelchair access to the trout pond, a fish cleaning building and other amenities make fishing popular for everyone. Check out Nicolle Flats, a popular bird watching area as well as the Bison Range. In 1972 buffalo were re-introduced to the park because of the area's historical importance as a buffalo pounding area. There are 5 campgrounds with a total of 262 sites: 60 at Maple Vale with electrical, 25 at Lower B Chalet with no service, 36 at Elm View with electrical, 25 full service sites at Valley and 116 electrical sites at Shady Lane. Other amenities include accessible washrooms with showers, beaches and change rooms and a boat launch.

Buffalo Pound Lake Recreation Sites (Map 28/E4) 🚤🚤🚤

This site is found within the resort village of South Lake is made of up of two different points. The first, also known as Loney's Point, provides a boat dock and parking area access to Buffalo Pound Lake. The second site only offers a boat launch and is situated on the north side of the Highway 2 causeway.

Bug Lake Recreation Site (Map 78/F4) 🚻🚻⛵🚤🚤🚴🚤🚤🏃

Bug Lake is found just off of Highway 945, 3 km south of the junction with Highway 943. This is a nice spot for an overnight visit or a day trip and is frequented by anglers and picnickers.

> For more information on Saskatchewan's Provincial Parks and Recreation Sites, visit www.saskparks.net or call 1-800-205-7070. To reserve a campsite, visit saskparks.goingtocamp.com or call 1-855-737-7275.

Cabri Regional Park (Map 25/C4) 🚻🚻⛵🚤🚤🚤🎿🏃🚤🚤🚤

This beautiful park is situated in the South Saskatchewan River Valley on the west end of the man-made Lake Diefenbaker. Accessed by 20 km of grid roads from Cabri and Highway 32, the valley emerges as a surprise due to the quick drop along the winding hillside road. From the cement boat launch canoeists and boaters can enter the winding pathways of the South Saskatchewan. Lake Diefenbaker has several kinds of fish, while the hills surrounding the park provide excellent opportunities to explore nature. The campground has over 130 sites, 100 with full service, 8 with water and electric and another 9 with electrical, tenting sites, group camping, accessible washrooms with showers, firewood and water. Other features include a concession, fish cleaning station, picnic shelter, playground, sandy beach with swim dock and sani-dump station. There are mature aspens, maples and willows to provide shade and privacy throughout the park.

Camp 10 Lake Recreation Site (Map 80/F1) 🚻🚻⛵🚤🚤🚤🚤🏃

Camp 10 Lake is a small lake located in between Prince Albert National Park and Montreal Lake. This 51 hectare (126 ac) recreation site is found on the southern shore of the lake, just off of Highway 916 – you will see it on your right, just past the junction with Highway 2 if travelling north.

Candle Lake Provincial Park (Map 81/F6)
🚻🚻⛵🚤🚤🚤🚤🎿🚤🚤🚤🛖♿

Candle Lake is home to 7 km of beaches, including three that are considered some of the finest inland beaches in the country and 254 campsites (179 with electric hook-ups). Amenities include accessible washrooms with showers, a boat launch, laundry and a sani-dump station. A mecca for watersports, the lake offers fishing, boating and plenty of beach for relaxing. In winter, the lake freezes over and snow sports like snowmobiling on the more than 300 km of trails, as well as cross-country country skiing, prevail.

Canoe Lake [Cole Bay] Recreation Site (Map 98/B5) 🚻🚤🚤🚤🚤

Found in Cole Bay on Canoe Lake, this 1,585 hectare (3,915 ac) site has been leased to a private operator. There are 46 campsites and a boat launch here. Lodging and supplies are also found in the area.

Canwood Regional Park (Map 70/B4) 🚻🚻⛵🚤🚤🚴🏃

Found 5 km east of Canwood in the Canwood Provincial Forest, this park has been a popular destination for locals for over 50 years. The park features a 9-hole golf course and 20 campsites, ten with electric hook-ups, ten without, washrooms with showers, a concession, playground and three ball diamonds. There is fishing in nearby Fish Lake.

Carlton Trail Regional Park (Map 33/C4)
🚻🚻⛵🚤🚤🚤🚴🚤🚤🏃🛖🚤

Carlton Trail Regional Park is situated on the historic Carleton Trail that was an overland route for settlers, linking Fort Garry in Manitoba with Edmonton House in Alberta during the fur trade. The park has two man-made lakes on its boundaries, one designated for recreational purposes with a fine sand beach and one for fishing. The campsite has 48 electrical and water sites and 8 other sites, well treed with mature aspens and willows and showers. Amenities include accessible washrooms with showers, a concession stand, grocery store, picnic shelter, playground and sani-dump station. Nature and hiking trails are available, along with a nearby 9-hole grassed green golf course.

PARK ADVENTURES

Ceylon Regional Park (Map 7/G3) 🚻🏕🏊🎣🛶⛺👣🚴🛒⛵♿
Set in a flat plain area of southern Saskatchewan, the park distinguishes itself by offering ash and poplar trees for shade in the picnic area. Ceylon Reservoir is part of the park, providing access to a beach and fishing area. There are accessible washrooms with showers, a concession, picnic shelter, playground and swimming pool. While there are no marked hiking or biking trails, there is lots of opportunity for these activities in the park. The campground has 33 full service, 3 electrical and 10 non-electrical sites, plus ample tenting sites. The park season runs from the long weekend in May through the long weekend in September.

Chitek Lake Recreation Site (Map 78/F6) 🚻🏕🏊🎣🛶⛺👣🚴🛒⛵♿
There are 15 lakes found within about 50 km of this 50 site campground at Chitek Lake, 42 with electric hook-ups at the main site and 15 non-electrical sites at the west site. Amenities include accessible washrooms with showers, cook shelters and a playground. Visitors come primarily to fish, boat, paddle, swim or otherwise enjoy the water. In the winter, there are also 400 km of snowmobile trails to explore.

Clarence-Steepbank Lakes Provincial Park (Map 81/G2–91/E7) 🏕🛒
As a 17,550 hectare (43,350 ac) wilderness park, there is very little infrastructure at this park next to Highway 927. Most people come here to fish, although there are five primitive campsites here as well.

Clearwater Lake Regional Park (Map 25/F2) 🚻🏕🏊🎣🛶⛺👣🚴🛒⛵♿
Clearwater Lake Regional Park is nestled in the Coteau Hills. With its spring-fed lake, it has been a natural recreation site since the first settlers arrived. The lake is an oasis of trees and natural grasslands, while the hillsides provide a beautiful backdrop. Bird watching is popular in this wildlife haven. The park has 60 campsites including 30 full-service sites, 15 electric only sites and 6 basic sites and cabins. Extras include accessible washrooms with showers, mini golf and a 9-hole golf course, picnic shelter, playground, a store and fast food outlet, tennis court and sani-dump station.

Clearwater River Provincial Park (Map 116/C5) 🏕🚻🎣👣🛒
The Clearwater River is a Canadian Heritage River. Many of the visitors to this park, 700 km northwest of Saskatoon, come to paddle. Rapids range from Class II to Class IV+, and there is one waterfall that paddlers should avoid. The park is remote, but accessible from Highway 955. There are 17 rustic campsites and hiking trails within the park.

Coldwell Park Recreation Site (Map 37/G4–38/A4) 🏕🚻🎣🐟
Although mainly a day-use site, there are 19 rustic campsites along with a picnic shelter on the flood plain of the South Saskatchewan River below the Gardiner Dam.

Condie Nature Refuge Recreation Site (Map 29/E5) 🚻👣🎣
This site was established in 1924 when the Canadian National Railway dammed Boggy Creek to provide a steady supply of water for their steam engines. Today, it is a habitat for waterfowl and wildlife. There is a picnic area and a 4 km (2.5 mi) nature trail here as well.

Courtenay Lake Recreation Site (Map 118/B3) 🚻🎣⛵🛒
This very remote site is found 170 km north of Southend along Provincial Road 905. There are eight campsites that are rarely full with a fish cleaning station and a natural boat launch. Fishing is the main pastime here.

For more information on Saskatchewan's National Parks, visit www.pc.gc.ca. For reservations visit www.reservation. pc.gtc.ca/ParksCanada.

Cowan Dam Recreation Site (Map 79/B2) 🎣🚻🛶🎣🛒⛵
Located south of Green Lake on Highway 5, this small site is best known for providing a boat launch for anglers. There is a campground here as well, with 17 rustic sites and a picnic shelter.

Craik & District Regional Park (Map 39/C7) 🚻🏕🏊🎣🛶⛺👣🚴🛒⛵♿
The Craik and District Regional Park is located in a small valley, alongside the man-made Craik Reservoir. There are tall elms and poplars to provide lots of shade for camping and picnics. The park has 58 serviced campsites and tenting sites, a large round swimming pool as well as a boat launch. Recreational pursuits include fishing, hiking and golf. Facilities include mini-golf, camp kitchens, food service, a playground and accessible washrooms with showers.

Crooked Lake Provincial Park (Map 32/B4) 🚻🏕🏊🎣🛶🛒🏌♿
Crooked Lake Provincial Park is situated in the Qu'Appelle Valley south of Melville, on Highway 247.The area has mixed prairie grass, groves of trembling aspen, American elm, Manitoba maple and green ash. The camping area offers 111 sites (all with electrical except for 5 tenting sites), group camping, a boat launch, camp kitchen, picnic area, playground, washrooms with showers and a sani-dump station. The beach is sandy, making it popular with swimmers. Three resorts and the Last Oak Golf Course are also found near the park.

Culdesac Lake Recreation Site (Map 85/E7) 🏕🎣🛒🎣
This 60 hectare (150 ac) site, established in 1986, can be found south of Highway 9 near the Manitoba border. Look for the turnoff about 15 km east of the junction with Highway 55 – another 15 km or so will bring you to the recreation site, located on the north end of the lake.

Cypress Hills Interprovincial Park (Map 12/B7; E7) 🚻🏕🚻🏊🎣🛶⛺👣🐎🏌🚴🛒⛵♿
Cypress Hills features four distinct habitats making it a nature lover's paradise. It also has the highest elevation between the Rocky Mountains and Labrador, due to millions of years of sedimentary build-up and erosion. The area has steep inclines, lush valleys and is the only spot in Saskatchewan where you will find Lodgepole pine. More than 700 species of plants thrive in the park, including 18 types of orchids. There are many types of wildlife including elk, deer, moose, antelope and coyote. Bird watching is also a popular activity, with over 220 species to look for. Covering 18,400 hectares (45,450 ac), there are multiple campgrounds hosting a total of 525 campsites, over half of which have electric hook-ups, along with several group sites. The West Block contains two rustic and one equestrian campground, as well as the Fort Walsh National Historic Site.

Deer Hollow Campground
Another smaller campground, the Deer Hollow campground only has 35 sites in one big loop. This site is the most rustic of the five with no showers or electricity in the sites.

Lodgepole Campground
Located off of Valley Trail Road, this campground is rather tight and only has 25 sites, 20 of which have electricity.

Meadows Campground
Just off Bold Butte Road, this campground has 143 sites, 57 of which have electricity and water. Amenities include washrooms with showers and a playground.

Rainbow Campground
The Rainbow Campground has a campground host on site as well as 59 sites with electricity and 10 with full service. Amenities in this campground include washrooms with showers.

Terrace Campground
This campground is one of the smaller ones. It is located in between Warlodge and Rainbow. There are 90 sites here all of which have electricity and washrooms with showers.

Warlodge Campground
There are 79 sites in this campground and all of them have electricity. The only amenity here besides the washrooms is a playground. There is a trail through to the Pinelodge Service Centre where there is a washroom with showers.

Core Area Cypress Hills Interprovincial Park
Just after visitors enter the park gates they will find a wide variety of amenities including a visitor centre with café, community centre, leisure centre with pool, many cabins, gas station, grocery store, laundry services and park administration building. Along Loch Leven there is a picnic area with playground, change rooms, equipment rentals and swimming beach. The Resort at Cypress Hills provides higher end accommodations for visitors as well as dining. There is also a zip line canopy tour available.

Cypress Lake Recreation Site (Map 1/E2) 🏕🎣🛶🏊🎣🛒
Not to be confused with nearby Cypress Hills Provincial Park, this day-use site has a boat launch, dock, fish cleaning station, picnic facilities and pit toilet. Activities include swimming and fishing for walleye year-round along with other watersports. Rustic camping is also permitted.

D. Gerbrandt Recreation Site (Map 83/F7)
Next to Squaw Rapids on Highway 123, this site is used by anglers and paddlers to access the east side of Tobin Lake or the Saskatchewan River. The nearby E.B. Campbell Dam is an impressive site.

Dagg Creek Recreation Site (Map 65/A4)
Located along Highway 9 south of Hudson Bay, just south of the junction with Highway 982, this recreation site features six picnic tables, four barbecues and a picnic shelter.

Dana Recreation Site (Map 50/D2)
This 6 hectare (15 ac) recreation site is used primarily as a rest area by those travelling along Highway 2. If travelling north from Meacham, look for the recreation site on your left after about 17.5 km.

Danielson Provincial Park (Map 37/G5–38/A5)
Located just above Gardiner Dam, one of the largest earth filled dams in the world, this park provides access to Lake Diefenbaker for thousands of people each summer. The area's large beaches draw sun worshippers from all across the province, while boaters, sailors, waterskiers, windsurfers and paddlers ply the lake's 225 km length. The lake is considered one of Saskatchewan's best fishing lakes for walleye. Hikers and bikers will find trails in the park, including a section of the Trans Canada Trail. The trails can be sandy, making for difficult riding. There are three campgrounds with a total of 94 powered sites. Shady Lane Campground has 25 sites with electricity and washrooms with showers. Bayside has 22 sites with electricity, washrooms and a playground. Lastly, Elmview Campground is the largest at 47 sites with electricity, washrooms with showers and playground. The park also hosts a boat launch and sani-dump station.

Davin Lake Recreation Site (Map 118/C4)
Davin Lake is a remote fishing lake found along Provincial Road 905, approximately 75 km north of the junction with Provincial Road 102. Look for this rustic 165 hectare (407 ac) recreation site on your left when travelling north.

Deer Creek Recreation Site (Map 66/E1)
Deer Creek Recreation Site is found where Highway 3 crosses the North Saskatchewan River, approximately 10 km west of Paradise Hill. This 14 hectare (35 ac) site is a popular spot for anglers, either as a day trip or an overnighter.

Delarond Lake (Zig Zag Bay) Recreation Site (Map 79/F4)
This 745 hectare (1,840 ac) site is found at Delaronde Lake's south end along Highway 922. There is a marina and boat launch here, as well as a long sandy beach to relax on.

Deschambault Lake (Southeast Arm) Recreation Site (Map 93/G3)
This small recreation site is found about 100 km west of Creighton off the Hanson Lake Road (Highway 106). The ten site campground with boat launch is leased to a private operator.

Devil Lake Recreation Site (Map 102/B1; 112/B7)
Devil Lake is located north of Missinipe. The site is a popular place to get onto the water, especially by paddlers looking to explore the impressive number of canoe routes around Otter Lake. There are 4 rustic campsites and a washroom with showers, a boat launch and fish cleaning station at this site.

Dickens Lake Recreation Site (Map 112/C6)
This site is found 20 km north of Missinipe off the Canam Highway (Provincial Road 102). The small, 2 unit campsite with boat launch and pit toilet sees light usage, mostly by anglers and boaters heading out onto the lake.

Doré Lake Recreation Sites (Map 89/D3)
There are a few different sites located around Doré Lake that were created to allow public access to the big lake. The Michel Point site is maintained by the local cottage owner's association and provides a campground (for a fee), which is primarily used by anglers. Nearby Tower Beach also offers a campground along with picnic and beach area. There are also many trails for hiking, interpretive walks, nature viewing and ATV riding. In the winter there is snowmobiling and cross-country skiing.

Douglas Provincial Park (Map 27/D1–38/D7)
Located on the shores of Lake Diefenbaker, Douglas Provincial Park is one of Saskatchewan's premier fishing and boating destinations. The natural environment park provides a diverse landscape ranging from sand beaches and massive sand dunes to secluded campsites tucked into the lush aspen forest. There is 20 km of park shoreline, including a natural sand beach. The park is named in honour of Tommy Douglas, the Saskatchewan Premier who created the first publicly funded health-care system in North America. There is a total of 350 campsites, most with electric hook-ups, located in three campsites, all with accessible washrooms with showers. The park also has a change room at the beach, grocery store, food service, playground and sani-dump station.

Dragline Channel Recreation Site (Map 84/C6)
This site is located along the South Saskatchewan River. Highway 123 crosses the channel and, if heading north, the recreation site will be on your left just before the bridge. As of this writing, the water at this site was unsafe to consume due to an oil spill.

Duck Mountain Provincial Park (Map 44/C1–55/C6)
Providing an oasis of boreal uplands in a sea of wheat, this popular park provides the most infrastructure of any Saskatchewan park. The camping is divided into three areas with Spruce Campground having 83 sites with electricity, washrooms with showers, a dock and fish cleaning station; 207 sites all with electricity in Birch Campground, accessible washrooms with showers and sani-dump station; 59 sites with electricity at Poplar Campground with washrooms with showers and a sani-dump station; and three group camping areas, some with electricity. Amenities located at the centre of all three campgrounds include an amphitheatre, laundry facilities, a playground and store. There is wilderness camping (Little Boggy Creek Valley) as well as lodges to stay at. Swimming, hiking and golfing are possible. In the winter, Duck Mountain offers cross-country skiing with over 60 km (37 mi) of groomed trails. You will also find a toboggan hill and over 70 km (44 mi) of snowmobile trails.

Dunnet Regional Park (Map 18/C4)
Built near the dam and reservoir that restrict Avonlea Creek, this park is found 5 km southeast of Avonlea. The park covers 20 hectares (50 ac) of naturally treed valley, with the nearby Blue Hills featuring the Bearpaw rock formation, the result of 70 million years of rock exposure. There is also a buffalo jump site for hikers to explore. The campground has 91 campsites 22 with electric hook-ups and 50 other sites with power and water, washrooms with showers, a swimming pool, play area and eight ball diamonds and mini-golf. The reservoir is stocked with walleye and there is a boat launch at the dam on Dunnet Lake.

Eagle Creek Regional Park (Map 48/D2)
Found in the Eagle Creek Valley, the big draw to the park, outside of the 85 site campground (including 67 sites with water and electricity and two cabins), is the 9-hole Eagle Creek Golf Course. A playground, accessible washrooms with showers and laundry service, a concession and store, disc golf, picnic shelter, riding arena, sani-dump station and even a church for weddings are also found here. The creek is home to pike, while a stocked trout pond is also on-site.

East Trout–Nipekamew Recreation Site (Map 91/G7–92/A7)
This large recreation site is leased to a private operator and sees moderate use. The 575 hectare (1,420 ac) site was originally designed for a cottage subdivision, but is now a recreation area providing good access to East Trout Lake.

Echo Valley Provincial Park (Map 30/E3)
Echo Valley Provincial Park is nestled in the Qu'Appelle Valley, situated on both prairie landscape and valley lowland. Part of the park is built on a delta between Pasqua Lake and Echo Lake. Both lakes have great beaches popular for day visitors as well as overnight stays. Nearby attractions include the Fish Culture station, Echo Ridge 9-hole golf course and the W.R. Motherwell Homestead National Historic Park (see above). There are 340 sites available within 5 different campsites: 173 sites in Valleyview, 170 of which have electrical, along with accessible washrooms with showers, a playground, sani-dump station and laundry facilities; 81 sites with electricity at Aspen with the same amenities as Valleyview; 22 sites in Lakeview A and 64 in Lakeview B all with electricity; and several group campgrounds. Amenities include baseball diamonds and a volleyball court.

Elaine Lake Recreation Site (Map 90/C6)
Located at the south end of Elain Lake, just north of Prince Albert National Park of Canada, Elaine Lake Recreation Site is a popular stop for anglers and can be accessed just off of Highway 916. Look for the turnoff to this 86 hectare (212 ac) recreation site on your right about 3.8 km past the junction with Highway 921 if travelling south.

Elbow Harbour Recreation Site (Map 38/C6)
Elbow Harbour Recreation Site is a day-use area. It has a 110-slip fully serviced marina, grocery store, laundry facilities and a beautiful 18-hole championship golf course. For more information about the Lake Diefenbaker Yacht Club see www.ldyc.org.

Elstow (Dr Bicum) Park (Map 50/A4)
This rest area is found just west of Elstow along Highway 16. There is room for RVs here and the site features a sani-dump as well as toilets and picnic tables.

Emerald Lake Regional Park (Map 69/E5)
Emerald Lake is located 30 km northwest of Leask and has 38 campsites, 13 with electrical and 18 with both water and electrical. Amenities include washrooms with showers, a concession, fish cleaning station, picnic shelter, store and sani-dump station. While the lake is the big draw here, with fishing for stocked pike and pickerel, swimming and a pretty beach are also major attractions, and there is also a challenging 9-hole golf course.

Esterhazy Regional Park (Map 32/G4)
Esterhazy Regional Park is situated on the northeast corner of the town of Esterhazy, the site of the world's largest potash mine. The park is treed with planted poplars, although they provide limited shade. A 9-hole golf course and the nearby Kaposvar Historic Site are worth a visit. Campers will find 35 sites, 33 with electric hook-ups and water, group camping and accessible washrooms with showers. The park also has food service, a picnic area with playground, ball diamonds and nature trails. There is even an outdoor swimming pool with lifeguards and lessons available.

Eston Riverside Regional Park (Map 35/F7)
Situated along the banks of the South Saskatchewan River, people often launch onto the river from the beach area. There is an outdoor pool that is popular with swimmers, while the 9-hole golf course attracts golfers. The campground has some trees for shade along with accessible washrooms with showers, food service, a picnic area, playground and sani-dump station. There are 85 sites, 40 with electrical hook-ups and 35 with full service.

Etter's Beach Recreation Site (Map 39/G5)
Found on the west side of Last Mountain Lake 10 km east of Stalwart, this recreation site protects wildlife habitat within an agrarian area. The site is currently leased to the village of Etter's Beach. There are 41 full services sites, 29 of which are available for seasonal rental, group campsites and washrooms with showers. Amenities include ball diamonds, a fish cleaning station and sani-dump station.

Fir River Road Mile 16 & 21 Recreation Site (Map 74/E6)
These little-used day-use sites provide access to the Fir River and its ecological reserve. There is a warm-up shelter at Mile 16 maintained by the local snowmobile club as well as one just north of Mile 21. Fishing, hunting and ATVing are some of the summer and fall activities here.

Fowler Lake Recreation Site (Map 76/G3)
This 70 hectare (170 ac) site, established in 1986, is located just south of Highway 699. If travelling east, look for the turnoff on your left about 12 km from the junction with Highway 21. The recreation site actually sits on the shore of Hoffman Lake, which is separated by a thin isthmus of land from Fowler Lake.

Fur Lake Recreation Site (Map 69/E4)
This 76 hectare (188 ac) recreation site is located at the south end of the southernmost Fur Lake, and you can access the site by a branch road off of Highway 3, about 8.5 km east of Shell Lake. This series of interconnected lakes are known for excellent fishing for walleye and northern pike, and you can find a boat launch at the recreation site to help you access the many fishing hotspots here.

Geikie River Recreation Site (Map 118/B2)
This remote recreation site, found 210 km north of Southend, still sees moderate use in the spring when the fishing is strong. Along with a boat launch for anglers and paddlers, there are 8 rustic campsites, a fish cleaning station and pit toilet.

Glenburn Regional Park (Map 58/F5)
Found in the North Saskatchewan River Valley, this natural park is found between Maymont and Sonnigdale, near the former site of the Maymont Ferry. There is a man-made swimming pond, a golf course and a hand launch for small boats on the river, where anglers will find walleye, goldeye, pike and sturgeon. There are 62 campsites, 16 with electrical hook-up and 24 with full service. Amenities include accessible washrooms with showers, concession, a grocery store, laundry services, picnic shelter and sani-dump station.

Good Spirit Lake Provincial Park (Map 43/B2)
Maclean's Magazine named the beach at Good Spirit Lake one of the best in the country, so is it any surprise that it attracts flocks of people? In addition to the beach, there are plenty of water-based activities here, from swimming to fishing to paddling to boating. While the day-use area is popular, there is a campground with over 200 sites, 126 with power, as well as group camping. Amenities include accessible washrooms with showers and laundry facilities, change rooms and a dock at the beach, playgrounds, recreation hall, tennis court and sani-dump station. The Trans Canada Trail passes through the park, while the Dune Discovery Interpretive trail follows the lake's shoreline into the dunes.

Gordon Lake Recreation Site (Map 110/B6)
The 15 unit campsite here is run by private operators. The 370 hectare (915 ac) site is a popular access point onto the Churchill River and is easily accessed from Provincial Road 914 northeast of Lac la Plonge.

Granite Lake Recreation Site (Map 94/E2)
The boat launch on Granite Lake is used by local cottage owners to access their remote cottages, but there is also a small campsite here with 6 sites, boat launch and a fish cleaning station. Fishing is popular in the area.

Grasslands National Park (Maps 3, 4, 5)
Made up of an East Block and West Block, Grasslands National Park is accessible from Highways 4 and 18. The wilderness park is full of unique flora and fauna. In fact, there are 15 species of wildlife listed at risk. The area is also rich in history. Ecotours can be explored by vehicle, while hiking and backcountry camping are also possible in the park, which currently has little development.

The park office and Visitor Information Centre are located in the village of Val Marie, close to the West Block. Although the park is open year-round, the Visitor Centre is only open from May long weekend to Labour Day in September. The Frenchmen Valley Campground is found in the West Block with 24 sites, 18 with electrical service. The Belza Day Use Site is also found here. In the East Block you will find the Rock Creek Campground with plenty of tent sites, 10 RV site, 2 teepee sites, as well as the Two Trees Day Use site nearby. To reserve a campsite, visit reservation.pc.gc.ca or call 1-877-737-3783.

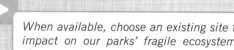

When available, choose an existing site to reduce your impact on our parks' fragile ecosystems. Otherwise, choose rock, gravel, dry grass, or snow for a camping surface to minimize signs of your presence.

Great Blue Heron Provincial Park (Map 70/F1–80/G6)
This newly formed 11,168 hectare (27,585 ac) provincial park encompasses both the former Anglin and Emma Lake Recreation Sites and a massive amount of Crown land. The park also borders Prince Albert National Park and because of all this protected land, the wildlife viewing opportunities are top notch. There are both spruce and aspen forests in the park and plenty of lakes for watersports and, of course, fishing. Camping opportunities are plentiful with three sites, Anderson Point, Spruce River and north at Anglin Lake, as well as a large site; Murray Point at Emma Lake, with a total of 294 sites, some with electric. Amenities include boat launches, day-use areas, group camping sites, wheelchair access, washrooms with flush toilets and showers, beach volleyball and a park store. Activities include swimming, hiking, biking and, in the winter, cross-country skiing on the many trails in the park. Reservations can be made online at www.saskparks.goingtocamp.com.

Greenbrush River Recreation Site (Map 64/E2)
This site is little more than a rest stop found west of Hudson Bay on Highway 3. The camp kitchen is used as a warm up shelter in the winter by snowmobilers.

PARK ADVENTURES

Greenwater Lake Provincial Park (Map 63/E5–64/A5)

Greenwater Lake is a four-season playground. While the lake is the heart of the park in summer, with swimming, fishing and boating equally popular, the 125 km (78 mi) of trails (100 km of snowmobile trails and 25 km of cross-country ski trails) draw visitors in winter. Skating is also popular. In summer, the trails are open to hiking and mountain biking and there are the Highbush and Marean Interpretive Trails to explore. There are 5 campgrounds with a total of 252 campsites, all of which have electric hook-ups group camping, rental cabins and an 18-hole championship course along with mini-putt. Amenities include accessible washrooms with showers and laundry facilities, a concession and grocery store, playgrounds, tennis courts and sani-dump station. The park is southeast of Melfort on Highway 38.

Grenfell Municipal Park (Map 31/G6)

Grenfell Regional Park is found at the northern edge of the town of Grenfell on the Trans-Canada Highway. The park has a full range of facilities, including swimming pool, mini-golf, 9-hole golf course, playground and recreation area for baseball. The campsite has 49 sites, 27 with power, another 11 with power and water and 8 with full service. Amenities include washrooms with showers, sani-dump station and two dining shelters for use during poor weather.

Hackett Lake Recreation Site (Map 79/F3)

Hackett Lake is found approximately 44 km north of the junction between Highways 55 and 922 near Big River. If travelling north, the recreation site will be on your left. This is a popular day-use and overnight spot for anglers.

Halfway House Recreation Site (Map 78/A6)

This 60 hectare (150 ac) site, established in 1977, can be found along Highway 4, about 47 km south of Meadow Lake. Look for the site on your left when travelling south.

Hanson Lake Recreation Site (Map 94/C4)

There are a dozen campsites in this moderately well-used recreation site, some with electricity. As with most recreation sites found adjacent to a lake, fishing is one of the most popular recreational activities around here along with cycling, hiking and boating.

Hazlet Municipal Park (Map 24/F6)

Hazlet Park is found 2.5 km northwest of Hazlet off Highway 332 on the edge of the Great Sand Hills. There is a body of water in the middle of the park created by a dam built in 1937 with horses and scrapers. There are over 30 electric and non-electric sites at the campground, a play and picnic area, golf course, tennis court along with a sprinkler pool. Two camp kitchens with wood burning stoves are available for groups, while short trails through the trees around the park are available for hiking or biking. White-tailed and mule deer frequently walk through the park, while other wildlife and many species of birds can often be seen in the trees. Birdwatchers can even see the endangered long-billed curlew and loggerhead shrike on occasion.

Helene Lake Recreation Site (Map 68/B1)

Maintained occasionally by the staff at nearby Candle Lake Provincial Park, this recreation area offers little more than a boat launch onto Helene Lake.

Herbert Ferry Municipal Park (Map 26/C4)

This park is located 26 km north of Herbert and the Trans-Canada Highway on winding backroads. The park surrounds a natural cove formed by Lake Diefenbaker that is a popular place to swim due to the nice beach area and shallow water with a sandy bottom. In addition to paddling and boating on the big lake, fishermen often catch whitefish in the bay. The campground has 30 non-electrical sites, non-modern toilets, a boat launch, picnic area and playground.

Heritage Lake Recreation Site (Map 81/F5)

This recreation site is located on the eastern shores of Heritage Lake, about 10 km north on Highway 913 from the junction with Highway 120. If travelling north, the site will be on your left. This 12 hectare (30 ac) site was established in 1986.

Hudson Bay Regional Park (Map 65/A2)

Located 2 km south of the town of Hudson Bay, this popular regional park is located near the junction of the Fir, Red Deer and Etomami Rivers, where a fur trading fort was built nearly 300 years ago. There are 46 camping spots, including 33 with electrical hook ups and six tenting sites. In addition to the beach, there is a spray park for the kids, a 9-hole golf course, accessible washrooms with showers, picnic shelter and sani-dump station. In winter, there are 30 km (19 mi) of groomed cross-country trails.

Hudson Bay Regional Park – Ruby Lake (Map 65/A1; 75/A7)

Maintained by the Hudson Bay Regional Park Authority, this site is found north of town off Highway 9. There are two 30-amp sites, two 15-amp sites and 5 unserviced campsites along with a boat launch here. Swimming, sailing, windsurfing, water skiing, wakeboarding, tubing, canoeing and kayaking are all popular activities on the lake.

Island Lake Recreation Site (Map 78/F4)

This site is best known for its 6 km (3.7 mi) trail featuring black spruce and jackpine. Wildlife, including moose, are often seen. The remote site is found north of Highway 943.

Ituna & District Regional Park (Map 42/B6)

This park is just south of the town of Ituna and is linked by a paved biking or hiking trail. The park has a 9-hole golf course, junior-sized Olympic swimming pool and a 17 site shaded campground with 12 electric sites. Amenities include washrooms with showers, beer garden, concession stand, ball diamond, beach volleyball, horseshoe pitch and a playground. There are lakes in the area to canoe as well.

Jan Lake Recreation Site (Map 94/C1)

This 2,095 hectare (5,175 ac) recreation site is located 81 km west of Creighton along Highway 135, just north of the junction with Highway 106. Offering spacious treed campsites, potable water, firewood, washrooms, a boat launch, fish filleting facilities, a large beach, playground and a convenience store, this is one of the better developed and maintained campgrounds in northern Saskatchewan. The site is open from May to September; call 306-632-2004 for more information.

Jayjay Lake Recreation Site (Map 92/F5)

Jayjay Lake is located just northwest of the much larger Big Sandy Lake and can be reached via Provincial Road 165, just off Highway 106. This rustic recreation site is found on the north end of the small lake, to your left when travelling north.

Jean Louis Legare Regional Park (Map 6/D4)

This park is located just south of the town of Willow Bunch on Highway 36 in a picturesque natural valley shaded with tall trees. Two natural hiking trails lead from the campground allowing visitors to enjoy wildlife and bird watching. Other sports in the park include a 9-hole golf course, horseshoe pits and a baseball diamond. The key local attraction is the Heritage Museum, which features the famous Willow Bunch Giant, Edouard Beaupré. The campground has 45 campsites, 41 with electric hook-ups, and group camping. Amenities include accessible washrooms with showers, a concession stand, picnic area with shelter, playground and sani-dump station.

Katepwa Point Provincial Park (Map 31/A4)

This is an 8 hectare (20 ac) recreation area on the shores of Katepwa Lake in the Qu'Appelle Valley. The valley, created during the ice age, comes as a lush green surprise to travellers passing through the otherwise arid prairie area. This is a day-use park with a shaded, family picnic area, a great beach with changerooms and good fishing facilities, including a boat launch. The park is open from late May until the September long weekend. Contact (306) 332-3215 for more information. A privately owned campground and 9-hole golf course are within walking distance outside of the park. Year-round accommodation and seasonal cabins are across the road from the park.

Kemoca Regional Park (Map 20/B2)

Kemoca Regional Park is situated just off Main Street in the south part of Montmartre. There is a 9-hole golf course with a historic rural school as a clubhouse. Campers will find 62 sites, 52 with full service and amenities including washrooms with showers, multi-purpose dining areas, basketball and volleyball courts, horseshoe pits, a swimming pool and sani-dump station. Each campsite is well grassed and trees provide some privacy.

Kindersley Regional Park (Map 35/C2)

There are 45 campsites, 24 full service site and 21 with power and water. Amenities include accessible washrooms with showers, a concession, picnic shelter and sani-dump station. The park is on the edge of a reservoir created by the Mothwell Dam. Small, non-motorized boats are allowed out on the reservoir, where there are some pretty hefty pike to be found. The main draw to the park is a 9-hole golf course.

PARK ADVENTURES

Kipabiskau Regional Park (Map 62/G5)

Called "Kip" by locals and folks in the know, this park is found in the Barrier Valley, on the shores of a long, narrow lake. While the park surrounds most of the lake, only the northern portion has been developed, with 25 campsites, 10 with power and water and 7 with just power, and two cabins. Amenities include accessible washrooms with showers, a concession, fish cleaning station, grocery store, laundry services and picnic shelter. The lake holds pike, perch and walleye for anglers, but other watersports are popular. In fact, the local watersport club is the largest waterskiing club in the province. There is a network of 10 km (6 mi) of hiking trails, a large floating dock and marina and boat launch, sandy beach and playground.

Lac La Plonge Recreation Site (Map 99/B5)

Not to be confused with Lac La Ronge, this large, 120 hectare (295 ac) site has a rustic 19-site campground that is rarely full. The lake is the main draw here and fishing is popular, with a boat launch, fish cleaning station and picnic tables found on-site. There is a beach at a nearby resort.

Lac La Ronge Provincial Park (Map 91/F1–100/C4)

This is one of Saskatchewan's largest and best-known parks. Mostly inaccessible by anything other than float plane or canoe, the park is 51% covered by water and is one of the best canoe destinations in the country, with more than 30 documented canoe routes that follow old fur trader routes. The signature lake, Lac La Ronge, is Saskatchewan's fourth biggest lake. There are over 1,300 islands to explore by canoe or boat. There are also four campgrounds: Missinipe has 15 sites, 13 with power, washrooms with showers, fish cleaning station, boat launch and dock and sani-dump station; Nemeiben has 52 sites, 29 with power, washrooms with showers, playground, boat launch and dock and sani-dump station; Nut Point has 85 sites, 46 with power, washrooms with showers, boat launch and sani-dump station; and Wadin Bay has 57 sites in 5 loops, 44 with power, washrooms with showers, playground, group camping, fish cleaning station, marina, boat launch, sani-dump station and picnic shelter.

Lac Pelletier Regional Park (Map 14/E4)

This park offers a full range of services from a 9-hole golf course and mini-golf through to a restaurant. Set in a scenic valley on the east side of Pelletier Lake, the park also permits all types of watercraft. There are two boat launches, one at Darling Beach and one north of Ona's Beach. The lake is excellent for fishing and is naturally stocked with perch, walleye, pike and whitefish. A year-round park, you can ice fish, cross-country ski or snowmobile during the winter. Six campground areas offer 262 campsites, 204 with power and water, 8 with full hook-ups, accessible washrooms with showers, a fish cleaning station, food concession, grocery store, picnic area with shelter, playgrounds and free WiFi.

Lady Lake Regional Park (Map 54/B4)

On a scenic lake stocked annually with rainbow and tiger trout. There is a launch for boats with electric motors at the north end of the lake along with a small dock. Visitors will find 58 grassy campsites, 30 with power, accessible washrooms with showers, a concession, fish cleaning station, a large group area for picnics, a playground and sani-dump station. The sandy beach features a diving dock.

Lake Charron Regional Park (Map 62/F6)

Lake Charron is well known as a wildlife watching destination, as the lake is home to pelicans. There are 73 sites, 67 with electrical hook ups. Amenities include accessible washrooms with showers, laundry services, picnic shelter and sani-dump station. But the lake itself is a popular destination for watersports and there is a boat launch on the lake. Fishing is possible, but isn't the best. In the winter, there are snowmobile trails in the area.

Last Mountain Regional Park (Map 40/A4)

Found at the north end of Last Mountain Lake, this park is found inside the oldest bird sanctuary in North America. As you might expect, wildlife watching is a prime activity here. There is also swimming pool, a beach, boat launch, 94 powered campsites and 14 sites without, washrooms with showers and laundry services, a grocery store, picnic shelter and sani-dump station. Anglers will appreciate the fish cleaning station and some fine fishing for pike, perch, walleye, whitefish and carp. There is even a nature trail for folks looking to get out for a stroll.

Leaf Rapids Recreation Site (Map 94/E2)

This tiny site has an eight unit campground that sees light use. There is a washroom and a fish cleaning station. It is on the banks of the Sturgeon-Weir River next to Highway 106 and the public can access the river here. In fact, paddlers are the main visitors to the site. There is a fee to camp here.

Lemsford Ferry Regional Park (Map 35/C7)

Located south of Glidden along Provincial Road 649 on the banks of the South Saskatchewan River, this 11 hectare (27 ac) park is nestled between the coulees and hills of the river basin. The fishing is good here for walleye, northern pike, goldeye and sturgeon, and hiking trails can be found nearby. The park also offers powered and unserviced camping sites, firewood, washrooms with showers and a playground.

LeRoy Leisureland Regional Park (Map 51/D4)

One of a handful of regional parks in the system that isn't built on a lake or river, this site has 20 campsites with full hook-ups and 3 more with power only. Amenities include accessible washrooms with showers, a food concession, picnic shelter and sani-dump station. There is also a 9-hole golf course and a man-made swimming pool here.

Leslie Beach Regional Park (Map 53/B6)

A prime wildlife watching area, this park is home to Pikezilla, built in honour of the 18.1 kg (39.9 lb) pike caught here in 2009. With a giant fish at the entrance and a lake called Fishing, you can probably guess the most popular activity here. But fishing is not all the park has to offer. In the winter, there are snowmobile trails in the area. In summer, the park features one of the best sand beaches in the province. Campers will find 51 sites with power and water, accessible washrooms with showers, food concession, grocery store, fish cleaning station, playgrounds, picnic areas with shelter and two cement boat launches. Nearby Foam Lake Golf & Country Club offers a 9-hole course.

Limestone Lake Recreation Site (Map 93/G4)

This 50 hectare (125 ac) site, established in 1991, is found on the northern shore of Limestone Lake. Look for the turnoff along Highway 106, about 8.5 km east of the junction with Highway 911. The recreation site will be on your right when travelling west and offers an informal area to camp or access the lake.

Little Amyot Lake Recreation Site (Map 98/F5)

The five site campground at Little Amyot Lake is leased to the resort next door. The site doesn't see much use, but there is a boat launch for access onto the lake.

Little Bear Lake Recreation Site (Map 82/C1)

This popular site is leased to a private operator. There is camping as well as a picnic area, fish cleaning station, playground, camp kitchen and a boat launch. For summer reservations call 306-426-2280, 306-764-3638 during winter or email littlebear@littlebearlake.ca.

Little Loon Regional Park (Map 68/A3)

Found 5 km east of Glaslyn on Highway 3, this park is a popular destination with boaters, anglers and people just coming to hang out on the beach. However, the golf course is also quite popular and is considered one of the best in the area. There are 59 campsites here, 25 with power and water, several of which are leased seasonally. Amenities include accessible washrooms with showers, a fish cleaning station, food concession, laundry services, picnic shelter and sani-dump station.

Lovering Lake Recreation Site (Map 28/D2)

Found along Highway 733 southwest of Chamberlain, this 153 hectare (378 ac) site features a boat launch along the isthmus that separates the two Lovering Lakes. Look for a turnoff on your right when travelling west along 733, 4 km from the junction with Highway 2.

Lucien Lake Regional Park (Map 61/D6)

Like many parks in the system, Lucien Lake became a regional park in the 1960s. There are 94 campsites, 70 with power and 16 with full service, set in mature aspen to provide shade and privacy. The beach is popular, as is fishing for pike, perch and walleye. Mini-golf, a boat launch, canoe rentals, a concession, four ball diamonds, a large playground and accessible washrooms with showers are some of the amenities.

MacKay Lake Recreation Site (Map 102/A3)

This site is used primarily by paddlers, although there is a boat launch for people looking to get out on the lake fishing, as well as a six unit campground that is open year-round with a washroom and fish cleaning station.

MacLennan River Recreation Site (Map 80/F2)

Conveniently located halfway between Prince Albert and La Ronge, this campground features 6 unserviced sites with picnic tables and fire pits. This is a popular spot for walleye fishers in the springtime, and a hiking trail follows the river to nearby Prince Albert National Park. Look for this site on your left if travelling north on Highway 2 – if you reach the turnoff to Highway 916, you have gone about 4 km too far.

Macklin Lake Regional Park (Map 56/A6)

Like many regional parks, Macklin Lake has both a lake and a golf course to draw visitors. The lake is a popular destination for watersports like boating, waterskiing and swimming. A stocked trout pond is found in the southeast corner of the park. The lake is also stocked with perch, which have historically suffered from winterkill, although an aerator has been installed to help with that. The park has over 160 campsites, 96 with full service and another 50 with power. Amenities include accessible washrooms with showers and laundry services, food concession, picnic shelter and sani-dump station.

Mainprize Regional Park (Map 9/B4)

Mainprize Regional Park is situated on rolling land that borders the Rafferty Reservoir, providing fishing and boating opportunities in the southeast "walleye hotspot." In addition to camping in the 217 sites, 170 with full service, 10 with power and water and another 36 with power only, there are 8 cabins available. Amenities include accessible washrooms with showers, fish cleaning station, food concession, grocery store, laundry services and picnic shelter. The boat launch features a concrete pad, while the professionally designed 18-hole golf course is rated one of the best in the province.

Makwa Lake Provincial Park (Map 77/A3)

The word Makwa is Cree for Loon. While the park is 5 km from Loon Lake, the loon is a common sight (and sound) on any of this park's five lakes. There are 273 campsites spread between four campgrounds, 220 of which have electric hook-ups, and group camping. Amenities include accessible washrooms with showers, a boat launch and dock, changerooms, a horseshoe pitch, picnic area and playground. Like most parks with the word "lake" in their name, Makwa Lake is known for its watersports: swimming, boating and fishing. In addition, the park has six hiking trails, the longest of which is 2.4 km long, which are used in the winter by cross-country skiers.

Manitou & District Regional Park (Map 50/F7)

Little Manitou Lake is not the only saline lake in the province, but it is the most famous, with people coming from across the world to soak in the "healing waters" here. The lake has such a high mineral content that it is nearly impossible to sink. Although there are no fish, the lake is popular for boating and sailing. The park includes a campground with 175 sites, 98 full service sites, 28 with power and water, 28 with power, camp kitchens, a large group site, playground, sani-dump station and washrooms with showers. Visitors can enjoy the 9-hole golf course, use the boat launch or explore the trail along the beach area.

Margo Recreation Site (Map 53/B5)

Margo Recreation Site is found within a protected wildlife area surrounding Sakwasew Lake. The site is found just off of Highway 5, 5 km northwest from Margo – look for the turnoff to the site on your right.

Martins Lake Regional Park (Map 69/E7)

Martins Lake is a quiet, pretty campground found northwest of Blaine Lake. There are 80 sites for campers, 73 of which have power. Amenities include accessible washrooms with showers, beach volleyball court, food concession, grocery store, playground and sani-dump station. The lake is the main draw to the park, with a large sandy beach for swimming and lots of pike and walleye for anglers. There is a nice concrete boat launch and dock. In addition to the lake, there is a 9-hole golf course.

McBride Lake Recreation Site (Map 65/A6)

Located in the Porcupine Hills south of Hudson Bay on Highway 983, this site is run by a private operator. The lake is the draw here, especially for the fishing. There is a 50 unit campground as well as a boat launch, but most of the sites are rented seasonally.

McLaren Lake Regional Park (Map 23/B7)

This park is found 8 km west and 18 km south of Richmound on grid roads. It is often a green oasis around McLaren Lake, with fertile grassland and well-aged elms, trees and shrubs. The lake is open to all types of watersports, excepting dry years, and has a sandy beach. Pike and perch provide good fishing, while golfers can enjoy the 9-hole course. The campground has 74 campsites, 44 with power hook-ups, accessible washrooms with showers and laundry services, a concession, grocery store, a picnic area with shelter and playground.

McLennan Lake Recreation Site (Map 112/F4)

Most of the facilities have been removed from this site, but the boat launch remains. The site is found about 50 km north of Missinipe on the Canam Highway (Provincial Road 102) and is often utilized by area paddlers.

McNab Park (Map 51/G3)

Featuring 16 full hook-up sites, as well as a number of electric-only and tenting sites and one of the region's best golf courses, this park can be found on Highway 6 at the south end of Watson. Visitors to the park will also find a swimming pool, washrooms with showers, firewood, food service, a picnic area and playground. For more information and reservations call 306-287-4240.

Meadow Lake Provincial Park (Map 86/D4–88/B6)

Found north of the actual Meadow Lake, this 1,600 km² (995 mi²) park is home to a few dozen lakes stretched along the Waterhen River. There are 919 campsites spread between Greig Lake, Kimball Lake, Murray Doell, Sandy Beach and Matheson Lake Campgrounds. There are also several day-use areas, boat launches and hiking trails, including the 120 km (75 mi) Boreal Trail. In winter, there are 20 km (12 mi) of cross-country ski trails and 45 km (28 mi) of snowmobile trails.

Greig Lake Campground

Located on the east side of the lake, this campground has 143 sites (124 with power, 9 with full service), washrooms with showers, tennis courts, concession, baseball diamonds, laundry, group camping sites and a grocery store.

Kimball Lake Campground

This campground features 190 sites (150 with power), along with accessible washrooms and showers, group campsites, baseball diamonds, tennis courts, a playground, laundry, change rooms, beach, day-use area, and sani-dump station.

Mistohay Lake Campground

Found near the eastern end of Mistohay Lake, this campground features 20 rustic tenting sites along with a picnic shelter, sewage disposal and a fish cleaning facility.

Murray Doell Campground

Located on the north shore of Lac des Iles, this campground features 125 sites (97 with power), accessible washrooms with showers, group camping, a boat launch and sani-dump station.

Matheson Lake

This campground has 42 sites, a boat launch, playground, picnic area and sani-dump station.

Rusty Lake Day Use Area

Found along Highway 223 about 9 km from the Dorintosh Park Administration office, this site features washrooms, picnic tables, barbecues and a fish cleaning area.

Sandy Beach Campground

Found on the south shore of Pierce Lake along Highway 919, this campground has 83 sites (61 with power), washrooms with showers, a playground, group campsites, concession, changerooms, a beach, boat launch and sani-dump station.

South Greig Picnic Area

Found a few kilometres west of the Greig Lake Campground, this day-use area features washrooms, picnic tables and a picnic shelter.

Waterhen Lake Campground

22 sites with electricity can be found at this campground, along with a picnic shelter, fuel, fish cleaning area, groceries and sewage disposal.

Waterhen River Picnic Site

This day-use site is found 500 metres north of the Dorintosh Park Administration Office at the junction of Highways 4 and 904. The site features picnic tables, a barbecue and washrooms.

Meeting Lake Regional Park (Map 68/F5)

Meeting Lake is stocked with pike and perch annually, and, as with most parks built on lakes, sees its most use from boaters, anglers and sunbathers. There is an 18-hole mini-golf course, ball diamonds, beach with volleyball court, dance hall and chapel and horseshoe pitch. The campground has 37 sites, 23 with power and water, cabins for rent, accessible washrooms with showers and laundry services, food concession and grocery store, fish cleaning station and marina, and picnic shelter. There are random hiking trails and ATV/snowmobile trails found nearby the park.

Melville Regional Park (Map 32/A1)

The Melville Regional Park is a popular park situated within the city of Melville on 121 hectares (300 ac) of land on Highway 10. The park has 7 professional standard ball diamonds that were built to host the Canada Cup championships. It also has an excellent 18-hole golf course. The shaded campground features 105 campsites including 85 fully serviced sites, accessible washrooms with showers, a full food service area, horseshoe pitch, outdoor swimming pool, playground facilities and tennis courts.

Memorial Lake Regional Park (Map 69/D4)

Found on the shores of beautiful Memorial Lake, this regional park is a popular destination, with 111 powered sites and group camping. The park is well maintained with clean, sandy beaches, an 18-hole golf course, museum and accessible washrooms with showers. Other amenities include a cement boat launch, marina and fish cleaning station, food concession and store, laundry services, playground, free WiFi and sani-dump station. The lake holds large populations of pike, perch and walleye, while local trails are used for hiking and cycling in summer and cross-country skiing and snowmobiling in the winter.

Meota Regional Park (Map 67/G6)

The name Meota comes from the Cree words Mewasin and Ota, which literally translated means "Good Here." The park is located 20 minutes north of North Battleford on Jackfish Lake. The swimming area is closed in from the main lake, with a spacious beach and greenbelt area that includes a playground. There is also mini-golf, baseball diamonds, basketball, tennis and volleyball courts. The lake is home to good populations of pike, walleye and whitefish, while golfers can test their skill at the Meota and District Golf Club, a 9-hole course that is just down the road. The campsite has 49 sites, 35 with power, a group camping area, accessible washrooms with showers, fish cleaning station, food service, grocery store and sani-dump station. There is also a trail along the lake that is partially paved.

Meridian Creek Recreation Site (Map 95/B5)

Located on the western shores of Amisk Lake, this 47 hectare (116 ac) site is easily accessed from Highway 167. Look for a turnoff to the site on your left about 15 km south of Denare Beach. The rustic area offers little more than a rest stop or a place to set up camp.

Missinipe Recreation Site (Map 102/B1)

This site is used by paddlers as a staging area onto the Churchill River/Otter Lake area. Fishing and paddling are both popular activities here; there is a 15 unit campsite, including 13 units with power. Amenities include washrooms with showers, fish cleaning stations and sani-dump station.

Montreal River Recreation Site (Map 91/B3)

Found about two hours north of Prince Albert, there are some picnic tables here, although it is maintained by the Department of Highways as a roadside pull-out. There are 6 rustic campsites here.

Moose Creek Regional Park (Map 10/G4)

One of Saskatchewan's newest parks, Moose Creek Regional Park is the first park available to visitors entering the province from North Dakota or southwest Manitoba. It is 3 km north of the Alameda Dam on the eastern shore of the Alameda Reservoir. Sand has been spread to create a beach setting for swimming. Two floating docks and a concrete boat launch allow good access for boating, waterskiing and year-round fishing. There is also golf at the 9-hole course. The campground has 83 sites, including 31 full service sites, 48 with power and water and 2 with just power, as well as accessible washrooms with showers, a fish cleaning station, food service, picnic shelter, playground and sani-dump station.

Moose Mountain Provincial Park (Map 21/C6–F5)

The park is situated in the Moose Mountain highland area, making it a bit of a cooler place to camp during the summer. The park itself covers approximately 388 km^2 (240.5 mi^2) of land, of which 80% is aspen poplar and balsam poplar forest, with another 15% as lake. It is home to various forms of wildlife and is a great spot to enjoy many outdoor activities. Visitors will find more than 328 campsites between the much larger Fish Creek Campground on Little Kenosee Lake and the smaller Lynwood Campground on Kenosee Lake, all with power and 20 with full service. Other facilities in the park range from waterslides, a playground, sani-dump station and an 18-hole golf course. The beach has a change house with accessible washrooms with showers open until 9:00 PM daily. Camping is available from May into September, but year-round accommodation is available.

Moosomin & District Regional Park (Map 22/D3)

Located 14 km southwest of Moosomin and the Trans-Canada Highway, this park provides a scenic lakeside location along Pipestone Creek. It offers a full range of activities including boating, swimming, fishing, hiking, 9-hole golf and ball diamonds. A boat launch is available on the 13 km long, 1 km wide Moosomin Reservoir and there is a great natural beach area. The campground has 167 sites, 112 with power and water, 5 with full services, accessible washrooms with showers, a fish cleaning facility, food and laundry services, a picnic shelter and playground, trails, sani-dump station and free WiFi.

Morin Lake Regional Park (Map 69/E2)

Located in the hamlet of Victoire, this 42 hectare (104 ac) park was established in 1984. There are 54 campsites, 40 with power and water and one with just power, in addition to a large overflow area and accessible washrooms with showers. Visitors can also find ball diamonds, fish cleaning stations, food services, a playground and picnic shelter. Morin Lake has natural sand beaches and the lake holds good populations of pike, perch, walleye and whitefish.

Mountain Cabin Recreation Site (Map 75/C1)

Found just off of Highway 9, on your left 500 metres past Bypass Road if travelling south, this forested recreation site features a picnic area with a shelter.

Narrow Hills Provincial Park (Map 82/C1–D5)

There are four vehicle accessible campsites in this provincial park. The largest of which, Lower Fishing Lake, has 77 sites all with power, and three satellite sites with a total of 24 rustic sites. Amenities include group camping areas, accessible washrooms with showers, a boat launch, playground and sani-dump station. While the park is called Narrow Hills, the real draw here are the 25 lakes, lakelets and ponds within the park boundaries. Many of the lakes in the park and nearby are stocked, making this a popular basecamp for anglers. There are a number of trails in the park used by hikers and bikers in the summer and by snowmobilers in the winter. This is also one of the province's only parks that have designated ATV trails.

Ness Lake Recreation Site (Map 79/F5)

This 13 hectare (32 ac) site is found at the northwestern reach of these fine fishing lakes. A short branch off of Nesslin Lake Road leads to this recreation site, about 3.2 km from the Highway 922 turnoff.

Nesset Lake Recreation Site (Map 77/F3)

This 532 hectare (1,315 ac) site can be found along Highway 304, about 10 km southwest of Meadow Lake. If travelling west, look for the turnoff to the recreation site on your right shortly after the gradual left turn.

Nesslin Lake Recreation Site (Map 79/G4)

Found on the west side of Prince Albert National Park, this site sees a lot of use, especially by anglers. However, this 510 hectare (1,260 ac) site offers a lot more, with a beautiful beach and a large lake and an annual music festival in July. The campground is well treed and there are large and small yurt rentals available, accessible washrooms with showers, a boat launch and camp store with a confectionary. Reservations are available by emailing nesslininfo@nesslinlake.com.

Nickle Lake Regional Park (Map 8/G2)
Nickle Lake Regional Park is situated around Nickle Lake, which was created by a dam on the Souris River. It is 11 km southeast of Weyburn off Highway 39. The lake and park are entirely man-made with planted trees and beach area with boat launch. Heritage Village is a nearby attraction, as well as the Weyburn's Soo Line Historical Museum. The campground features nice shade from tall, mature cottonwood trees, 302 campsites, 265 with power and water and 31 with full service, accessible washrooms with showers and laundry services, children's activities, equipment rentals, a fish cleaning station, food service, grocery store, mini-golf, playground and sani-dump station.

Nipiwan & District Regional Park (Map 73/A3)
Found in the northwest corner of Nipiwan, this is a four-season park, with cabins to rent for winter camping. There are 180 campsites, all of which have power and water. The Saskatchewan River bounds the park and offers great fishing. In fact, many of the largest walleye caught in the province have been caught along this stretch of river. Add to that a golf course and many other amenities and you have a great recreation destination. Reservations are available online at www.nipawinpark.com/campground_info.html.

> When building a campfire, don't gather firewood from the area around your campsite or elsewhere in the park. Dead wood is an important habitat element for many plants and animals; it adds organic matter to the soil.

Nisbet Trails Recreation Site (Map 70/F5)
Found west of Prince Albert, this large recreation site covers 1,754 hectare (4,330 ac). Home to a trout pond that is well used, the site is best known for its ATVing and motorcycle trails, although the trails are also used by mountain bikers and even hikers.

Notukeu Regional Park (Map 15/B6)
This small, beautifully treed park is adjacent to the town of Pontiex alongside Notekeu Creek. Fish from Gouverneur Dam make their way to the creek so you can lay back on the banks with a fishing pole and relax. Nearby Pontiex also offers history buffs the Notekeu Heritage Museum with artefacts of the early Plains Indians, the Roman Catholic Church, which is the largest column-free church in Southwest Saskatchewan and the Pheasant Farm. The campground has 30 sites, 17 with full service and another 13 with power and water, and a host of tenting sites, washrooms with showers, a picnic area, swimming pool, 9-hole golf course and playground.

Ogema Regional Park (Map 7/D2)
This campground is situated on the south side of the town of Ogema, on Highway 13. Ogema is home to the Deep South Pioneer Museum, which consists of dozens of heritage buildings set up in a village format, along with artefacts specific to each, such as the telephone exchange office and general store. Pioneer Days are held the second Sunday in July annually with a parade of dozens of tractors and other farm equipment. The campground has 70 campsites, 50 with power and water, a roofed picnic area, playground with wooden play train, washrooms with showers and laundry facilities, three ball diamonds and swimming pool. A 9-hole golf course is found 3 km south of the park.

Oro Lake Regional Park (Map 17/G6)
You can find this park about 10 km north of Ormiston along Ormiston Grid Road. The park features 10 unserviced campsites, picnic tables, firewood, pit toilets and a playground, and is situated in a grassland area surrounded by a few cottonwoods, chokecherries and Hawthorne trees. Oro Lake is often victim to droughts and usability for sports is not predictable.

Oungre Memorial Regional Park (Map 8/F6)
The Oungre Memorial Regional Park, located near the US border, features a Communiplex open year-round with recreational activities such as skating, swimming and bowling. Nearby Oungre Reservoir provides fishing. The campsite has numerous willow and poplar trees providing shade for 77 serviced sites, washrooms with showers, laundry and a playground. Visitors will also find a 9-hole golf course and mini-golf, ball diamonds, pool and hot tub.

Outlook & District Regional Park (Map 37/F2)
Voted Regional Park of the year a few years ago, this well-kept park is home to the "SkyTrail," an old CPR train bridge that is the longest walking bridge spanning a body of water in the country. The SkyTrail is part of the Trans Canada trail. There are 84 campsites with power and water and group camping. There is a junior Olympic sized swimming pool, camp kitchen, playground, volleyball court and washrooms. There is also an excellent golf course and a number of hiking trails.

Overflowing River Recreation Site (Map 75/B7)
Found along Highway 9, this 15 hectare (37 ac) recreation site was established in 1986 – look for it on your right when heading north, about 20 km from Hudson Bay.

Pagan Lake Recreation Site (Map 88/B7)
This recreation site is a popular getaway for people in the Meadow Lake area. The site is found next to Highway 903 and has a campground with 12 rustic sites and picnic area, as well as a boat launch and fish filleting table.

Palliser Regional Park (Map 26/G2)
The park is named for the illustrious surveyor, John Palliser, who identified what later became known as Palliser's triangle, where the prairie wheat fields were eventually planted. From Rusty Coulee Marina, with its boat launches and 120 host docks, to the nearby free Riverhurst Ferry that crosses Lake Diefenbaker every half hour, there's a lot to attract visitors to the area. The marina is open to all types of watercraft, from houseboats to jet-skis. There are 162 campsites with hook-ups along with 143 other sites, washrooms with showers and laundry service, food service and a playground. Native chokecherry and Saskatoon bushes along with aspen trees provide shade for campers, while the surrounding hillsides are great for hiking, biking and wildlife viewing. Other park features include a 9-hole golf course, mini-golf, nature trail, an outdoor swimming pool, accommodations and fine dining. Reservations are available online at www.palliserregionalpark.com.

Parr Hill Recreation Site (Map 65/C6)
While the site is named Parr Hill, it is found in the Porcupine Hills and was built on the shores of Parr Hill Lake off Highway 982. Most of the action here comes in the form of fishing. This popular site has a boat launch and dock along with a 12 unit campground that is run by a private operator, as well as a fish cleaning station, picnic shelter and outhouses.

Pasquia Hills North Recreation Site (Map 75/A2)
There are no fees or services at this 136 hectare (336 ac) site, located next to the Rice River Canyon Ecological Reserve. The site is found along Highway 55, about 17 km west of the junction with Highway 9.

Pasquia Regional Park (Map 73/E5)
Found 10 km south of Carrot River off Highway 23, the big draw here is the golf course. However, there is also a pool and a recently upgraded playground area for the kids. For campers, there are 108 sites, 100 of which have power, and there is a café, mini golf and sani-dump station.

Pasquia River Recreation Site (Map 75/C4)
Found off Mile 31 Road to the west of Highway 9, this rustic site offers camping and access to the river. There are no services or fees here.

Pepaw Lake Recreation Site (Map 65/B6)
This lightly used day-use site is found in the Porcupine Hills off Highway 982. There is a small picnic area, a boat launch and a couple of docks. Fishing is popular, as you might have guessed.

Petrofka Recreation Site (Map 59/F4)
Found along Highway 12 just west of the North Saskatchewan River, this is a popular spot for picnickers, campers and hikers. A freshwater spring is located at the site.

Pike Lake Provincial Park (Map 49/B5)
Located a short drive from Saskatoon, Pike Lake is a popular recreation destination. An outdoor pool with a waterslide is not a typical fixture of a provincial park, but then this is not your typical park. While you can do the more outdoorsy things here—fish, paddle, hike—you can also golf, play mini-golf, tennis or beach volleyball. The campground has 220 sites, 210 with power, group camping, accessible washrooms with showers, laundry facilities and a sani-dump station.

Pine Cree Regional Park (Map 2/E1–13/E7)
A small park located in the Cypress Hills between Shaunavon and Eastend along the South Fork Grid Road 633, there are 29 rustic campsites for visitors to enjoy. The private, treed sites are found next to Swift Current Creek, which offers fine brook trout fishing. There are also larger group sites with camp kitchens. The playground is a hit with the kids, while trails lead to the Top of the World and above the Hermits Cave. One of the most complete Tyrannosaurus Rex skeletons in the world was found in this area, and there have been numerous fossils discovered. Hikers can enjoy looking for fossils as well as the excellent bird watching opportunities.

Pine Woods Recreation Site (Map 87/C7)
Located in a forested area just south of where Highway 55 crosses the Beaver River, this 58 hectare (143 ac) recreation site offers a place to camp or picnic while exploring the area. Fishing, hunting and exploring the old roads on an ATV are some of the possible activities here.

Piprell Lake Recreation Site (Map 82/A2)
This 69 hectare (170 ac) site was established in 1986 and can be found along the Trans Canada Adventure Trail (Highway 912) about 5 km west of the boundary of Narrow Hills Provincial Park. This is a popular spot for anglers.

Piwei River Recreation Site (Map 64/C5)
The Piwei River crosses Highway 984 about 13 km south of Somme, and this 8 hectare (20 ac) recreation site is found just before the river on your right. There is a snowmobile shelter and some extended riding in the area too.

Prairie Lake Regional Park (Map 26/D3)
This park is located 21 km south of Beechy on an isthmus of Lake Diefenbaker, making it a great spot for fishing, swimming and other water pursuits. One of its key features is a deep marina capable of taking fixed-keel sailboats. The park is naturally divided into two areas by the folding of the shoreline. Ash and poplar trees have been planted to provide shade throughout, while naturalists can enjoy hiking and wildlife viewing. The campground offers 10 sites, including 9 with power, in addition to the seasonally rented sites. There is a concession and grocery store in the park, along with a marina, a separate beach area, fish cleaning station, picnic shelter, playgrounds and washrooms with showers.

Prince Albert National Park (Maps 70, 80, 89, 90)
This is a four-season recreational destination. The park, which covers both southern plain and northern boreal forest habitats, hosts a variety of wildlife and has over 99 km (60 mi) of trails as well as over 1,500 lakes and streams to explore. Discover historical aboriginal and fur trading routes or look for the lakeside cabin of conservationist Grey Owl from the 1930s. Both back and frontcountry camping are available in this 388,000 hectare (958,360 ac) national park. 14 backcountry campsites can be found spread between Kingsmere Lake, the Bagwa Canoe Route, Crean Lake and the Elk Trail. There are 5 vehicle accessible campsites located in three different regions in the park. Red Deer and Beaver Glen are the larger campgrounds with over 360 reservable sites. Amenities at these two sites include power, modern washrooms with showers, beaches, picnic areas and playgrounds. There are restaurants and hiking trails nearby as well. The Narrows, Namekus Lake and Sandy Lake sites are for group camping.

Red Deer Campground
This vehicle access campground has 161 reservable sites all of which have full services. Amenities include accessible washrooms with showers and a fish cleaning station. Found within walking distance of the centre of Waskesiu, you can make reservations for this campground by calling 1-877-RESERVE or going to *reservation.pc.gc.ca*.

Beaver Glen Campground
This vehicle access campground has 200 reservable sites, all with power and 10 oTENTik sites. Amenities include accessible washrooms with showers, a beach, camp kitchens and sani-dump station. The campground is located just outside of Waskesiu and you can make reservations by calling 1-877-RESERVE or going to *reservation.pc.gc.ca*.

The Narrows Campground
Although this campground has vehicle access, the 87 sites are rustic and non-reservable. Found nearby the boat launch and marina, amenities include solar powered washrooms with cold water and no showers and a sani-dump station. This non-reservable campground is located 25 km from Waskesiu along the Narrows Road.

Namekus Lake Campground
The Namekus Campground is much smaller with only 21 sites, 15 rustic car sites and 6 walk-in tenting sites. Amenities include a long beach, fish cleaning station, picnic area and toilets. You can find this non-reservable campground 10 km south of Waskesiu off of Highway 263.

Sandy Lake Campground
Sandy Lake has 25 non-reservable rustic sites and 6 walk-in tenting sites. Amenities include a boat launch, beach area with buoyed swimming area, fish cleaning station, lakefront camp kitchen and accessible pit toilets. This non-reservable campground is found near the park's South Gate, 35 km south of Waskesiu off of Highway 263.

Puskwakau River Recreation Site (Map 93/D6)
The Puskwakau River connects with the south end of Deschambault Lake allowing for some decent stream fishing in the lower reaches. The recreation site is found along Highway 106, just east of where the highway crosses the river, about 50 km east of Big Sandy Lake.

Radville-Laurier Regional Park (Map 8/B3)
Located on the outskirts of the town of Radville, this park has special attractions for those interested in plains history. The park has self-directed tours that cover the effects of the Ice Age on the area, including the nearby Big Muddy, Buffalo rocks and wallows. Buffalo rocks were large surface rocks exposed enough for the animals to scratch their horns against, while the wallows are surface hollows where buffalo rolled in the dirt to protect against summer insects. The campground is well treed with tall elms and poplars, so that there is lots of shade and privacy. There are 32 sites, 12 of which have power, group camping and washrooms with showers. Visitors will also find a 9-hole golf course and large outdoor pool, ball diamonds, curling rink, playground, recreation centre and skating rink.

Raymore Recreation Site (Map 40/G3)
This forested recreation site is found just off Highway 6, about 5 km north of Raymore. Look for the site on your left if travelling north from town.

One of the first faux-pas of backcountry sanitation is to use soaps in lakes or streams. For any soap or shampoo to biodegrade, they must be disposed of on land a good distance from water sources.

Redberry Lake Regional Park (Map 59/C3)
Redberry Lake is famous for its great white pelicans. While not everyone who comes to the lake is a birdwatcher, most take some time to watch the birds. The lake is salty, which means it does not host any native sportfish, but there is a well-stocked trout pond at the north end of the park. There is a boat launch and dock, while canoeing, sailing and waterskiing are all popular pursuits. In addition to 127 campsites, 102 with power, accessible washrooms with showers, a concession, fish cleaning station, food service, picnic shelter and sani-dump station there is a challenging 9-hole golf course on site.

Regina Beach Recreation Site (Map 29/C3)
This is a day-use site situated on Last Mountain Lake that offers a picnic area, beach, change house, boat launch and parking space. The lake is one of the premier fishing lakes in southern Saskatchewan. There are also trails to explore in the area.

Reindeer Lake (Norvil Olson) Recreation Site (Map 118/D6)
Found at the southern tip of Reindeer Lake (on Numabin Bay), this recreation site can be reached via Provincial Road 102. Supplies and fuel can be found in the nearby community of Southend, while angling licenses can be picked up at the nearby Nordic Lodge. This recreation site is open year-round.

Riverhurst Ferry Recreation Site (Map 26/G1)
This is a day-use site is situated where the free Riverhurst Ferry crosses Lake Diefenbaker, connecting the east and west sides of Highway 42.

Roche Percée Recreation Site (Map 10/B6)
This 62 hectare (153 ac) site was established in 1962 and can be found off of Highway 39. Look for the turnoff on your left about 1.4 km south of the Roche Percée Sandstone Caves.

Rockin Beach and Campground (Map 6/B5)
Located on the south end of Fife Lake, you can find this park by heading 6 km east and 3 km north of Rockglen. The campground has 47 electrical sites (some with water) and 10 unserviced tenting sites, as well as picnic tables, firewood, washrooms with shower, sani-dump, laundry, hiking trails, a playground, picnic shelter, boat launch and concession store. For more information call 306-476-2388.

Round Lake Recreation Site (Map 63/F7)
This low-use site protects 1,035 hectares (2,555 ac) of land on the east side of Round Lake. Found south of Provincial Road 678, there is a campground and boat launch here.

Rowan's Ravine Provincial Park (Map 29/A1–40/A7)
This recreation park features one of southern Saskatchewan's longest and safest sand beaches. Large lawns with picnic tables and barbeques are available on the beach for day trippers, while two campgrounds offer a total of 312 sites, 200 with power, as well as group camping spots and rental cabins. Amenities include accessible washrooms with showers, a beach with swimming area, boat launch, grocery store, laundry facilities and playground. There park also features a licensed restaurant and 18-hole mini-golf course. There is even a first class-marina with 85 slips and twelve lakeside cabins.

Saginas Lake Recreation Site (Map 65/B5)
Found in the Porcupine Hills off Highway 982, this site is maintained by the Hudson Bay Regional Park Authority and is quite popular. The small site is not RV accessible, but has space for 6 to 8 tenters. There is a boat launch, dock and fish cleaning station.

Saint Cyr Hills Trails Recreation Site (Map 78/C2)
This 455 hectare (1,125 ac) site is found along Island Hill Road, just north of Highway 55. Look for the Island Hill Road turnoff on your left when travelling from Meadow Lake, about 19.5 km west of town.

Saltcoats Regional Park (Map 43/F7)
This small park offers 15 campsites, 11 with power, in a pine-covered setting. There are accessible washrooms with showers, a concession, food service, picnic shelter and a sani-dump station. The park provides access to Saltcoats Lake, also known as Anderson Lake. Although the lake is not deep enough to support fish life, watersports are popular so there is a boat launch, beach and swimming dock. Hiking around the lake area is popular as well.

Sandy Beach Lake Regional Park (Map 66/B2)
As the name indicates, this park is built around the beach. The lake that the beach is on is not well known for its fishing, but boats are allowed on the lake. The park, 12 km from Lloydminster, also has a 9-hole golf course and day-use area with picnic shelter. The campsite offers full service and non-serviced sites, washrooms with showers, a concession, hall and playground.

Saskatchewan Beach Regional Park – Robbie Park (Map 29/C3)
Found on the north shore of Last Mountain Lake alongside the resort village of Saskatchewan Beach, this day-use park has two beaches, a boat launch and playground area. The Last Mountain Lake Sailing Club also operates out of this site.

Saskatchewan Landing Provincial Park (Map 25/E4)
This 5,500 hectare (13,585 ac) park was once the site of a steamboat landing and ferry crossing for settlers on the historic Battleford Trail. Situated at the western end of Lake Diefenbaker, the park office rests on Highway 4 in a restored century-old stone property called the Goodwin House that was built by a North West Mounted Police officer. Paddling and boating are popular, and the lake is considered one of the best walleye lakes in the province. There is also a beach area, while horseback and hiking trails cut through the coulees of the park. Rock hounding is popular in the hills that are rich in fossils from dinosaurs and ice age mammals. Camping is available at any of the four campgrounds: Bearpaw with 218 sites, all with power; Sagebrush has 54 sites all with power; Nighthawk has 25 rustic sites; and Riverside has 42 rustic sites. Campground amenities include accessible washrooms with showers, a concession, grocery store, laundry facility, playgrounds and sani-dump station.

Saskatchewan River Forks Recreation Site (Map 71/F5)
Found where the North and South Saskatchewan River meet, this is a day-use site with picnic area and pit toilet. There is a trail that leads down from the parking lot at the top of the valley to the river that paddlers can use to launch.

Secretan Recreation Site (Map 27/D6)
Secretan Recreation Site is found on Secretan Road, just south of where it intersects Highway 1. Look for the turnoff to Secretan Road about 13.5 km east of Chaplin.

Shamrock Regional Park (Map 16/D3)
This park is one of the oldest natural parks in the province and was originally part of the W-Bar Ranch. Cradled by the Wood River, it is a popular site for nature walks, picking wild berries and fishing from the riverbank. There is also a 9-hole golf course and an outdoor swimming pool. Campers will find 100 campsites with electric hook-ups and 40 non-electrical sites, washrooms with showers and laundry facilities, a ball diamond, beach volleyball court, horseshoe pitch, play area, picnic sites and public hall that can be rented. The campsites are first-come, first-served.

Shell Lake Recreation Site (Map 78/G5)
Also known as Big Shell Lake, this site found northeast of Chitek Lake is quite popular with anglers looking for pike and perch. There are 15 basic campsites, a boat launch, dock and fish cleaning station found here, while most of the other lakes in the Porcupine Hills offer a similar fishery.

Shirley Lake Recreation Site (Map 89/C6)
Shirley Lake is found next to the larger Beaupre Lake and is accessible via Highway 924 – look for the turnoff about 2.5 km north of the junction with Highway 916. This 42 hectare (103 ac) site was established in 1986 and mainly used by anglers looking for stocked rainbow trout.

Silver Lake Regional Park (Map 66/G4)
Located 15 km northeast of Maidstone, this park is home to a walking trail with a birding tower, 156 campsites, 107 with power and water and another 41 with full hook-ups, and the titular lake. There is a 9-hole golf course and mini golf, accessible washrooms with showers and laundry facilities, ball diamonds, a boat launch, concession and food service, picnic shelter, swimming area and sani-dump station.

Smoothstone Lake Recreation Site (Map 89/F5)
This 9 hectare (22 ac) recreation site is found at the southwest corner of Smoothstone Lake and is accessed via Charbonneau Road. Look for the Charbonneau Road turnoff along Highway 916, about 100 km north of Big River – the recreation site will be a further 5.5 km along this road. There is a boat launch and beach for visitors to enjoy.

Souris Recreation Site (Map 10/F6)
This 11 hectare (27 mi) recreation site is, as the name suggests, found along the Souris River, near where it intersects the Sakota Flyway (Hwy 9) – look for the turnoff to the recreation site about 250 metres south of the bridge over the river. This is a popular stopping point for anglers and paddlers.

> *Each year dozens of forest fires are started by human negligence. Be sure your fire is completely out and cool to the touch before moving on.*

Spring Fountain Recreation Area (Map 32/F5)
This is a day-use area providing access to the Qu'Appelle River near the junction of Highway 9 and 247.

St. Brieux Regional Park (Map 62/A4)
St. Brieux is found southwest of Melfort. The long, narrow lake offers great fishing for pike, perch and walleye and connects to Lake Lenore, which offers more of the same. There are 54 powered campsites and a group camping area along with a 9-hole golf course and mini golf, a beach with swimming area, boat launch, Centennial Gazebo, fish cleaning station, playground, sani-dump station and washrooms with showers.

St. Walburg Recreation Site (Map 77/A7)
This forested site is found in a protected wildlife area just south of the town of St. Walburg, at the junction of Highway 26 and Highway 3 – look for the site on your right about 3.2 km south of town.

PARK ADVENTURES

Struthers Lake Regional Park (Map 61/E2)
This park features 51 campsites with electric hook-ups and five without, seven rental cabins, a boat launch, concession, grocery store, laundry facilities, playground and waterslide. People who come to camp can swim at the beach, go for a hike on the park's trails (the longest of which is just over 4 km), go boating or fishing for walleye, perch or northern pike.

Sturgeon Lake Regional Park (Map 70/E3)
Found 50 km northwest of Prince Albert, Sturgeon Lake is a quiet family park that was named 2014 Saskatchewan Regional Park of the Year, featuring 55 campsites, including 40 with power, and is best known for water-based activity. There is a sandy beach and swimming area and the lake is stocked with pike, perch and walleye. Amenities include accessible washrooms with showers, a concession, food service, grocery store, marina, fish cleaning stations and a sani-dump station.

Sturgeon River Recreation Site (Map 70/G5)
This larger recreation area features a fully serviced campground (run by a private operator), but doesn't see much use. There is a picnic site as well.

Suffern Lake Regional Park (Map 56/B3)
Suffern Lake has a sandy beach, sand dunes and sandy hills nearby that are ripe for exploring. The small lake is quiet and has a speed limit of 5 km for those looking for stocked rainbow trout. The park offers 66 campsites, 36 with power and water, a 9-hole golf course, volleyball and bunnock courts, accessible washrooms with showers, a fish cleaning station, picnic shelter and sani-dump station.

Sylvan Valley Municipal Park (Map 6/C3)
Sylvan Valley is a secluded, scenic park nestled in a valley right next to the tall hill that is home to the St. Victor Petroglyph Provincial Historic Park. The park has a freshwater spring that creates the St. Victor Pool, a refreshing site with a man-made beach. Visitors can explore the area by hiking or biking, or camp at the developed camping area. There are 21 campsites with electric hook-ups and 30 non-electrical sites, washrooms with showers, and a play and picnic area.

Taylor Lake Recreation Site (Map 116/D7)
There are 13 rustic sites and a picnic shelter at the campground here that are leased to a private operator. The site sees low use. Most of the people who come here are heading out onto the lake to go fishing or participate in bird watching.

Thomson Lake Regional Park (Map 16/C6)
The park, the first regional park in Saskatchewan, is located on Highway 58, 8 km north of Lafleche and Highway 13, or 12 km south of Gravelbourg and Highway 43. It sits on 45 hectares (110 ac) of gracefully treed and grass covered lakeside land and is a popular watersport destination. In addition to a marina there is a half-size Olympic pool and a 9-hole golf course. The lake is regularly stocked with jackfish (pike), walleye and perch, while nature hikes are popular with bird watchers. Sports enthusiasts will find a challenging BMX bike course behind the ball diamonds. The large campsite offers 130 sites, 85 with full hook-ups, 10 with power and water, 35 with power only, a group site, accessible washrooms with showers, a boat launch and fish cleaning station, concession, children's activities, grocery store, laundry facilities, picnic shelter, playground and sani-dump station.

Tobin Lake Recreation Site (Map 73/C2)
Resting on the shores of the big lake south of Highway 35, this is a low use site offering camping and a boat launch. It is leased to a private operator.

Top Lake Recreation Site (Map 79/F4)
Top Lake is located next to the much larger Delaronde Lake and is accessed off of Highway 922. When travelling north, look for the recreation site on your right about 25 km from the turnoff to Big River.

Turtle Lake Recreation Site (Map 77/F7)
This recreation site is run by a private operator. It sees lots of use on summer weekends. There is a campground and a day-use area that are popular, but many people come here to fish.

Tyrrell Lake Recreation Site (Map 95/B1)
The local cottage owners use the launch at this site to access their cabins on the lake, which can only be accessed by boat. There is a six-site campground that sees some use over the summer, mainly by paddlers, and there are pit toilets and a fish cleaning station.

Valeport Recreation Site (Map 29/D3)
This is another day-use facility providing access to the south end of Last Mountain Lake. Visitors not interested in venturing out on the lake can explore the unique flora and fauna of the nearby Valeport Marshes or do some geocaching.

Valley Centre Recreation Site (Map 30/F3)
This is a day-use facility providing access to Echo Lake. It is usually a quieter destination than the nearby provincial park.

Valley Municipal Park, Waldheim (Map 60/A4)
The main activity in the park itself is the 9-hole golf course. However, campers will find 14 camping sites here, 8 with power, next to a dugout that was once stocked with trout. The pond has not held fish for many years and the old snowmobile race track from the heady days of the 1970s, when snowmobile racing was a big-time sport, surrounds a pair of ball diamonds. Other amenities include a basketball court, beach volleyball, food concession, horseshoe pitch and sani-dump station.

Keep black flies away with a safe homemade formula. Combine four parts vegetable oil with two parts aloe vera gel and one part citronella, cedar oil or sassafras oil (available at pharmacies). Apply liberally and remember to wear light-coloured clothing.

Valley Regional Park, Rosthern (Map 60/C4)
The well-manicured park offers 76 campsites, 41 with full hook-ups and 32 with power only, an extensive playground for the kids (including one of the longest slides you ever did see), accessible washrooms with showers, food concession, free WiFi, picnic shelter, sani-dump station and one of the nicest 18-hole golf courses north of Saskatoon.

Wakaw Lake Regional Park (Map 61/B4)
The regional park is found on the west shores of Wakaw Lake. The lake offers great fishing for pike, perch and walleye, but nearly as many people come here for the golf course. There is a 125 site campground, 79 with full hook-ups and another 46 with power only, accessible washrooms with showers, boat launch and marina, fish cleaning station, food service, laundry facilities, mini-golf, a playground and public day-use dock along with a beach and concession.

Wapiti Recreation Site (Map 72/D4)
This 17 hectare (42 ac) recreation site is located to the north of the town of Wapiti, across the Saskatchewan River just off of Highway 6. The treed site has a boat launch and was established in 1986.

Wapiti Valley Regional Park (Map 72/E4)
Known as much for its winter sport as its summer, Wapiti Valley is one of the few places in the area (and indeed, the province) that offers downhill skiing. There is also cross-country skiing and snowmobiling trails in the area. In the summer, there are 26 campsites, 10 of which have power. Other amenities include year-round rental luxury cabins, washrooms with showers, a boat launch and marina, concession with food service, fish cleaning station, picnic shelter, playground, sani-dump station and free WiFi.

Wascana Valley Nature Area Recreation Site (Map 29/D5)
As the name suggests, this recreation site features a series of trails; notably mountain bike trails that are also used for hiking and trail running. Visitors also come here to enjoy the flora and fauna of the area. Wascana Creek flows through the area and is bordered by American elms and Manitoba maples. The fairly steep banks not only challenge bikers, but are also home to a wide variety of wildlife. In winter, the trails are used for cross-country skiing and snowshoeing.

Waskateena Beach Recreation Site (Map 81/E7)
This day-use site is found on the south side of Candle Lake near a cottage area. It sees heavy use during the summer and also offers a series of ski and snowmobile trails for winter visitors.

PARK ADVENTURES

Waskesiu River Recreation Site (Map 80/F3)
Located just north of where Highway 2 crosses the Waskesiu River, this 8 hectare (20 ac) site is well-treed and provides river access. Look for the river crossing about 4.5 km north of the Highway 969 turnoff.

Waterhen River Recreation Site (Map 88/F4)
The Waterhen River Recreation Site can be found on the south shore of the Waterhen River at the bridge along Highway 155. This 12 hectare (30 ac) site is well treed and is popular with anglers looking to drop a line in the Waterhen. Paddlers also run through the area.

Welwyn Centennial Regional Park (Map 33/E7)
Welwyn Regional Park is situated 2 km north of Welwyn off Highway 308. There is a beach, picnic area and playground, along with a boat launch and fishing on the reservoir. This simple campground features 47 sites, 22 with power, picnic shelter and pit toilets.

Weyakwin Lake [Ramsey Bay] Recreation Site (Map 90/F6)
This popular recreation area is leased to a private operator. There is not one, but two boat launches, and the campground has 75 sites, 27 with power and 12 with power and water. Amenities include washrooms with showers, laundry facilities, fish cleaning station, grocery store, playground and sani-dump station. There is also extensive cottage development in the area. The 590 hectare (1,460 ac) site is found 144 km north of Prince Albert west of Highway 2.

White Butte Trails Recreation Site (Map 30/A6)
The White Butte Trails Recreation Site is a day-use trail park next to the community of Pilot Butte, just east of Regina. The trails can be used year-round and provide a nice outdoor retreat from the city. Amenities include a warm-up shelter and outdoor washrooms.

Whitesand Regional Park (Map 42/G2)
This scenic park is best known for its treed campsites, golf course and its fishing. The Theodore Reservoir has been stocked with walleye and perch and there is a good boat launch and docks to help anglers access the lake. There are two campgrounds. Whitesand Drive Campground is in the southeast corner of the park and offers 20 sites, 3 of which have full hook-ups and 15 have power and water, and a group camping area. Poplar Lane Campground is located northwest of the concession building and has 33 sites with hook-ups and 22 seasonal sites. Amenities include accessible washrooms with showers, a concession, fish cleaning station and playground.

Whiteswan Lake [Whelan Bay] Recreation Site (Map 81/F4)
Found between Narrow Hills and Candle Lake Provincial Parks on Highway 913, this is one of the largest recreation sites in the province, covering 1,785 hectares (4,410 ac). The site rests on Whelan Bay and has a campground that is run by a nearby lodge owner.

Wildcat Hill Provincial Wilderness Park (Map 74/G4–75/A4)
This undeveloped 21,752 hectare (53,730 ac) park is located northeast of Saskatoon and protects a portion of the Pasqua Hills. The area is mostly used by snowmobilers in winter, but anglers come here in summer as well.

Trails are planned to take you safely through the most interesting and beautiful parts of our parks without damaging sensitive and unique plant and wildlife habitats. Please stay on the trails!

Wilkie Regional Park (Map 57/D6)
Found along Highway 29 on the west side of Wilkie, this well-treed park offers 22 sites, 15 with power, children's activities, a picnic shelter, playground, washrooms with showers and sani-dump station. There are also ball diamonds within the park and golfing in town.

Wollaston Lake [Hidden Bay] Recreation Site (Map 118/B1)
One of the most remote recreation sites in the province, Wollaston Lake is found 260 km north of Southend. It sees little use. There is a 12 unit campground, fish cleaning station and a boat launch on Hidden Bay. As you might expect, fishing is popular here.

Wood Mountain Regional Park (Map 5/E4)
Wood Mountain Regional Park is 8 km south of Wood Mountain off of Highway 18. The area hosts a variety of trees including poplar, birch, willow, native cherry and Saskatoon trees that offer shelter and beauty. As a centre of rodeo country, the park is well known for its Rodeo Ranch Museum with over 1,200 historical photos and 2,000 artefacts. In fact, the Wood Mountain Stampede is found on site and is one of the biggest events in the area. This park is only 4 km away from the Wood Mountain Post Provincial Historical Park, which is accessible by trail. The campground offers 99 sites, 32 sites with power and 27 with power and water and an overflow camping area for the large crowd that the rodeo always draws. Accessible washrooms with showers and laundry facilities, a concession, conference facilities, a museum, picnic area, playground, and a large outdoor heated swimming pool are also available.

Woodlawn Regional Park (Map 9/G6)
Featuring two locations south of Estevan, Woodlawn Regional Park has been reopened after the flooding in 2011. The Souris River site offers 40 well-treed full service campsites and another 108 sites with power and water, group camping, cabins, a concession, ball diamonds, beach volleyball courts, a soccer and football field, two rental halls and washrooms with showers. The river has a dock that is popular with swimmers and paddlers, while there are trails around the bird sanctuary. The Souris Valley Theatre offers shows and there is golfing at the 18-hole Estevan Woodlawn Golf Course. The Boundary Dam site also offers well-treed 30 full-service campsites, group camping, a concession and washrooms with showers. The beach is popular with families, with a picnic and barbeque area, while the boat launch gives access to the reservoir for some rare bass fishing in the province.

Woody River Recreation Site (Map 65/G5)
This 2,200 hectare (5,435 ac) site is comprised of several smaller sites in the Porcupine Hills on Highway 980. Each of the sites; Elbow Lake, Isbister Lake, Smallfish Lake, Spirit Lake, Townsend and Woody Lake, is different with the main draw being the fishing. Townsend Lake is the largest and most developed site, but there is also camping at Isbister, Spirit and Smallfish Lakes. Elbow and Woody Lakes are day-use only and there is a grocery store and food services. Be wary of the hunting restrictions in the area.

Isbister Lake Campground
The Isbister Campground has three quiet campsites that are rarely full. Offering good northern pike fishing, there is a boat launch, dock, bathroom, picnic tables and fish cleaning station for anglers to use.

Smallfish Lake Campground
Smallfish has six RV accessible sites along with a grassy area for tenters. Anglers will find fishing for pike and perch along with a boat launch, dock, bathrooms and fish cleaning building.

Spirit Lake Campground
Spirit Lake offers camping, as well as a boat launch, dock, bathrooms and fish cleaning facilities. Known for its good walleye fishing, ATV trails also lead east to Armit Lake in Manitoba.

Townsend Lake Campground
Townsend is the biggest and most popular campground with 27 regular and 6 overflow sites in tall spruce and balsam tree forest. There is a boat launch, dock, bathrooms, playground and picnic area in the campground. Fees are required.

Wynyard & District Regional Park (Map 52/C6)
There are 22 campsites with power at this quiet well-treed park, which offers good fishing for stocked rainbow trout. Canoes, kayaks and electrical powered boats are allowed on the reservoir, while a picnic area, playground, washrooms with showers and two sani-dump stations are available. A hiking trail leads around the coulee and golfing is found in town.

York Lake Regional Park (Map 43/C6)
Found 5 km south of Yorkton on Gladstone Avenue, this park offers access to the lake, which is too shallow to support fish, but paddling and waterskiing are popular, as is swimming or just hanging out on the beach or picnic area. There is a nature trail along the north edge of the lake, a playground and a boat launch for water enthusiasts and paddlers. The campsite features 39 shaded sites, 33 of which offer power and water, a group site near the beach, accessible washrooms with showers, a picnic shelter and sani-dump station.

Prince Albert National Park, Saskatchewan
©Tourism Saskatchewan / Greg Huszar Photography

TRAIL ADVENTURES

When visitors think Saskatchewan, hiking is not typically the first activity that jumps to mind. While the province is traditionally viewed as flat grassland prairie from top to bottom and from side to side, that is far from the truth. In fact, southwest Saskatchewan has the highest elevation point between the Rocky Mountains and Labrador, in Cypress Hills Interprovincial Park. Visitors can also walk in soft desert-like sand across ever-drifting hills, or explore the Canadian Shield in the east and north. For the more adventurous, there are multi-day hikes to be found in Prince Albert National Park and Meadow Lake Provincial Park.

Trails are generally easy to moderate, although visitors need to be prepared for summer heat. Saskatchewan's weather can best be described as one of extremes. Midale and Yellowgrass in southern Saskatchewan hold the record for highest temperature ever recorded in Canada at 45° C (113° F). Anyone engaging in physical activity should be prepared for the heat, which can also be accompanied by strong winds. Backpackers spending a few nights out also need to be prepared for cooler evenings. There are often summer thunderstorms in the evening, although rainfall is usually limited.

Wood ticks can be a problem in the spring and early summer for anyone who spends time outdoors. To protect against wood ticks, wear slippery finished clothes with elastic cuffs to protect the body. Once inside, do a thorough body check and use proper techniques for the removal of wood ticks that have bitten into the flesh. Mosquitoes can carry West Nile disease, so use recommended types of mosquito repellents and appropriate clothing.

This section is written from a hiker's point of view, but there are many other types of trail uses out there. Horseback riding is a popular pursuit, with riding opportunities available in Cypress Hills Interprovincial Park, Moose Mountain Provincial Park, Grasslands National Park and numerous sections of the Trans Canada Trail. Mountain biking trails are also available. The most popular system for those looking for semi-technical trails is in Buffalo Pound Provincial Park, which hosted the Canada Cup in 2000. Cypress Hills Interprovincial Park has trails suitable only for experts, while many trails in the northern parks (Prince Albert National Park, Meadow Lake Provincial Park) are also open to bikers. ATVers will find the following ATV/OHV section full of many good riding areas. Also, look for the ATV symbol in trails listed below.

TRAIL ADVENTURES

Andy Jamault Nature Trail (Map 73/E5) 🥾🚵🐎⛷🔍

Also known as the Pasquia Paleontological Site, this 5 km (3 mi) one-way trail was named after a local farmer. However, the highlight of the route is the so called Fern Gully area where "Big Bert," a crocodilian fossil, was found imbedded in shale. Other marine-like fossils (fish, plesiosaurs, turtles, etc.) from 92 million years ago are also exposed. This area is accessed off the main trail along the Carrot River via Shorty's Trail and will add another 1 km to the route.

Anglin Lake Trails (Map 80/G7) 🥾🚵⛷🔍

While this area is better known for its winter activities, the 12.5 km (7.8 mi) of trails can be hiked or biked. A bridge over the narrows at Jacobsen Bay accesses the main body of the trails, which can be accessed from either the Anglin Lake Recreation Site or the Land of the Loon Resort. The best views can be found at the northwest corner of the trail system at a fire lookout tower atop a hill near the Prince Albert National Park boundary.

Battlefords Provincial Park Trails (Map 68/A6) 🥾🚵🔍

Next to Jackfish Lake, this park offers a large campsite and a few trails to explore. Notably, the park features one of the few mountain-bike specific trails in the area, this 4 km (2.4 mi) trail can be quite challenging, despite its fairly short distance. The Wintergreen Nature Trail is a short 1.2 km (0.7 mi) trail that passes through a wooded ravine and over a rolling hill to views over Jackfish Lake.

Beaver Creek Conservation Area (Map 49/C4) 🥾🚵⛷🔍

Best known for its wildlife watching, this area also has 8 km (5 mi) of trails for hikers. The main trail follows the creek down to the South Saskatchewan River, with several other trails to explore. The conservation area is found 13 km south of Saskatoon. There is little elevation gain along this loop trail.

Beaver Pond Trail (Map 71/A1) 🥾

As astute readers might gather, this trail leads to a beaver pond. The trailhead is at the Lakeland Art Gallery. But wait, the beaver pond is only part of the draw to this 2 km (1.2 mi) one-way trail. Past the beaver pond the trail leads down to a lake.

Blue Mountain Outdoor Adventure Centre (Map 58/C1) 🥾🚵⛷🔍

There are several trails at this privately-owned adventure centre, including a hiking trail to the second highest point between Labrador and the Rocky Mountains. In the winter, there are 40 km (24 mi) of cross-country ski trails and snowshoe trails here as well. Look for the Adventure Centre northeast of North Battleford along Highway 378.

Borden Bridge Route (Map 59/D7) 🥾🔍🔍

Although there are no marked trails here, you can pull off of Highway 16 and take a 3 km (1.9 mi) round-trip hike to a 1930s bridge through deer, coyote and beaver habitat. This hike follows along the banks of the North Saskatchewan River through dense bush and marshland, making it easier to hike when the water is frozen.

Boreal Trail (Map 86/D4–87/E6) 🏕🥾🔍

Spanning 120 km (74.5 mi) in Meadow Lake Provincial Park, the Boreal Trail is the only destination backpacking trail in the Saskatchewan park system. Offering a variety of access points, it is possible to do the trail as a multi-day trip or as shorter day trips. Those going for extended outings can stock up (and shower) at any of the main campgrounds, while backcountry camping is also possible. The western trailhead can be found just south of the Cold River Campground, while the eastern trailhead is located on the west side of Greig Lake. The trail leads past several lakes and along the Waterhen River, with stands of jack pine and spruce mixed with poplar and birch providing homes for song birds and red squirrel. Beaver, moose, wolf and black bear can also be seen on occasion. If you plan to overnight on the trail, please register at least two weeks prior to your trip.

Brightsand Lake Regional Park Trails (Map 77/D7) 🥾🚵

There is a network of trails in this regional park. All told, there are over 15 km (9 mi) of trails here, including the ever-popular Esker Trail.

Buffalo Pound Provincial Park (Map 28/F5–29/A5) 🥾🚵⛷🐎🔍

Although the lake provides the focal point for activities, the area abounds in wildlife and opportunities to explore the natural environment. About 8 km (5 mi) of the Trans Canada Trail are found around Nicolle Flats along the Dyke Trail, while a few interpretive trails and an elaborate cross-country ski/mountain bike system is also found within the park. Mountain bikers can enjoy around 32 km (20 mi) of mixed single track and dirt road trails that climb up to 50 m (165 ft) in elevation, while cross-country skiers have 7 km (4.5 mi) of ungroomed trails to explore in winter. The Bison View Interpretive Trail is a 3 km (1.9 mi) trail that passes by a bison enclosure. The 3 km Nicolle Flats Trail passes through prairie, wooded coulee and past a turn-of-the-century homestead. Those wishing to explore the confluence of the Moose Jaw and Qu'Appelle Rivers can hike the 1.5 km Valley Interpretive Trail.

By drinking plenty of water and knowing your limits, heat stroke/exhaustion can be easily avoided.

Candle Lake Provincial Park (Map 81/F6) 🥾🚵⛷🔍

The Nordic ski trail system is mostly used by bikers in the summer, but hikers do venture here as well. The 14 km (8.7 mi) of trails range from easy to challenging, and if you tire of the official trails, there are several fire roads in the park.

Carlton Trail Regional Park (Map 33/D3) 🥾🔍

Home to 3 natural trails, visitors can explore the mature parklands forest area of aspen and willow, along with a marsh area. The trails cover 1.6 km (1 mi) and are popular with birdwatchers.

Chinook Pathway – Swift Current (Map 14/G1) 🥾🚵⛷🔍🔍

The Chinook Pathway meanders from one end of Swift Current to the other, along Swift Current Creek. It covers a total distance of 8 km (5 mi) and provides a protected ecosystem for over 60 different types of wildflowers, along with habitats for songbirds and waterfowl. The plant life ranges from cattails, to prickly pear cactus, to wild liquorice. You can expect to enjoy the beauty of nature at the heart of this city along this trail.

Christopher Lake White Spruce Trail (Map 70/G1) 🥾

Found in the Prince Albert Model Forest, this easy trail is not quite 3 km (1.8 mi) return. The trail showcases regeneration methods used in the forest.

Clarine Lake Hiking Trail (Map 80/G7) 🥾

Found in the Clarine Lake Demonstration Forest, this 2.5 km (1.5 mi) loop trail passes through a managed forest.

Clearwater Lake Regional Park (Map 25/F2) 🥾🚵

Clearwater Lake Regional Park provides great opportunities to hike around its natural, spring-fed lake. The lake is nestled in the Coteau Hills, so there is a wide range of flora and fauna.

Craik and District Regional Park (Map 39/C7) 🥾🚵🐎🔍🔍

This park is in a small valley, alongside the Craik Reservoir. There are several trails here that lead alongside a flood plain, wetlands and to viewpoints.

BUFFALO POUND PROVINCIAL PARK	MAP	DIFFICULT·	LENGTH	ELEVATION GAIN	CAMPGROUND	HIKE	BIKE	HORSE	XC-SKI	SNOWSHOE	INTERPRETIVE	VIEW
Bison View Interpretive Trail	Map 28/G5	Easy	2.9 km (1.8 mi)	20 m (65 ft)		•				•	•	•
Dyke Trail	Map 28/G5	Moderate	8 km (5 mi)	Minimal		•				•		
Mountain Biking Trails	Map 28/F5	Varying Difficulty	32 km (20 mi)	50 m (165 ft)			•					
Nicolle Flats Marsh Boardwalk Interpretive Trail	Map 28/G5	Easy	0.5 km (0.3 mi)	Minimal		•			•		•	•
Nicolle Flats Trail	Map 29/A5	Easy	3 km (1.9 mi)	60 m (200 ft)		•				•	•	•
Valley Interpretive Trail	Map 29/A5	Easy	1.5 km (0.9 mi)	Minimal		•				•	•	•

Cypress Hills Interprovincial Park Centre Block (Map 12/E7)

Cypress Hills is one of southwest Saskatchewan's best destinations for hikers, bikers and nature enthusiasts. The Trans Canada Trail cuts through both blocks of the park, but most developed hiking trails are found in the Centre Block, where there are about 28 km (17.5 mi) of trails and another 15 km (9 mi) of groomed ski trails. There are many varieties of flora to be viewed along the trails; please remember to not disturb or pick the wildflowers here. Moose, deer, elk and antelope are common sights within the park.

Highland Rotary Trail

You can find parking for this trail off Ben Vannoch Drive, just south of Loch Lomond. The 2 km loop takes you south along Lonepine Creek and around a couple of small lakes, bordered by wooded hills on either side. This easy trail has little elevation gain.

Loch Leven Trail

This 4 km (2.5 mi) loop circumnavigates Loch Leven and can be accessed from numerous points along its length. The easy trail has minimal elevation gain and accesses several excellent fishing holes.

Lodgepole Trail

This 5.5 km (3.5 mi) one-way trail incorporates part of the Loch Leven Trail, running along the east side of the lake before extending north and exploring the ridge above Boiler Creek. A trailhead can be found at the south end of Loch Leven and taking this trail to its end will lead you to the Lynx Trail. The moderate trail gains around 60 m (200 ft) in elevation.

Lynx Trail

This 3 km (1.9 mi) one-way trail connects with the Twisted Tree trail at its south end and the Lodgepole Trail at its north end. The trail loses and gains up to 20 m (65 ft) of elevation throughout its length.

Moose Trail

From the trailhead near the Poplar Picnic Area, this 3 km (1.9 mi) one-way trail runs south for a short distance before hooking northwest and running parallel to Bald Butte Road, eventually linking up with the Twisted Tree Trail. This moderate trail gains and loses up to 30 m (100 ft) of elevation.

Native Prairie Trail

Found southwest of the Terrance Campground this 2 km (1.2 mi) trail passes through grassland ecosystems with minimal elevation gain.

Trans-Canada Trail

Within the Saskatchewan side of Cypress Hills Interprovincial Park there is over 31 km (19 mi) of the TCT in both the Centre and West Blocks. Open to hiking, biking, cross-country skiing and, in the western block, horseback riding, this wilderness trail can be challenging. There is also 20 km (12.4 mi) of trail on the Alberta side, but there is no official TCT joining Alberta with Saskatchewan.

Valley of the Windfall Trail

This trail starts at the parking lot for the main beach at Loch Leven and passes through marshland and forests. The 1 km loop climbs and descends around 30 m (100 ft) throughout its length.

Valley View Trail

This 2.5 km one-way trail climbs around 60 m (200 ft) in elevation to one of the highest points in the park, offering excellent views of the surrounding area. The northern trailhead can be found at the south end of Loch Leven, while the southern trailhead is located at the Poplar Picnic Area.

Whispering Pines Trail

Beginning near the Cypress Bible Camp, this 4 km (2.5 mi) return trail heads north along the western shore of Loch Leven before climbing around 20 m (65 ft) to a sweeping viewpoint over the park.

Cypress Hills Interprovincial Park West Block (Map 12/E7)

This portion of Cypress Hills Park is more rustic and challenging than the Centre Block. Horseback riding and camping is a popular activity in the West Block and maps are available at the Ranger Station near the park entrance. In addition to the Trans Canada Trail, there are numerous backroads in the West Block that can be explored on foot or horseback. Since a portion of the trails are over cobblestones you may want to have your horse shod prior to entering the park. Mountain bike trails in the park are designed for experts only.

La Barge Trail

This 5 km (3 mi) one-way trail zig-zags from the southern boundary of the West Block, briefly linking up with the Trans Canada Trail before entering the park's central core. Be prepared for a 200 m (655 ft) elevation gain if travelling this trail from north to south.

North Benson Trail

Stretching for 4 km (2.5 mi) one-way, this trail links the West Block's central core with Meier's Road to the north, gaining around 200 m (655 ft) along the way.

Old Fire Tower Trail

This 4 km (2.5 mi) one-way trail runs north from Ranger Station Road to Tower Road, gaining about 190 m (625 ft) of elevation.

South Benson Trail

This 5 km (3 mi) one-way trail climbs around 200 m (655 ft) as it makes its way to the southern boundary of the park's West Block from its central zone.

West Benson Trail

Stretching for 5 km (3 mi) one-way, this trail runs from the Alberta-Saskatchewan border into the West Block's central core, linking up with the North Benson Trail and the Trans Canada Trail. If travelling from east to west, be prepared for a 220 m (720 ft) climb.

CYPRESS HILLS - CENTRE BLOCK

	MAP	DIFFICULTY	LENGTH	ELEVATION GAIN	CAMPGROUND	HIKE	BIKE	HORSE	XC-SKI	SNOWSHOE	INTERPRETIVE	VIEW
Highland Rotary Trail	Map 12/E7	Easy	2 km (1.2 mi)	Minimal		•	•					•
Loch Leven Trail	Map 12/E7	Easy	4 km (2.5 mi)	Minimal		•	•				•	•
Lodgepole Trail	Map 12/E7	Moderate	5.5 km (3.5 mi)	60 m (200 ft)		•	•					•
Lynx Trail	Map 12/E7	Easy	3 km (1.9 mi)	20 m (65 ft)		•	•		•			
Moose Trail	Map 12/E7	Moderate	3 km (1.9 mi)	30 m (100 ft)		•	•					•
Native Prairie Trail	Map 12/E6	Easy	2 km (1.2 mi)	Minimal		•						•
Trans-Canada Trail	Map 12/E7	Varying Difficulty	31 km (19 mi)	120 m (395 ft)	•	•	•	•	•		•	•
Valley of the Windfall Trail	Map 12/E7	Easy	1 km (0.6 mi)	30 m (100 ft)		•						•
Valley View Trail	Map 12/E7	Moderate	2.5 km (1.5 mi)	60 m (200 ft)		•						•
Whispering Pines Trail	Map 12/E7	Easy	2 km (1.2 mi)	20 m (65 ft)		•						•

CYPRESS HILLS - WEST BLOCK

	MAP	DIFFICULTY	LENGTH	ELEVATION GAIN	CAMPGROUND	HIKE	BIKE	HORSE	XC-SKI	SNOWSHOE	INTERPRETIVE	VIEW
La Barge Trail	Map 12/B7	Difficult	5 km (3 mi)	200 m (655 ft)		•		•				
North Benson Trail	Map 12/A7	Difficult	4 km (2.5 mi)	200 m (655 ft)		•		•				
Old Fire Tower Trail	Map 12/B7	Difficult	4 km (2.5 mi)	190 m (625 ft)		•		•				
South Benson Trail	Map 12/A7	Difficult	5 km (3 mi)	200 m (655 ft)		•		•				
West Benson Trail	Map 12/A7	Difficult	5 km (3 mi)	220 m (720 ft)		•		•				

Danielson Provincial Park (Map 38/B5) 🥾🚴🎿📷

There are several informal trails found within the park. In addition, almost 24 km (15 mi) of the Trans Canada Trail passes through the park, including a short stretch of road. This section of the trail offers views of Lake Diefenbaker and cuts through woodlands. A nature loop can be found near the campground.

Doghide River Trails (Map 63/A2) 🥾🚴🎿📷

Around 2 km (1.2 mi) of walking, cycling and skiing trails follow along the Doghide River in Tisdale. The trails can be accessed from Kinsmen McKay Park. Highlights include a natural wetland with a trout pond, observations deck and boardwalks, flower beds and a gazebo that overlooks the river.

Douglas Provincial Park (Map 27/E1–38/D7) 🥾🚴🎿🚶📷

There are several marked trails to explore the dunes, prairie and forests within the park. A 12 km (7.4 mi) section of the Trans Canada Trail passes through the park and incorporates portions of several of the park's trails. The 6 km (4 mi) Cacti Trail links up with the 2.5 km Juniper Trail, passing through some arid landscapes, while the Sunset Trail stretches for 2 km between the Homestead Campground and the Trans Canada Trail. For a longer distance hike, the Wolf Willow Trail stretches for 12 km (7.5 mi) along the eastern shore of the Gordon McKenzie Arm of Diefenbaker Lake.

Duck Mountain Provincial Park (Map 44/C1–55/D7) 🥾🚴🎿🚶📷

An oasis of boreal forest surrounded by prairie, Duck Mountain is a popular destination for hikers and mountain bikers. The Trans Canada Trail winds its way east across the entire park for over 14 km (9 mi) before leaving the park and the province. Other trails in the park include the 1 km Boreal Forest Nature Trail, the 4.5 km (2.5 mi) Pelly Point Trail and the 2 km Nature Woodland Trail. Cross country skiers can explore the 12.5 km (7.5 mi) return Moose Lake/Sergeant Lake Trail and a 28 km (17 mi) loop that leads to the south from Madge Lake Golf Course.

Boreal Forest Nature Trail

Weighing in at 1 km (0.6 mi), this is the shortest trail in the park. However, it is quite scenic as it passes through an old growth forest, by a marsh bog and to a great view of the lake.

Duck Mountain Ski Trail

A 28 km (17 mi) loop heads south from the Madge Lake Golf Course past a series of lakes, including Sergeant, Moose, Rundle and Spruce. Expect about a 50 m (165 ft) elevation gain on the more difficult trails.

Moose Lake/Sergeant Lake Trail

Part of the cross-country ski network, this route can also be hiked in the summer. The trail starts at Batka Lake and loops around the two titular lakes before returning to the trailhead 12.5 km (7.7 mi) later. Expect muddy sections even in summer.

Pelly Point Trail

Passing through a variety of scenery, this 4.4 km (2.7 mi) trail is moderately challenging as it climbs a hill near the beginning of the route. The rest of the trail is relatively level.

Woodland Nature Trail

This 2 km (1.2 mi) trail runs from the campground to Ministik Beach. While it is often used just to get from one place to the other, birdwatchers and nature lovers will find it an interesting hike as well. There are some lovely views of the lake along the way.

Dunnet Regional Park (Map 18/C4) 🥾📷

Dunnet Park is in a naturally treed valley that provides great opportunities for long or short nature hikes. It is adjacent to the Blue Hills, which are part of the Bearpaw Rock formation. The Blue Hills are estimated at 70 million years old and have numerous interesting formations. There is also a buffalo jump site near a First Nations ceremonial site with a sweat and healing lodge, along with First Nations effigies.

Echo Valley Provincial Park (Map 30/E3) 🥾🚴🏇🎿🚶🧗📷

Echo Valley Provincial Park has many opportunities to hike through the valley and upper prairie regions. Formal trails are also found in the cross-country ski network as well as on the Qu'Appelle Interpretive Trail. The cross-country ski trail system is mainly used by mountain bikers. The 10 km (6 mi) of trail are rated novice to intermediate trails. The park also has some great single track trails that wind up and down the valley through forests of poplar and aspen and open prairie grassland. You can get a trail map from the park office.

The Qu'Appelle Interpretive Trail takes about an hour and provides information about the valley formation and plant life. The trail leaves from the parking and picnic area, and leads to a series of stairs to climb up the hillside. Park interpreters offer guided hikes regularly over the summer.

Esterhazy Regional Park (Map 32/G4–33/A4) 🥾🚴🎿🚶🧗📷

This park has 6 km (3.7 mi) of maintained nature trails that wind around the golf course in the scenic Kaposvar Valley. In the winter, 26 km (16 mi) of trails are groomed for cross-country skiing.

Foam Lake Marsh Trails (Map 53/A7) 🥾📷

There are two trails through Foam Marsh, which is part of the Quill Lakes International Bird Area. The Vatnabyggd Trail is a 3.5 km (2.2 mi) one-way trail and can be accessed from the Lure Crop and Bertdale entrances. The Engitrod Trail forms a 1.2 km (0.7 mi) loop and is accessed only from the Bertdale Viewing area. There are also a couple short spur trails that can be hiked.

Fort Carlton Trail (Map 60/B2) 🥾

Starting at the campground at Fort Carlton, this 1.5 km (0.9 mi) loop trail climbs up to the top of the hill overlooking the Fort. The climb is not extremely hard, but it will be a challenge for some.

Gem Lakes Trail (Map 82/B2) 🏕🥾🛶

A 5.5 km (3.5 mi) loop takes you through this group of small lakes in Narrow Hills Provincial Park. There are 7 lakes in total and the trail is well marked, with some moderately steep sections. Several sites for backcountry camping can be found along the trail, and the lakes are stocked making for some decent angling.

Good Spirit Lake Provincial Park Trails (Map 43/B2) 🥾🚴🎿🚶

The longest single trail in Good Spirit Lake Provincial Park is the 18 km (11 mi) section of the Trans Canada Trail that starts across from the recreation hall. However, it is not the only trail here. A 3 km (1.8 mi) easy return hike will take hikers into the complex of sand dunes at the edge of the lake. In the winter, there are 18 km (11 mi) of cross-country trails in the park. There is also a short interpretive woodland trail.

DOUGLAS PROVINCIAL PARK	MAP	DIFFICULTY	LENGTH	ELEVATION GAIN	CAMPGROUND	HIKE	BIKE	HORSE	XC-SKI	SNOWSHOE	INTERPRETIVE	VIEW
Cacti Trail	Map 38/D7	Moderate	6 km (3.7 mi)	Minimal		•	•					
Juniper Trail	Map 38/D7	Easy	2.5 km (1.6 mi)	Minimal		•						•
Sunset Trail	Map 38/D7	Easy	2 km (1.2 mi)	Minimal		•						•
Wolf Willow Trail	Map 38/D7	Moderate	12 km (7.5 mi)	Minimal		•						•
DUCK MOUNTAIN PROVINCIAL PARK												
Boreal Forest Nature Trail	Map 55/D7	Easy	1 km (0.6 mi)	Minimal		•	•				•	•
Duck Mountain Ski Trail	Map 55/D7	Varying Difficulty	28 km (17 mi)	50 m (165 ft)		•	•		•		•	•
Moose Lake/Sergeant Lake Trail	Map 44/D1	Difficult	12.5 km (7.7 mi)	40 m (130 ft)		•			•			•
Pelly Point Trail	Map 55/C7	Moderate	4.4 km (2.7 mi)	20 m (65 ft)		•					•	•
Woodland Nature Trail	Map 55/D7	Easy	2 km (1.2 mi)	Minimal		•					•	•

Grasslands National Park (Maps 3, 4, 5) 🏕️🥾🚴🏇⛷️🚶❄️

Grasslands National Park provides a unique opportunity for hikers to explore the traditional prairie landscape. The park offers short interpretive hikes of less than a kilometre and long backcountry camping trips along unmarked routes. Those interested in the backcountry routes should pick up a copy of the field guide developed by the Prairie Wind and Silver Sage Ecomuseum.

Shorter marked trails include the 70 Mile Butte Trail, which is 5 km (3 mi) long, the rugged Broken Hills Trail that stretches for 11 km (7 mi), the easy 2 km Eagle Butte Trail and the 500 metre Larson's Interpretive Trail. The 2.5 km Rim Trail leads through some stunning scenery, the Riverwalk Trail stretches for 2 km along the Frenchman River and the 2 km Rock Creek Trail explores some beautiful grasslands. Hikers looking to explore the Laouenan Coulee can take the 500 metre interpretive Top Dogtown Trail, while the Two Trees Trail is another interpretive trail which explores the Frenchman River over a 3.5 km (2 mi) loop.

Long distance and unmarked trails in the park include the 16 km (10 mi) Butte Creek/Red Butte Trail (a popular overnighter), the 9 km (5 mi) Eagle Butte – Ecotour Route, the 15 km (9 mi) North Gillespie Trail and the 16 km (10 mi) Timbergulch Route. Zahurkis's Point Trail, a difficult 11 km (7 mi) trek, runs over three different routes through badlands and rugged gullies.

70 Mile Butte Trail (Map 3/G5–4/A5)

This moderately difficult 5 km (3 mi) trail leads you up to the 70 Mile Butte. Along the way you will be treated to views of the natural prairie landscape and once on top you will get fantastic views of the surrounding area.

Broken Hills Trail (Map 4/A6)

A more difficult 11 km (6.8 mi) trail takes hikers, bikers and those on horseback into some rugged prairie landscapes. Bikers and horseback riders should note that after the 3 km (1.9 mi) mark the trail does get more rugged and steep and it is best left for those hiking.

Butte Creek Trail (Map 5/C6)

With a camp for both hikers and horses at the 8 km (5 mi) mark, this is a popular 16 km (10 mi) overnight trip. From McGowan Ranch, you will cross Rock Creek and continue past the butte to the Four Corners. From the northwest corner of the ranch there is a narrow corridor of parkland to cross in order to reach Hellfire Creek, which marks the midway point of the hike. The trail crosses Hellfire Creek and leads to a scenic gap between a pointed butte and rounded butte to the west. Continue west over a series of ridges and draws until you reach the extraordinary Red Buttes. These are remnants of the prehistoric landscape, turned red by shattered fragments of scoria.

Eagle Butte – Ecotour Route (Map 3/G5–4/A5)

This trail is a 9 km (5.5 mi) one-way hike requiring up to 5 hours to complete. The trail begins at Ecotour Stop 1, proceeding in a northwest direction to the 70 Mile Butte Kiosk. The trail passes through the Laouenan Coulee Flats and along game trails to a former ranch dugout. At about 3.4 km you will see the Snake Pit Prairie Dog Colony. Next up is Lizard Draw, which twists down to Bog Coulee. This is a great place to search for the endangered short-horned lizard. The hike continues up a small knoll to the draw, around to the head of the north draining channel and finally to the north end of Eagle Butte and the 70 Mile Butte Kiosk.

North Gillespie Trail (Map 4/D6)

This moderate hike can be enjoyed as an overnighter or challenging single day route. It is 15 km (9.3 mi) return and starts from the roadside south of Gillespie Ranch. Hiking and horseback riding are recommended, with mountain biking possible for the first 3 km. The hike follows an old fence west to the ridge of Otter Creek Valley, where there are two campsites available. From Otter Creek Valley you cross the ridge to the gap, continue west and then take a north turn up the coulee to see the Little Breed Creek Valley and the prairie dog town, which marks the halfway point. To return, travel southeast across Little Breed Creek to the gap in the slope on the other side of the valley, then cross into Otter Creek Valley. Otter Creek Ridge will return you to the start.

Rim Trail (Map 5/D7)

This is an easy 2.5 km (1.6 mi) hike taking about 1 to 2 hours. The departure point is McGowan Kiosk and the halfway point is a small sandstone outcrop on the southwest edge of the rim. The hike takes you along the rim of the butte above Hellfire Creek overlooking the McGowan Ranch. You may choose to add an additional loop to Rock Creek, or continue to the east end of the upland rim. You can also to descend into the Kildeer badlands. At the east edge of the rim you head back to the kiosk.

Timbergulch Route (Map 4/A5)

This is a 5 to 8 hour hike covering 16 km (10 mi) return to the Ecotour Stop 1. The route requires some bushwhacking and is used by hikers and horseback riders. Your starting point leads you through the bushy Timmons Coulee to a scenic gap that separates this coulee from Police Coulee. Continue east into Police Coulee and then turn north to cross the meandering stream bed to climb to the tabletop and Maple Draw. An old Manitoba Maple tree is the marker of a shallow point to continue east across the draw in the Timbergulch Coulee, marking the halfway point of the hike. Rather than retracing your steps you can hike 5 km into the Frenchman River Valley. Once in the valley you will pass a prairie dog colony and continue until you are once again at the opening to Police Coulee and the gap at Timmons Coulee. Finish your hike back to the Ecotour Stop.

Zahurski's Point Trail (Map 5/D7)

Covering 11 km (7 mi) of moderate to difficult terrain, hikers and horseback riders often take two days to explore this trail. The point of departure is the East Block McGowan Kiosk, with Zahurski's Point the halfway landmark. The portion from the McGowan Creek to the confluence of Hellfire and Rock Creek can be biked. The hike leaves from the kiosk heading west to the edge of the valley, then south to sandstone outcroppings. Two trees on the tabletop provide you with markers to follow; Zahurski's Point is to the west. There are three different routes, all of which provide you with an opportunity to cover intriguing terrain and see various wildlife.

GRASSLANDS NATIONAL PARK	MAP	DIFFICULTY	LENGTH	ELEVATION GAIN	CAMPGROUND	HIKE	BIKE	HORSE	XC-SKI	SNOWSHOE	INTERPRETIVE	VIEW
70 Mile Butte Trail	Map 3/G5	Moderate	5 km (3 mi)	90 m (295 ft)		•	•	•				•
Broken Hills Trail	Map 4/A6	Difficult	11 km (6.8 mi)	90 m (295 ft)		•	•	•				•
Butte Creek Trail	Map 5/C6	Moderate	16 km (10 mi)	60 m (195 ft)	•	•		•				•
Eagle Butte Trail - Ecotour Route	Map 3/G5 - 4/A5	Difficult	9 km (5.5 mi)	110 m (360 ft)		•		•				•
Eagle Butte Loop Trail	Map 3/G5	Easy	2 km (1.2 mi)	50 m (165 ft)		•		•				•
Larson Interpretive Walk	Map 4/B6	Easy	0.5 km (0.3 mi)	Minimal		•					•	
North Gillespie Trail	Map 4/D6	Moderate	7.5 km (4.5 mi)	140 m (460 ft)	•	•	•	•				•
Rim Trail	Map 5/D7	Easy	2.5 km (1.6 mi)	Minimal		•						•
Riverwalk Trail	Map 3/G5	Easy	2 km (1.2 mi)	Minimal		•						•
Rock Creek Trail	Map 5/C7	Easy	2 km (1.2 mi)	Minimal		•						•
Timbergulch Route	Map 4/A5	Difficult	8 km (5 mi)	70 m (230 ft)		•		•				•
Top Dogtown Trail	Map 4/A5	Easy	0.5 km (0.3 mi)	Minimal		•					•	
Two Trees Trail	Map 3/G5	Easy	3.5 km (2 mi)	Minimal		•						•
Zahurski's Point Trail	Map 5/D7	Varying Difficulty	11 km (7 mi)	90 m (295 ft)		•		•				•

Greenwater Lake Provincial Park (Map 63/E5) 🥾🚴🛶🏕🏊🐾🎣

Greenwater Lake Provincial Park offers some spectacular interpretive trails prefect for nature viewing and birdwatching. The Highbush Interpretive Trail offers two loop trails. The longer Donald Hooper Loop is 3.3 km (2 mi) while the shorter Greenwater loop is less than 2 km (1 mi) long. The trail can be muddy in low spots. The Marean Lake Birding Interpretive Trail gives you the chance to see some of the more than 200 species of birds that have been recorded in the area. This is an easy, wide trail that is surfaced with crusher dust, and a viewing tower can be found along the way. For the more adventurous, there are over 25 km (15 mi) of cross-country ski and extended snowmobile trails that can be hiked or biked in the summer – look for the trailhead to the ski trails across from the park office on Highway 38. You can find this park 20 km south of Porcupine Plain.

Hudson Bay Trails (Map 65/A2) 🥾🚴🛶🎣

Found south of town, the regional park offers a series of nature trails that feature bridges, stairways and hand rails guiding hikers up the side of the hill and along the banks of the Fir and Red Deer Rivers. The wooded trails also lead past an old cabin and down to the river junctions. In winter, the Pineview system offers about 30 km (19 mi) of cross-country ski trails to explore as well.

> *Short breaks taken at regular intervals will optimize your overall performance and keep your hiking rhythm steady. You will have an easier time maintaining a consistent speed if you take a two-minute break every 25 to 30 minutes.*

Hjertaas Nature Trail (Map 43/C5) 🥾🚴

Part of the Trans Canada Trail, the Ravine Ecological Preserve in Yorkton was once a landfill. The area has been restored, becoming "a multi-purpose jewel" in the heart of the city. The trail here is only 2.8 km (1.7 mi) long, but includes a boardwalk over the water at the mid-point of the trail, which will allow hikers to either shorten the route, or hike a figure eight pattern. The trail passes through grassland and aspen parkland as well, with little elevation gain.

Indian Head Shelterbelt (Map 31/A5) 🥾🏠

The Indian Head Shelterbelt facility is located 2 km south of the town of Indian Head. The National Migratory Bird Sanctuary has been operating for over a century here, growing trees to fill the needs of prairie farmers. It is 259 hectares (640 ac) in size and produces 29 hardy varieties of trees and shrubs. A parking area and self-guided hiking trail are available year-round. The Sunbeam Nature Trail allows you to view a variety of plants, and often, small animals.

Jean Louis Legare Regional Park (Map 6/D4) 🥾🚴🏠

This regional park is next to the historic community of Willow Bunch, which was settled more than a century ago by Métis people. The town's museum provides a wealth of information for visitors. Inside the park there are two natural hiking trails that are especially popular with birdwatchers and wildlife lovers.

Kaposvar Trail (Map 33/B5) 🥾🚴🏕🛶🏊

Stretching for 7 km (4.5 mi) from the Qu'Appelle Valley to Hazel Cliffe, this moderate trail follows along Kaposvar Creek for its entire length. From the trailhead off Grid Road 637, you will head northwest and, for the first 2 km, the path is flat and easy. Beyond this, water erosion has washed out sections of the trail, forcing you into detour up the ravine. There are several creek crossings along the way, including at 3.5 km and at 5.3 km. Hazel Cliffe, a historic settlement, is now just a small park and a house with a couple of outbuildings. It is possible to extend this trail for a 20 km (12.5 mi) one-way route to Esterhazy along a popular snowmobile route.

Katepwa Point Provincial Park (Map 31/A4) 🥾🚴🥾🛶🏊🐾🎣

Katepwa Point Provincial Park has an interpretive exhibit that explains the geology, ecology and recreational history of the area. The exhibit is also the trailhead for two hiking trails. The Cutout Coulee Trail is a 1.6 km (1 mi) return trail winds through a scenic coulee to the top of the valley for a panoramic view of Katepwa Point. The Hillside Nature Trail stretches 8 km (5 mi) and includes a portion of the Trans Canada Trail on the east side of Katepwa Lake.

Kipabiskau Regional Park Trails (Map 62/G5) 🥾🚴🎣

There are about 10 km (6 mi) of trails here, although few of them are more than a kilometre or two long. The main trails run across the hillside, but side trails do climb up the hill. There are some nice views of the lake along the Lakeview Trail.

Kristi Lake Nature Trail (Map 71/A5) 🥾🐾

Located about 5 km north of Prince Albert, this is an easy 2 km (1.2 mi) interpretive trail.

Lac La Ronge Provincial Park (Map 101/D6) 🏕🥾🚴🛶🏊🐾🎣

Found at the south edge of the Canadian Shield, Lac La Ronge is Saskatchewan's largest provincial park. This is a land defined by water and only has two designated trails. The Nemieben Trail is an easy 1.5 km (0.9 mi) long interpretive trail along the shores of Nemieben Lake. The trail features interpretive signs on how glaciers shaped this landscape and about the current natural environment. Those wishing to venture further can explore the Nut Point Trail. This overnight trail is 30 km (18 mi) return and features a trio of rustic camping sites along the way, including Nut Point itself. The trail begins at Nut Point Campground near La Ronge and takes its name from the abundance of hazelnuts found along the trail. The moderate trail has several places where you will need to climb up and down off rocky ridges, which can be slippery. A third trail leads to the sand cliffs on a river bank south of La Ronge. Although it is not a formal trail, it is fairly well used.

Lac Pelletier Regional Park (Map 14/E4) 🥾🚴🥾🏊🎣

Lac Pelletier is a spring-fed waterbody and is central to this scenic year-round park. Natural trails through the valley and along the lake provide opportunities for nature hikes and wildlife viewing.

Last Mountain Lake National Wildlife Area Trails (Map 40/A3) 🥾🏠

Best known as the first bird sanctuary in North America, the two trails, located on opposite sides of the wetlands, are both fairly short. The Grasslands Nature Trail is a 1.5 km (0.9 mi) loop through the grasslands at the southeast end of the wetlands. The Wetland Trail, as the name would lead you to believe, is a 2.5 km (1.5 mi) loop through the wetlands, including some boardwalk sections. Both trails are popular with birdwatchers.

Laurier Regional Park (Map 8/B3) 🥾🚴🐾🎣

Located on the outskirts of the town of Radville, this park has a self-guided trail. The trail shows the effects of the Ice Age on the area, including the nearby Big Muddy. There are also examples of Buffalo rubbing rocks and wallows.

Leflay Nature Trails (Map 43/F7) 🥾🚴🏠

Found in Saltcoats Regional Park, next to Anderson Lake, there are about 4 km (2.5 mi) of trails to explore here. The trails lead through the pine forest to a wildlife observation stand.

Little Bear Lake Trail (Map 82/C2) 🥾🚴🏊

From just north of Route 913, a 15 km (9 mi) one-way trail leads through some remote wilderness to Little Bear Lake Resort on the south end of Little Bear Lake. The trail gains and loses up to 50 m (165 ft) of elevation throughout its length, passing by numerous small lakes and streams.

Little Red River Park Trails (Map 71/A5) 🥾🚴🛶🏕

Home to the Kinsmen Ski Hill, the 485 hectare (1,200 ac) Red River Park is also home to many kilometres of multi-use trails. In summer, the trails are used by hikers and bikers while cross-country skiers and snowshoers explore the system in winter. The local ski club maintains about 35 km (22 mi) of trails in winter, most of which are open to hiking and mountain biking in summer. Red River Park is on the north side of the river, just minutes from Prince Albert. The trails wind around the Spruce River, past Coubeaux Lake and a sports field, covering an area between Highways 2 and 55. There are several access points to the trails, which lose and gain up to around 30 m (100 ft) of elevation throughout. Highlights include a pedestrian suspension bridge over the Spruce River and a picnic area complete with camp kitchens and barbecue pits.

Luck Lake Heritage Marsh (Map 37/F6) 🥾🚴🏠

A hiking trail along the northeast corner of the marsh allows for a closer view of this ecosystem's inhabitants. There is also a 35 km (21.7 mi) self-guided nature tour that circles the marsh and makes for an interesting bicycle ride. From this tour, people can access the various public observation points for wildlife viewing, particularly birdwatching.

TRAIL ADVENTURES

Makwa Lake Provincial Park Trails (Map 77/A3)
The Mewasin Trail is a 3 km (1.8 mi) trail that runs from the Mewasin Campground over one small pond and past an old cabin on the shores of a second pond. There is a secondary trail that shortens the trip by about a kilometre. During winter there are about 18 km (11 mi) of trails to explore with trail maps at the park office.

Meadow Lake Provincial Park (Maps 86–88)
This park features the only destination backpacking trail in the Saskatchewan park system, the 120 km (75 mi) long Boreal Trail. There is no shortage of shorter trails to hike, ski or even snowmobile, either, with over 100 km (60 mi) of snowmobile trails available. Several frontcountry and backcountry campsites can also be found throughout the park.

It is possible to connect with the Boreal Trail via numerous branch trails, including the 4 km (2.5 mi) Da Balinhard Trail, the 3.5 km First Mustus Lake Trail, the 7.5 km (4.5 mi) Mistohay Lake Trail, the 11 km (7 mi) Newbranch Trail and the 4.2 km (2.6 mi) Vivian Branch Trail. The Humphrey Lake Trail is a 7 km (4.3 mi) return hike through an area rich with wildlife, while the Kimball Lake Trails lead hikers around the titular lake as well as Little Raspberry Lake.

Several cross-country ski trails are used by hikers in the summer, including the 5 km (3 mi) Hay Meadow Trail and the St. Cyr Trails. The 500 metre Boreal Forest Interpretive Trail and the 2 km White Birch Nature Trail offer some easy treks through stunning scenery.

De Balinhard Lake Trail (Map 87/B5)
This 4 km (2.5 mi) one-way trail branches off the Boreal Trail and leads hikers to a campsite on the south shore of De Balinhard Lake. The moderate trail gains up to 30 m (100 ft) of elevation along the way.

Hay Meadow Trail (Map 87/F5)
From the road to the campground at Greig Lake, this 4.8 km (3 mi) loop trail is used by cross-country skiers in the winter. While most of the other trails are not passable in summer, this trail is maintained for hiking through a forest of trembling aspens.

Humphrey Lake Trail (Map 86/E5)
Removed from the other trails in the park, this 7 km (4.3 mi) return trail passes through an area that has lots of wildlife. Indeed, the shallow lake is home to many waterfowl and there is a viewing tower near the lake. It is only about twenty minutes from the trailhead near Sandy Beach Campground to the lake itself, but the trail circumnavigates the lake, with a spur to the viewing tower.

Mistohay Lake Trail (Map 87/C5)
This 7.5 km (4.5 mi) one-way trail leads south from the campground on Mistohay Lake to link up with the Boreal Trail, losing about 60 m (200 ft) of elevation along the way.

Newbranch Trail (Map 87/D5)
This is the longest trail in Meadow Lake Provincial Park, at 11 km (7 mi). The trail starts off Highway 224 west of Kimball Lake and takes hikers through an area thick with wildlife. There are a couple difficult sections, but the hiking is mostly easy and will take about four hours to complete. Hikers looking for a longer experience on the trail can stay at one of two primitive campsites; one at Peitahigan Lake, the other at Third Mustus Lake, and continue along the Boreal Trail. The trail loses and gains up to 40 m (130 ft) of elevation throughout its length.

Methye Portage Trail (Map 116/B5)
From Wallis Bay at the northwest end of Lac Loche, the Methye Portage is a 20 km (12 mi) one-way hike to the Clearwater River. This is a historic portage trail, and the only way to get to the trail at either end is by water. Most people hiking the trail arrange for a boat to drop them off and pick them up, although it is possible to paddle the 18 km from the town of La Loche to the trailhead. It is even possible to portage your canoe into the Clearwater, but bear in mind the first section of the trail features several boggy areas and creek crossings. The farther you go the drier it becomes. The trail is mostly level, save for the descent into the Clearwater River Valley. Allow for three or four days to do this hike.

Milligan Creek Trail (Map 42/A1)
This short, 1.5 km (0.9 mi) loop trail starts right beside the visitor centre in Foam Lake. It can also be accessed from the nearby campground.

Moose Mountain Provincial Park (Map 21/F5)
Moose Mountain Provincial Park is an excellent spot for hiking in southeast Saskatchewan. With about 80% of the park's land set in aspen forest dotted with small lakes, the area is very scenic. Due to its higher elevation, the area also provides more moderate summer temperatures than southwest portions of the province. Hiking trails in the park include the 2 km Birch Forest Interpretive Trail, the 4.5 km (3 mi) Beaver Lake Trail and the 2 km Wuche Sakaw Interpretive Trail. The easy, paved Lakeview Trail stretches for 900 metres around the eastern side of the Fish Creek Campground. Close to 30 km (19 mi) of cross-country ski trails can also be found northwest of Kenosee Lake, while some of the park's trails are open to ATV use from June 15th through the Labour Day Weekend.

MEADOW LAKE PROVINCIAL PARK

	MAP	DIFFICULTY	LENGTH	ELEVATION GAIN	CAMPGROUND	HIKE	BIKE	HORSE	XC-SKI	SNOWSHOE	INTERPRETIVE	VIEW
Boreal Forest Interpretive Trail	Map 87/F5	Easy	0.5 km (0.3 mi)	Minimal		•						•
Boreal Trail	Map 86/D4-87/F6	Varying Difficulty	120 km (74.5 mi)	90 m (295 ft)	•	•						•
De Balinhard Lake Trail	Map 87/B5	Moderate	4 km (2.5 mi)	30 m (100 ft)	•	•						•
First Mustus Lake Trail	Map 87/E6	Easy	3.5 km (2 mi)	Minimal	•	•						•
Hay Meadow Trail	Map 87/F5	Moderate	4.8 km (3 mi)	Minimal		•				•		•
Humphrey Lake Trail	Map 86/E5	Moderate	3.5 km (2.1 mi)	30 m (100 ft)		•						•
Kimball Lake Trails	Map 87/E6	Moderate	5 km (3 mi)	Minimal		•					•	•
Mistohay Lake Trail	Map 87/C5	Moderate	7.5 km (4.5 mi)	60 m (200 ft)		•						•
Newbranch Trail	Map 87/D6-F6	Varying Difficulty	11 km (7 mi)	40 m (130 ft)	•	•						•
St. Cyr Trails	Map 87/A5	Varying Difficulty	n/a	40 m (130 ft)					•	•		•
Vivian Lake Trail	Map 87/D6	Moderate	4.2 km (2.6 mi)	Minimal		•						•
White Birch Nature Trail	Map 87/G4	Easy	2 km (1.2 mi)	Minimal		•					•	•

MOOSE MOUNTAIN PROVINCIAL PARK

	MAP	DIFFICULTY	LENGTH	ELEVATION GAIN	CAMPGROUND	HIKE	BIKE	HORSE	XC-SKI	SNOWSHOE	INTERPRETIVE	VIEW
Beaver Lake Trail	Map 21/F5	Moderate	4.5 km (2.8 mi)	Minimal		•	•					•
Birch Forest Interpretive Trail	Map 21/F6	Easy	2.1 km (1.3 mi)	Minimal		•					•	•
Kenosee Lake Riding Stables	Map 21/E6	Easy	n/a	Minimal				•				•
Lakeview Trail	Map 21/F5	Easy	0.9 km (0.6 mi)	Minimal		•	•					•
Moose Mountain Park Ski Trails	Map 21/F5	Varying Difficulty	27 km (17 mi)	Minimal					•			•
Wuche Sakaw Interpretive Trail	Map 21/F5	Easy	2 km (1.2 mi)	Minimal		•					•	•

Moose Jaw Trails (Map 28/E7)

Around 80 km (50 mi) of walking, hiking and biking trails can be found in and around the city of Moose Jaw. This includes a 40 km section of the Trans Canada Trail which extends north of the city and the 15 km Rotary Trail, which forms a loop around the city. The shorter 4 km Rotary Cove Trail explores the wetlands of Sunningdale Park, and the beautiful Wakamow Valley offers around 20 km of multi-use trails. In the winter, cross-country skiers and snowshoers use many of these trails.

Moose Jaw and Area Trans Canada Trail

Around 40 km (25 mi) of paved and gravel trail leads north from Moose Jaw to link up with the proposed Trans Canada Trail. Following along this route will eventually lead you to Buffalo Pound Provincial Park.

Rotary Trail

This 15 km (9 mi) paved and dirt loop circles around the city and is relatively easy, though several branch trails offer more of a challenge. This trail can be accessed from many different points, allowing you to pick and choose the length of your hike.

Wakamow Valley Trails

Around 20 km (12 mi) of trails can be found in the Wakamow Valley, just south of downtown Moose Jaw. The scenic Moose Jaw River runs through the valley, creating a fertile habitat for over 190 species of birds, as well as offering opportunities for canoeing and kayaking. The 4 km (2.5 m) Devonian Trail is a popular choice for walkers and cyclists, following the banks of the Moose Jaw River.

Moosomin & District Regional Park (Map 22/D3)

Found 14 km from the Trans-Canada Highway, along Moosomin Reservoir, this park offers hiking and biking trails in a natural prairie environment. Cross-country skiers and snowshoers also use the natural trails in the winter.

Mount Blackstrap Trails (Map 49/E6)

This man-made mountain was constructed to host the 1971 Canada Winter Games in nearby Saskatoon. The Mount Blackstrap Ski Hill was closed in 2009 (although there is a proposal to reopen the hill), but there are 5 km (3 mi) of trails here that are used for mountain biking and cross-country skiing and, to a lesser extent, for hiking.

To protect against wood ticks, wear slippery finished clothes with elastic cuffs to protect the body. DEET repellants can protect against ticks on exposed skin. Once inside, thoroughly inspect your body and clothing for ticks.

Mud Lake Trail (Map 52/C5)

Part of the Quill Lakes International Bird Area, the prime reason people come here is to watch birds. Access is not permitted in the fall, but during the rest of the year there is a 2.7 km (1.7 mi) trail to a Ducks Unlimited Dam.

Nipawin and District Regional Park Trails (Map 73/A3)

If a hiker were to walk all the trails in this regional park, they would cover about 10 km (6 mi). However, they would have to hike seven main and a handful of minor trails to do so.

North Battleford Trails (Map 58/A3)

The city of North Battleford offers a variety of walking, cycling and winter-use trails for users of all skill levels. Long-distance trekkers can take on a 30 km section of the Trans Canada Trail. The north shore of the North Saskatchewan River offers about 25 km of hiking and biking trails that can be found around the Battleford River Valley Visitor Centre. Mountain bikers can also check out the 6.5 km Peagee Man Trail, one of the most challenging biking trails in the province. Finlayson Island is another hiking, walking and cycling hotspot, with 20 km of mostly easy trails. Within the city itself, Centennial Park offers several easy walking trails along a variety of recreation activities such as soccer and baseball.

Palliser Regional Park (Map 26/G2)

Palliser Regional Park is a very large, full-service park situated near the town of Riverhurst, on Lake Diefenbaker. The Eric Kurz Memorial Nature Trail provides opportunities to explore the area and its wide range of flora and fauna.

Pine Cree Regional Park (Map 2/E1–13/E7)

Found along the South Fork Road 633, this park sits in the Cypress Hills north of Eastend. There are three trails covering about 6 km (3.7 mi). The Top of the World Trail is about 4 km long and climbs to the highest point in the park. The Short Loop Trail branches from this trail and back down to the park, while the Everett Baker Trail is also 1 km. It takes you above the Hermits Cave along a historic trail. The area around the park is also noted for its fossils (including one of the most complete Tyrannosaurus Rex skeletons ever found), and hikers often search for these hidden gems.

Prince Albert National Park (Maps 70, 79, 80)

Saskatchewan's largest National Park offers the biggest and arguably the best selections of hiking trails in the province, with 21 main trails that cover over 150 km (90 mi) of terrain. Many of the trails are open to mountain bikers and horseback riders in the summer and cross-country skiers and snowshoers in the winter. Notable trails include the Amyot Lake Trail, which combines with the West Side Boundary Trail to form a 15.5 km (9.5 mi) loop. The Elk Trail is a 40 km (25 mi) one-way trail that leads from near Sandy Lake all the way to the west side of the park. The Freight Trail is a 27 km (17 mi) trail that offers multiple access points for shorter treks. The 20 km (12 mi) Grey Owl Trail leads along the shore of Kingsmere Lake to Grey Owl's historic cabin. The Red Deer Trail's 17 km (10.5 mi) is composed of three separate loops, while the 8.5 km (5 mi) Spruce River Highlands Trail is one of the more difficult trails in the park.

Amyot Lake Trail (Map 79/G7–80/A7)

If hiked/biked/skied or ridden in conjunction with the West Side Boundary Trail, this moderate trail forms a 15.5 km (9.6 mi) loop. The sedge meadows along the way are home to a free roaming herd of bison. Care must be taken around these big animals.

Elk Trail (Map 70/C1–80/E7)

At 40 km (25 mi) one-way, this is one of the longer trails in the park. Taking hikers from near Sandy Lake on Highway 263 all the way to the west side of the park and the West Side Boundary Trail, hikers still have several kilometres to walk before finding the nearest road. The moderate out-and-back trip trail hooks up with the Fish Lake Trail and the Hunters Lake Trail, which can be used to create shorter loop, although a shuttle is needed for all options. The trail is also open to mountain bikers and horseback riders and, in the winter, cross-country skiers.

Fisher Trail (Map 80/F5)

This easy 7.2 km (4.5 mi) trail passes through some great scenery near Waskesiu. The trail is open to hiking and mountain biking in summer and cross-country skiing in winter.

Fish Lake Trail (Map 70/E1–80/E7)

This 12 km (7 mi) one-way trail starts on Cookson Road near the southern boundary of the park. The trail takes hikers, bikers and horseback riders to Fish Lake and a backcountry campground.

Freight Trail (Map 80/E5)

This easy 27 km (17 mi) one-way trail was once used as a fur and supply trail between Prince Albert and La Ronge. Fortunately, hikers (and mountain bikers and cross-country skiers) do not have to do the whole trail in one shot. There are alternate trailheads (four in total) that break the trail into smaller portions, the longest of which is 10 km (6 mi) one-way.

Grey Owl Trail (Map 80/C3)

If you don't have a boat, the only way to get to the historic site of Grey Owl's cabin is via this 20 km (12 mi) one-way trail that follows the Kingsmere Lake shoreline. There is a campsite at the 17 km mark on the lake. Boaters will only have to hike about 3 km (1.9 mi) one-way to the cabin. Paddlers can also portage 600 metres to Lake Ajawaan Lake and paddle to the cabin.

Hunters Lake Trail (Map 70/C1–80/C7)

Starting from Cookson Road, this challenging 22 km (13.6 mi) trail has some steep hills as it makes its way to Hunters Lake. The route can be hiked, biked, ridden on horseback, snowshoed or skied as a partial loop with the Elk Trail, which connects to this trail at Hunters Lake.

Kingfisher Trail (Map 80/E4)

This 13 km (8 mi) trail begins at the Waskesiu Marina and crosses the Waskesiu River to hook south past the community of Waskesiu Lake. This trail has minimal elevation gain.

Red Deer Trail (Map 80/E5)

This relatively new trail, or rather, trio of interlocking loop trails covers 17 km (10.5 mi) of moderately difficult terrain. Open to hiking and mountain biking, the trailhead is found at the corner of Waskesiu Drive and Lakeview Drive in Waskesiu.

Spruce River Highlands Trail (Map 80/F7)

This 8.5 km (5.2 mi) loop is one of the more difficult trails in the park. It features a lot of up and downs that will challenge most hikers and cross-country skiers.

West Side Boundary Trail (Map 70/C1–79/G4)

Covering 59.5 km (37 mi), this trail follows the west side of the park from the South Gate on Cookson Road to the north end of the trail near Nesslin Lake. The trail can be broken into two shorter trips, with the dividing point at the Sturgeon Crossing Picnic Area at the 37.5 km (23 mi) mark. The trail is not maintained and can be difficult, especially for mountain bikers, as there are several hidden washouts and fallen trees hidden by tall grass.

Prince Albert Rotary Trail (Map 71/A5)

This 26 km (16 mi) trail circumnavigates much of Prince Albert, missing only the southwest corner of the city. The longest section of the route follows the Saskatchewan River, but is not contiguous in nature due to private lands and natural obstacles. Near the eastern side of the city, the trail heads south, passing through parks, green spaces and sometimes along sidewalks as it circumnavigates most of the city. A 3 km (1.8 mi) spur connects to the trails in Little Red River Park.

Qu'Appelle Valley Trails (Map 29/D4)

5 km (3 mi) of easy walking trails extend into the hills east of Lumsden. The looping trails gain up to 40 m (130 ft) in elevation and can be accessed from Qu'Appelle Drive. In the winter, this is a popular Nordic skiing destination.

Redberry Lake Biosphere Reserve (Map 59/C3)

This is Saskatchewan's only UNESCO world biosphere reserve, providing protected habitat for nine endangered or threatened species of wildlife, as well as over 180 other species. The reserve is centred around the saline lake and also features rolling prairie, seasonal ponds and marshes and aspen groves. Designated hiking trails include the 2 km Millennium Point Trail, which wraps around Pelican Bay, the 2 km Lookout Trail, the 2 km Grassland Golf Course Walking Trail and the 200 metre Crooked Bush Trail, which leads to a stand of uniquely shaped aspens. The reserve is found just outside of Hafford.

Regina Beach Trail (Map 29/C3)

On the southern shores of Last Mountain Lake, an old railway bed has been converted into a broad, easy trail that stretches from the resort community of Regina Beach to the mouth of the Arm River. The portion from Regina Beach to Buena Vista is paved. The main trail is 11 km (6.7 mi) one-way, but mountain bikers have built several trails that fall off from the main route. Between the main trail and the lake is considered easy single track, while heading away from the lake brings mountain bikers into some fairly technical terrain.

Regina Trails (Map 29/F6)

The city of Regina offers an excellent multi-use trail system that stretches across the entire city. Many of the trails are paved, allowing wheelchair access, and the use of bicycles, rollerblades and skateboards is encouraged. Paved multi-use pathways in the city include the 8 km Devonian Pathway, the 4.5 km North Storm Channel Pathway, the 3 km Pilot Butte Creek Pathway, the 9.5 km Wascana Park Pathway (Southside) and the 1 km South Storm Channel Pathway. Wascana Centre, one of North America's largest urban parks, is found in the heart of the city and offers the 12 km Wascana Lake Trail, among others. Another park in the city that is great for hiking and walking is the McKell Conservation Park, which offers 4 km of easy trails. Hikers and bikers can also explore close to 20 km of the Trans Canada Trail that passes through the city.

Rocanville to Tantallon Trail (Map 33/D6–B5)

From Rocanville, this trail runs north-northwest along an abandoned CPR line for 22 km (13.5 mi). This wide dirt, gravel and cinder trail was established by local ATVers but is a welcome route for hikers, mountain bikers, cross-country skiers and snowshoers as the Scissors Creek Coulee that it runs through is now a provincial wildlife area. In Rocanville, you can find the old railway adjacent to Provincial Road 601. After 2 km of pastureland you will dip into the ravine that contains Scissors Creek – be prepared for the occasional creek crossing. Near the middle of the trail there is a steep drop to the ravine floor where a railway bridge used to stand. You can either turn back to Rocanville for a 20 km (12.5 mi) return trek or continue towards Tantallon along the railway (following another creek crossing).

Rowan's Ravine Provincial Park (Map 29/B1)

Rowan's Raving Provincial Park has a self-guided hiking trail called the Prairie Whispers Nature Trail. The trail offers a wide variety of flora and fauna. Mountain biking is popular here.

PRINCE ALBERT NATIONAL PARK	MAP	DIFFICULTY	LENGTH	ELEVATION GAIN	CAMPGROUND	HIKE	BIKE	HORSE	XC-SKI	SNOWSHOE	INTERPRETIVE	VIEW
Amyot Lake Trail	Map 79/G6	Moderate	15.5 km (9.6 mi)	20 m (65 ft)		•						•
Beach Walk	Map 80/F5	Easy	2.8 km (1.7 mi)	Minimal		•				•		
Boundary Bog Trail	Map 80/F5	Easy	2 km (1.2 mi)	Minimal		•					•	
Elk Trail	Map 70/F1	Moderate	40 km (25 mi)	130 m (425 ft)		•	•	•	•			
Fisher Trail	Map 80/F5	Easy	7.2 km (4.5 mi)	10 m (30 ft)		•	•					•
Fish Lake Trail	Map 70/D1	Difficult	12 km (7 mi)	20 m (65 ft)	•	•	•		•			
Freight Tait Springs Trail	Map 80/F7	Easy	2 km (1.2 mi)	Minimal		•						•
Freight Trail	Map 80/E5	Easy	27 km (17 mi)	40 m (130 ft)		•	•	•				
Grey Owl Trail	Map 80/C4	Moderate	20 km (12 mi)	30 m (100 ft)	•	•						
Hunters Lake Trail	Map 70/D1	Difficult	22 km (13.6 mi)	70 m (230 ft)		•	•	•	•	•		
Kingfisher Trail	Map 80/E5	Moderate	13 km (8 mi)	10 m (30 ft)		•						
Kingsmere River Trail	Map 80/C4	Easy	1.5 km (0.9 mi)	Minimal		•						
Kinowa Trail	Map 80/F7	Moderate	5 km (3 mi)	50 m (165 ft)		•						•
Mud Creek Trail	Map 80/E5	Easy	2 km (1.2 mi)	Minimal		•						
Narrows Peninsula Trail	Map 80/D4	Easy	3 km (1.8 mi)	Minimal		•						•
Red Deer Trail	Map 80/F5	Moderate	17 km (10.5 mi)	30 m (100 ft)		•	•					
Shady Lake Trail	Map 80/E5	Moderate	1.7 km (1 mi)	45 m (148 ft)		•						
Spruce River Highlands Trail	Map 80/F7	Difficult	8.5 km (5.2 mi)	30 m (100 ft)		•			•			
Sturgeon Lookout Trail	Map 80/A7	Easy	0.8 km (0.5 mi)	Minimal		•						•
Treebeard Trail	Map 80/D4	Easy	1.2 km (0.7 mi)	Minimal		•					•	
Valleyview Lookout Trail	Map 79/G7	Easy	0.2 km (0.1 mi)	Minimal		•						•
Waskesiu River Trail	Map 80/F4	Easy	2.5 km (1.5 mi)	Minimal		•						
West Side Boundary Trail	Map 70/D1-79/G5	Difficult	59.5 km (37 mi)	80 m (260 ft)		•	•					

TRAIL ADVENTURES

Saskatchewan Landing Provincial Park (Map 25/E4)
Situated along the southern shore of Lake Diefenbaker, this park offers an equestrian campsite and a few maintained trails for all trail enthusiasts to enjoy. The Brunyee Ridge Trail offers fantastic views of Lake Diefenbaker. The Cactus Coulees Trail comes alive with blossoming cacti in June and July and the Coulee Trail is an interpretive trail composed of loops that vary between 1 and 3 km in length. Hikers wishing to visit a lookout over the Brunyee Coulee and South Saskatchewan River Valley can take the 3.5 km return Prairie Vista Trail, while the 1.2 km Ridges and Ravines Interpretive Trail explores a ravine bottom and ridge top. For a fascinating look into the area's First Nations history, the 2.5 km Rings, Ruts and Remnants Trail is an excellent choice.

Saskatoon Trails (Map 49/C3)
The city of Saskatoon offers an extensive system of well-maintained, scenic trails for walkers, hikers and bikers to explore. One of the premiere destinations for outdoor adventurers in Saskatoon is the Meewasin Valley area, where a series of nature trails are complemented by a 13.5 km paved section of the Trans Canada Trail. The Cranberry Flats Conservation Area is another hub for nature lovers and features 3 km of trails. Just south of the city, 3 km of trails can be found in Chief Whitecap Park, running along the South Saskatchewan River. Additionally, a 2 km trail runs through the Saskatoon Natural Grasslands, a pristine patch of untouched prairie.

Skytrail (Map 37/G2)
This 4 km (2.5 mi) urban trail is located in Outlook. Used year-round, the trail is not a difficult one and will take about an hour to navigate for the average walker. Overlooking the South Saskatchewan River, the Skytrail is home the longest pedestrian bridge in Canada at over a kilometre wide and 48 metres (157 ft) tall. Part of the Trans Canada Trail, the bridge was a rail bridge from 1912 until the mid-1980s lying dormant for years until it was donated for conversion to a pedestrian bridge in 2003. The views from the bridge are spectacular and very popular with birdwatchers.

St. Cyr Trails (Map 78/C2)
Better known for its cross-country skiing, this 8 km (5 mi) trail system is also used by mountain bikers in the summer. There are a few steep, technical areas, but most of the area is rolling hills. Look for the trails east of Meadow Lake off Island Hill Road.

St. Victor Petroglyphs Historic Park (Map 6/B3)
From the bottom of the hill parking lot to the enclosure for the rock carvings at the top parking lot it is about a 1 km (0.6 mi) hike. Self-guiding interpretive information is provided. The hillside provides a panoramic view of the region's plains and bluffs, as the hill towers over the surrounding countryside. The exact creators and history of the petroglyphs are not known.

Struthers Lake Trails (Map 61/E2)
The regional park offers a pair of short hiking trails (750 metres to 2.5 km) that provide glimpses of the lake and a chance to see small wildlife and birds. There is also a longer 4.4 km (2.7 mi) hike that may offer a chance encounter with a deer or elk that often migrate from the nearby farmland to the lake.

Tatagwa Parkway (Map 8/F1)
The city of Weyburn has numerous trails through the Tatagwa Parkway along the Souris River banks. The main access to the trails is from the Signal Hill Arts Centre and Heritage Village. The parkway consists of 73 hectares (198 ac) of native prairie lands dedicated to the preservation of native fauna and flora. Look for such plants as the yellow goat's beard, Canada anemone, green needle grass, wild liquorice, common broomweed, pasture sage, and silver buffaloberry.

Trans Canada Trail
The Trans Canada Trail is an ambitious trail building project that aims to span the entire length of Canada. Although the entire trail is not yet completed, Saskatchewan boasts an impressive system that runs across the whole province, from Duck Mountain Provincial Park in the east to Frenchman Butte in the west. Saskatchewan's TCT is a mix of roads, dirt and gravel pathways and urban trails. Hikers, walkers, bikers, ATVers, snowmobilers, cross-country skiers, snowshoers and equestrians all use the trail, but it should be noted that certain modes of transport are restricted in certain trail sections. The trail also features two paddling routes (including the Qu'Appelle which needs to be run west to east). Additionally, many portions of the trail feature multiple access points, allowing you to choose the length, direction and difficulty of your journey. The following chart lists trail segments from east to west.

Valeport Marshes Trail (Map 29/D3)
Located near the southwest tip of Last Mountain Lake, 3 km (1.9 mi) of easy trails lead through the Valeport Marshes Conservation Area, an important habitat for many bird species. Much of the trail follows along a dyke and there is a shaded picnic area available for visitors. These trails can be found off Highway 20 just south of Last Mountain House Historic Park.

Wadena Wildlife Wetlands Trails (Map 52/E5)
Part of the Quill Lakes International Bird Area, these two marshes are found on the eastern shores of Little Quill Lake and offer great birdwatching opportunities. There are five trails totaling 8 km (5 mi) with boardwalks and two interpretation towers for viewing Milligan Creek Marsh and Jesmer Marsh. Plover's Path also takes hikers to the shores of Little Quill. There are also bathrooms, a picnic shelter and a canoe launch.

Wanuskewin Heritage Park (Map 49/D2)
This historical park contains a 6 km (4 mi) trail that offers views of the South Saskatchewan River and Opimihaw Creek and passes by a number of historical sites. This is an area of traditional First Nations importance and there is an interpretive centre on site – you will have to pay to use the trails, but this will grant you access to the centre as well. You can find the heritage park north of Saskatoon along Highway 11.

When hiking with a backpack, your heaviest items should be packed in the middle of your bag (not at the bottom) and as close to your back as possible. This will stabilize you and your pack, and keep it from pulling you in different directions.

Wascana Valley Nature Area Trails (Map 29/D5)
Along with hiking, snowshoeing and cross-country skiing, this is the main mountain biking destination in the Regina area. Wascana Creek flows through the area dividing the trails into east and west. Mountain bikers, in particular, will enjoy exploring the number of off-the-beaten-path type trails that range from easy to advanced. In total, there are around 15 km (9 mi) of trails in the area, climbing up to 30 m (100 ft) in elevation. The more challenging trails feature sharp corners along winding descents, while the valley bottom trails are generally easier. The well-maintained system even has trails designed specifically for Handcycling. Access is found west of Exit A on Highway 11 off the 734.

White Butte Trails Recreation Site (Map 30/A6)
Next to the community of Pilot Butte, this site features 12 km (7.5 mi) of hiking, biking and cross-country ski trails, as well as a 5 km (3 mi) year-round pet-friendly hiking trail. There is also a warming shelter and outdoor washrooms. White Butte Recreation Site is located bout 20 minutes east of Regina in between Highways 1 and 46.

Woodlawn Bird Sanctuary (Map 9/G6)
Found south of Estevan in Woodlawn Regional Park, the bird sanctuary offers 3 km (1.9 mi) of nature trails to explore.

Wood Mountain Nature Trail (Map 5/E4)
Wood Mountain Post Historical Park is the historical site of the North West Mounted Police post established in 1874 by a detachment moving into buildings put together by a Boundary Commission Crew moving on. The police referred to the area as an oasis in the middle of the semi-arid desert-like region they had travelled through, due to the lush green around the Wood River. The historic site has an interpretive centre and buildings. A 4 km (2.5 mi) nature trail cuts through bluffs and prairie from the Wood Mountain Post Historic Site to the Wood Mountain Regional Park Campgrounds and rodeo grounds.

Wynyard Regional Park (Map 52/C6)
Found south of town, this park sits next to a small reservoir. Trail enthusiasts will find a nice 3 km (1.9 mi) trail around the coulee. There is also a short 500 metre nature trail in the park.

York Lake Nature Trail (Map 43/C6)
Found in York Lake Regional Park, 5 km south of Yorkton, there is a 4 km (2.5 mi) self-guided nature trail along the north edge of the lake. It is common to see wildlife such as birds, deer and beaver along the well-treed trail. The 1.5 km (0.9 mi) one-way Isabel Priestly Nature Trail is also found in the park and is popular with birdwatchers.

TRAIL ADVENTURES

SASKATCHEWAN TRANS CANADA TRAILS (TCT)

	MAP	DIFFICULTY	LENGTH	ELEVATION GAIN	TRAIL TYPE	BIKE	CANOE	HIKE	HORSE	SKI	SNOWMOBILE	SNOWSHOE	VIEW
Duck Mountain Provincial Park	55/D7-44/C1	Moderate	14 km (8.7 mi)	40 m (130 ft)	Gravel Trail	•		•	•	•	•		•
Two Rivers Trail	44/C1-43/G1	Difficult	52 km (32.5 mi)	180 m (590 ft)	Paved Road	•		•	•	•	•		•
Veregin	43/G1	Easy	3 km (1.9 mi)	Minimal	Dirt Trail	•		•	•	•	•		•
Veregin to Canora	43/G1-D1	Difficult	31 km (19.5 mi)	20 m (65 ft)	Gravel Road	•		•	•	•	•		•
Canora	43/D1	Easy	6 km (3.7 mi)	Minimal	Dirt Trail	•		•	•	•	•		•
Good Spirit Lake Trail	43/D1-B2	Moderate	36 km (22.5 mi)	Minimal	Dirt Trail, Gravel Road	•		•	•	•	•		•
Good Spirit Lake Trail to Yorkton	43/B2-D5	Difficult	41.5 km (26 mi)	30 m (100 ft)	Gravel Road	•		•	•	•	•		•
Yorkton to York Lake Park	43/C5-D6	Easy	22.5 km (14 mi)	Minimal	Dirt Trail, Paved Road	•		•	•	•	•		•
York Lake Regional Park to Melville	43/D6-32/A1	Difficult	46.5 km (29 mi)	40 m (130 ft)	Gravel Road	•		•	•	•	•		•
Melville Trans Canada Walking Trail	32/A1	Easy	4.5 km (2.8 mi)	Minimal	Gravel Trail	•		•				•	•
Melville to Rural Municipality of McLeod	32/A1–31/G4	Varying	45 km (28 mi)	110 m (360 ft)	Gravel Trail	•		•	•	•	•		•
McLeod Trail	31/G4	Easy	5.8 km (3.6 mi)	30 m (100 ft)	Dirt Trail	•		•	•	•	•		•
Crooked Lake Trail - Sunset Beach to Melville Beach	32/B4	Easy	9.3 km (5.8 mi)	20 m (65 ft)	Dirt Trail	•		•	•	•	•		•
Rural Municipality of Elcapo	31/G4-F5	Moderate	11.5 km (7.3 mi)	40 m (130 ft)	Dirt Trail	•		•	•	•	•		•
Rural Municipality of Wolseley	31/F5-D5	Difficult	23 km (14.5 mi)	20 m (65 ft)	Dirt Trail	•		•	•	•	•		•
Rural Municipality of Abernathy	31/D5-A4	Difficult	27 km (16.5 mi)	10 m (35 ft)	Dirt Trail	•		•	•	•	•		•
Katepwa to Lebret	31/A4-30/G3	Easy	11 km (6.9 mi)	20 m (65 ft)	Dirt Trail	•		•	•	•	•		•
Tansi	30/G3-F3	Moderate	13 km (8 mi)	20 m (65 ft)	Dirt Trail	•		•	•	•	•		•
Fort San Walkway Trail	30/F3	Easy	5.4 km (3.4 mi)	10 m (35 ft)	Dirt Trail	•		•	•	•	•		•
Fort San to Lumsden	30/F3-29/D4	Easy	4.5 km (2.8 mi)	20 m (65 ft)	Gravel Road	•		•	•	•	•		•
Qu'Appelle River Paddling Route	29/D4-30/F3	Difficult	149 km (92.5 mi)	Minimal	Water Trail		•						•
Qu'Appelle Valley Waterway to White Butte Trails	30/B3-B6	Difficult	39.5 km (24.5 mi)	200 m (655 ft)	Gravel Road	•		•	•				•
Pilot Butte Trail	30/B6	Easy	11 km (6.9 mi)	10 m (35 ft)	Dirt Trail, Gravel Road, Paved Road	•		•	•	•	•		•
White Butte to Regina	30/B6-29/G6	Easy	6.5 km (4 mi)	20 m (65 ft)	Gravel Road	•		•	•	•	•		•
Regina	29/G6-F6	Varying	25.5 km (16 mi)	10 m (35 ft)	Gravel Road, Paved Road, Paved Trail	•		•	•	•	•		•
Regina to Wascana Trails	29/F6-E5	Moderate	17.5 km (11 mi)	10 m (35 ft)	Gravel Road	•		•	•	•	•		•
Wascana Trails	29/E5-D5	Easy	6 km (3.7 mi)	30 m (100 ft)	Dirt Trail - Proposed	•		•	•				•
Saw Whet Trail	29/D5-D4	Moderate	15 km (9.4 mi)	60 m (195 ft)	Dirt Trail	•		•	•	•	•		•
Lumsden	29/D4-C5	Moderate	18.5 km (11.5 mi)	60 m (195 ft)	Dirt Trail	•		•	•	•	•		•
Lumsden to Buffalo Pound Park	29/C5-A5	Varying	20.5 km (12.5 mi)	70 m (230 ft)	Paved Road	•		•	•	•	•		•
Buffalo Pound Provincial Park	29/A5-28/F5	Easy	16 km (9.9 mi)	80 m (260 ft)	Paved Road, Dirt Trail	•		•	•	•	•		•
Mount Pleasant Trail – Buffalo Pound Park to Moose Jaw	28/F5-E7	Difficult	40.5 km (25 mi)	50 m (165 ft)	Paved Road	•		•	•	•	•		•
Mount Pleasant Trail – Buffalo Pound Park to Sand Point Beach	28/F5-E4	Moderate	24 km (15 mi)	70 m (230 ft)	Paved Road	•		•	•	•	•		•
Sand Point Beach to Tugaske	28/E4-27/F2	Difficult	71 km (44 mi)	120 m (395 ft)	Paved Road	•		•	•	•	•		•
Tugaske to Craik	27/F2-39/C7	Difficult	55.5 km (34.5 mi)	110 m (360 ft)	Paved Road	•		•	•	•	•		•
Tugaske	27/F2-E1	Varying	24 km (15 mi)	50 m (165 ft)	Paved Road, Dirt Trail	•		•	•	•	•		•
Rural Municipality of Maple Bush to Douglas Provincial Park	27/E1-38/E7	Easy	7 km (4.3 mi)	30 m (100 ft)	Gravel Trail	•		•	•	•	•		•
Douglas Provincial Park	38/E7-D7	Moderate	13 km (8 mi)	Minimal	Dirt Trail	•		•	•	•	•		•
Piping Plover Trail	38/D7-C6	Easy	6.8 km (4.2 mi)	10 m (35 ft)	Dirt Trail	•		•	•	•	•		•
Elbow View	38/C6-B5	Difficult	28.5 km (17.5 mi)	30 (100 ft)	Dirt Trail	•		•	•	•	•	•	•
Danielson Provincial Park	38/B5-37/G5	Varying	25.5 km (16 mi)	20 m (65 ft)	Dirt Trail, Paved Road	•		•	•	•	•		•
Chief Whitecap Waterway	38/A4-49/C3	Varying	120.5 km (75 mi)	20 m (65 ft)	Water Trail		•						•
Outlook	37/G2	Easy	4.5 km (2.8 mi)	30 m (100 ft)	Dirt Trail, Paved Trail	•		•	•	•	•		•
Meewasin Trail	49/C3-D2	Moderate	25 km (15.5 mi)	20 m (65 ft)	Gravel Trail, Paved Trail - Proposed	•		•	•				•
Northern Trails – Louis Riel Trail – Saskatoon to Duck Lake	49/D2-60/D2	Difficult	150 km (93 mi)	80 m (260 ft)	Paved Road	•		•	•	•	•		•
Northern Trails – Carlton Trail – Duck Lake to Turtleford	60/D2-67/C3	Difficult	226 km (140 mi)	280 m (920 ft)	Paved Road	•		•	•	•	•		•
Northern Trails – Fort Pitt Trail – Rural Municipality of Frenchman Butte	67/C3-76/B7	Difficult	84.5 km (52.5 mi)	110 m (360 ft)	Paved Road	•		•	•	•	•		•
North Battleford to Prince Trail	58/A2-68/A7	Difficult	23.5 km (14.5 mi)	70 m (230 ft)	Paved Road	•		•	•	•	•		•
Battleford	58/A2-A3	Easy	8.4 km (5.2 mi)	20 m (65 ft)	Paved Trail	•		•	•	•	•		•
Cypress Hills Interprovincial Park West Block	12/A7-B7	Moderate	19 km (12 mi)	240 m (785 ft)	Dirt Trail	•		•	•	•	•		•
Cypress Hills Interprovincial Park Centre Block	12/E7-F7	Moderate	12.5 km (7.6 mi)	120 m (395 ft)	Dirt Trail	•		•	•	•	•		•

ATVing, Northern Saskatchewan
©Tourism Saskatchewan / Greg Huszar Photography

ATV [OHV] ADVENTURES

Although private lands affect the ability for ATVs and OHVs to explore much of the south, as you work your way north you will find some fine riding areas where ATVs are welcome. Many riders also take advantage of the snowmobile trail system in Saskatchewan as many of the trails are on Crown land.

One of the known hot spots is around Hudson Bay. No, not that Hudson Bay! The small Saskatchewan community offers endless riding, with many of the trails shared with the elaborate snowmobile system in the area. Other hot spots include Narrow Hills Provincial Park and Nisbett Forest. In the south, Moose Mountain Provincial Park is a popular destination. Or, for something different, why not follow the Trans-Canada Adventure Trail?

Riders should remember to respect these trails and to cooperate with the snowmobile clubs in maintaining the trail systems. Popular ATVing areas, including the provincial parks, are considering shutting down the trails in the summer for motorized users, so remember to pack out what you packed in. Some of these snowmobile trails are on private land – always get permission from the landowner before riding. Getting permission is not only the law, but it is good for public relations to ensure future access to lands.

Riders in Saskatchewan should also be aware of their legal responsibilities. All riders are required to wear an approved motorcycle helmet and appropriate eyewear when riding on public land. When riding in public areas, operators of ATVs must be 16 years old and hold a valid driver's license. Younger riders between 12-15 years old can operate an ATV in public areas if they have passed an approved safety course or are supervised by someone that has a driver's license. ATVs cannot be registered in Saskatchewan, but must have liability insurance ($200,000) when being operated in a public area. And it is considered a criminal code offense to operate an ATV in any way that endangers the public, including operating under the influence of drugs or alcohol.

As a general rule riders are allowed to operate their machines on Crown land including the non-traveled parts of roadways such as shoulders and medians (that are at least 50 meters/165 feet wide). In some areas riders are allowed to drive their ATVs along roads and across bridges. Be sure to check provincial and local regulations before riding along roadways.

The Saskatchewan ATV Association and its associated clubs offer a wealth of information on trails, poker rides and more. Be sure to visit *satva.ca* before heading out on the trails. Riders should also check into many of the outfitters and lodges that are found in Saskatchewan as many of them have their own trail systems.

DID YOU KNOW?

OUR BACKROAD GPS MAPS FEATURE OVER 5,700 KM OF ATV/MOTORIZED TRAILS.

 ROAD CLASSIFICATION

Know which roads can be driven in a car and which ones should be left to a four-wheel drive vehicle or ATV. Our enhanced road classifications help you distinguish the highways from the logging roads and the main roads from the side roads.

 POI & WRITE-UPS

From trail heads, staging areas, and nearby activities to elevation gain, trail conditions and access, our POI and accompanying descriptions will have you riding with confidence.

 backroadmapbooks.com/gps-maps

ATV [OHV] ADVENTURES

Big River (Map 79/E5)

With more than 300 km (180 mi) of ATV trails in the area this spot has something for every level of rider. There are 40 lakes within an hour's ride of Big River, providing trail access to some excellent fishing spots. Routes here vary from old logging roads and old exploration routes to small muddy trails, open meadows and summer access snowmobile routes. One of the best areas to ride is the so-called Timberlost area, where five of the 40 lakes are found. The area was settled in the 1930s and then reclaimed in the 1960s, although some of the old buildings can still be found along the older routes.

Big Sandy Lake (Map 92/F7)

Located 196 km north of Prince Albert, Big Sandy Lake is off kilometre 132 on Hanson Lake Road. Trails are found to the southwest of Big Sandy Lake, and riders can find trails and backroads that lead to Little Bear Lake and the Narrow Hills Provincial Park area. Camping can be found at Big Sandy Lake and there are plenty of ATV-access fishing holes.

> *ATVs and motorbikes can have a dramatic effect on trails, so pitch in and help with trail maintenance.*

Brightsand Lake (Map 77/D7)

The Brightsand Lake Regional Park is a very popular location with a beautiful sandy beach and good sized campground. You can ride to and from your campsite with a permit, but no pets or ATVs are allowed on the beach. Trails lead all around the area and to Turtle Lake, with some forested trails and long muskeg lines with the occasional deep hole. It is recommended to have a four-wheel drive ATV and winch, or at least to stick with a riding buddy.

Bronson Forest (Map 76/E4)

Offering over 20 km (12.5 mi) of trails, the Bronson Forest area is found around Little Fishing Lake, located off Highway 21 20 km south of Secondary Highway 699. Although the trails are mostly intermediate to advanced, there are some trails suitable for beginner riders, others are mud bogs and may require winches to pull you out. It is recommended you travel with someone else as the area is very remote and some trails are not well maintained. There are several camping options here and some nice fishing opportunities, making this a good all round recreation destination.

Candle Lake (Map 81/E6)

Riders going to the Candle Lake area will find a multitude of winding trails that travel through thick pine forests. Some of these trails go as far as the Christopher Lake area near Prince Albert National Park. You can ride to Narrow Hills Provincial Park along an 85 km (53 mi) route ending at Lower Fishing Lake. Around Candle Lake there are loops, one-way trails, trails to beaches and trails in deep muskeg. The village now allows ATVs on any road except for the paved highway (maximum speed of 20 km/h).

Chitek Lake (Map 78/F6)

In and around the Chitek Lake area riders will find a vast network of remote trails, suitable for all skill levels. Most of the trails are unmaintained and range from muskeg and mud bogs to sandy trails near the lake. Riders will find good campgrounds in the Chitek Lake Recreation Site, but remember to not ride within the site and to gas up in the village. If you head east of town you can find the Boundary Road that hooks up with trails to the area north of Leoville. The site does make a good base for family riding trips as the non-riders can keep busy with many water sport activities, including some excellent fishing. Chitek Lake is located off Highway 24, 150 km northeast of North Battleford.

East Nisbet Trail (Map 60/E2)

To find these trails look for a turn-off east of the highway, about 10 km north of Duck Lake. Turning west will take you to the popular Nisbet Forest Trails, but on the east side of Highway 11 there are approximately 20 km (12 mi) of trails to explore. Trails are mostly sandy and run through the forest with some spots running alongside the river and its sandbars.

Emma and Christopher Lakes (Map 70/F1–71/A2)

This vacationing area is not only good for it's boating and swimming, but also for its ATV riding opportunities. Riders here will find some very good marked trails and some remote trails with deep mud bogs that may require a winch to get out of. Some of these trails hook up to ATVing areas to the north and northwest, including trails that continue towards the Candle Lake area.

Fort a La Corne Trails (Map 72/E6)

Found in the Gronlid Area, access can be found by travelling 15 km north of Gronlid on Highway 6 and turning west, just south of the bridge and Wapiti Valley Ski Resort. As you head west there are many sandy and dirt roads that make up miles of trails to enjoy. Many are good quality routes for beginners, whereas the more advance riders can explore some side trails. Amongst the wooded trails there is the Sandberg Creek Rest Stop, a native burial site with some beautiful views.

Glaslyn (Map 68/A3)

Glaslyn is located at the intersection of Highways 4 and 3, 150 km north of North Battleford. The community offers a great trail network for four-wheel drive enthusiasts and ATVers. Most of the trails are remote; some lie in heavily forested areas and others run through mud bog areas.

Good Spirit Lake (Map 43/B2)

The Good Spirit Lake and Wildlife Area is located off Highway 229. It is a remote provincial park with a vast network of informal trails. Most trails are not maintained and many are mud bogs suitable for four-wheel drive enthusiasts and four-wheel drive ATVs only. It is advisable to have at least two ATVs in case you do get stuck in the mud. Trail conditions can vary greatly, depending on the time of year. Carry extra clothing and be prepared for snow from November to April and rain in the spring months. GPS units are highly recommended for those not familiar with this area.

Holbein Area (Map 70/D5)

Found 32 km west of Prince Albert, this ATV area is located south off Highway 3. Follow 5th Street and look for D Avenue to take you south of the community. Riders can make a 53 km (33 mi) loop heading south to the North Saskatchewan River, before looping west along some old washed out paths and roads. The trails are muddy with numerous mud bogs for four-wheel drive enthusiasts and ATVers.

Hudson Bay Area (Map 65/A2)

Around the Hudson Bay area riders can find trails and routes all over the place. You can go as far east as the Manitoba border. Or go as far west/southwest as Porcupine Plain or Preeceville. There is something for just about every rider here, from easy trails to expert terrain that will challenge the seasoned rider. Many of the trails follow the well-established snowmobile system in the area. Riders are asked to respect these trails and ask permission before crossing any private lands. In 2015, the Hudson Bay area was awarded five Riders West ATV Awards in Saskatchewan, chosen by Riders Choice. These include platinum for Favourite Family Riding Area and multiple silvers for Most Challenging, Scenic and Favourite Overall Area, plus Bronze for Favourite Campground at McBride Lake Recreation Site.

Lady Lake Area (Map 54/B4)

ATVers can find some great trails north of Preeceville and around Endeavor, where there are some excellent trails leading into the Porcupine Forest. For family friendly riding, the area around Lady Lake is a great choice. These trails stretch as far north as Porcupine Plain and Hudson Bay. The Trans Canada Adventure Trail can be found nearby, as well.

La Ronge Area (Map 101/E6)

La Ronge is located off Highway 2, 240 km northeast of Prince Albert. South of the city is a vast network of trails and forestry roads where ATVs are permitted. The area has over 320 km (200 mi) of snowmobile trails to explore, although not all of them are suitable for ATV use. There are a lot of muskeg, sand trails, sand pits and even a mile-long beach along these routes.

Lintlaw Trails (Map 53/D3)

Outside of Lintlaw is a forest reserve that offers fairly easy trails with a touch of history. Trails are a mixture of farmland and forested trails, while riding look for the abandoned farm houses that are slowly fading back into the bush. There are also lakes to explore and wildlife to see if you ride slowly enough.

Little Bear Lake (Map 82/C1–92/D7)

The Little Bear Lake area can be found just north of Narrow Hills Provincial Park. There are hundreds of kilometres of trails here, with something for everyone. Trails head out towards Big Sandy Lake and around the Narrow Hills area. The trails are generally wide and pass through forest, ranging from dry to muddy. Do not forget your fishing rod; some of the best brook trout fishing in the province can be found here.

Love (Map 72/F2)

Northwest of the town of Love riders can find some nice ATV trails. There is a poker ride here in February that features 80 km (50 mi) of trails and a good variety of terrain to explore for riders of all skill levels.

McPhee and Yotin Lakes Area (Map 80/F5)

Located just north of Anglin Lake and just east of the boundary of Prince Albert National Park, this area is home to some great ATV riding trails. From here riders can make their way over to Candle Lake, Emma Lake and Christopher Lake. This area would make a great family destination as there are several other outdoor activities to be found nearby in Prince Albert National Park or Anglin Lake Provincial Park. ATVers can get accommodations from the Elk Ridge Resort and ride directly from the lodge, cabin, townhouse or cottage.

Meadow Lake Provincial Park (Map 86/D4–88/B6)

A large network of snowmobile trails, suitable for ATVing in the off-season, can be found in this park, located 130 km north of Saskatoon off Highway 55. A nice ride of about 25 km (15 mi) can be found around Jeanette Lake starting from the Camp Oshkidee turn-off. Please refrain from riding the trails during excessively wet weather. There is plenty of camping to be found along this extensive trail system.

Moose Jaw Motocross Park (Map 28/D7)

Located off Highway 363 about 10 km west of Moose Jaw, this motocross track offers an established track and staging area. Both ATVs and dirt bikes are welcome, although there tend to be a lot more two wheelers present than four wheelers.

Moose Mountain Provincial Park (Map 21/F5)

Moose Mountain Provincial Park features around 120 km (75 mi) of trails, and ATVers are allowed to ride on designated trails from June 15th until the end of Labour Day Weekend in September. Some trails may be closed following heavy rain, so check with the park before you go. The main ATV trail that runs through the park is the 21 km (13 mi) Centre Road Trail. This trail runs east to west and most of the park's other trails connect with it. These include the 7 km (4.5 mi) Bennet Lake Trail, the 9.5 km (6 mi) Gillis Lake Trail, the 11 km (7 mi) Horse Lake Trail, the 17.5 km (11 mi) Long Lake Trail and the 19 km (12 mi) Harmon Lake Trail. Other trails in the park include the 13 km (8 mi) Boundary Trail and the 9.5 km (6 mi) Stevenson Lake Trail, which both run south of Kenosee Lake. If you plan on exploring these trails then head to the park office and pick up the no-charge permit and information package, which comes with a trail map.

Narrow Hills Provincial Park (Map 82/C3)

Narrow Hills is one of two parks in Saskatchewan open to ATVs. Upon arrival, riders will want to check in at the park office to get a trail map. Remember that ATVs are only allowed on designated trails and that a lot of the trails are multi-use, so it is important to ride with caution. There are well over 200 km (124 mi) of trails, some well signed, that wind in and around the 25 lakes within the park boundary, plus the dozens more just outside the borderline. In fact, some of the best fishing holes are better accessed by ATV. However, some trails are very remote and muddy and only suitable for four-wheel drive ATVs. It is recommended to travel with a friend in case you need a pull.

Nisbett Forest Trails (Map 60/D2–70/E6)

Over 100 years ago this area was logged and mined for its raw materials. Today, the Nisbett Forest is a protected area that allows motorized recreation and just about all outdoor activities; you will find lots of designated ATV trails and hundreds of kilometres multi-use trails. Riders should expect to find snow free trails from mid-April to October with rainy and muddy conditions in the spring. The area leading north from Duck Lake off Highway 11 provides gravel roads where you can find staging areas close to the trail system. There are trails for every skill level. Cell coverage is spotty at best in this area, so you should plan accordingly.

North Battleford (Map 58/A2)

Mostly used by snowmobilers, ATV riders can find some nice open grassy fields that lead down to the North Saskatchewan River with some more challenging side trails. The views can be inspiring and there are pocket beaches to explore. However, riders need to be wary of private property in the area. Please respect the wishes of the land owners and be sure to close all gates after you get permission to ride in these areas.

Onion Lake (Map 76/B6)

Onion Lake is located off Secondary Highway 641, north of Lloydminster on the Saskatchewan/Alberta border. There is a good network of remote trails, with some more than 80 km (50 miles) in length. There is also an annual ATV Rally held in May when the trails are still quite wet, although most hazards feature easy detours. The area has enough variety that it is suitable for riders of all skill levels, including families.

Pleasantdale Area (Map 62/D5)

Located off Highway 6, 200 km northeast of Saskatoon, is a network of local trails through forested areas set among a large group of lakes and streams. These are generally open pasture trails with nearby trails to help winch you out of the sticky mud. A four-wheel drive ATV and riding partner are recommended.

Porcupine Hills (Map 65)

Riders heading to the Porcupine Hills area can find many places to explore along the gravel roads and ATV trails that can be found here. Remember to bring your fishing rod as many of these roads and trails lead to some nice fishing spots.

Tobin Lake (Map 73/D2)

Located 164 km east of Prince Albert off Highway 35, Tobin Lake offers a ton of trails that are unofficial and unsigned. There is family and ATV friendly camping available in the area as well.

Trans-Canada Adventure Trail (Maps 12, 13, 24–25, 36–38, 49, 55, 60–61, 65, 70–71, 73–75, 80–82)

Part of a coast-to-coast trail system, the TCAT route stretches approximately 1,700 km (1,055 mi) across Saskatchewan. From the Manitoba border, the route runs north into Hudson Bay, then heads west to Nipawin along a mix of highway, canal and grid road. Continuing northwest, the route passes through Narrow Hills Provincial Park then resumes along highways to Montreal Lake. From here you will head southwest to Waskesui in Prince Albert National Park, past Christopher Lake and along grid roads to Prince Albert. The route then leads through the mud and ruts of the Nisbet Forest Trails before leading east across the South Saskatchewan River via the St. Laurent Ferry to Alvena. From here, head south then southwest past the Gardiner Dam to Kyle and White Bear, then past the Great Sand Hills into Cypress Hills Interprovincial Park and the Alberta border. Supplies and accommodations can be found at most towns along the route. Visit *graveltravel.ca* for more details.

GENERAL SAFETY

▶ **Take a Course**
Taking a basic ATV safety course is the best way to get acquainted with safe riding techniques. A good course will also teach you about local laws and regulations surrounding ATV use.

▶ **Inspect Your Ride**
Always check tire pressure, fuel level, oil level, chain slack and lube and tightness of all nuts and bolts before going out riding.

▶ **Be Alert**
ATV trails do not have a uniform surface and are not as well kept as normal roads, so keep a constant eye out for hazards.

▶ **Check the Weather**
Rain and wind can be serious hazards while ATVing, so check the forecast and avoid riding in inclement conditions.

▶ **Slow Brake**
Avoid sudden braking. You could be flung forward off your ATV.

▶ **Hills**
Avoid sudden braking or acceleration when travelling up or down a hill. Keep your weight toward the front while ascending, and towards the back when heading downhill.

Snowmobiling, Elk Ridge Resort, Saskatchewan
©Tourism Saskatchewan / Greg Huszar Photography

SNOWMOBILE ADVENTURES

Snowmobiles are often used as a form of transportation in Saskatchewan just as much as a recreational sport. A lot of snowmobiling takes place on roadsides moving from one community to another. While snow levels, especially in the southern portions of the province, can sometimes be low, Saskatchewan still has some great snowmobiling opportunities. From organized trails to random riding in fields or along unplowed grid roads and along lakes and rivers, there is no shortage of places to sled.

The Saskatchewan Snowmobile Association is the main governing body for recreational snowmobiling in the province. They help to build and maintain most of the 10,000 km (6,200 mi) of trails; they do this with the assistance of their over 60 clubs. Most of these systems are well maintained and include signage, warming huts and easy access to fuel and accommodations. There are many opportunities for extended riding including linking to neighbouring club trails or sampling portions of the Trans Canadian Trail.

The association's main goals are centred around safety, public relations, developing clubs, trails and tourism. One of the association's biggest contributions to safety in the sport is by holding Snowmobile Safety Courses. This course is required by law for anyone operating a snowmobile on public land in Saskatchewan that was born after January 1, 1989.

As with many adventure sports, safety is a primary concern. The most basic of the safety rules are governed by law: always wear a helmet and never drink and ride. Also, all snowmobiles being used on public lands must be registered and show plates. Ice, or the lack thereof, is a huge concern for anyone riding a snowmobile. Riders should know where they are riding as small water bodies might be hard to identify when covered in windblown snow. Early season and late season are the times that riders should be extremely careful when riding as the ice might be too thin to support a rider and their snowmobile. The minimum safe ice thickness is considered to be 12 cm (5 in); remember to check in several areas.

Riders who are planning to ride on slopes that are 25 degrees or more should take an avalanche safety course. Also, be mindful of ditches and other small slopes; even a small slope can slide with deadly consequences. Other things to consider when riding is dressing for the weather and never riding alone.

For more information, including maps and trail updates visit *www.sasksnow.com* or call 306-729-3500.

DID YOU KNOW?

OUR BRMB NAVIGATOR APP HAS WEBMAPS FOR YOUR DESKTOP WITH EVEN MORE SPECIAL FEATURES

 TRIP PLANNING

Discover and use great tools that you won't find on the app, such as drawing tracks, to creating custom trips. Mark them with waypoints, save them, and they will automatically sync with your phone. Plan your trips online ahead of time and view them on your device through the BRMB Navigator app.

 IMPORT GPX FILES

Got GPX tracks from friends, your favourite adventure website, or your latest GPS-logged trip? Import your GPX files here and save to My Trips.

 brmbnavigator.com

SNOWMOBILE ADVENTURES

Zone 1 Northwest Saskatchewan

Close to 2,000 km (1,240 mi) of trails extend northwest of Saskatoon, reaching as far as the area around Cold Lake on the Alberta border. The most extensive trail network can be found around the city of North Battleford, maintained by the Battleford Trail Breakers Snowmobile Club. Other clubs and trail systems in this region can be found in Canwood, Chitek Lake, Leoville, Spiritville, Big River and Goodsoil.

Club #101 - Battleford Trail Breakers (Maps 57, 58, 67, 68, 69)

With nearly 500 km (300 mi) of trails, the Battleford Trail Breakers have one of the most extensive trail systems in the province. The trails are laid out in a series of loops, both big and small, mostly north and east of North Battleford, which is on the northeast side of the North Saskatchewan River. There are 11 huts and shelters around the system and nearly as many places to fuel up.

Trail 101A
Starting in North Battleford, this trail travels northeast for 64 km (40 mi) before its terminus just north of Hatherleigh Station Shelter where it hooks up with Club Trail 114A. Along the way you will encounter numerous lakes and rivers to explore and a chance to re-fuel at the Blue Mountain Resort approximately half way along the trail, north of Gordie's Shelter warming hut.

Trail 101I
If you're looking for a long ride, look no further than Trail 101I. Starting at the Phil Billy Inn Shelter, you will travel 105 km (65 mi) crossing Dewan Creek and skirting the northeast corner of Maiden Lake. Continuing southward, you will hit the community of Glaslyn (re-fueling and provision opportunity) which sits approximately half way into your journey. Two more warming huts await as you pass by the Rider Villa Shelter and Noble's Nook Shelter at the north end of Jackfish Lake. This trail connects to Trail 101B at the community of Meota.

Club #103 - Canwood Sno Blazers Trails (Map 69/F2–70/C5)

The Canwood Club maintains three trails. The longest route is the Trans Canadian Trail which follows The Northern Woods and Water Route through the heart of this region. There are three shelters and three gas up opportunities in this area.

Trail 103A (Trans Canadian Trail)
Starting in the western portion of this club, a 67 km (42 mi) trip begins at a 24-hour gas-up card lock station near the community of Debden. Travelling southwest, this trail will take you through Mattes and Polwarth before hitting another 24-hour card lock station at Canwood. At this juncture, you may take Trail 103C south, or continue north to rest and warm up at the Rasmussen Shelter. The Sturgeon River Shelter is found further north at the trail's terminus, where you can continue east along Trans Canadian Trail (Club #212A) towards Emma Lake.

Trail 103C
Found off the southern part of Trans Canadian Trail 103A, this trail can be accessed from two regions. Both trails will take you to the community of Shellbrook, (the western trail accesses the Pile of Bones Shelter) approximately 51 km (32 mi) away, where there is a 24-hour card lock gas station.

Club #104 - Chitek Lake Bush Buddies Trails (Maps 78, 79)

Chitek Lake is a hub of the Saskatchewan snowmobile trail system, spanning over 180 km (112 mi) with 17 different trails to explore ranging from a couple of kilometres to the 42 km (26 mi) Trans Canadian Trail. Many of these trails travel along frozen lakes, so be sure to check ice thickness before venturing out. Look for three warm up shelters along the main route and two gas up stations.

Trail 104A (Trans Canadian Trail)
The main trail in this region, the Trans Canada, encompasses 42 km (26 mi) from the Pipeline Junction Shelter in the western sector south through Chitek Lake (gas up and provision opportunities), Huard Guard Shelter and its terminus where it continues into Club #107.

Trail 104M-Y
Encompassing another series of trails in this club's region, approximately 25 km (16 mi) of winding tracks await you in the central portion of this area with Lac des Joncs, Shell Lake, Muskak Lake, Bug Lake and portions of Chitek Lake part of this trail system. Be aware of ice thickness levels on these (and any) lakes, as they can change throughout the season.

Club #107 - Leoville Snow Drifters Trails (Maps 69, 78, 79)

As you might expect, this trail system is found around Leoville. The local snowmobile club maintains 110 km (68 mi) of trails that connect to Big River in the east, Chitek Lake in the west, and Spiritwood in the south. The remaining 65 km (40 mi) within this club's zone consist of four trails which meander along the outskirts of Leoville and beyond. Bear Lake Shelter and Huard Hill Shelter warming huts are always a favourite in these parts as are Sandy Lake, Deep Lake and Magalki Lake (always check ice levels before venturing out on lakes).

Trail 107A (Trans Canadian Trail)
At over 38 km (24 mi), this trail starts at the Huard Hill Shelter warming hut and travels south past Gagne Lake before hitting the community of Leoville. Continue north from here for the second part of the trip until a merge with 107G, then onwards to Big River.

Club #109 - Northern Lights Snowmobile Association Trails (Maps 67, 68, 77, 78, 87)

There are five trails maintained by the Northern Lights Snowmobile Association, including a 128 km (80 mi) section of the east/west running Trans Canadian Trail. In and around this club's limits you will find four warm up shelters and four gas up/provision centres as well.

Trails 109C/D
Long and relatively straight, Trail 109D begins as an off-shoot trail from the Trans Canada and travels south for approximately 30 km (19 mi) to Chumbs Road House Shelter, where Trail 109C starts and branches off to the east for 32 km (20 mi). Trail D ventures off to the west and follows Turtle Lake for another 40 km (25 mi) where it ends at the southern tip of the lake. Trail C ends at Pearl Lake where you can warm up at Phil Billy Inn Shelter warming hut.

Club #112 - Saskatoon Snowmobile Club (Maps 49, 60)

Saskatoon is the largest city in the north half of the province, so you will be forgiven for assuming that there would be an extensive trail system around the city – there isn't. The local club maintains about 130 km (80 mi) of trail, mostly an out-and-back trail from the SSC Clubhouse north of the city to Duck Lake. There is an alternate loop between Rosthern and Duck Lake as well as a smaller loop at the south end of the main trail to south of Martensville.

Trail 112A
This easy, groomed trail heads out in a north-easterly direction from Saskatoon towards the community of Hague. The trail is an out-and-back style ride along primarily flat terrain for 86 km (53 mi) past the North 40 Shelter, the community of Rosthern (gas up opportunities) to Duck Lake.

Trail 112B
Starting at the community of Duck Lake and travelling south, you will find a small off-shoot trail about 12 km (7 mi) in, which leads to the Lac D' Quack Shelter warming hut. Alternatively, you may continue for another 15 km (9 mi) past Rempel Lake and gas up opportunities near the community of Rosthern.

Club #114 - Thickwood Trail System (Maps 68, 69)

The Spiritwood Snowmobile Club maintains nearly 300 km (180 mi) of trails, mostly south of Spiritwood. The trail system is built around a rather large loop that features four warm up shelters; Fuzzie's, Jim's, Edgewater and Perogies Place.

Trail 114A
At 82 km (51 mi) this trail is the second longest in this club's zone. Starting near the community of Rabbit Lake (gas and provision opportunities), this trail takes you past Meeting Lake and veers north towards Fuzzie's Shelter then east onwards towards Jim's Shelter and more gas up opportunities at Spiritwood. From here this trail follows the southern shores of Witchekan Lake north along Highway 24.

Trail 114C
This trail is approximately 120 km (75 mi) long and is the largest within this club's boundaries, looping from Meeting Lake in the western region east through long stretches of isolated, rugged terrain with no gas up stations until the halfway point off Trail 114E near the community of Shell Lake in the extreme east. If you choose to begin your trek in the opposite direction, you will start off along 114A until it separates at Spiritwood and heads east towards Edgewood Shelter and follows the same route in the opposite direction.

Club #115 - Timber Trails Sno Riders Trails (Maps 69, 79)

Located around the town of Big River, the Timber Trails Sno Riders maintain 187 km (116 mi) of snowmobile trails. The main trail in the area is the Trans Canadian Trail. There are a handful of lengthy secondary trails falling off the main trail as well as trails connecting to the Chitek Lake Club as well.

Trail 115A (Trans Canadian Trail)

Starting just south of Otter Lake near the Timberlost Shelter, this major snowmobile trail is 83 km (52 mi) long, ending at the community of Debden, where there is gas up and provision opportunities. Along the way, you will pass through several communities including Big River, Bodmin, Erinferry and Eldred. Look for several off-shoot trails leading to isolated frozen lakes and rugged landscape as you plan your route(s). As always, be aware of ice thickness levels when venturing out onto frozen lakes and rivers.

Trails 115B-E

These trails vary in length with the smallest being 115E at 9 km (6 mi) and 115D the longest at 35 km (22 mi). All these trails offer shortcuts to other longer trails or create loops for those not wishing to spend all day following one trail. These trails often lead to gas up opportunities or to access frozen lakes for some high speed snowmobiling.

Club #125 - Goodsoil Ridge Riders Trails (Maps 86, 87)

The Goodsoil Ridge Riders maintain approximately 150 km (93 mi) of trails. The main trail through the area is 125A (Trans Canadian) with 125B, C and D Trails providing short loops or alternate routes for riders. There is one warm up shelter, found near where the trail systems meets the Northern Lights Snowmobile Association Trails, and fuel stops at Howe Bay, Bousquet Lake and Goodsoil. The main trail crosses Lac des Iles, while the C and D Trails cross Pierce Lake.

Trail 125A

Part of the Trans Canadian Trail, this trail runs south of Cold Lake, crosses the Cold River and passes north of Pierce Lake and Lepine Lake before crossing Lac de Illes about halfway along its length. The trail then runs south to Bousquet Lake and through the community of Goodsoil, continuing east to meet up with Trail 109 and the Northern Lights Snowmobile Association trails.

Zone 2 Northeast Saskatchewan

Over 4,000 km (2,500 mi) of snowmobile trails can be found in the northeast section of the province, stretching as far north as the area around Flin Flon, Manitoba. The most extensive trail systems can be found around the city of Hudson Bay, where the local club maintains around 700 km (435 mi) of trails, and around Kelvington, with 450 km (280 mi) of trails. There are many other snowmobiling hotspots in this region, with well-established clubs located in Archerwill, Candle Lake, Mistatim, Naicam, Porcupine Plain, Tisdale and beyond.

Know before you go! Visit www.sasksnow.com or call 306-729-3500 for the latest trail updates and map information.

Club #201 - Archerwill Drift Riders Trails (Maps 52, 63)

Archerwill is a small village of less than 500 people. The small club here maintains 155 km (96 mi) of groomed riding, spread out across five trails. There are four warming huts and three gas up/provision opportunities within this club's boundaries.

Trail 201A

The beginning of this trail is actually the end of Trail 219B travelling east. Kletteberg Shelter greets you as start your 53 km (33 mi) trek following the long snake-like George Williams Lake to the community of Archerwill and gas up opportunities. From here, you will continue northeast to the Red Deer Shelter after crossing the frozen Red Deer River.

Trail 201B

This trail follows a similar pattern as 201A, but is a more northerly route through the Burn Shelter and the communities of Barford and Merle. Look for gas up opportunities just off trail 201E at Barrier Lake west of Merle. This trail is slightly longer at just over 46 km (29 mi) and ends at the Red Deer Shelter.

Club #203 – Border Explorers Snowmobile Club (Map 95)

This club is based in Manitoba but many of its trails cross west into Saskatchewan. The majority, however, are tightly packed together in the northern sector here with approximately 100 km (62 mi) of routes to follow through the communities of Creighton and Denare Beach, where you can find gas. There are several lakes in this region as well, including Meridian, Wolverine, Amisk and Spectral so be prepared to measure the ice thickness (minimum 12 cm or 5 in) before hitting the high speeds only a frozen lake can offer.

Trail 203A/C

These trails make a loop to the southwest of Flin Flon. Heading in a clockwise direction, 203C runs south past Douglas Lake to meet up with the much longer 203A at Mystic Lake. From here you can follow 203A west to Denare Beach where you can find gas. Heading north from here, along the East Bay of Amisk Lake, you can stop at a warming shelter near Magdalen Lake before cutting east to Creighton.

Club #205 - Candle Lake Sno Drifters Trails (Maps 71, 81, 82)

The local club maintains 352 km (218 mi) of trails around Candle Lake. While the Trans Canadian Trail makes its way through this area, it is only a fraction of the total system, with other main trails heading south to Prince Albert and north to Esker.

Trail 205A (Trans Canadian Trail)

Cradling Candle Lake, this part of the Trans Canadian Trail is 70 km (43mi) long and continues where TC212A ends, south of the Clear Sand Shelter, before winding its way east through the community of Minowukaw Beach, north along the eastern shores of the big lake and onwards north to the Ice House Creek Shelter.

Club #208 - Esker Bear Trails (Maps 81, 82, 92)

The Esker Bear Trails Inc. Club maintains over a dozen trails and five warm up shelters in the Esker area, many of which are in Narrow Hills Provincial Park. The longest single trail is a section of the Trans Canadian Trail, which passes through the area. Most of the trails can be done as loops, although there are a few out and back trails, as well as trails that connect to Steepbank Lake, Arborfield, White Fox and Candle Lake.

Trail 208A (Trans Canadian Trail)

By far the longest trail within this club's boundaries, this section of the Trans Canadian Trail continues from TC 232A and travels east from Scott's Shelter near Tent Lake. Continuing along after hitting Memorial Ridge Shelter you will head straight south through numerous lakes and rivers before another rest stop at the Pine Junction Shelter where there is food, lodging and gas up opportunities at Caribou Creek. There are several options here for taking short trips between 10 km (6 mi) to 30 km (18 mi) in length in the surrounding area, or you can choose to continue south through endless kilometres of rough, isolated snowmobiling.

Club #210 - Hudson Bay Trail Riders Inc (Maps 64, 65, 74, 75)

No, your geography isn't completely screwed up, this is not the actual Hudson Bay found in northern Manitoba, Ontario and Quebec. Instead, the town of Hudson Bay is found a few hours northeast of Saskatoon. The club has one of the most extensive trail systems in the province, with just under 700 km (435 mi) of trails spread out across 21 trails. The longest single trail, at just over 140 km (87 mi), is the Trans Canadian Trail. Below are a few of the more notable groomed trails:

Trail 210A

Found southeast of Hudson Bay, this 130 km (81 mi) one-way trip starts out easy, but gets more difficult as you make your way towards the lodge located in the Porcupine Hills. The first part of the trail heads east along an old rail bed before making a turn to the south and progressively more turns as you head into the hills. Once at the Moose Range Lodge you will find hot meals to help refuel your body and fuel for your ride. The lodge also offers cabins for those wanting to stay the night.

Trail 210P

Heading north from the town, this trail leads you 100 km (62 mi) from Hudson Bay to Wild Cat Hill Provincial Park. The trail starts out gentle enough, but as you enter the park you will encounter more difficult terrain. The park is a remote destination location in all seasons, but especially so in the winter months. There are no amenities here. Remember to take along emergency gear and never ride alone.

SNOWMOBILE ADVENTURES

Club #211 - Kelvington Trail Blazers Trails (Maps 52, 53, 63, 64)

With nearly 455 km (282 mi) of terrain spread out across 22 trails, the Kelvington area is a great place for riders to explore. The many trails loop close to Kelvington, including around and over the many lakes found to the northeast. Like most trails in the area, there are a number of connecting trails. Look to the communities of Archerwill, Rose Valley, Porcupine Plain, Weekes, Preeceville and Quill Lake for many of the more popular routes. Additionally, there are close to 20 warming huts found within this club's boundaries. Be sure to check ice thickness levels before venturing out onto the many barren isolated lakes and rivers in this region. Ice should be 12 cm (5 in) thick and should be checked at several points.

Trail 211B/I/J/K/W/X

These trails make a loop to the west of Kelvington. In a clockwise direction, trails run south past the Wadena North Shelter before looping up to Hendon, past Fosston and continuing north to Rose Valley. From here you make an abrupt turn south to head back to Kelvington. From near the Wadena North Shelter, the 211W and 211X run south to Wadena and continue to Fishing Lake.

Club #212 – Lakeland Snowmobile Club (Maps 70, 71, 80, 81)

Prince Albert National Park encompasses a big chunk of the northwest region of this club so be aware of your boundaries as there is no snowmobiling here. Eight warming huts and 10 gas up stations (including 3 just north of the major city of Prince Albert) can be found along the way.

Trail 212A (Trans Canadian Trail)

From the Sturgeon River Shelter north of the community of Blue Heron, this part of the Trans Canadian Trail begins as you trek through numerous lakes and rivers eastward to the Trail Head Shelter and Emma Lake. Choosing to continue north, your last shelter is the Chris Can before its terminus south of Candle Lake.

Trail 212R

This trail heads due north out of Prince Albert and travels over 50 km (31 mi) through rural areas with communities dotted along the way until Christopher Lake where you will find ample gas up opportunities and provisions. Continuing approximately another 50 km (31mi) north will take you through more remote and rugged sections of this club before connecting with 212B north of McPhee Lake.

Club #217 - Melfort and District Trails (Maps 62, 63, 72, 73)

The Melfort Snowmobile Club has five trails they look after, offering a total of 223 km (139 mi) of trails to explore. This system connects to the Naicam Trails in the south and the Tisdale Trails in the east, while the rest of the trail system is laid out in large loops. There are six warming huts and several gas stations dotted throughout this club's boundaries.

Trail 217A

The primary route connecting Naicam to Melfort before venturing on to the Wapiti Valley Ski Resort, this trail is 88 km (55 mi) in length. Not overly challenging, this trail is more of a scenic route as you pass through the communities of Clemens and Glenlid and the city of Melfort. Look for Lenvale Shelter found just east of Lenvale.

Trail 217D

This trail originates from the Wapiti Ski Resort and ventures east past the Ratner Shelter following Little Bridge Creek. At Buffalo Junction, this trail veers directly south past two gas up stations and countless rivers and lakes. This trail is approximately 75 km (47 mi) from start to finish.

Club #218 - Mistatim Snow Packers Trails (Maps 63, 64, 73)

If stretched end to end, the Mistatim Trails would be about 167 km (103 mi) long. However, none of the club's six trails is more than 50 km (31 mi) long. While there are a few loops in the system, most of the trails are connectors, to Tisdale, Hudson Bay, Carrot River and Kelvington. There are three warming huts within this club's region; Wilkinson's Inn Shelter, Connell Creek Shelter and Marlin's Place Shelter. There are two gas up stations at the communities of Mistatim and Prairie River.

Trail 220A (Trans Canadian Trail)

Cutting across the northern section of the Mistatim Snow Packers riding area, this trail passes through Arborfield, where you can find gas, continues past Jordan River and eventually leads to the Jubilee Shelter. Continuing east will lead you to Hudson Bay, while following this trail west will eventually take you to Nipawin.

Trail 218A/B/C/D/E/I

From Mistatim it is possible to ride east past Orley and Peesane, eventually heading towards Tisdale. To the north, the trail passes the Connell Creek Shelter to connect with the Trans Canadian Trail. To the east, riders can access Prairie River, where you can find gas, while Porcupine Plain and Chelan can be reached to the south.

Club #219 - Naicam Snowblasters Trails (Maps 51, 62, 63)

With 267 km (166 mi) of snowmobile trails, the Naicam system is not the most extensive in the province, but the six trails that make up the system offer some excellent riding. North and east of the town, the trails allow riders to explore the many lakes in the area as the trails pass around and sometimes over these lakes, including Charron Lake, one of the more popular recreation lakes in the area.

Trail 219AA

Starting from Humboldt, this trail travels approximately 75 km (46 mi) in a general northeast direction through the Wolverine Creek Shelter and Hergott Shelter, just west of Naicam. From here it is a short trip east past Gosselin, Charron and Edourad Lakes before hitting the Kitako Shelter and the Kletteberg Shelter at its terminus.

Club #220 - Pasquia Snow Goers Club Trails (Maps 73, 74)

The Pasquia Club maintains 250 km (155 mi) worth of groomed trails east of Nipawin. There are a handful of warming huts and places to fuel up along the trails such as Carrot River, Zenon Park and Arborfield. These trails generally travel east-west through many frozen lakes, rivers and streams and are mainly used as connector trails.

Trail 220A (Trans Canadian Trail)

The community of Aylsham is where this part of the Trans Canadian Trail begins, travelling in an easterly direction through suburban to rural areas and then on to more remote regions as the route moves east to Jubilee Shelter and Dahl Lake Shelter at its eastern borders. This part of the TCT is approximately 87 km (54 mi) long.

Trail 220B

This trail is an off-shoot of the Trans Canadian Trail and follows a more north-easterly route. At 88 km (55 mi) it is only slightly longer than its southern cousin, but does travel through similar conditions. The big difference however is that there are no warming huts or gas up stations along this route. Snowmobilers will have to use one of the many connector trails for access to gas and shelter.

Club #221 - Porcupine Trail Blasters Trails (Maps 63, 64)

The town of Porcupine Plain is found between Archerwill in the west, Hudson Bay in the east, Mistatim in the north and Kelvington in the south. Like most of the clubs in the area, the trails here are mostly designed to connect with the other club trails, encompassing approximately 163 km (101 mi) in total. There is one rather large loop south of town, with three warming shelters along the route; Timberwolf, Pei Wei and Stromberg Shelters. Gas up at the communities of Porcupine Plain and Greenwater Lake.

Trail 221A

From the town of Porcupine Plain, this trail runs southeast between Carragana and Piwei Lakes, eventually leading to the Pei Wei Shelter. From here, the trail cuts south past Cougar Canyon and across Big Valley Lake. Alternately, heading west from Porcupine Plain will lead to the small community of Chelan.

Club #223 – Roughrider Snowmobile Club (Maps 53, 54, 64)

With five trails at over 275 km (170 mi), this club's trails centre around the community of Preeceville and Lintlaw, except the Trans Canadian Trail which heads northwest from May Lake Shelter all the way up to the Reserve Shelter. There are three gas up opportunities along the way plus four warm up shelters.

Trail 223A (Trans Canadian Trail)

A continuation of Trail TC324A out of Canora, this section starts just west of the community of Stenen and proceeds west until gas up opportunities at Preeceville. From here, its due north for approximately 80 km (50 mi) through Hinchliffe Shelter, Ushta Shelter and its terminus at the Reserve Shelter.

SNOWMOBILE ADVENTURES

Club #225 - Tisdale Snowmobile Club Trails (Maps 62, 63, 73)

The Tisdale Club is a nexus of sorts, with trails to Melfort, Naicam, Archerwill, Mistatim, Hudson Bay and Nipawin all diverging from the rather short system of trails the local club maintains. There are four groomed trails covering approximately 150 km (90 mi) maintained by the Tisdale Club as well as five warming huts shelters (Darren's Den, Barrier, Dog River, Leather River and Wilkinson's Inn) all found in and around these trails. Look for gas up opportunities in the communities of Ridgedale, Zenon Park and Tisdale.

Trail 225A

From Tisdale, this trail cuts due south, passing by Darren's Den Shelter before zig-zagging to the southwest just before the community of Lightwood. The trail then takes you to Hidden Meadow Golf Course where you can find gas and food.

Trail 217D

From Star City, this trail leads northeast past the Leather River Shelter to Ridgedale, where you can find gas. The trail then continues in the same direction to terminate at Buffalo Junction, near the community of Pontrilas. Heading west from Star City, trails lead to Melfort.

Club #226 - Twin Lake Trail Blazer Trails (Maps 72, 73, 82)

Found around Nipawin, these trails connect in the southeast with Arborfield and Hudson Bay, in the northwest to Candle Lake, and the western extremes of this club's borders through Whiteswan Lake and Esker Bear. In between, there are approximately 230 km (143 mi) of trails, mostly off shoot trails found along the Trans Canadian Trail, as well as a few other primary trails.

Trail 226A (Trans Canadian Trail)

Another section of the TCT, this portion continues from Trail 208A in the western region of this club's management, heading in a southern direction from the Horseshoe Bend Shelter for over 85 km (53 mi). This route takes you through several arms of the Torch and Fern Rivers before skirting the western limits of the community of Nipawin (accessed from connector rail 226E) following Highway 35 then turning sharply east and its terminus where TC220A takes over at Aylsham. Strangely, there are no warming huts along this route so appropriate dress is essential.

> Carry a first-aid kit, an emergency tool kit (with spark plugs, and drive and fan belts), an extra key, and a survival kit that includes flares. Also, a cellular phone is invaluable if you are in an area with service.

Club #232 - Whiteswan Snow Hawks Trails (Maps 81, 82)

There are over 150 km (90 mi) of trails in the Whiteswan Lake area. The main trail here is the Trans Canadian Trail, but there is a series of primary and secondary routes as well.

Trail 232M

Starting from Scott's Shelter warming hut, this trail is approximately 74 km (46 mi) long, looping north through more remote and rugged conditions, travelling past Clarence and Steepbank Lakes before the Cat Shelter warming hut. From here, this route heads directly south crossing TC232A at its mid-point and ending at the Lorentz Shelter.

Club #236 - Quill Lake Trails (Maps 51, 52, 62)

The local Trail Twister Club maintains a trio of trails. The longest of these is 236C at 75 km (47 mi) long. The other two, 236B and 236A are 50 km (31 mi) and 45 km (28 mi) respectively. The two shorter trails form two loops northeast and southeast of the town of Quill Lake, where there are provision and fuel opportunities. Meiklejohn's, Clair, Scrip, Nicholl's and Pruden Shelters can all be accessed along this route.

Trail 236B

This 50 km (31 mi) trail extends west of the town of Quill Lake, past the small community of Wimmer to Watson, where you can find gas. From here, the trail cuts southeast along the way. The trail runs along Quill Lake before meeting up with the 236A trail. Alternately, heading east from Quill Lake leads to a junction with the 236A and 236C trails.

Zone 3 Southeast Saskatchewan

Over 4,000 km (2,500 mi) of maintained trails can be found in the southeast part of Saskatchewan, with most of the trails found close to the Manitoba border in the eastern part of this subsection. The most extensive trial systems can be found around the towns of Carlyle and Oxbow as well as around Yorkton. There are many other excellent trail systems in this region, with active snowmobile clubs found in Fort Qu'Appelle, Stoughton, Estevan, Weyburn and beyond.

Club #301 - Broadview Snow Busters Snowmobile Club (Maps 21, 32)

The Broadview Snow Busters Club grooms and maintains five trails, approximately 159 km (99 mi) in total length, north and south of the focal point of Broadview on the Trans-Canada Highway. These trails go as far north as Crooked Lake and into the Qu'Appelle Valley. There are four warm-up huts, with three of them north towards the valley, and one to the south through the Pipestone area. Fuel stops are available on the Sakimay First Nation, Marieval and Broadview. Accommodations are available in Broadview, with the Ochapowace Ski Resort just north of town.

Trail 301A

This is the main trail within this club's boundaries, beginning just south of Crooked Lake in the community of Marievo and the Last Oak Country Club Shelter. Travelling south, you will skirt the edges of Ekapo Creek before passing the Chinook Shelter and the town of Broadview where there are fuel up opportunities. Start to finish, this is a 70 km (43 mi) trek through scenic hills, valleys and treed areas.

Club #302 - Calling Lake Cruisers Snowmobile Club (Maps 30, 31)

Based in the town of Fort Qu'Appelle, the Cruisers maintain seven groomed trails over 294 km (183 mi) through some of the most scenic snowmobiling in southern Saskatchewan—the Calling Lakes area of Pasqua, Echo, Mission and Katepwa Lakes, as well as other sections of the Qu'Appelle Valley. There are six well-maintained and equipped warm-up shelters on the trails for the use of snowmobilers. Fuel stops are available at Fort Qu'Appelle, Balcarres, Lipton, Dysart and Southey.

Trail 302A

Beginning in the community of Balgonie (gas up stations), this 108 km (68 mi) trail is nothing short of spectacular as far as the scenery goes. Travelling north, this trail splits with one route following Highway 364 north, and the other following Highway 10 northeast before meeting up again at Edgeley, just south of Rooster's Retreat Shelter. A short ride from here takes you into the town of Fort Qu'Appelle where more gas and provisions can be attained. Here there is a hub of different trails both long and short, and continuing along 302A will lead you to the terminus at Balcarres, where you can find gas.

Club #303 - Cupar Snowmobile Club Trail (Maps 29, 30, 41)

This club maintains three trails that total just over 150 km (93 mi) in length. Small towns litter this area of Saskatchewan and you will find four shelters and fuelling opportunities at Cupar, Southey and Dysart. These trails are scenic in nature and not really for the thrill seeker as they travel a direct east-west route.

Trail 303A/B

Start to finish, these two trails account for 90% of the trails within this club's boundaries, starting near the community of Earl Grey and travelling east through Southey (gas available), Markinch, Cupar and ending in Dysart where they hook up with Trail 302B west of Qu'Appelle.

Club #304 - Esterhazy Super Sledders (Maps 32, 33)

The Esterhazy Super Sledders maintain four groomed and ungroomed trails approximately 162 km (100 mi) in length, found around Bear Creek and the Qu'Appelle Valley. There are four warm-up huts (The Dubuc, The Cook Shack, The Shack and the New Finland) and fuel stops in Esterhazy, Spy Hill, and Stockholm. The area includes some of the scenic Qu'Appelle Valley, plus rolling agricultural land with scattered bluffs.

Trail 304A

Starting in the far western corner of this club's boundaries near the town of Grayson, this 72 km (45 mi) trail follows in a general west-east direction paralleling Highway 9 until Stockholm. The next stop along this route is in Esterhazy, where you will find ample gas and provision opportunities before moving on to Tantallon where it merges with Trail 312D and 312H.

SNOWMOBILE ADVENTURES

Club #308 - Kamsack Snow Drifters Trails (Maps 43, 55)
The Trans Canadian Trail passes through Kamsack and is the longest of the five groomed trails which total approximately 88 km (55 mi). Most of the other routes are short, but when combined with the park trails in the northeast corner they combine to stretch over 190 km (117 mi). Look for five warming huts along the trails in this region, with fuelling opportunities in the communities of Norquay, Kamsack and just south of Benito.

Trail 308A (Trans Canadian Trail)
This stretch of the TCT begins where it takes over from TC318A at the Snodrifters Hideaway Shelter southeast of Kamsack and travels in a relatively straight line northeast for 35 km (22 mi). This route follows Highway 57 until it hits the southern shores of Madge Lake and the 100 km (62 mi) of park trails to the north.

Club #309 - Last Mountain Lake Drifters (Maps 29, 30)
The Last Mountain Lake Drifters groom and maintain approximately 217 km (135 mi) spread out over six trails, with the majority of them through the scenic Qu'Appelle Valley and around Last Mountain Lake. There are two warm up huts around Last Mountain Lake, with 10 fuel stops available in small towns through the area, including Lumsden, Craven, Regina Beach, Bethune, Dilke, Bulyea, Earl Gray, Southey and Cupar. Accommodations with direct trail access are found in Lumsden, Craven and Regina Beach.

Trail 309A
Starting at the major city of Regina, this trail is the predominant route here at 78 km (48 mi) in length, presenting a variety of terrain. Flat prairie landscape greets you along the outskirts of the big city, but the further out along this route you go past Lumsden and Regina Beach you will experience more hills and valleys. After crossing Last Mountain Lake, it's a short trip along Highway 20 to the community of Earl Grey and this trail's terminus.

Club #311 - Moose Mountain Snowmobile Club (Maps 9, 10, 20, 21)
With the rolling Moose Mountain Highlands encompassing a vast area here, you will find lots of trees, small lakes and streams; the perfect club for those looking for spectacular landscapes. It is one of the most popular riding areas in the southeast and maintains six groomed trails covering approximately 321 km (200 mi). There is an extensive park trail system in the northeast corner as well with 124 km (78 mi) of trails through hundreds of small lakes, rivers and streams. There are nine warm-up huts for the convenience of riders with fuel stops available at Lampman, Carlyle, Arcola, Kisbey, Stoughton, Corning, Kennedy, Langbank, Kipling and Windthorst. Stoughton is the largest town in the area, but there are good overnight facilities at many of these towns.

Trail 311A
The predominant trail within this cub's limits, you will travel over 186 km (116 mi) meandering across all types of landscapes. There are ample gas up opportunities along this trail and several warming huts including Rae Johnson Shelter, Norm's Palace and Beaver Lodge Shelter. As there are hundreds of lakes and rivers along this route, so be sure to check ice levels in several spots before venturing out.

Club #312 - Tri-Valley Trails (Maps 22, 33)
The Tri-Valley Trails Snowmobile Club maintains eight snowmobile trails that add up to over 268 km (166 mi) in length, running through the communities of Maryfield, Moosomin, Rocanville, Welwyn, St. Lazare, Spy Hill, Bear Creek and Tantallon. Moosomin is the largest community in the area, offering a full range of services and conveniently located on the Trans-Canada Highway just a short distance west of the Manitoba border. These trails are well marked and have a nice range of terrain to interest riders.

Trail 312A
Beginning near the community of Spy Hill (fuel and provision stock up), this route takes you through rolling hills in a fairly straight line south past the Qu'Appelle River and more gas up opportunities at Rocanville and Moosomin. This route runs parallel to Highway 8 and, at 67 km (42 mi), it is the longest trail within this club's boundaries.

Club #313 - Grenfell Snowdrifters (Maps 21, 30, 31)
The Grenfell Snowdrifters groom most of the same trails as the Broadview Snow Busters Snowmobile Club, plus an additional small stretch around Grenfell; two trails approximately 75 km (47 mi) in length. There are several warm up shelters within this club's boundaries. Look for fuel stops and accommodations in the town of Grenfell.

Trail 313A
From the community of Goose Lake this trail runs for a short distance along the shores of Crooked Lake before cutting south, passing by Ed's Shelter and leading to the community of Grenfell, where you can find gas. The trail then continues south past the Pipestone Hideaway Shelter, eventually linking with trails that lead to Windthorst.

Club #316 - Prairie and Pine Sno Riders Trails (Maps 54, 55, 65)
The Prairie and Pine Sno Riders Club is based out of the town of Norquay. The club looks after three trails at over 200 km (124 mi) which radiate out from the town and connect with trails from other clubs around Elbow Lake, Sturgis, Kamsack and Canora. There are four warming huts within this club's boundaries with two gas up locations. The Manitoba border can be found along the eastern limits of this club's riding area.

Trail 316A
Beginning at the town of Elbow Lake in the extreme northern part of this club, you will travel 81 km (50 mi) in a general southwest direction past the Trickett Lake and Boiler Junction shelters and numerous frozen lakes and rivers. The landscape along this route is predominantly hills and valleys, with more level ground the closer you get to the small communities you get.

Club #318 - Rhein Sno Cruzers Trails (Maps 43, 44)
The Rhein Club maintains a 38 km (22 mi) portion of the Trans Canadian Trail which passes through the town of Rhein as well as a secondary trail which can provide a nice side route for riders or be utilized as a loop trail from the town, depending on if riders are passing through or starting and ending at Rhein. In total, the club maintains 72 km (45 mi) of trails.

Trail TC318A
This portion of the Trans Canadian Trail runs for 38 km (22 mi) from near the Eagle Peak Shelter in the southwest to near the Snodrifters Hideaway Shelter in the northeast, passing through the town of Rhein along the way, where you can find gas.

Club #320 - Showstoppers Snowmobile Club (Maps 31, 32, 42, 43)
The Showstoppers Snowmobile Club grooms and maintains four trails spread out over approximately 208 km (130 mi) of parkland and natural forest areas north of the Qu'Appelle Valley, as well as dipping down into the valley along Crooked Lake. There are five warm up huts in the area, while fuel stops are in Melville and at two of the resort villages along Crooked Lake: Grenfell Beach and Marieval. The city of Melville has a full range of accommodations and facilities.

Trail 320A
Starting from Yorkton in the eastern region of this club, this 109 km (68 mi) trail follows a southwest route and connects with Melville in the south, past Rousay Lake and Mark Lalonde Shelter. There are no refuelling stations along this route, so make sure you gas up in either Yorkton or Melville.

Club #322 - Souris River Snowmobile Club (Map 8/F1–20/G4)
The Souris River Snowmobile Club maintains the region east of the city of Weyburn. There are only three groomed trails totalling approximately 164 km (103 mi), with warm-up shelters including the Weyburn, Griffin, Melrose Place and Lionel's Shelters. These trails are mostly scenic in nature as this area of Saskatchewan is rich with agricultural, flat landscapes and scattered bluffs.

Trail 322A
From Weyburn, this trail runs in a straight line to the east, parallel to Highway 13. The trail passes through Griffin, where it is possible to branch off to Trail 322B and head north to Creelman. Continuing east will lead you past Froude to the town of Stoughton, where you can find gas and link up with a number of other trails.

Club #324 – Trakkers Snow Club (Maps 43, 54)
This club's main trails are found around the towns of Preeceville, Sturgis and Canora, encompassing approximately 82 km (51 mi). You will find two fuelling stations and three warm up shelters within this region.

Trail 324A (Trans Canadian Trail)
As a continuation of Trail 327A, this section of the Trans Canadian Trail starts off just east of the Moose Lodge Shelter, taking you past the town of Canora and the Stumble Inn Shelter. From here, this route turns sharply north as you cross the Assiniboine River, Whitouche Lake and pass just south of the community of Stenen where this section ends.

Club #327 - Yorkton Sno-Riders Trails (Maps 42, 43, 53)

The Yorkton Sno-Riders maintain 12 trails totalling 387 km (240 mi), mainly north of Yorkton and in and around the massive Good Spirit Lake area. There are only three trails that are greater than 50 km (31 mi), while shorter trails break off for a series of small loops that can be strung together into rides as long or as short as desired. There are warming huts littered across this region as well as refuelling stations.

Trail 327A (Trans Canadian Trail)

Starting in the southeast corner of this club's boundaries, this section of the TCT is approximately 87 km (54 mi) of zig-zagging routes past countless frozen lakes, rivers and streams. The further your adventure takes you from the bigger cities and towns along this route, the hillier and more rugged the terrain gets. This trail ends near the Moose Lodge Shelter and Good Spirit Lake and connects with TC 324A east of Canora.

Club #329 - Springside Snowmobile Trails (Map 43)

The Springside Club maintains a pair of trails totalling approximately 34 km (21 mi). These two routes are basically connectors to the Trans Canadian Trail which passes east of the town. There is gas at Springside and the Four Corners Shelter about halfway up Trail 329A.

Trail TC327A

This portion of the Trans Canadian Trail zig-zags in a southeast direction across this group's riding zone. From the northwest, this trail passes between Whitesand and Horseshoe Lake, continuing to the Southern Comfort Shelter and linking up with trails that lead to Yorkton.

Club #332 - South East Saskatchewan Stubble Jumpers (Maps 10, 11, 21)

Situated in the Redvers, Carnduff, Oxbow, and Carlyle area, the Stubble Jumpers Club maintain approximately 391 km (244 mi) of marked, groomed trails. For the convenience of riders, there are half a dozen warm-up huts in this region and fuel stops in the towns of Carlyle, Redvers, Alida, Alameda, Oxbow, Carnduff and Gainsborough. The terrain is slightly rolling, with some natural bush and small creeks for an interesting ride. Carlyle is the largest community in the area, but there are good overnight facilities at many of these towns.

Trail 332A

At 98 km (61 mi) this is the longest trail within this club's boundaries and basically loops around several warming huts such as the Braap Shack Shelter, the North Shelter and the South Shelter. On the eastern section of this loop you will straddle the Saskatchewan – Manitoba provincial border for a good chunk of this ride. There are gas stations near the communities of Redvers and Alldo.

Club #333 - Estevan Snowmobile Club (Maps 9, 10)

The Estevan Snowmobile Club has eight marked trails totalling about 278 km (172 mi) in length. The area is mainly flat, with natural bush and several large water reservoirs for some interesting riding. The area around Bienfait and Roche Percee also has lots of intriguing geography to explore around the Souris Valley. For the convenience of riders, there are five warm-up shelters on the trails and fuel stops at Macoun, Bienfait and Lampman.

Trail 333A

Starting from the Blueline Shelter, this route meanders southwards for 61 km (38 mi) through the communities of Bensen, Hitchcock and the much larger Estevan, where the trail ends. This trail runs parallel to Highway 47 north south past several frozen lakes and rivers.

Trail 333E

At 92 km (57 mi), this is the largest trail within this club's limits. Access to this trail is from the town of Estevan, where you can find gas. Head south across the Rafferty Dam Reservoir then west to the Lord's Grove Shelter warming hut before riding due north where you will cross the Reservoir again and pass through the communities of Macoun and Bensen where it connects with 333A.

Club #335 - Crossroad Sno-Diggers (Maps 21, 32, 33)

The Crossroad Sno-Diggers develop and groom three trails north and south of the Trans-Canada Highway from Percival to Wapella. There are approximately 105 km (65 mi) of trails in the area, with rolling terrain scattered with bluffs, including the spectacular scenic views of Pipestone Creek Valley. There are two warm-up huts along these routes with fuel stops available at Kennedy, Langbank, Whitewood and Wapella. Whitewood has good accommodations and is situated conveniently on the Trans-Canada Highway.

Trail 355B

This trail forms an almost complete loop to the north of Whitewood, where you can find gas. The trail zig-zags to the northeast past Clayridge to the New Finland Shelter before cutting west toward Round Lake, turning south just after crossing Iskwaohead Creek. The trail then heads southwest to Percival where it links up with the 301D and 335A trails.

Club #339 - Trans Canada Trail Drifters Inc (Maps 30, 31)

Strangely, the Trans Canadian Trail doesn't touch the boundaries of the Trans Canada Trail Drifters Inc. Trails 339A and 339B, at 60 km (37 mi) and 48 km (30 mi) respectively, do parallel the Qu'Appelle River however, with numerous creeks and smaller rivers shooting off from the big river. You will find Mac's Shelter and Dicks Place at opposite ends of these trails, while gas stations can be found at the towns of Grenfell, Wolselley, Sintaluta and Indian Head. All together, this club maintains 109 km (68 mi) of trails.

Trail 339A

From Grenfell, this trail runs west past Summerberry to Wolsely, where you can find gas. From here, continuing west will lead you to Dicks Place Shelter, Sintaluta (more gas) and eventually Indian Head as you parallel the Trans Canada Highway.

Club #343 - Elbow Lake Sno Drifters Trails (Maps 55, 65)

Running into Zone 2, the Elbow Lake Sno Drifters maintain a single 56 km (35 mi) long route made up of several trails that connects to Norquay and to Hudson Bay. The eastern portion of the route teases its way along the boundary between Saskatchewan and Manitoba. The trail then heads east through Elbow Lake before bending south to Norquay. Unlike many trails in the province, there are no easy loops here; instead, you will be heading out-and-back from Elbow Lake or Norquay.

Trail 343A

From just north of Whitebeech, this trail runs directly north to Elbow Lake, straddling the Saskatchewan-Manitoba border and dipping back and forth between the two provinces. Along the way you will pass Norm's Place Shelter, Whitefish Lake, Oops/Boundary Shelter, Smallfish Lake and Pickerel Lake. You can find gas in Elbow Lake.

Trail 316A/B/C

From Elbow Lake, this trail runs west past Trickett Lake and the Trickett Lake Shelter, meandering south towards the Boiler Junction Shelter. From here the trail runs due south parallel to the Swan River, passing the Valley Inn Shelter, eventually leading to Norquay. From Norquay you can continue east past Pelly and Arran to a gas station just south of Benito.

Park #346 - Moose Mountain Provincial Park (Map 21)

Moose Mountain Park, with its natural aspen forests and numerous small lakes, makes an ideal spot for snowmobilers. With its higher elevation, it also receives more snow and has fewer winter thaws than many other areas of southern Saskatchewan. The park has a nice mix of 89 km (55 mi) of groomed and ungroomed snowmobile trails to suit all riders. Facilities are available year-round in the resort village of Kenosee Lake. The main trail through the park is the Centre Road Trail, which runs for 21 km (13 mi) east to west across the park. A series of shorter trails branch off this trail, mostly to the south, connecting to the various 311 trails. These trails include the 7 km Bennet Lake Trail, the 11 km Horse Lake Trail and the 10 km Stevenson Lake Trail. To the north, the 19 km Harmon Lake Trail makes a loop across a series of lakes.

Boundary Trail (P346B)

The Boundary Trail is groomed and suitable for novices. It runs for 13 km (8 mi), connecting with Trail 311A in the south near Camerons Slough. The trail runs across Hewitt Lake, past Little White Bear Lake and across Kenosee Lake to link up with the Centre Road Trail. This trail also connects with the Stevenson Lake Trail in its southern section.

Centre Road Trail (P346A)

Centre Road is rated a novice trail. It is groomed and runs for 21 km (13 mi), cutting east to west across the park and connecting with most of the park's other trails throughout its length. Gas can be found at the trail's eastern terminus, near the north shore of Kenosee Lake. From here, continuing south will lead to Trail 311B and the Bear Claw Casino. The trail also joins with Trail 311B at its western end, while riding south from its western end leads to Trail 311C and the town of Kisbey.

Moose bull, cow and calf in Cypress Hills Provincial Park, Saskatchewan
©Shutterstock / Pictureguy

WILDLIFE ADVENTURES

Saskatchewan is a premier destination for wildlife viewing, particularly for migratory birds. The province acts as a natural flyway for many species of birds and is one of the most important preservation areas in the Western Hemisphere, providing a sanctuary for millions of migrating birds each fall. With over 300 species of birds spotted in the province, Saskatchewan is second to none in North America for migratory bird watching.

Southwest Saskatchewan's thousands of acres of wetlands are an important ecosystem with over 45 kinds of waterfowl and 80 species of other birds that make their homes in these wetlands. Unfortunately, there are many threatened species of birds found in this region. The Loggerhead Shrike is important to the rural economy as they feed extensively on grasshoppers, beetles, rodents and other agricultural pests. Restoring them to healthy numbers will be beneficial in many ways. The Sage Grouse is also threatened, due to the loss of its native sagebrush habitat. Drought conditions have affected their environment, as has over hunting. The Ferruginous Hawk and Burrowing Owl are two additional threatened species that are important in Southern Saskatchewan.

While birding is one of the most popular forms of wildlife watching, there are other animals to spot. The mixed grasslands of southern Saskatchewan have one of the highest concentrations of species in the world. It is estimated that there are no less than 13 species of amphibians, 18 reptiles, 72 mammals, 160 butterflies, 222 birds and around 1,595 species of grasses, sedges and wildflowers in this one bioclimatic region alone. That creates a total of about 2,095 on the species richness index used by the World Wildlife Fund. When compared to California's rainforests at 1,710 and Florida's Everglades at 1,855 you will see that southern Saskatchewan is indeed home to an impressive variety of wildlife.

Farther north, the province transitions to Canadian Shield. Here you will find large ungulates such as moose and deer, as well as larger predators: foxes, wolves and black bears. However, wildlife is less concentrated here since it is a much larger habitat.

In most areas of the province, a leisurely drive at dusk will often provide glimpses of a variety of animals. Provincial and most regional parks also offer good nature viewing opportunities. Even in the heart of urban Saskatoon or Regina, wildlife can be spotted, including birds and small mammals. This section provides a good sampling of notable wildlife viewing areas to help get you started as you begin your search for Saskatchewan Wildlife.

Plains Bison in Grasslands National Park
©Shutterstock / BGSmith

WILDLIFE ADVENTURES

Assiniboia (Map 6/A1)
Bird watchers flock to the area during the fall and spring migrations of the whooping crane that fly from their wintering grounds in Texas to their summering spots in the north. Assiniboia is on the diagonal flyway for the birds. To narrow your search, contact the Canadian Wildlife Service at 306-975-4109 or the Whooping Crane Hotline at 306-975-5595. An estimated 2 to 3 million snow geese also gather in the area during the fall migration, making it a popular spot for bird watchers.

Basin and Middle Lakes Migratory Bird Sanctuary (Map 61/E4)
Located 40 km north of Humboldt, this Bird Sanctuary was established all the way back in 1925. The two lakes are saline, with Basin Lake being much deeper, at 9 metres (30 ft) on average, versus Middle Lake at 1 m (3 ft) on average. Basin Lake used to support a whitefish fishery until its salinity increased. Both lakes are important migratory stopovers, with Basin Lake hosting up to 20,000 ducks, 400 geese and 600 tundra swans, and Middle Lake about half of that number. Several hundred ducks also use the lakes during their molt in the summer.

Battleford Area (Map 58/A3)
The Battleford area has many walking trails and an urban park. Here, birders can spot waterfowl, shorebirds, songbirds and raptors. Jackfish Lake, just north of the city, has a 526 hectare (1,300 ac) marsh where waterbirds are common.

Beaver Creek Conservation Area (Map 49/C4)
Located 13 km south of Saskatoon along Highway 219, this conservation area protects pristine prairie grassland, wetland, forest and creek habitat. Beavers are very active here, and their dams create habitat for many other species. Chickadees are very social and will often fly up to eat out of your hand. You will find a series of nature trails and an interpretive centre here.

Berube Lake Game Preserve (Map 69/E2)
Lining the shores of Berube Lake, this game preserve is found southwest of Prince Albert National Park and can be accessed via grid roads from Highway 55 and Provincial Road 793. A variety of water birds, marsh birds and shore birds can be found here.

Boggy Creek Game Preserve (Map 30/A6)
Found just northeast of Regina, this game preserve sits at the intersection of Gottselig Road and Tower Road. Much of this preserve is located on the grounds of Tor Hill and Murray Golf Courses, offering the chance to spot a variety of songbirds.

Bradwell National Wildlife Area (Map 49/F5)
Located about 48 km southeast of Saskatoon, this 128 hectare (316 ac) site can be accessed by grid roads south of Highway 16. Consisting of a mix of wetlands and grasslands, this is an important nesting habitat for waterfowl including canvasbacks and redheads, as well as shorebirds, songbirds and hawks. Coyotes, deer and ground squirrels are also common here.

 Early morning and late evenings are generally the best times for wildlife viewing.

Brandon Land Nature Sanctuary (Map 54/G5)
Highway 49 cuts through this nature sanctuary, located 8 km east of Norquay. The preserve was set aside to protect the flora of the area, but this is an important wildlife habitat as well.

Buffalo Pound Provincial Park (Map 28/F5)
Nicolle Flats is the premier bird watching area within the park. The flats refer to an area between the Qu'Appelle Valley, Buffalo Pound Lake and Moose Jaw Creek to the east. A 3 km trail connects the marsh area with the historic Nicolle Homestead and provides excellent opportunities for birders. Expect to see great blue heron, sora and Virginia rails, yellow-headed blackbirds, American bitterns, ducks, coots and grebes. A boardwalk over the marsh offers ducks, willow flycatchers, veeries and wrens, while Le Conte's sparrow, bobolinks and say's phoebes, American white Pelicans and western grebes are also spotted here.

In addition to birding, one of the key attractions at the park is the Buffalo Pound Bison Range. The 2.9 km Bison View Interpretive Trail provides an opportunity for you to view these animals without encroaching on their habitat. Other animals to see throughout this park include western painted turtles, white-tailed deer, raccoons, muskrat, coyote and beaver.

Candle Lake Game Preserve (Map 81/D6)
Candle Lake is found north of Prince Albert along Highway 120. Along the western shore of the lake sits Candle Lake Provincial Park, while the game preserve is located on the lake's eastern side. This area is known for mammals such as bears, coyotes, deer, elk, foxes, and wolves, as well as blue herons and loons.

Chaplin Heritage Marsh (Map 16/E2)
Located southeast of Chaplin and 7 km north of the rural municipality of Rogers, this area has four fresh water basins covering 1,325 hectares (3,270 ac) that are dyked from the lake. Offering a variety of habitats including wet meadow, sedge, cattail marshes and open water, a great variety of birds are found here. Look for American bittern, cinnamon teal, marsh wren, yellow-headed blackbird, western grebe, Forster's tern, black-crowned night heron, black-necked stilt and many others.

Chaplin Lake Shorebird Reserve (Map 18/D2–27/C6)
Conveniently located alongside the Trans-Canada Highway, this reserve, along with the nearby Old Wives Migratory Bird Sanctuary, is a designated Western Hemispheric Shorebird Reserve Network site, the highest designation possible. Easily recognized by the mounds of snow-white salt, Chaplin Lake is Canada's second largest inland saline water body, covering over 6,000 hectares (14,820 ac). Giving the illusion of snow in summer, the area provides an ideal environment for numerous shorebirds. Migrating birds that winter in South America travel more than 5,000 km each fall and there are many shorebirds that spend their summers here as well. Counts of all shorebirds have exceeded 100,000. The Chaplin Nature Centre offers information on the area and its birds and features a 12 metre (40 ft) diorama. There is even an interpreter-led shorebird shuttle bus tour available from the Nature Centre, while the Chaplin Lake Shorebird Festival is held the first weekend of June each year.

Species found here include the piping plover, American avocet, sanderling and Baird's sandpiper. You can also bird watch along Highway 58, south of Chaplin. Here, the highway passes through the lake offering a chance to see ferruginous hawk, long-billed curlew, upland sandpipers, sharp-tailed grouse and lark bunting. You will also see a wide variety of waterfowl, shorebirds, gulls, and terns. Other birds to see include chestnut-collared longspur, Baird's sparrow, Sprague's pipit and the northern mockingbird.

Chappuis-Fontane Lakes Special Management Area (Map 120/C3)
Jutting against the Northwest Territories above Lake Athabasca, this Special Management Area contains countless lakes, rivers and streams. In addition to many bird and fish species, bear, caribou, moose and wolf can be seen here.

Chitek Lake Recreation Site (Map 78/F6)
There are 15 lakes found within about 50 km of the Chitek Lake. Wildlife is abundant, including bear, beaver, coyote, deer, elk, fisher, fox, moose, muskrat, otter, wolf, woodchuck and more than 75 species of birds.

Condie Nature Refuge Recreation Site (Map 29/E5)
This site was established in 1924 when the Canadian National Railway dammed Boggy Creek to provide a steady supply of water for their steam engines. Today it is an ideal habitat for waterfowl and wildlife.

Crooked Lake Fen Nature Sanctuary (Map 32/A4)
Containing a rare seepage fen, this small sanctuary in the Qu'Appelle River Valley has lush vegetation which in turn attracts birds during migration and breeding seasons.

Cypress Hills Interprovincial Park (Map 12/B7)
Cypress Hills are an anomaly rising out of the prairie as the highest elevation east of the Rocky Mountains and west of Labrador. You will find lodgepole pine forests and multiple ecosystems providing habitat for a variety of birds. Unique to the area is the opportunity to see most of the birds you would expect to see in Alberta's Rocky Mountains. Cypress is also a stronghold for the common poorwill. Other species include dusky flycatcher, MacGillivray's warbler and the red-napped sapsucker. In the West Block you can easily spot such birds as violet-green swallow and lazuli bunting at Fort Walsh, the turkey vulture and Townsend's solitaire at the Conglomerate Cliffs. Even the graceful trumpeter swan has been seen nesting in the area. Exploring in Cypress Hills, you will also encounter large mammals from moose, deer, antelope and elk, to much smaller mammals such coyote and Red Fox. The park is open year-round. For more information contact 306-662-5411.

WILDLIFE ADVENTURES

Dafoe Game Preserve (Map 51/G6)
Located at the southwest corner of Big Quill Lake, Dafoe Game Preserve can be accessed off of Highway 6 and Highway 16. Quill Lakes are Canada's largest saline lake, with the three interconnected lakes covering around 635 km² (245 mi²). Studies have shown that up to 200,000 birds can be found on the lakes at one time, including 100,000 ducks, 85,000 ducks, 12,000 cranes as well as smaller numbers of black-bellied plover, Hudsonian godwits, lesser yellowlegs, long-billed dowitchers, red-necked phalaropes, red knots, sanderlings, semipalmated sandpipers, stilt sandpipers and white-rumped sandpipers. The endangered piping plover stages and breeds here as well, and islands on the lake are home to double-crested cormorants and American white pelican.

Danielson Provincial Park (Map 38/A5)
Found next to Gardiner Dam, which was built in the 1960s to create Lake Diefenbaker, this provincial park is home to diving ducks and other waterbirds. Along the shoreline are piping plover and other shorebirds, while the scattered stands of trees in and around the park provide the opportunity to see songbirds.

Doré Lake Recreation Site (Map 89/D3)
Doré Lake is a big lake with interpretive walks and lots of wildlife, including several species of birds. A good place to start looking for these birds is from the recreation site found near Michel Point.

Douglas Provincial Park (Map 27/D1–38/E7)
Douglas Provincial Park covers 20 km of natural sand beach on Lake Diefenbaker. A series of nature trails also offer bird watching opportunities. The park is home to over 170 bird species, abundant mule deer, white-tailed deer, coyotes and fur-bearing animals. Expect to see birds such as Cooper's hawks, veeries, gray catbirds, warbling vireos and spotted towhees. Fifteen species of rare plants and animals are located within or near the park, including the western spiderwort and the endangered piping plover, which nests on the beach.

Duck Mountain Provincial Park (Map 44/C1–55/C6)
The northern boreal forests of Saskatchewan stretch farther south along the eastern side of the province than in the west and it is at Duck Mountain that they find their southernmost limit. Here, birders will find species common to more northern areas without having to go north. Warblers such as Nashville, Magnolia and Blackburnian are among the most common, but yellow-bellied sapsuckers, flycatchers and rose-breasted grosbeaks. The birds can be seen along the park's many trails, including Pelly Point and the Boreal Forest Trail. Madge Lake is also home to a variety of waterbirds with loons, grebes, scaups and terns often seen here.

Duncairn Reservoir Migratory Bird Sanctuary (Map 14/D3)
This sanctuary is located 32 km southwest of Swift Current and can be reached via Provincial Road 631. Duncairn Reservoir is also known as Reid Lake, and is fairly deep, allowing it to maintain consistent water levels even during drought. This reservoir is an important area for mallard ducks, geese and tundra swans.

Eastend (Map 2/D2)
Birding is offered right in the town's campsite, along the Frenchman River Valley or from Pine Cree Regional Park. One of the best places to bird, or hunt for fossils, is at Jones Peak in the Valley of the Hidden Secrets. Here you have a vista of the whole valley below. Expect to see species such as the white-crowned sparrow, rock wren, prairie falcon, say's phoebe and the violet-green swallow. Contact the T-Rex Discovery Centre in Eastend at 306-295-4009 for more information.

E.B. Campbell Game Preserve (Map 83/F7)
This preserve is found on the eastern end of Tobin Lake, which is known for its incredible fishing – the ice fishing world record walleye was caught here. The preserve is home to a number of marsh birds and shorebirds, as well as frogs and other amphibians. Highway 123 passes by the preserve.

Echo Valley Provincial Park (Map 30/E3)
Echo Valley Provincial Park is nestled in the Qu'Appelle Valley, situated on both prairie landscape and valley lowland. Part of the park is built on a delta between Pasqua Lake and Echo Lake creating great habitat for wildlife. Birders will appreciate the more than 225 species of birds, including mountain bluebirds, found in the valley. There are also interpretive programs for young and old alike.

Etter's Beach Recreation Site (Map 39/G5)
Found of the west side of Last Mountain Lake, 10 km east of Stalwart, this recreation site protects an area of wildlife habitat in an agrarian area. There is excellent bird watching here including for ducks and geese, as well as mammals such as deer and rabbits. There are many other species of migratory waterfowl found here, including the occasional whooping crane.

Foam Lake Heritage Marsh (Map 53/A7)
Foam Lake Heritage Marsh was the third major wetland to be dedicated as part of the Saskatchewan Heritage Marsh Agreement. Ducks Unlimited Canada has restored the 2,630 hectare (6,500 ac) area that lies in the main central flyway for many species of migratory birds. The wetland and surrounding upland areas are used for nesting, moulting and staging and are also home to other aquatic and terrestrial wildlife. Abundant wildlife can be seen in the area including mule and white-tailed deer, moose, elk, coyote and fox. Song birds, swans and pelicans, bald and golden eagles and blue heron are some of bird species seen.

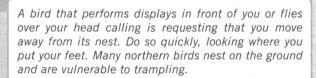

A bird that performs displays in front of you or flies over your head calling is requesting that you move away from its nest. Do so quickly, looking where you put your feet. Many northern birds nest on the ground and are vulnerable to trampling.

Fort Qu'Appelle Fish Culture Station (Map 30/F3)
The Fort Qu'Appelle Fish Culture Station is the major breeding station for restocking southern Saskatchewan's lakes. There is a visitor centre open from the first of May until the Labour Day weekend, where you will find displays and audio visual materials to explain how the culture station works. To arrange a tour, contact the Fish Culture Station at 306-332-3200.

Good Spirit Lake (Map 43/A1–B2)
This area is often called Canada's Duck Factory, since the small ponds and pothole lakes here produce millions of ducks each year. Good Spirit Lake is home to grebes, grosbeaks, herons, blackbirds, sharp-tailed grouse, wrens, waxwings and sparrows. The best place to access the lake is from the provincial park or through the private resort at the north end of the lake. Nearby, Horseshoe Lake Heritage Marsh offers good birding opportunities as well. Access to the marsh is on foot and across private property. Make sure to keep gates closed. Watch for deer, coyote, fox and rabbit in the dunes area, and elk and moose elsewhere.

Grasslands National Park (Map 3/G5–5/D7)
Grasslands National Park is extremely important to the preservation of a variety of bird and animal species at risk. Made up of two distinct blocks, it is accessible by Highway 4 and Highway 18. Visitors can explore the West Block by vehicle using the self-guided Frenchman River Valley Ecotour brochure or audiocassette tour, as well as take a guided tour. The East Block is found around Killdeer and the Killdeer Badlands. Grasslands National Park is open year-round, with the park office and Visitor Centre open daily from May long weekend to Labour Day in September. For more information, contact the park office at 306-298-2257.

Due to its unique environment, the park is home to some of the rarest birds found in Saskatchewan. Along the Frenchman River, you can listen for shrub birds such as the loggerhead shrike and yellow-breasted chat. Burrowing owls are often found in the prairie dog towns. You may also see mountain plover, golden eagle, prairie and peregrine falcons and ferruginous hawks. In the sagebrush and greasewood flats you will see such rare birds as the brewer's sparrow, and greater sage grouse. Other species at risk include Eskimo curlew, mountain, piping and sage plover and Sprague's pipit.

The park list has 43 mammals you may see. These include masked and prairie shrew, bats, American badger, beaver and porcupine, Nuttall's cottontail, snowshoe hare, white-tailed jackrabbit, Richardson's and thirteen-lined ground squirrel, northern pocket gopher, black-tailed prairie dog, Norway rat, muskrat, voles, mouse, coyote, red and swift fox, ermine, long-tailed weasel, mink, striped skunk, raccoon, bobcat, mule and white-tailed deer as well as pronghorn antelope.

Great Sandhills (Map 24)

The Great Sandhills are a vast 1,900 km² (1,180 mi²) area of desert-like golden sands. The sandhills drift east at a rate of about 4 metres (13 ft) per year because of winds from the west and northwest. Not all of the Sandhills are completely bereft of vegetation as there are small clumps of aspen, birch and willow trees scattered about the fine sand, all held together by native prairie grass. Also low brushes such as rose, chokecherry and sagebrush feed the antelope in the area. You can expect to see birds such as the sandhill crane, partridge, prairie chicken, hawks and sharp-tailed grouse.

The main viewing area for the Great Sandhills is reached south of the town of Sceptre on Highway 32. The viewing area is on private property and visitors are asked to respect the property without damaging the delicate ecosystem. From the parking area, you climb the 30 metre (100 ft) sandhills to experience the incredible sight. You can also visit the Great Sandhills Museum in Sceptre for an interpretive experience. There is another private property viewing area that requires permission before entering found east of Highway 21 at Liebenthal.

Hazlet Municipal Park (Map 24/F6)

Hazlet Park is 2.5 km northwest of Hazlet off Highway 332 on the edge of the Great Sandhills. White-tailed and mule deer frequently walk through the park, while other wildlife and many species of birds can often be seen in the trees. Birdwatchers can even see the endangered Long-billed curlew and loggerhead shrike on occasion.

Indian Head National Migratory Bird Sanctuary (Map 30/G6)

This 32 hectare (79 ac) sanctuary was established in 1924. It is located 3 km south of the town of Indian Head at the PFRA Shelterbelt and is made up of 8% wetland and 92% tree nursery.

Jean Louis Legare Regional Park (Map 6/D4)

This park is located just south of the town of Willow Bunch on Highway 36 in a picturesque natural valley shaded with tall trees. Two natural hiking trails lead from the campground, allowing visitors to enjoy wildlife and bird watching.

Jewel Creek Nature Conservancy (Map 9/A3)

The Jewel Creek Nature Conservancy is created from the parcels of land surrounding the Rafferty Reservoir project. The 469 hectare (1,160 ac) piece of mixed-grassland habitat is large enough to support and maintain numerous species including the northern pintail, blue-winged teal, ferruginous hawk, red-tailed hawk, sharp-tailed grouse, white-tailed deer, Baird's sparrow, mink, western painted turtle and the nationally threatened Sprague's pipit. Vegetation includes western porcupine grass, fringed sage, wood's rose, snowberry and wolf willow.

Kendal Game Preserve (Map 20/B2)

Located around the Chapleau Lakes east of Kendal and south of Highway 48, this is an excellent place to view birds of all kinds.

Lake Charron Regional Park (Map 62/F6)

Lake Charron is well known as a wildlife watching destination, as the lake is home to pelicans. There's also a nature trail with native flowers, plants and animals found at the regional park on the lake.

Lake Diefenbaker (Maps 25–28, 38)

Lake Diefenbaker, which is a 42,000 hectare (103,740 ac) bowl between the Gardiner Dam and the Qu'Appelle Valley Dam, provides a habitat for the piping plover, as well as numerous other birds. The plover was listed as an endangered species in 1985. You may have many opportunities to spot the plover with nearly 800 km (500 mi) of shoreline on Lake Diefenbaker.

Last Mountain Lake (Map 29/D4–40/A4)

Due to its location in the central flyway for migration and its excellent habitats, Last Mountain Lake has always been an important area for birders. It was the first Federal Bird Sanctuary reserved in North America. More recently, Last Mountain Lake National Wildlife Area has been designated as a Wetland of International Importance along with 30 other sites in Canada and over 700 locations worldwide. During the fall migration you can expect to see up to 280 species of birds in this area. Thousands of cranes, geese and ducks fill the skies and resting areas when migration peaks. There are also scores of songbirds, shorebirds and birds of prey in the area. Mammal species include deer and rabbits. You can access the lake from the Regina Beach Recreation Site, Saskatchewan Beach Regional Park, Valeport Recreation Site, Rowan's Raving Provincial Park and any of a few dozen small resort communities along its shores.

Leader (Map 23/F1)

The town of Leader has the most extensive woodlands in southeast Saskatchewan, making it home to many species of birds and animals. Stop at the Estuary Ferry and explore the cottonwood forest, where you may see the willow flycatcher, warbling and redeyes vireos, yellow-breasted chat or northern saw-whet. While crossing on the ferry you may get glances of the belted kingfisher, northern rough-winged swallow or even the violet-green swallow, which are at their northeastern limits.

Lenore Lake Migratory Bird Sanctuary (Map 61/G5–62/A6)

Lenore is a slightly saline lake with an average depth of 5 metres (16 ft), though water levels fluctuate considerably throughout the seasons. The lake is found 25 km north of Humboldt and can be reached by branch roads from Highway 368 and Provincial Roads 773 and 777. Over 30,000 ducks, primarily mallards but assorted diving ducks as well, stage here during the fall, as do 700 Canada Geese and 300 Tundra Swans. The lake's protected bays and many islands make an ideal breeding habitat for diving and dabbling ducks, as well as geese. This is also a major fishing lake and contains northern pike, perch, walleye and whitefish.

Lloydminster (Map 66/A3)

Found on the Saskatchewan/Alberta boundary (not border despite its moniker as the "border city"), Ducks Unlimited has created a driving tour around the city to sites of interest for birders: marshes and other wetlands.

Luck Lake Heritage Marsh (Map 37/F6)

The Luck Lake Heritage Marsh features a 35 km self-drive nature tour. There are various public access and observation points for wildlife viewing, particularly bird watching. Alternatively, a hiking trail along the northeast corner of the marsh allows hikers even closer views of this ecosystem's inhabitants. Contact 306-858-2624 for more information.

Marsden Game Preserve (Map 56/B1)

This game preserve straddles the south and east shores of Wells Lake, just outside of the town of Marsden. Marsden Lake is part of the Manitou Lake Area, which is known to support some of the largest shorebird concentrations in Western Saskatchewan. Species that have been observed here include dunlin, red knot, red-necked phalarope, ruddy turnstone, sanderling and stilt sandpiper. This area is also home to nesting endangered piping plovers.

A good set of binoculars or spotting scope will allow you to observe birds and animals more easily and from further distances.

Maurice G. Street Wildlife Sanctuary (Map 73/B3)

This nature reserve is found 17 km northeast of Nipiwan and is home to over 245 identified species of birds including bald eagles, golden eagles, pileated woodpeckers and many more. Many beautiful species of flower are found within the thick boreal forest setting, including large yellow lady's-slippers and ram's-head lady's slippers. Mammal species found in the sanctuary include, but are not limited to, black bear, bobcat, elk, red fox and river otter.

Maymont Conservation Area (Map 58/F5)

This ecologically diverse area straddles the boundary between open grasslands and closed forest, facilitating biodiversity and creating habitat for at least 33 endangered species, including the whooping crane. You can also find some rare stands of cottonwood here. This area is located south of Maymont along Highway 376.

Misaw Lake Special Management Area (Map 121/E2)

This area encompasses the northeastern tip of Saskatchewan, meeting the borders of Manitoba, the Northwest Territories and Nunavut. This is a popular fishing area and contains countless lakes. In addition to many bird and fish species, bear, caribou, moose and wolf can be seen here.

Moose Mountain Provincial Park (Map 21/C6–G5)

Moose Mountain Provincial Park provides a rare forest habitat in southeast Saskatchewan. In addition to a wide range of animals and birds, you will find Cooper's hawk at home here. This threatened species nests in hardwood trees during the summer, then migrates south through Mexico to Guatemala and Honduras for the winter. At last count, there were also 400 moose known to roam the park.

WILDLIFE ADVENTURES

Morse Viewing Tower on Reed Lake (Map 26/F7)

Reed Lake, a smaller inland saline lake, has a variety of shorebirds, both migratory and resident. There is an observation tower and picnic area about 2.4 km west of the town of Morse. Caspian terns are on a small island just to the west of the southern end of the causeway. Other nesting birds here include the double-crested cormorant, common tern, ring-billed, California and herring gulls. There are also eared, western and occasionally some Clark's grebe nesting in the reed beds of the lake. Migrating birds seen from the viewing tower include the black-bellied plover, ruddy turnstone, red know and sanderling. Contact the Morse Museum for more details at 306-629-3230.

Murray Lake Migratory Bird Sanctuary (Map 68/B6)

Murray Lake is a relatively large and deep lake that maintains steady water levels throughout the year, thanks to several creeks and a canal that connects to Jackfish Lake. The lake is used primarily as a staging area in the spring and fall and over 6,000 ducks have been observed here. You can find this lake 30 km north of Battleford, off of Highway 4.

Never approach an animal directly and do not try to bring animals to you by offering them food. This is dangerous for both you and the animal.

Neely Lake Migratory Bird Sanctuary (Map 64/D3)

Located 50 km southwest of Hudson Bay, this shallow lake is surrounded by forest and peatland and can be reached by grid roads off of Highways 3, 23 and Provincial Road 677 followed by a short stretch of trail. This is an important fall staging area for white-fronted geese, tundra swans and ducks. There are a few pairs of ducks who nest here, and the lake is used for breeding by ducks including blue-winged teal, bufflehead, canvasback, common goldeneye, lesser scaup, mallard and ruddy duck.

Nickle Lake (Map 8/G1)

Nickle Lake, a reservoir located just south of Weyburn on the Souris River, has numerous water birds. Look for loons, Piping Plover and all three species of scoter during the fall migration.

Old Man on His Back Prairie Preserve (Map 12/A5)

This 5,302 hectare (13,101 ac) mixed prairie grass preserve is part of the Old Man on His Back Plateau. The land was donated by Sharon and Peter Butala, while several organizations including the Nature Conservancy of Canada and Saskatchewan Environment (through the Fish and Wildlife Development Fund) donated money for the project. A small herd of 50 bison were set loose to roam freely on the preserve in December of 2003; there is still a sustainable herd found on this preserve.

Old Wives Lake Migratory Bird Sanctuary (Map 16/F2–17/C3)

Old Wives Lake is the fourth largest inland saline lake in North America. Along with the Chaplin Lake Shorebird Reserve it was designated a Western Hemispheric Shorebird Reserve Network site in 1997. Wood River flows into the west end of this 285 km2 (110 mi2) dry lake bed that is approximately 32 km (20 mi) long and 19 km (12 mi) wide. The town of Mossbank is the southern gateway to the sanctuary, while numerous grid roads provide access for birdwatchers around the lake.

The natural wetlands ecological area around the lake makes it a favourite habitat for many species of waterfowl. Further off shore, the Isle of Bays is known to have had colonies of pelicans and gulls nesting on it for centuries. An aerial survey once counted more than 64,000 shorebirds lining Old Wives' edges. During the same count, a total of almost 30 thousand Baird's sparrows—roughly 40 per cent of the world's population—were counted at Old Wives and Chaplin Lakes.

Opuntia Lake Migratory Bird Sanctuary (Map 47/A5)

Opuntia Lake is a shallow, saline lake located 60 km southwest of Biggar. This is an important fall staging area for 15,000 to 20,000 geese, including Canada, white-fronted, snow and Ross's geese, up to 30,000 ducks, including mallard, pintail and assorted diving, 2,000 sandhill cranes and 500 tundra swans. The lake also supports a number of shorebirds, including snowy owls. You can access the lake via grid roads from Highways 31, 51 and Provincial Road 657.

Outlook Game Preserve (Map 37/F1)

Located on the west bank of the South Saskatchewan River, just north of Outlook, this preserve can be accessed by branch roads off of Highways 15 and 45. Birders will find many different species of songbirds and water birds to look for here.

Patterson Lake Game Preserve (Map 43/A1)

Patterson Lake is located just north of Provincial Road 746 and the much larger Good Spirit Lake. This is a small game preserve, wrapping around the southern shore of the lake. This area is known as a habitat for coyote, deer, fox and rabbit, as well as birds such as grosbeaks, waxwings, sharp-tailed grouse and a variety of water birds.

Pelican Lake (Map 28/B6)

Pelican Lake is located right off of the Trans-Canada Highway, providing another easy bird watching stop. Good places to watch from include Besant Recreation Site and a Ducks Unlimited Viewing Area that are both well signed. Fall provides spectacular views as tens of thousands of migrating geese stop to rest on these waters. You can also see a variety of species of ducks, including ruddy duck, northern pintail, canvasback and mallard. Some of the bird species you can expect to see in Besant Provincial Recreation Site include ruby-crowned kinglets, magnolia and Canada warblers, blackpoll, gray catbirds, bank swalls, yellow-breasted chat, great horned owls and Cape May.

Pine Cree Regional Park (Map 2/E1–13/E7)

This small park, located in the Cypress Hills between Shaunavon and Eastend along the South Fork Grid Road 633, is the location of the discovery of one of the most complete Tyrannosaurus Rex skeletons in the world, along with numerous other fossils. In addition to fossil hunting, visitors can also enjoy some excellent birdwatching.

Prairie National Wildlife Areas
(Maps 3, 4, 12, 13, 20, 23, 24, 27, 33, 37, 48, 56, 60)

A number of Prairie National Wildlife areas are distributed throughout southern Saskatchewan. These areas protect different ecodistricts and improve potential wildlife habitat in a region of Saskatchewan that is being progressively degraded of wildlife habitat. These areas are available for public use for nature watching and other eco-friendly pursuits, such as hiking. Usage is monitored by the National Wildlife Area Regulations. The wildlife areas are marked on the maps.

Prince Albert National Park (Maps 79, 80, 90)

This national park sits on the transition zone between parkland and the northern forest. The park has Canada's only fully protected nesting colony of white pelicans, many species of waterfowl and plenty of mammals. Moose, wolf and caribou inhabit the northern forests while elk, deer and badgers inhabit the southern parkland region. But the park's signature species is the Sturgeon River Plains Bison, Canada's only free ranging plains bison. Bison roam freely in the southwest corner of the park, where pockets of fescue grassland can be found. This herd is one of only two such herds protected within a Canadian national park. At last count the herd numbered 400. While this is only a pittance compared to the millions that once ranged the plains, it is far better than the 50 animals that were originally moved here in 1969.

Quill Lakes International Bird Area (Map 51/G6–52/E5)

The Quill Lakes Marsh Network has been identified as internationally important wetlands and is a Western Hemisphere Shorebird Reserve Network Site. More than 300 species come to this one site alone and over one million birds pass through Quill Lakes annually. Despite the number of birds, it can be hard to get a good look at the birds because the area is so big including three big lakes: Big Quill, Little Quill and Mud Lake. There are three visitor centres here that can direct you to the best birding opportunities at the time you show up. The best time for viewing is during spring and/or fall migrations, when over 200,000 shorebirds, 400,000 ducks, 130,000 snow geese, 80,000 Canada geese and 40,000 sandhill cranes stop here along with smaller populations of other waterfowl and shorebirds. The lakes are home to breeding colonies of American White Pelicans. The area is also home to deer, fox, badger, coyote, muskrat and beaver.

Radisson Lake Game Preserve (Map 59/A5)

Radisson Lake is found just north of the town of Radisson, sandwiched between Highways 16 and 340. This saline like is roughly 4.5 km² (1.7 mi²) and is a stopping point for a variety of waterfowl. The endangered piping plover breeds here in small numbers. The whooping crane, also endangered, can be seen here from mid-September to mid-October.

WILDLIFE ADVENTURES

Raven Island National Wildlife Area (Map 61/G6)

Raven Island is found at the south end of Lenore Lake (see Lenore Lake Migratory Bird Sanctuary). The island is an important feeding, breeding and nesting area for cormorants, grebes, great blue herons, gulls, terns and songbirds. In the summer, Canada geese, ducks and passerines nest on the island.

Red Coat Nature Habitat – Weyburn (Map 8/F1–19/F7)

The Red Coat Nature Habitat is in Weyburn's Tatagwa Parkway, a 73 hectare (180 ac) conservation area along the Souris River. You can expect to see such species as the ferruginous hawk, rough-legged hawk, ring-necked pheasant, prairie falcon, snowy owl and burrowing owl. Call 306-848-3233 for more information.

Redberry Lake World Biosphere Reserve (Map 59/C4)

Designated as a World Biosphere Reserve by United Nations Education, Science and Cultural Organization (UNESCO), the Redberry Lake Watershed is presently the only UNESCO designated biosphere reserve in the province. Included here is the saline lake, a regional park, a research and education centre and 112,200 hectares (277,135 ac) of rolling prairie, dotted with seasonal ponds and marshes. The lake provides habitat for nine endangered species as well as over 180 other species of birds including migrating shorebirds and waterfowls. Threatened birds like piping plover and colonial birds like American white pelican are unusual species here. Moose and fox are also found in the area.

Rendek Elm Forest Nature Sanctuary (Map 65/C1)

Found at the confluence of Smoking Tent Creek and the Red Deer River, this area, prone to flooding, is mostly covered with American elms, although there are maples and poplars on the east side. The elms were stricken with a case of Dutch elm disease and many of the trees are dying or dead. While the area has many birds, few people have spent much time bird watching here, as the area is more noted for its trees than its wildlife.

Saskatchewan Burrowing Owl Interpretive Centre – Moose Jaw (Map 28/E7)

The city of Moose Jaw is located on the Trans-Canada Highway. Birders will love a visit to the Saskatchewan Burrowing Owl Interpretive Centre, located on the Moose Jaw Exhibition Grounds, as they have been nesting inside the racetrack for many years.

Saskatchewan Landing Provincial Park (Map 25/E4)

Saskatchewan Landing is an important stop of the Birding Trail in Southwest Saskatchewan. The Coulee Trail in the park is one of the best hikes for birders. It is located on the south side of the lake, west of the bridge. On your walk you will encounter everything from beaver dams to thick growths of shrubbery. It is likely you will see yellow-breasted chat, spotted towhee, willow flycatcher, gray catbird and common yellowthroat. If you camp or walk through the northeast corner of the park during the summer you may see resident northern flickers, lark sparrow and Baltimore orioles.

Saskatoon (Map 49/C3)

The green spaces along the shores of the South Saskatchewan River in Saskatoon, including Diefenbaker Park, Sutherland Beach and Cosmopolitan Park are great places for birding. The weir and the area around the Queen Elizabeth Power Plant do not freeze in the winter and are among the best places to see early migratory birds in spring as well as in late fall. Away from the river, President Murray Park is home to a stand of mature white spruce, which attracts merlins, blue jays, red-breasted nuthatches, olive-sided flycatchers, woodpeckers and chickadees, just to name a few.

Scentgrass Lake Migratory Bird Sanctuary (Map 68/B7)

Fed by runoff and rain, several springs and Page Creek, and enclosed by a dyke and an earthen dam, this lake maintains steady water levels in an area subject to drought, making it an important refuge for many types of birds. This is crucial moulting and breeding area for ducks, including mallards, northern pintails and various diving ducks – up to 2,000 ducks have been observed here. There are also 7,000 geese who use the lake in the fall, including Canada, lesser snow, Ross's and white-fronted geese. The lake is also home to many other birds, including American bittern, black-crowned night heron, black tern, franklin's gull, killdeer, marbled godwit, marsh wren, pied-billed grebe, red-winged and yellow-head blackbird, spotted sandpiper, Wilson's pharalope and Wilson's snipe.

Shamrock Regional Park (Map 16/D3)

This park is one of the oldest natural parks in the province and was originally part of the W-Bar Ranch. Cradled by the Wood River, it is a popular site for nature walks, picking wild berries and birding since it is part of the Saskatchewan Birding Trail.

Shawaga Game Preserve (Map 64/E4)

This small game preserve measures about 800 metres by 800 metres and can be found north of Highway 23, south of Neely Lake. The preserve protects a small patch of forest in an area otherwise cleared for farming, creating a refuge for many birds and small mammals.

Silver Lake Regional Park (Map 66/G4)

Located 15 km northeast of Maidstone, this park is home to a walking trail with a birding tower. A wide variety of birds can be seen here, along with various wildlife.

St. Denis National Wildlife Area (Map 50/A2)

Found about 40 km east of Saskatoon, this 360 hectare (890 ac) area was established for research into the effects of agriculture on waterfowl habitat in the unique prairie pothole region. Over 100 species of birds have been recorded in the area. Some of the most common species include American crow, American widgeon, black-billed magpie, blue-wing teal, canvasback, gadwall, green-wing teal, lesser scaup, mallard and tree swallow. Common species of mammals include American mink, coyote, Franklin's ground squirrel, mule and white-tail deer, muskrat, red fox, striped skunk and thirteen-lined ground squirrel.

St. Walburg District (Map 77/A7)

The St. Walburg District is found along Highway 26 and is near the transition between rolling farmlands and Canadian Shield. Here, birders will find wetlands and eskers. Over 250 species of birds have been spotted in this region; this is over 80% of all the birds seen in the province. The area is called the Hummingbird Capital of the Province and it is not a surprise to see the tiny birds. But there are also warblers, waterbirds, owls, woodpeckers, cranes, terns and many more. Check out Spruce Lake southeast of town, Frenchman's Butte to the west, the salt water Stony Lake and the Turtle Lake Nature Sanctuary.

Stalwart National Wildlife Area (Map 39/G5)

This 1,525 hectare (3,770 ac) wildlife area includes 600 hectares (1,480 ac) of managed wetland, including 50 nesting islands constructed by Ducks Unlimited Canada. Over 115 bird species are observed here, including thousands of ducks and geese. Canada geese and canvasback and redhead ducks breed in the marshes. Nesting species include coot, grebe, kingbird, oriole, marsh wren, tern, thrasher and vireo. Mammals that can be seen here include ground squirrels, deer, jackrabbits, meadow voles, mice, muskrats, pocket gophers and skunks. This is also a breeding site for amphibians such as the boreal chorus frog, leopard frog and tiger salamander. This area can be accessed from Highway 2, southeast of Saskatoon and north of Regina and Moose Jaw.

Do not disturb plants, branches or bushes around dens or nests. By making a den or nest more visible to people, you also make it more visible to predators.

Suffern Lake Regional Park (Map 56/B3)

Suffern Lake features a sandy beach, sand dunes and sandy hills nearby. The small, quiet lake is also home to a few birds, deer, ducks and geese for visitors to look for.

Sutherland Migratory Bird Sanctuary (Map 49/D2)

This bird sanctuary is located within the city of Saskatoon and includes a park and zoo. This sanctuary is unique in that it consists of manicured lawns and exotic vegetation, creating an artificial environment that is used by a variety of captive native and exotic species of ducks, geese and swans. Other birds who use the sanctuary include blackbirds, chickadees, grosbeaks, gulls, hawks, kingbirds, owls, sparrows, swallows, warblers and woodpeckers. This sanctuary can be reached via Forest Drive, off of Attridge Drive in northeastern Saskatoon.

Swift Current (Map 14/G1)

The Swift Current Chinook Pathway begins at Swift Current Creek near the Trans-Canada Highway at the north end of the city. The trail wanders west through the city alongside the creek to the southern edge and provides a fabulous opportunity to view birds. During the winter, birders can also visit the Semi-Arid Prairie Agriculture Research Centre, which is adjacent to Highway 4 on the southeast edge of the city. You will see birds such as the red-breasted nuthatch, golden-crowned kinglets and brown creepers. Contact the Swift Current Tourism Centre, situated at the junction of Highway 4 and the Trans-Canada Highway, by telephone at 306-778-2775.

Taylor Lake Recreation Site (Map 107/G3)

Located just 28 km north of Buffalo Narrows on Highway 155, this recreation site sits at the southwest end of Taylor Lake. The easy access makes this a popular birding site.

Tazin Lake Special Management Area (Map 119/D2)

This area is found in Saskatchewan's northwest corner, just above Lake Athabasca. The remote area is home to eagles and ospreys, as well as bears, caribou, moose and wolves.

Turtle Lake Nature Sanctuary (Map 77/F7)

One of the main birding destinations in the St Walburg District, 177 different species of birds have been seen here. May is one of the best times to be here. The forests are also home to mammals like deer, elk, wolves and fishers.

Tway National Wildlife Area (Map 61/D3)

This marsh complex is found at the headwaters of the Carrot River, near the intersection of Highways 20 and 320. This waterfowl staging area is surrounded by rolling uplands and trembling aspen forest. Canada geese, coots, divers and grebes stage and breed in the marsh. Hawks, owls, songbirds and small mammals can also be found here.

Upper Rousay Lake Migratory Bird Sanctuary (Map 43/C5)

This sanctuary can be found 6 km east of Yorkton, in between Highways 52 and 10. The lake is part of a large wetland complex of interconnected shallow lakes. Upper Rousay Lake has an average depth of 0.5 metres (1.5 ft) and includes many bays and islands, including artificial islands constructed by Ducks Unlimited. Many dabbling and diving ducks, as well as Canada geese, nest on the lake. The lake also serves as a fall staging area for ducks and geese. Other water and marsh birds that can be found at the lake include eared, horned, pied-billed and red-necked grebe, marsh wren, red-winged and yellow-headed blackbird and sora. In the summer you can observe American bittern, American white pelican, black-crowned night heron, common loon, great blue heron, herring gull, ring-billed gull and western grebe. Shorebirds in the area include American avocet, Baird's and spotted sandpiper, killdeer, marbled godwit, upland sandpiper, willet, Wilson's phalarope and Wilson's snipe. During migration you can also find greater and lesser yellowleg, pectoral, least and solitary sandpiper, semipalmated plover and short-billed dowitcher here.

Val Marie Reservoir Migratory Bird Sanctuary (Map 3/F4)

Located 10 km northwest of Val Marie along Newton Lake Road, this reservoir was created from the Frenchman River, and water levels here fluctuate significantly according to irrigation needs of the surrounding farms. This is an important spring and fall staging area for several hundred Canada geese and ducks. Birds that nest on the lake's islands include black-crowned night heron, California gull, common tern, double-breasted cormorant, great blue heron and ring-billed gull. In the summer you can also find American white pelicans, black terns and Franklin's gulls.

Valeport Marshes (Map 29/D3)

The Valeport Marshes are along Highway 20, near the town of Craven at the south end of Last Mountain Lake. The marshes are a perfect nesting place for numerous waterfowl and serve as an ideal spawning ground for local game fish.

Van Brienen Land Nature Sanctuary (Map 52/G3)

Found about 11 km southwest of Kelvington, this preserve protects a portion of the uplands around Meadow Bank Lake as well as part of the lake. The lake attracts waterfowl and shorebirds, while the forest is home to 18 observed species of mammals. Access to the sanctuary by land is across private property and permission is needed to cross. However, it is possible to canoe to the sanctuary from the east end of Meadow Bank Lake. Note that the boundaries of the sanctuary are not marked.

Wakamow Valley (Map 28/E7)

Over 191 species of birds have also been sighted in the Wakamow Valley Authority area, as well as four different species flying over without stopping— the tundra swan, greater white-fronted goose, snow goose and sandhill crane. The Kingsway Park Ecological Zone is a great place to begin your bird watching experience in Moose Jaw's Wakamow Valley. It is an 800 metre (2,625 ft) self-guided nature trail through a variety of habitats. You will find more than 100 bird species in this small area. This Ecological Zone is comprised of four distinctly different ecosystems and is also home to 140 different plant species, 12 species of amphibians and reptiles, along with 20 animal species and numerous insects.

Wascana Centre—Regina (Map 29/G7)

The Regina area has the longest bird list of any area in the province. The Wascana Centre is a Migratory Bird Sanctuary and one of North America's largest urban parks. Wascana Creek flows through the park providing an important staging area for Canada geese in the fall and thousands of birds are often seen overhead or heard throughout the area. Another common viewing area is Warbler Alley found in trees north of the legislature buildings.

In order to improve your chances of spotting birds and animals, wear natural colours and unscented lotions.

Wascana Lake Migratory Bird Sanctuary (Map 29/G7)

This sanctuary is part of the larger Wascana Centre park complex, located in downtown Regina. Human-made islands on Wascana Lake provide nesting habitat for over 200 pairs of Canada geese. Blue-winged teal, mallard and northern pintail ducks also nest here. There are up to 115 species of migrant birds that use the area as well, including up to 7,500 Canada geese.

Webb National Wildlife Area (Map 14/D2)

Located about 28 km west of Swift Current, this wildlife area can be found along Highway 1. The area consists of a mix of wetlands and uplands, including the saline Goose Lake and a variety of marshes and coulees. About half of this area is used for agricultural production. There have been approximately 115 bird species, 20 mammal species and 6 amphibian species observed here. Waterfowl and shorebirds use Goose Lake as a staging area, while migratory birds that pass through here include Sprague's pipit, western meadowlark and willet.

Whiteswan Lakes Game Preserve (Map 81/F3)

This series of lakes are popular with anglers and can be found along Highway 913, northeast of Prince Albert. The lakes are surrounded by forest which shelters several mammal species and song birds, while waterfowl and other birds can be found all along the lakes.

Willow Bunch Game Preserve (Map 06/E3)

Located on the north shore of Willow Bunch Lake, this preserve can be accessed by branch roads reaching south from Highway 13. Willow Bunch Lake is a saline lake about 30 km (18.5 mi) long and 1 to 2 km wide. The mudflats which develop on the lake shore are important piping plover habitat, and over 120 breeding pairs have been observed here, representing around two percent of the global population.

Wood Mountain Area (Map 5/E4)

The Wood Mountain area includes the Wood Mountain Regional Park, the community of Wood Mountain and surrounding area that dips down into Killdeer and the Killdeer Badlands. The rolling hills and short prairie grass of this area provide a great habitat for various mammals. Look for mule and white-tailed deer, antelope, eagles, buzzards and even some cougars and elk wandering through the buttes and hoodoos.

The Wood Mountain Uplands have been home to a diverse assortment of wild animals since prehistoric times. Fossils of tyrannosaurus, brontosaurus and giant sea turtle fossils have been found there, as well as later primitive mammals such as three-toed horses and mastodons close to the town of Rockglen. Sharp-eyed visitors may still see the odd moose, lynx or bobcat preying on badgers, foxes, weasels and coyotes. You will certainly encounter beaver and muskrat in the small meandering creeks or marshy areas along the edge of grid roads.

Snowshoeing, Greenwater Lake Provincial Park, Saskatchewan
©Tourism Saskatchewan / Greg Huszar Photography

WINTER ADVENTURES

Saskatchewan winters are generally long and it is no surprise that there are a lot of things to do during this season: cross-country skiing, downhill skiing, snowshoeing, snowmobiling, ice fishing and outdoor skating are some of the favourite activities.

While Saskatchewan is a province of extremes and temperatures can readily drop to -40° C (-40° F) on a January day, there can also be long periods of beautiful winter weather. Many will tell you it is a "dry" cold. This makes it easier to stay warm than in more humid climates. However, the wind can also blow right through to the bone in Saskatchewan, so be very attentive to wind chill advisories. Dressed properly for the weather your body will stay comfortable on the most frigid of days. Always take precautions to ensure that you do not have exposed skin when preparing to participate in any outdoor activities.

Winter is a wonderful season if treated with respect. Always be prepared for unexpected disasters when you are travelling to a recreation site with your vehicle. What seems to be a light breeze can readily sift enough snow onto a grid road to create snowdrifts that make it nearly impossible to pass. Carry a shovel, along with all the usual emergency supplies, and be sure to keep your cell phone charged. Also, it is important to have emergency supplies on you when you are away from your vehicle. A twisted ankle can become a life and death struggle even when you are a kilometre from your vehicle. Always tell a responsible party where you are going and when you should be back.

Unlike other areas of the country where snow may be soft powder that makes finding a groomed trail mandatory, many skiers continue to enjoy the same woodland paths and trails they have hiked all summer. They also often utilize roadside areas that have been packed by snowmobiles. You can even expect to find cross-country skiers and snowshoers enjoying sunny afternoons on many streets in small towns and villages too.

Snow conditions in Saskatchewan, like the air temperature, are affected by the winds. The snow only remains soft and fluffy as it falls. After that, it gets packed into rippled drifts in fields and along fence lines in a consistency more like cement. As the temperatures rise in March the snow has a higher moisture content and different texture, so conditions will change somewhat after a fresh snowfall.

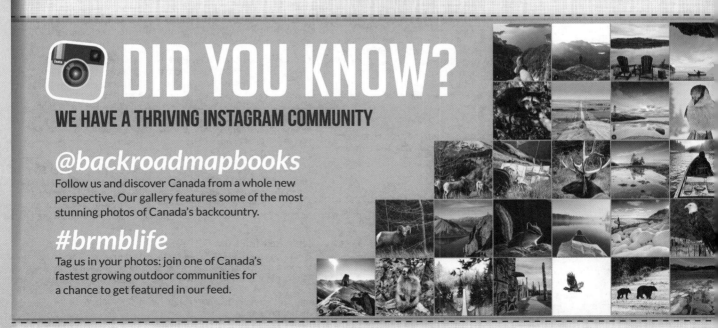

Argo Ski Trails (Map 47/F4)

Found just southwest of the town of Biggar, a series of classic and skate ski trails wind through a gorgeous deciduous forest. The trails are maintained by the Argo Ski Club and are dog-friendly.

Anglin Lake Recreation Site Trails (Map 80/G7)

Found just outside Prince Albert National Park (one trail even runs along the boundary for about a kilometre), there are six named trails in Great Blue Heron Provincial Park, totalling 16 km (10 mi). The park offers a warm-up shelter and the groomed trails are perfect for both beginner and intermediate skiers. If that is not enough, the Spruce River Highlands Connector trail heads west into the park, connecting up with another 18 km (11 mi) worth of trails.

Beaver Creek Conservation Area (Map 49/C4)

Located 13 km south of Saskatoon along Highway 219, the Beaver Creek Conservation Area hosts a nice system of ungroomed ski trails. When the temperature drops low enough and the creek that runs through the conservation area freezes over, staff clear a section of the creek to make an outdoor skating rink. Additionally, exploring the creek by snowshoe is an excellent way to take in some winter scenery in this beautiful location.

Blue Mountain Outdoor Adventure Park (Map 58/C1)

Offering some of the best skiing in the province, there are over 40 km (24 mi) of groomed classic and skate skiing trails along with a chalet that has a fireside den for those colder days. The trails range from easy to very difficult and have played host to the World Cup. Check out full details of all the winter activities including snowshoeing and sleigh rides on their website at *bluemountaincanada.com*.

Candle Lake Provincial Park (Map 81/F6)

In the winter, Candle Lake has two groomed sets of cross-country ski trails, at Bay Lake and Hilltop. There are 14 km (8.7 mi) of trails between the two areas, as well as several trails that have been set aside for snowshoeing.

Carlton Ski Club Trails (Map 51/A1)

The Carlton Ski Club operates two sets of trails. The first set of trails, along with the clubhouse, is situated approximately 15 km northwest of Humboldt. There is a good variety of trails here, ranging from the short, easy 1 km (0.6 mi) Jackrabbit Loop to the challenging 15 km (9.3 mi) long Trail 3. There are two other main loops and a total of about 30 km (19 mi) of trails, including 4.7 km (2.9 mi) of groomed trail for skate skiing. The club also maintains a warm-up cabin near Grouse Mountain. The rolling terrain accesses a few mountains for nice views of the surrounding area.

The other set of trails is found in Humboldt at the Humboldt Golf Club. You will find about 5 km (3.1 mi) of classic ski trails as well as 3 km (1.9 mi) of skate ski trails here.

Cypress Hills Interprovincial Park (Map 12/E7)

For those looking for groomed and backcountry ski trails, Cypress Hills Interprovincial Park is the premier destination in southwest Saskatchewan. All of the cross-country ski trails are in the montane ecosystem, with diverse forest protection to maintain snow quality for as long as possible. The park has 10 marked cross-country ski trails rated by terrain and degree of difficulty (beginner to intermediate); ranging from 0.5 to 7.5 km long, and totalling 17 km (10.6 mi). The Trans Canada Trail also traverses the park. Additional details can be found on the park website, *cypresshills.com*.

Douglas Provincial Park (Map 27/D1)

Located on the southeast end of Lake Diefenbaker, skiers and snowshoers can use the hiking trails and roadways within the park in the winter. The terrain is relatively easy, but the trails are not groomed.

Duck Mountain Ski Resort (Map 44/D1)

With 22 runs and a vertical drop of 120 metres (400 ft), The Duck is Saskatchewan's biggest ski area. It is open on weekends only and is about four hour's drive from both Saskatoon and Regina, making it a long haul for skiers from the province's biggest cities. For snowboarders, there is a terrain park and half pipe to play in, while the tube run is popular with the younger kids. However, it can be hit or miss whether the mountain is open or not; be sure to check conditions by calling (306) 542-4111 or visiting *skitheduck.com*.

Duck Mountain Cross-Country Ski Area (Map 44/D1)

Found just north of the Duck Mountain Ski Hill, there are over 50 km (30 mi) of cross-country ski trails in this area, the majority of which are rated intermediate or expert. However, there are enough novice trails to keep beginner skiers occupied for a few hours.

Eb's Trails (Map 60/E1)

Maintained by the Saskatoon Nordic Ski Club, Eb's Trails are found just north of Duck Lake on Highway 11. The trails vary, with routes for all to enjoy and over 52 km (32 mi) of groomed classic ski trails in the system. There are two entrances to the trails, both with a warm-up shelter and washroom facilities. No dogs are allowed on the trails.

Echo Valley Provincial Park (Map 30/F3)

Echo Valley Provincial Park is situated on both prairie landscape and valley lowland that offer a variety of trails to explore on skis. The 10 km (6 mi) of groomed trails are quite scenic and fast. Two warm-up shelters equipped with wood and wood stoves add to appeal of the area.

Esterhazy Regional Park (Map 32/G4–33/A4)

On the northeast corner of the town of Esterhazy, this park has 26 km (16 mi) of groomed cross-country ski trails. Part of the area is around the rolling golf course, which is nestled in the Kaposvar Hills that provide some shelter from the wind. Snowmobiling is also popular in and around the park.

Finlayson Island (Map 58/A3)

Cross-country ski trails are found on both the north and south side of Finlayson Island, which is accessibly from the town of Battleford. In total, there are 14 km (8.7 mi) of well-maintained ski trails, some of which are groomed for classic skiing and others for skate skiing. The trails are designed for beginner and intermediate skiers.

Good Spirit Lake Trails (Map 43/B2)

Located in Good Spirit Lake Provincial Park, there are 18 km (11 mi) of groomed trails here, designed for both beginner and expert skiers. The main trail is only 1.6 km long and leads to the ski shack. From here, the trails loop out to the park's northern boundary, with a total of about 10 km (6 mi) worth of skiing to be had.

Greenwater Provincial Park (Map 63/E5)

There are 25 km (15 mi) of groomed trails at Greenwater Provincial Park, set for both classic and skate skiing. The park is found 20 km south of Porcupine Plain. Watch for the trailhead across from the park office on Highway 38. There is a second entrance about 5 km north. The tracks are groomed weekly, while there are two warm-up shelters, a toboggan hill and ice skating that can also be enjoyed during the winter months here.

Kinsmen Ski Hill – Prince Albert (Map 71/A5)

Located in Little Red River Park near the city of Prince Albert, this small community ski hill is open daily unless the temperature falls below -25° C (-13° F). There are three runs here, the longest of which is 150 metres (500 ft). The runs are serviced by two cable tows. The ski area sports a terrain park and snowmaking equipment. The area is lit for night skiing. Red River Park is on the north side of the river, only a few minutes east of Prince Albert along Highway 55. Call the Little Red Log Cabin at (306) 763-5454 for current conditions.

Lac La Ronge Provincial Park (Map 101/D6)

Despite being a fair distance from the province's main population centres, Lac La Ronge Provincial Park has one of the most extensive cross-country trail systems. There are 62 km (39 mi) of trails groomed for classic and freestyle cross-country skiing, including a 5 km (3 mi) section lit for night skiing at Nut Point Campground. The other main group of trails are the Don Allen Trails, where you will find 14 km (8.7 mi) of trails. Connecting the two is a 32 km (20 mi) Loppet Trail.

Lac Pelletier Regional Park (Map 14/E4)

Lac Pelletier Regional Park is located about 30 km south of Swift Current on Highway 4, then 11 km west on Highway 343. This scenic park, with a year round full service restaurant, is a popular destination for cross-country skiers and snowshoers wanting to explore the valley around Lac Pelletier. There are tobogganing opportunities here as well, while snowmobiles are limited to the lake only.

Little Red Trails (Map 71/A5)

Found off Highway 55 on the northeast boundary of the city of Prince Albert, the local ski club maintains a series of looping trails in the Kristi Lake Area. There are over 35 km (22 mi) of Nordic trails in the city park, ranging from easy to difficult. There is also a network of trails open for snowshoeing and the Kinsmen Ski Hill to explore. Visit the club website, *paskiclub.ca* for more information.

Makwa Lake Provincial Park (Map 77/A3)

This park, located northwest of North Battleford, grooms their hiking trails in the winter. Around 18 km (11 mi) of trails cater to all skiing abilities, and you can find trails maps at the park office.

Meadow Lake Provincial Park (Map 87/F5)

Meadow Lake Provincial Park is located 7 km north of Dorintosh. There are 24 km (15 mi) of groomed trails located at Grieg Lake in the east central region of the park.

Melfort Cross-Country Ski Trails (Map 62/C2; 72/D5)

The local ski club track sets a series of cross-country ski trails in the Melfort Campground, which are lit for night skiing. In addition, there are also trails located nearby in Gronlid, with several loops totalling 20 km (12.5 mi) located in the Fort a La Corne Provincial Forest. Here you will find warm-up shelters, washrooms and lots of parking.

Melville Regional Park (Map 32/A1)

Groomed by the Melville Ski Club, the park offers a nice network of ski trails through its 121 hectares (300 ac). The woodland trails are open to the public and include the 3 km (1.9 mi) Green Trail and the 2.5 km (1.6 mi) Red Trail. The park can be accessed from Highway 10 or Prince Edward Street.

Mission Ridge Ski & Board Resort (Map 30/G3)

Mission Ridge Ski Area is located in the town of Fort Qu'Appelle, in the Qu'Appelle Valley. The hill features 36 runs, a terrain park, two bunny hills and a snowboard half pipe. Skiers and snowboarders are taken up the hill by three double chairlifts, one quad chairlift and two tow ropes. The hill has a vertical drop of 89 metres (290 ft), with the longest run, the Half-Mile Highway, measuring 792 metres (2,600 ft) long. The hill does have snowmaking equipment. More information can be found on their website, *missionridge.com*.

Moose Jaw River Park (Map 28/E7)

Moose Jaw Parks, Recreation and Culture maintain 20 km (12.5 mi) of groomed cross-country ski trails through the Wakamow Valley area. The trailhead is at the Speed Skating Oval and is rated for beginners and intermediate. It is a scenic, rolling, treed area that provides a great winter experience. There is a warm-up building open on weekends from 9 am to 4 pm. The park can be accessed from Wellesley Street in the south and River Street from east or west.

Moose Mountain Provincial Park (Map 21/F5)

Moose Mountain Park is one of the most popular winter destinations in southeast Saskatchewan. There are over 50 km (31 mi) of cross-country ski trails, groomed for classic and skate skiing, on 11 official trails of varying difficulty. Heavily treed, the park has lots of shelter from winter winds on its trails. There are also 10 km (6.25 mi) of snowshoe trails.

Mount Blackstrap Ski Area (Map 49/E6)

This 45 metre (150 ft) man-made mountain was constructed to host the 1971 Canada Winter Games in nearby Saskatoon. Although closed in 2009, there is a proposal to reopen the Mount Blackstrap Ski Resort with a new lodge, quad chair and Poma lift. The nearby provincial park currently grooms 5 km (3 mi) of cross-country ski trails.

Naicam Nordic Ski Trails (Map 62/D6)

These easy ski trails are found near the town of Naicam. There are five trails in total, the longest of which is 7.2 km (4.5 mi) long. The trails are all well-sheltered, tracked for classic skiing and relatively flat.

Pineview Cross-Country Ski Trails (Map 65/A2)

Found in the "Moose Capital of the World," the Pineview Trail System in Hudson Bay Regional Park offers skiers 30 km (18 mi) of groomed trails to explore. Be wary of the aforementioned moose as they can be spotted from time to time in the woods.

Prince Albert National Park (Maps 70, 79, 80)

Up to 50 km (30 mi) of groomed cross-country ski trails, maintained by the Waskesiu Lake Ski Club, and several more kilometres of backcountry ski and snowshoe trails invite winter enthusiasts to enjoy this winter wonderland. The park is vast wilderness area and the trails are not patrolled in winter; visitors must be self-reliant and prepared for emergencies. Park permits are required and visitors are asked to register at the Waskesiu Visitor Centre if planning an overnight trip. Call (306) 663-4522 for more information.

Amyot Trail (Map 80/A7)

This 9.6 km (5.9 mi) one way trail takes snowshoers from the west side of Prince Albert National Park to Amyot Lake. It is possible to return the way you came or along the West Side Boundary Trail, which is a slightly shorter route.

Anglin Lake Trail (Map 80/F7)

This 12 km (7.5 mi) one-way trail in Prince Albert National Park passes by Anglin Lake as it makes its way from the trailhead along Route 263 to a second trailhead along the 263. The trail is intersected by the Kinowa Trail. From here, enterprising skiers could head east across Anglin Lake (caution is needed when crossing ice) to hook up with the Anglin Lake Trails outside the park.

Crean Trail (Map 80/E4)

This 19 km (11.8 mi) trail takes skiers through the very heart of the park, following a patrol road past the Heart Lakes before cutting across Crean Lake to a winter campsite. Access is found 500 metres south of Birch Bay, 11 km north of Waskesiu on the Kingsmere Road.

Elk Trail (Map 70/C1–80/E7)

At 22 km (13.6 mi) return, this is one of the longest ski trails in Prince Albert National Park. The route follows an old fire road past Sandy Lake for about 10.6 km, where it hooks up with the Fish Lake Trail. Turning north (right) will bring skiers to Fish Lake and a backcountry campsite. Turning left will bring skiers to Route 240, for a 40 km (25 mi) out-and back trip (a second vehicle could be left at the Fish Lake Trailhead). Most people choose the first option. The middle section of the trail is not open in the winter, but 12.5 km one-way of the western section of the trail is open to form a loop with the West Side Boundary and Hunters Lake Trail, making a loop of nearly 40 km (18 mi).

Freight Trail (Map 80/F6)

This old fur trading route from Prince Albert to La Ronge is mostly gone, but there still is over 50 km (30 mi) of this trail found in the park. Open to cross-country skiing and snowshoeing, the North Freight Trail is an 8.6 km (5.3 mi) return section of the trail that has been turned into a loop. From the end of the North Freight Trail, a 7 km (4.3 mi) return out-and-back trail takes skiers to Beartrap Lake. The rest of the trail has been broken into three sections with access trails from Route 263 allowing snowshoers to travel each section independently. The longest of these sections is the South Freight Trail, at 23.4 km (14.5 mi) return.

Lee Trail (Map 80/F4)

Found along Kingsmere Road, this easy 15 km (9.4 mi) trail was once part of the Prince Albert to Lac La Ronge Freight Trail. The trail passes through a gently rolling aspen forest to the very edge of the park.

Spruce River Highlands (Map 80/F7)

There are 18 km (11 mi) of groomed ski trails in the Spruce River Highlands. The longest of the trails is the titular trail, an 8.5 km loop that connects to the Anglin Lake Trails and passes the Spruce River Tower, a perfect place to take a break and soak in the sites from the top.

West Side Boundary Trail (Map 70/C1–79/G4)

This 37.7 km (23.4 mi) hiking trail found in Prince Albert National Park becomes a truly epic snowshoe trip in the winter. While there are no formal winter camping sites along the way, it is nearly impossible to reach the Sturgeon Crossing Picnic Area in one day.

Qu'Appelle Valley Nordic Trails (Map 29/D4)

4 km (2.5 mi) of groomed Nordic trails can be found just east of Lumsden, easily accessible via Qu'Appelle Drive. These trails cater to all skill levels and are suitable for both classic and skate skiing. There is also a 30 lane shooting range for biathletes. Cycling, hiking and paddling are possible in the summer.

Redberry Lake Biosphere Reserve (Map 59/C3)

Snowshoeing and cross-country skiing are popular activities here in the winter, both on the 7 km (4.5 mi) of established summer hiking trails and elsewhere. If you visit the reserve at nighttime, you may get some breathtaking views of the northern lights. This is Saskatchewan's only UNESCO world biosphere reserve and your chances of spotting some wildlife, including a variety of birds, are very good.

WINTER ADVENTURES

Regina Toboggan Hills (Map 29/F6)

The city of Regina offers plenty of hills that are safely protected from traffic and perfect for spending an afternoon zipping down on a toboggan. A small hill, perfect for young children, can be found in French Park along McIntosh Street. Two toboggan hills can be found at Mount Pleasant, just off Winnipeg Street, with one of them lighted for evening tobogganing. Two more hills are located in North Regina behind the Ruth M. Buck school, and these are lighted as well. Just off of Garnet Street and Regina Avenue you will find the Kiwanis Park toboggan hill, also known as The Bowl. One of the more popular toboggan areas can be found in Regina's East end, just off Victoria Street, tucked behind Home Depot. Other hills in the city include the Douglas Park hill, found off a side road off MacDonald Street, the Southland Mall hill, the Shweitzer Park hill, located just off Prince of Whales Drive and the Northwest Leisure Centre hill.

Rocanville Cross-Country Ski Trails (Map 33/D6)

Offering over 10 km (6 mi) of sheltered, groomed trails, the clubhouse at the trailhead has a waxing station and ski equipment for rent. To reach the trails, take Highway 8 south of Rocanville, turn west at the Welwyn Road sign and travel 6.2 km, then turn north and travel 2.8 km to the clubhouse (on the left side of the road).

Rowan's Ravine Provincial Park (Map 29/B1)

Rowan's Ravine offers a short circuit of groomed cross-country ski trails through the park. The trails provide scenic views of Last Mountain Lake, shelter from the prairie winds, and warm-up huts.

Sanderson Ski Trails/Beauval Ski Club (Map 99/A5)

Located near the town of Beauval, there are 22 km (13.7 mi) of trail in the forest along the Beaver River. There are five loops here, with 10 km (6 mi) of these trails groomed for skate skiing as well as classic. The trails are a favourite of the Saskatchewan Ski Association and many provincial races and loppets have been held here.

Saskatoon Municipal Trails (Map 49/C3)

The city maintains over 18 km (11 mi) of ski trails. These trails are not interconnected, but are spread out throughout the city of Saskatoon. The trails range from 2 to 4.8 km (1.2-3 mi) long. There is a 3.5 km (2.2 mi) outside loop double track and skating track at the Holiday Park Golf Course accessed from Avenue U South. Lower Meewasin Park offers a 4.8 km (3 mi) single track loop, while Upper Meewasin Park has a 3.4 km (2.1 mi) single track loop. Both trails are accessed at Pinehouse and Whiteswan Drive. Diefenbaker Park has a 2 km (1.2 mi) single track trail accessed at Ruth Street and Henry Avenue.

Saskatoon Nordic Ski Club Trails (Map 49/C3)

In addition to maintaining the extensive Eb's Trails (listing above), the Saskatoon Nordic Ski Club also maintains three trails in Saskatoon. In Kinsman park, 3 km of relatively flat trails can be explored. Loops of 2.5 km and 6 km (3.7 mi) can be found at Wildwood Golf Club, while the Willows Golf Club offers loops of 1.5 km and 4 km (2.5 mi).

Kinsman Park (Map 49/C2)

Maintained by the Saskatoon Nordic Ski Club, there are 3 km (1.9 mi) of relatively flat terrain for cross-country enthusiasts to enjoy in the heart of Saskatoon. Parking is available in the two northernmost rows of the Kinsmen Park/YMCA parking lot.

Wildwood Golf Club (Map 49/D3)

Maintained by the Saskatoon Nordic Ski Club, there are two loops, a 2.5 km (1.5 mi) perimeter loop and a 6 km (3.7 mi) inside loop that winds through the area. The course offers a good balance of flat terrain with slightly rolling and more hilly sections. The clubhouse and parking is just east of McKercher Drive on 8th Street.

Willows Golf Club (Map 49/C3)

Maintained by the Saskatoon Nordic Ski Club, there are two loops, the south loop at 1.5 km (0.9 mi) and the northwest loop at 4 km (2.5 mi) in length. These trails take full advantage of the terrain and are not recommended for beginner skiers. Willows Golf Club is located off Cartwright Street, with the trails running out from the clubhouse.

Saskatoon Toboggan Hills (Map 49/C3)

Once the snow falls in Saskatoon, many of the city's hills are transformed into popular tobogganing destinations. You can find hills to zip down in a toboggan, sled, tube or saucer along the Meewasin Trail off 3rd Avenue South, at Forest Hill off of Attridge Drive in North East Saskatoon, at Pest Hill on Spadina Crescent (south of 42nd Street Bridge), at Silverwood Heights School off Silverwood Road, at Victoria Park Hill near Spadina Crescent West and at WJL Harvey Park off of Verbeke Road.

Ski Timber Ridge (Map 79/E6)

This community ski hill is found 3 km southeast of Big River. There are six runs here, the longest of which is 800 metres (2,625 ft). The area is serviced by a rope tow and a T-bar. Call (306) 469-4545 for more information.

Table Mountain (Map 57/E2)

The only ski hill in northwestern Saskatchewan, Table Mountain is found near North Battleford. The ski hill features two quad chair lifts and two magic carpets servicing 11 runs. The vertical drop of 110 metres (360 ft) is one of Saskatchewan's biggest. The longest run here is 1 km (0.6 mi) and there is a terrain park for snowboarders and adventurous skiers, as well as a tube park. There is snowmaking equipment and night skiing on Fridays. Visit their website at *tablemountainregionalpark.com* for additional details.

Wapiti Valley Ski Resort (Map 72/E5)

Found along the Saskatchewan River Valley about 50 km north of Melfort, this downhill ski area is one of Saskatchewan's biggest, with 12 runs, the longest of which is 1.2 km (0.75 mi) long. The area is lit for night skiing, but only on Fridays. There is a terrain park and four lifts, including one quad chair, along with snowmaking equipment. Call (306) 862-5621 or visit *skiwapiti.com* for more information.

Waskesiu Townsite Trails (Map 80/F5)

There are five cross-country ski trails in and around the Waskesiu townsite in Prince Albert National Park, totalling 25 km (15 mi). These include the 5.8 km (3.6 mi) Beaver Glen Loop, the 7.2 km (4.5 mi) Fisher Trail, the 8 km (5 mi) Red Deer Trails and the 5.6 km (3.5 mi) Wapiti Loop. Beaver Glen actually offers a pair of loop trails, the shorter of which is lit for night skiing.

Beaver Glen Trail (Map 80/E4)

This 5.8 km (3.6 mi) easy loop trail offers both classic and skate skiing as it parallels Waskesiu Drive and circles the Beaver Glen Campground. Linking to the Red Deer Yellow Trail, the section of trail along Waskesiu Drive is lit for night skiing. Access is from the Lakeview and Waskesiu Drive intersection.

Fisher Trail (Map 80/E4)

This 7.2 km (4.5 mi) classic ski loop makes a great family outing trip as it is scenic and stays close to Waskesiu. Access is adjacent to the Highway 264 entrance to Waskesiu or from the Lakeview and Waskesiu Drive intersection.

Red Deer Red Trail (Map 80/E4)

This 5.7 km (3.6 mi) one-way trail offers classic skiing with a few large hills that have challenging corners. Linking the Wapiti and Fisher Trails, access is from the Lakeview and Waskesiu Drive intersection.

Red Deer Yellow Trail (Map 80/E4)

This 2.7 km (1.7 mi) one-way trail is linked to the Red Deer Red, Fisher and Beaver Glen Trails. The trail is flat with a gentle roll. Access is from the Lakeview and Waskesiu Drive intersection.

Wapiti Trail (Map 80/E4)

This 7.6 km (4.7 mi) or 5.6 km (3.5 mi) loop trail is set for classic skiing. The rolling terrain trail follows the golf course and can be accessed from the Lakeview and Waskesiu Drive intersection or the south end of Montreal Drive.

White Butte Trails Recreation Site (Map 30/A6)

Next to the community of Pilot Butte, this site features over 15 km (9.3 mi) of ski trails regularly groomed by the Regina Ski Club. The trails lead through gently rolling, treed terrain. Amenities include a parking lot, warm-up hut and outdoor toilets.

WINTER ADVENTURES

Winter Safety Tips

While winter is indeed a magical time to explore Saskatchewan, special hazards exist in winter that require outdoor explorers to take some extra precautions. Here are a few tips to make sure you have a safe and fun adventure in Saskatchewan's great outdoors this winter.

Tell Someone
Always tell a responsible person where you are going and when you plan to come back. If you are heading out on an extended journey leave a detailed written itinerary in your car and at home.

Keep an Eye on the Time
Sunset can creep up sooner than you think during Saskatchewan's short winter days. While out exploring in the winter, keep an eye on the time and pack a flashlight or headlamp, just in case.

Check Equipment
Always check to make sure your gear is in good working order before heading out. A broken strap or loose binding is much easier to deal with at home than in the backcountry.

Dress Warmly
Be sure to dress in layers, so you can peel off or add clothing as needed to adjust your comfort level.

Trap in the Heat
Head wear, like a balaclava or wool toque, are essential on a winter trip since most of your body's heat loss is from your head.

Check Forecast
Winter conditions can change very quickly. Always check ahead for any storm warnings, and when travelling into the backcountry be mindful that you have to return the same way you came in.

Bring a Stove
Firewood will be much more difficult to find in the winter than in other seasons. When camping, don't rely on a fire for preparing meals or staying warm – pack a camping stove instead.

Stick to Water
Eating snow is never a good idea. It takes a tremendous amount of energy to transfer water from one state to another.

Check Ice Thickness
Before crossing ice on skis or on foot, make sure it is at least 15 cm (6 in) thick. Clear or blue ice is strongest, while darker coloured ice contains snow or water and should be avoided.

Get Some Grip
Take extra care when driving in snowy conditions. Drivers who are not used to winter conditions can find themselves in the ditch quite quickly if they are not careful.

Plan for Trouble
When driving in the winter it is always a good idea to pack an emergency kit in case you get stranded. Extra clothes, blanket, flashlight, signal flares, spare cell phone battery, food and water are a few items that can really come in handy if you get stuck on the road

WINTER IN SASKATCHEWAN

INDEX

The **Map Index** listings consist of: listing name, page number/coordinates. In the example found on the left, Duncan is found on page 11/E6.

For the **Adventure Index**, the listing also consists of the Reference Page number, where the description of the listing is found. In the example below, the Stuart Channel listing description is found on page 89.

Stuart Channel..........11/B1-G4;**89** ➤ Reference Page

Name   **Map Page/Coordinate**

The grid lines found in the example are used for illustration purposes only. The blue grid lines found on the maps refer to UTM coordinates.

Eastend, Saskatchewan
© Shutterstock / David P. Lewis

R.S. = Recreation Site   P.P. = Provincial Park
P.N.W.A. = Prairie National Wildlife Unit

ADVENTURE INDEX

BACKROAD ADVENTURES

70 Mile Butte Lookout Point 3/G5;**125**
Ambroz Blacksmith Shop 17/B5;**125**
Ancient Echoes Interpretive Centre ....
....47/C7;**125**
Athabasca Sand Dunes...119/D4–G4;**125**
Batoche National Historic Site of Canada
....60/E3;**125**
Battle of Tourond's Coulee / Fish Creek National Historic Site..........60/D5;**125**
Bear's Head – Sandfly Lake 110/F7;**125**
Beaver River Sand Cliffs..........88/B7;**125**
Big Muddy Badlands..............6, 7;**125**
Big Muddy Nature Centre and Museum...
....7/B6;**125**
Big Rock Buffalo Rubbing Stone..............
....57/D4;**125**
Brunyee Ridge 25/E4;**125**
Buffalo Jump 7/E5;**125**
Canada's Dead Sea 50/F7;**125**
Cannington Manor Provincial Historic Park
....22/A6;**125**
Carlton House Historic Site 60/B2;**125**
Castle Butte.........................7/A5;**125**
Checkerboard Hill 34/E7;**125**
Chimney Coulee Provincial Historic Site ..
....2/D1;**126**
Churchill River's Aboriginal Rock Paintings
........101, 102, 110–112, 118;**126**
Claybank Brick Plant National Historic Site
....18/A4;**126**

Cochin Lighthouse 68/A5;**126**
Crooked Bush 59/C3;**126**
Cumberland Delta Lookout Point ....
....75/C2;**126**
Cumberland House Provincial Historic Park................................85/A4;**126**
Cypress Hills P.P. 12/B7;**126**
Deep Bay Impact Crater........118/D6;**126**
Douglas P.P. Sand Dunes ....
....38/E7;**126**
Doukhobors at Veregin Historic Site.........
....43/G1;**126**
Duck Mountain Highlands Viewpoint ....
....44/D1;**126**
Eye Cave of Dead Man's River ....
....120/G4;**126**
Forestry Farm Park and Zoo Historic Site .
....49/D2;**126**
Fort Battleford National Historic Site........
....58/A3;**126**
Fort Carlton Provincial Historic Park.........
....60/B2;**126**
Fort Espérance National Historic Site ....
....33/D5;**127**
Fort Livingstone National Historic Site......
....55/A5;**127**
Fort Pelly National Historic Site................
....54/G6;**127**
Fort Pitt Provincial Historic Park..............
....76/C7;**127**
Fort Qu'Appelle Trading Post ..30/F3;**127**
Fort Walsh National Historic Site ....
.....................................1/B1, 12/B7;**127**
Frenchman Butte National Historic Site....
....76/E7;**127**
Gardner Dam 38/A5;**127**
Good Spirit Sand Dunes 43/B2;**127**
Goodwin House...................25/E4;**127**
Government House Regina 29/F6;**127**
Gow Lake Impact Crater........117/G6;**127**
Great Sandhills 24;**127**

Great Sandhills Museum........24/A1;**127**
Grey Owl's Cabin 80/B2;**127**
Highest Point in Saskatchewan ..1/A1;**127**
Holy Trinity Anglican Church..102/D3;**128**
Humboldt Historic Murals 51/B2;**127**
Hunt Falls 120/C3;**127**
Jones Peak..........................2/C2;**127**
Keyhole Castle Historic Site 71/A5;**127**
Killdeer Badlands..................5/C6;**128**
La Roche Percee Provincial Historic Site & Short Creek Cairn.................10/A6;**128**
Lacolle Falls Hydroelectric Dam ....
....71/F5;**128**
Lake Athabasca 119;**128**
Last Mountain House Historic Park ....
....29/E3;**128**
Last Mounted Horse Patrol.....7/B7;**128**
Limestone Crevices of Amisk Lake...........
....95/B5;**128**
Little Manitou Lake 50/F7;**128**
Little Swan River Viewpoint.....65/C6;**128**
Lund Wildlife Exhibit 71/A5;**128**
Manitou Falls 121/A5;**128**
Maple Creek Museums 12/F4;**128**
Marr Residence Historic Site ...49/C3;**128**
McNichol Lake Plaque..........102/C2;**128**
Mennonite Heritage Village......14/G1;**128**
Mistusinne Cairn 38/C6;**128**

Moose Bay Mound 32/B4;**128**
Murals of Nipawin 73/A3;**128**
Murals of Whitewood 32/F7;**128**
National Doukhobor Heritage Village ......
....43/G1;**128**
Natural Prairie Grasslands.......................
...................................3/G5–5/C7;**129**
Ness Creek Site 79/F5;**129**
Next of Kin Memorial Avenue Historic Site
....49/C2;**129**
Nicolle Flats Homestead 28/G5;**129**
Nipekamew Sand Cliffs..........91/G3;**129**
Nitenai Salt March 75/B1;**129**
Notukeu Heritage Museum......15/B6;**129**
Parr Hill Springs 65/C6;**129**
Percival Windmill 32/D7;**129**
Popoff Tree 59/F4;**129**
Prince Albert Visitor Centre ....71 /A5;**129**
Regina Floral Conservatory ....;**129**
Rice River Canyon.................74/G2;**129**
Roan Mare Valley 7/E5;**129**
Roche Percee Sandstone Caves & Hoodoos
....10/B6;**129**
Royal Saskatchewan Museum ....
....29/G6;**129**
Sam Kelly's Caves 7/D7;**129**
Sandcastles........................26/B4;**129**
Saskatchewan Railway Museum ....
....49/B3;**130**

Saskatchewan River Forks......71/G5;**130**
Saskatchewan Science Centre ....
....29/F6;**130**
Saskatoon Forestry Farm & Zoo...............
....49/D3;**130**
Short Creek Cairn..................10/B7;**130**
Skytrail Pedestrian Bridge.......37/G2;**130**
Smoothrock Falls 116/C5;**130**
St. Victor Petroglyphs Historic Park ....
....6/B3;**130**
Standing Rock......................24/F6;**130**
Steele Narrows Provincial Historic Park....
....77/A3;**130**
Sukanen Ship Pioneer Village & Museum .
....17/E1;**130**
Sunken Hill 26/B4;**130**
Swift Current Petroglyph Boulder..............
....14/G1;**130**
Touchwood Hills Post Provincial Historic Park..................................41/D4;**130**
Tunnels of Moose Jaw 28/E7;**130**
W.R. Motherwell Homestead National Historic Park...........................31/C3;**130**
Wanuskewin Heritage Park......49/D2;**130**
Waskwei River Shale Outcrops..................
....75/C3;**130**
Wood Mountain Post Historic Park............
....5/E4;**130**
World's Largest Coffee Pot 39/B5;**130**

©Shutterstock/Tom Clausen

BOOT HILL, GREAT SANDHILLS, SK.

ADVENTURE INDEX

HUNTING ADVENTURES

STOCKING CHART
Northern Pike
PAGE.....................146
TOTAL LAKES...........9

WATERS EDGE ECO LODGE, GREIG LAKE, SK.

©Jenna Gall

©flymetoanywhere

PADDLING PRINCE ALBERT NATIONAL PARK, SK.

ADVENTURE INDEX

©ragnarrobinson

CYPRESS HILLS PROVINCIAL PARK, SK.

TRAIL ADVENTURES

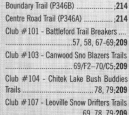

ATV (OHV) ADVENTURES

SNOWMOBILE ADVENTURES

©shutterstock/Scott Prokop

ATV BRIDGE, NORTHERN SK.

ADVENTURE INDEX

©chelseyoyka

MOOSE MOUNTAIN PROVINCIAL PARK, SK.

WETLANDS, SK.

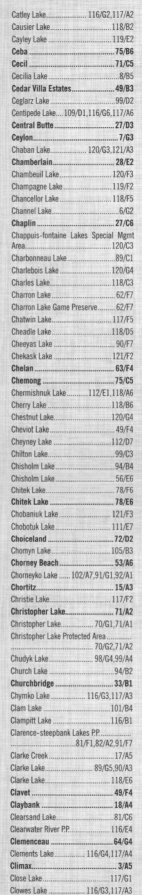

©shutterstock/pictureguy

AN OTTER IN PRINCE ALBERT NATIONAL PARK, SK.

Crawford Lake ... 117/D3
Crawford Lake ... 49/F3
Creelman ... 20/D6
Creighton ... 95/D3
Crellin Lake ... 116/E1
Crescent Lake ... 43/C7
Crichton Lake ... 120/B6
Crimes Lake ... 118/F1
Crockett Lake ... 116/G3,117/A3
Crooked Lake ... 32/B4
Crooked Lake ... 121/B6
Crooked Lake P.P. ... 32/B4
Crooked River ... 63/D2
Crowe Lake ... 112/B4,117/G7
Crozier Lake ... 118/D4
Crump Lake ... 120/D6
Crutwell ... 70/E5
Crystal Bay-Sunset ... 67/D1
Crystal Beach Lake Game Preserve ... 37/B1,48/B7
Crystal Lake ... 54/D5
Crystal Springs ... 61/D2
Cub Lake ... 82/D1,92/D7
Cudsaskwa Beach ... 61/B4
Cudworth ... 61/A6
Cuelenaere Lake ... 118/B5
Cuillerier Creek ... 64/D3,65/A2
Culdesac Lake ... 75/E1,85/E7
Cumberland House ... 85/A4
Cumberland House P.P. ... 85/A4
Cumberland Lake ... 84/G3,85/A4,94/E7
Cumins Lake ... 107/F7,97/F1
Cumming Lake ... 113/E2,118/C6
Cunning Lake ... 118/C6
Cunningham Lake ... 121/C4
Cunningham Lakes ... 117/D3
Cunnings Lake ... 98/F6
Cupar ... 30/C1
Currie Lake ... 120/D4
Currie Lake ... 115/B2,118/F7
Cushing Lake ... 117/F1
Cut Knife ... 57/B2
Cutbank Lake ... 26/G5
Cybulski Lake ... 121/B2
Cypress Hills P.P. ... 1/A1,12/A7
Cypress Lake ... 1/E2
Cyprian Lake ... 121/A4

D

Dafoe ... 51/G7
Dafoe Game Preserve ... 51/G6
Dale Lake ... 116/G5
Dalmeny ... 59/F7
Dana Salt Lake ... 50/D2
Danchuk Lake ... 120/B6
Danielson P.P. ... 37/G5,38/A5
Dardier Lake ... 119/G2,120/A2
Darieu Lake ... 103/B5
Darlings Beach ... 14/E4
Daschuk Lake ... 121/F5
Dauk Lake ... 121/F7
Dautremont Lake ... 120/B7
David Lake ... 118/C5
Davidson ... 39/B5
Davies Lake ... 90/A4
Davies Lake ... 121/E2
Davin ... 30/D7
Davin Lake ... 118/C5
Davison Lake ... 120/E3
Davy Lake ... 119/F5
Dawson Lake ... 118/C3
Day Lake ... 120/E3
Day's Beach ... 68/A6

©shutterstock/Brendan van Son

CYPRESS HILLS PROVINCIAL PARK, SK.

de Balinhard Lake ... 87/B5
Deadmoose Lake ... 51/B1,61/F7
Debden ... 69/F2
Deep Lake ... 84/F5
Deep Lake ... 30/G6,31/A6
Deep Lake ... 105/A7
Deer Lake ... 76/D1
Deering Lake ... 121/F7
Degryse Lake ... 99/F1
Deighton Lake ... 117/F6
Deitsch Lake ... 118/D4
Delaronde Lake ... 79/E3
Delhaye Lake ... 121/D4
Delisle ... 48/F5
Delmas ... 57/F1,67/F7
Demaine ... 26/E2
Dempster Lake ... 117/B2
Denare Beach ... 95/B4
Denholm ... 58/C4
Dennis Lake ... 116/D2
Denzil ... 45/F1,56/C7
Derkson Lake ... 116/D2
Deschambault Lake ... 103/E7,104/A7,92/G5,93/E1,94/A2
Desjardins Lake ... 103/E6
Desnomie Lakes ... 117/B4
Devil's Lake ... 39/E1
Devils Lake ... 116/F5
Dewar Lake ... 116/G2
Dezall Lake ... 121/C4
Dezort Lake ... 104/G6
Dickens Lake ... 112/C6
Dicks Lake ... 116/F3
Dickson Lake ... 61/D2
Dilke ... 29/A2
Dinsmore ... 37/C4
Dinty Lake ... 119/G3
Dirks Lake ... 103/A1,113/A7
Disley ... 29/C4
Ditton Park ... 73/C6
Dixon Lake ... 116/D2
Dobbin Lake ... 117/F5
Dobson Lake ... 118/E2
Dockerill Lake ... 109/D7,99/D1
Dodge Lake ... 120/E2
Dodsland ... 46/F5
Dog River ... 18/D2
Dollard ... 2/F1,13/F7
Domremy ... 61/A3
Donaldson Lake ... 119/F3
Donnelly Lake ... 110/D3,117/C7
Dore Lake ... 89/B4
Dorintosh ... 87/F6
Dot Lake ... 117/B6
Dougal Lake ... 113/A1,118/B6
Dougherty Lake ... 104/G6
Douglas Lake ... 117/G2,118/A2
Douglas P.P. ... 27/D1,38/E7
Douglas River ... 119/C7
Dowler Lake ... 119/C5
Downie Lake ... 12/D5
Drackley Wildlife Refuge ... 37/G7
Drake ... 51/C7
Drake Lake ... 56/A5
Dreaver Lake ... 112/B5,117/G7
Dreyer Lake ... 110/F1,117/D6
Drinkwater ... 18/B1
Drumheller Wildlife Refuge ... 72/D2
Dubé Lake ... 88/E2
Dube Lake ... 120/F6
Dubets Lake ... 116/F1
Dubuc ... 32/D4
Duck Lake ... 60/D2
Duck Mountain P.P. ... 44/D1,55/C7
Duddridge Lake ... 100/E2
Duff ... 31/E2
Dufferin Lake ... 116/G3
Duffield Lake ... 118/D4
Dummer Lake ... 116/G4
Dumont Lake ... 118/F6
Dumville Creek ... 119/C4
Dunajski Lake ... 102/C7,92/C1
Dunbar Lake ... 89/F3
Duncairn Reservoir Migratory Bird Sanctuary ... 14/D3
Dundurn ... 49/D6
Dunlop Lake ... 121/C5
Dunlop Lake ... 111/F3,117/F7
Dunn Lake ... 114/F5,118/F7
Dunn Lake ... 111/F2,117/F7
Dunnett Lake ... 118/C3
Duns Lake ... 116/C3
Dunsmore Lake ... 117/C4
Duplex Lake ... 120/E3
Durocher Lake ... 88/F1,98/F7
Durrant Lake ... 120/G6,121/A6
Dutertre Lake ... 100/A1,99/G1
Dutton Lake ... 121/E3
Duval ... 40/C6
Dwyer Lake ... 118/B1
Dyck Lake ... 121/C3
Dyck Lake ... 116/D2
Dysart ... 30/D1

E

E.B. Campbell Game Preserve ... 73/F1,83/F7
Eadie Lake ... 107/E7
Eagle Ridge Country Estates ... 49/E2
Eaglehill Lake ... 57/B6
Eagles Lake ... 78/E2
Eaglestone Lake ... 117/B5
Ear Lake ... 46/C1,56/G7
Earl Grey ... 29/F1
East Anglia ... 67/G3
East Archibald Lake ... 119/F5
East Coteau Lake ... 8/A7
Eastend ... 2/D2
Eastley Lake ... 116/C1
Eastman Lake ... 108/E5,116/F7
Easton Lake ... 113/E6
Eastwood Wildlife Refuge ... 68/G4,69/A4
Eatonia ... 35/A4
Ebenezer ... 43/D3
Ebertheltuntue Lake ... 119/D3
Echo Bay ... 69/D5
Echo Valley P.P. ... 30/F3
Edam ... 67/D5
Eday Lake ... 120/B2
Edenwold ... 30/C4
Edgar Lake ... 121/A4
Edgeley ... 30/E4
Edward Lake ... 78/F7
Edwards Lake ... 86/F3
Egg Lake ... 84/G5,85/A5
Egg Lake ... 79/E4
Ehman Lake ... 80/G3
Einarson Lake ... 117/D3
Eisenhauer Lake ... 120/F4
Eisler Lake ... 103/E1
Ekapo Lake ... 21/C1,32/C7
Elaine Lake ... 90/C6
Elak Dase ... 110/A5
Elbow ... 38/C6
Elbow Lake ... 65/F5
Elder Lake ... 119/F3
Eldersley ... 63/C2
Eldridge Lake ... 103/A5
Elephant Lake ... 118/B6
Elfros ... 52/F7
Ellefson Lake ... 118/D5
Elleraas Lake ... 117/C5
Elliott Lake ... 118/E6
Ellis Lake ... 102/D6
Ellis Lake ... 121/C3
Ells Lake ... 116/B3
Elm Lake ... 85/D6
Elrose ... 36/E5
Elstow ... 50/A4
Emerson Lake ... 121/D3
Emma Lake ... 70/G1,80/G7
Emmeline Lake ... 100/C7,89/G2,90/C1
End Lake ... 56/G6
Endeavour ... 54/B2
Engemann Lake ... 117/B1
Englefeld ... 51/F2
Engler Lake ... 120/C4
Englishman Lake ... 67/A2
Ennis Lake ... 91/F4
Ens Lake ... 119/G7,120/A7
Ens Lakes ... 117/F1
Epp Lake ... 117/E2
Erickson Lake ... 84/A3
Erickson Lake ... 121/D4
Ernfold ... 27/A6
Errington Lake ... 94/F3
Erwood ... 65/B2
Esker Lake ... 116/G3
Estabrooks Lake ... 110/D4,117/C7
Esterhazy ... 32/G4

ESTEVAN
9/G6

ELEVATION
570 m (1,870 ft)

POPULATION (2011)
TOTAL: 11, 054

AREA CODE(S)
306

Eston ... 35/F5
Ethelwyn Lake ... 87/E1
Etters Beach ... 39/G5,40/A5
Ettinger Lake ... 121/F4
Eva Lake ... 120/G3
Evans Lake ... 121/E3
Evergreen Acres ... 67/F1
Evergreen Brightsand ... 77/D7
Ewonus Lake ... 116/E4
Eyahpaise Lake ... 103/D1
Eyapawutik Lake ... 78/F6
Eyebrow ... 27/G3
Eyebrow Lake ... 27/G1
Eyinew Lake ... 121/D4
Eynard Lake ... 120/E2
Eyre Lake ... 120/C2

F

Fafard Lake ... 103/G1,113/G3,114/A1,118/D7
Fafard Lake ... 68/E4
Fahlmann Lake ... 116/G4
Fairbairn Lake ... 118/D4
Fairholme ... 67/F2
Fairlight ... 22/D5
Fairy Glen ... 72/D7
Falardeau Lake ... 113/F1,118/C6
Fannon Lake ... 117/E6
Fansher Lake ... 117/B3
Faraud Lake ... 120/F2
Father Lake ... 120/F3
Fedun Lake ... 117/D5
Fengstad Lake ... 111/G4,117/F7
Fenuik Lake ... 120/E3
Fenwood ... 42/F7
Ferguson Lake ... 88/E6
Ferguson Lake ... 84/B3
Fern Lake ... 88/C2
Fichtner Lake ... 121/E4
Fidler Lake ... 118/B3
Field Lake ... 119/D6
Fields Lake ... 112/D1,117/G6,118/A6
Fiest Lake ... 111/B4,117/E7
Fife Lake ... 6/D5
Fife Lake ... 6/B5
Filion Lake ... 70/A2
Fillmore ... 20/C5
Findlater ... 28/G3
Findlay Lake ... 118/B3
Finlay Lake ... 106/E1,116/B6
Finlayson Lake ... 114/C1,118/E6
Finnie Lake ... 117/B5
Fir River Eco Reserve ... 64/F1,74/F7
Fire Lake ... 56/F5
Firebag Lake ... 116/B3
Firneisz Lake ... 117/F2
First Mustus Lake ... 87/E6
Fisher Lake ... 118/E5
Fishing Lake (Big) ... 53/B6
Fishing Lake Wildlife Refuge ... 53/A5
Fishley Lake ... 120/E3
Fiske ... 36/B2

G

H

©shutterstock/Tyler Olson

SWIFT CURRENT CREEK, SK.

©shutterstock/Kelsmead

PRINCE ALBERT NATIONAL PARK, SK.

SUNRISE OVER THE SOUTH SASKATCHEWAN RIVER, SASKATOON, SK.

©shutterstock/Richard Espenant

PRINCE ALBERT
71/A5

ELEVATION
440 m (1,440 ft)

POPULATION (2011)
TOTAL: 35,129

AREA CODE
306, 639

SASKATOON
49/C3

ELEVATION
482 m (1,578 ft)

POPULATION (2011)
TOTAL: 222,190

AREA CODE
306, 639

©ragnarrobinson
SAND CLIFFS ALONG NIPEKAMEW RIVER, SK.

REGINA
29/F6

ELEVATION
577 m (1,893 ft)

POPULATION (2011)
TOTAL: 193,100

AREA CODE
306, 639

©shutterstock/Mark Zulkoskey

PUMP JACKS, SHAUNAVON, SK.

SASKATCHEWAN

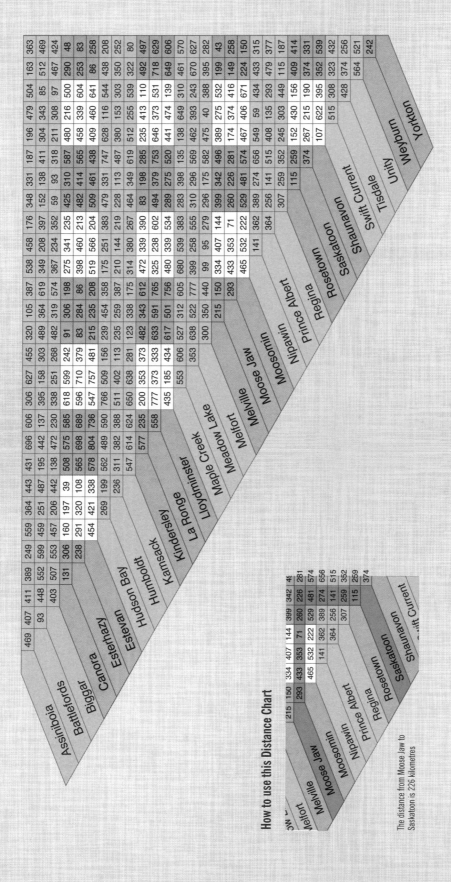

How to use this Distance Chart

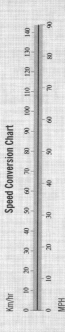

The distance from Moose Jaw to Saskatoon is 226 kilometres

1 Kilometre = 0.621 Mile   1 Mile = 1.6 Kilometres

Speed Conversion Chart

Km/hr 0 10 20 30 40 50 60 70 80 90 100 110 120 130 140

MPH 0 10 20 30 40 50 60 70 80 90

Contacts

 South Saskatchewan River
©Shutterstock / Chase Clausen

ADVERTISER LIST

TRAVEL SASKATCHEWAN

Saskatchewan Tourism ....sasktourism.com
....1-877-237-2273
Southwest Saskatchewan Tourism ....greatsouthwest.ca
....1-877-237-2273
Tourism Lloydminster..lloydminstertourism.ca
....1-780-875-8881
Tourism Moose Jaw...tourismmoosejaw.ca
....1-866-693-8097
Tourism Prince Albert...princealberttourism.com
....(306) 953-4385
Tourism Regina ....tourismregina.com
....1-800-661-5099
Tourism Saskatoon..tourismsaskatoon.com
....1-800-567-2444
Tourism Swift Current ....tourismswiftcurrent.ca
....(306) 778-9174
Tourism The Battlefords..battlefords.ca
....1-800-243-0394
Tourism Yorkton..tourismyorkton.com
....1-306-783-8707

IMPORTANT NUMBERS

GENERAL

Firewatch (Report a Wildfire) 1-800-667-9660
Highway Hotline...hotline.gov.sk.ca
....1-888-335-7623 or *7623
Saskatchewan Tourism ....sasktourism.com
....1-877-237-2273
Updates to Mapbooks ....email to: updates@backroadmapbooks.com
Weather Conditions...................................weatheroffice.ec.gc.ca/canada

FISH & WILDLIFE

Ministry of Environment.........................saskatchewan.ca/environment
....1-800-567-4224
Boating Safety 1-800-267-6687
Saskatchewan Anglers Guide ....publications.gov.sk.ca
Saskatchewan Anglers Information ....(306) 787-2847
Saskatchewan Hunting Guide ....publications.gov.sk.ca
TIPS (Report Poachers)..1-800-667-7561

PARKS

General information ....saskparks.net
Provincial Parks Reservations....................saskparks.goingtocamp.com
....1-888-737-7275
Parks Canada ....pc.gc.ca/eng/index.aspx
Parks Canada Reservations ....reservation.pc.gc.ca/ParksCanada
....1-877-737-3783
Saskatchewan Regional Parks ....saskregionalparks.ca
Saskatchewan Parks and Recreation Association ....spra.sk.ca

CLUBS & ASSOCIATIONS

Canoe Saskatchewan...................................canoesaskatchewan.rkc.ca
Cross Country Saskatchewan...................................crosscountrysask.ca
Nature Saskatchewan...naturesask.ca
Saskatchewan ATV Association ....satva.ca
Saskatchewan Cycling Association ....saskcycling.ca
Saskatchewan Golfing ....saskgolfer.com
Saskatchewan Horse Federation ....saskhorse.ca
Saskatchewan Snowmobile Association.............sasksnowmobiling.sk.ca
Saskatchewan Trails Association ....sasktrails.ca
Saskatchewan Outfitter's Association ....soa.ca
Saskatchewan Wildlife Federation ....swf.sk.ca

CHOOSE YOUR ADVENTURE

TRIP PLANNING
TRAILS
PARKS
SNOWMOBILE
BACKROADS
ATV [OHV]
FISHING
PADDLING
HUNTING
WINTER
RECSITES
WILDLIFE

Backroad Mapbooks

BRMB
backroadmapbooks.com

For a complete list of our products

Backroad Mapbooks

GPS Maps

Fishing Maps

BRMB Navigator

Waterproof Maps

TOPO Maps

Digital Maps